William Babcock Hazen

The School and the Army in Germany and France

With a Diary of Siege Life at Versailles

William Babcock Hazen

The School and the Army in Germany and France
With a Diary of Siege Life at Versailles

ISBN/EAN: 9783337015008

Printed in Europe, USA, Canada, Australia, Japan

Cover: Foto ©ninafisch / pixelio.de

More available books at **www.hansebooks.com**

THE SCHOOL AND THE ARMY

IN

GERMANY AND FRANCE,

WITH A DIARY OF

SIEGE LIFE AT VERSAILLES.

BY

B'V'T MAJ.-GEN'L W. B. HAZEN, U.S.A.,

COLONEL SIXTH INFANTRY.

NEW YORK:
HARPER & BROTHERS, PUBLISHERS,
FRANKLIN SQUARE.
1872.

INTRODUCTION.

THE first part of the following work is a faithful record of my personal observation of German military life and service during a part of the late Franco-Prussian war. As I believe that organization stands to successful action in the relation of cause to effect, I have devoted the remaining pages to an examination and comparison of the military and educational systems of France and Germany. It will be seen that in each of these countries the connection between the school and the army is intimate, and that the latter rests upon and corresponds in excellence to the former. I have preferred an exposition and discussion of these fundamental subjects to detailed descriptions of battles that I did not see, and which were only results.

In treating of the schools, I have been greatly aided by the reports of the various commissioners sent out by the British Government. It may be said that I am partial to Germany. I answer that I have written what I found to be true. That my convictions were not hastily formed, will appear by the following extract from a private letter:

"NUERMBERG, November 9, 1870.

" * * * I can not close this letter without thanking you for the great interest you have taken in our German question since I had the pleasure of meeting you first three years ago. Your views then were so correct, every thing that has happened since you foretold with such accuracy, that I look upon our first meeting with the deepest interest, while my political views have since been guided by your kind advice. * * *

"I have the honor to be, most respectfully,   EUGENE HURZ.
"To GENERAL HAZEN."

The first meeting spoken of in this letter took place in 1867, just after I had spent a few days at the head-quarters of General L'Admirault, commanding the camp of instruction at Chalons.

What I then saw and had previously observed of the tone and character of the French army and people, and their attitude toward Germany, made the result of the recent war a foregone event to me.

If this book shall serve to turn the attention of a single person to the moral and intellectual causes of German success and French disaster, it will not entirely fail of its purpose.

W. B. HAZEN.

FORT HAYS, KANSAS.

CONTENTS.

CHAPTER I.

Credentials.—Bismarck.—Ferrieres.—Sedan.—Versailles.—King William.—Cost and Management of Versailles.—General Burnside.—Peasants eating Royal Game.—Relics of St. Cloud.—Sortie from Mount Valerien.—Chateau Beauregard.—Chateau Balzac.—Prussian Military Burial.—Hôtel du Reservoir.—German Princes.. Page 9

CHAPTER II.

Types of German People.—Characteristics of Princes.—Prussian Officers.—Posting and quartering the German Army.—The Old Noblesse 55

CHAPTER III.

Fall of Metz.—Fortifications about Paris.—Americans from Paris.—The Mitrailleuse.—Roads in Europe.—Food about Paris.—Contumacy of the French People.—Alarm and Re-enforcements.—Promotion of Royal Princes.—Von Moltke.—France and her Situation.—The American Press.—Conduct of the Germans... 65

CHAPTER IV.

Guard-mounting.—Small-arms.—Prussian Uniform.—The Iron Cross.—The Crown Prince.—Army Police.—Americans.—Thiers in Paris.—Church at Versailles.—Revictualing of Paris.—Causes of the Fall of Metz.—Prussian Soldiers.—Their Equipment, Rations, Allowances, and Pay.—Retiring unworthy Officers.—Billeting.—Regimental Bands.—Brigade Commanders.—Chiefs of Regiments.—Ambulance.—Field Telegraph.—Transportation.—O'Sullivan... 82

CHAPTER V.

Von Roon.—Blumenthal.—Prussian Artillery.—Cavalry Equipments.—No Stragglers.—Keratry.—Society at Versailles.—Paris from the Lines.—Leaving Versailles.—Railway Terminus Supplies.—A Night among the Soldiers.—Soup Sausage... 117

CHAPTER VI.
THE PRUSSIAN ARMY.

The Great Elector.—Frederick the Great.—Blucher.—Conquest by Napoleon.—Short Terms of Service.—Local Distribution of Army Corps.—The Landwehr.—Officering the Army and Landwehr.—A weak Point.—Army Reform.—War of 1866.—The Breech-loader.—Operations against France.—Mobilization.—Dépôt Troops.—Garrison Troops.— Field Administration.—Observations..Page 136

CHAPTER VII.
THE FRENCH ARMY.

Origin of its Tactics.—The early Armies of the Revolution.—The Conscription.—Reorganization of the Army.—Vital Statistics.—Strength in 1867.—Trochu.—Administration.—The Intendant-general.—Infantry.—Cavalry.—Want of Simplicity.—Popular Enthusiasm.—Army Organization.—Observations.. 186

CHAPTER VIII.
COMPARATIVE OBSERVATIONS UPON THE UNITED STATES ARMY.

Remedy for Desertion. — Undue Size of the Staff. — Want of Unity. — Schenck's Salary Bill.—Sutler System.—Soldiers' Safe Deposit.—Officering of Troops.—Brevet Rank.—Extravagance...................................... 222

CHAPTER IX.
PRUSSIAN MILITARY SCHOOLS.

Plan of Officering the Prussian Army.—Cadet Schools.—Berlin Cadet School.—War Schools.—Artillery and Engineering School.—The War Academy.—Observations.. 247

CHAPTER X.
FRENCH MILITARY SCHOOLS—PLAN OF OFFICERING THE FRENCH ARMY.

Imperial Polytechnic School.—School of Application at Metz.—Saint-Cyr.—Staff School of Application.—La Flêche.—French Military Schools compared with West Point... 266

CHAPTER XI.
GERMAN CIVIL SCHOOLS.

Primary Education.—Inspection and Support of Schools.—Berlin Schools.—Method of Teaching.—Religious Instruction................................. 294

CHAPTER XII.

GERMAN CIVIL SCHOOLS—*continued*.

Elementary Teaching.—Teachers.—Higher Education.—The Real School.—The Gymnasium.—The Universities..................................Page 320

CHAPTER XIII.

FRENCH CIVIL SCHOOLS—EARLY HISTORY.

The University of Paris. — The College of France. — The Jesuits. — The Schools during the Revolution. — Municipal Divisions of France. — The Church in France.—Brethren of the Christian Schools.—Louis XIV.—Coercive Catholic Education.—Efforts of the Convention.—Napoleon and the Schools.—The University of France.—Schools under the Restoration.—Guizot.—The Monarchy of July.—Law of 1833........................ 340

CHAPTER XIV.

FRENCH CIVIL SCHOOLS—*continued*.

The Coup D'État and the Schools.—Present Condition of Schools.—School Buildings and Management.—Primary Normal Schools.—Secondary Instruction. — The Lyceums and Communal Colleges. — Superior Normal School.—The Seven Great Lyceums.—The University.—Popular Intelligence.—Conclusion,... 362

APPENDIX.

ORGANIZATION AND ADMINISTRATION OF THE GERMAN ARMY............ 383

THE SCHOOL AND THE ARMY

IN

GERMANY AND FRANCE.

CHAPTER I.

THE following official documents will exhibit my credentials, and show what facilities I had for gaining access to sources of original information. The letter from Count Bismarck is my authority for printing his interesting statements as to the origin of the war, made in the conversation recorded in my diary.

"WAR DEPARTMENT, ADJUTANT GENERAL'S OFFICE,
"WASHINGTON, August 29, 1870.

"*Special Orders, No.* 224.

[EXTRACT.]

"* * * By direction of the President, leave of absence until further orders, with permission to go beyond the sea, reporting his address monthly to this office, is hereby granted Colonel W. B. Hazen, Sixth Infantry.

"By order of the Secretary of War.

"(Signed) E. D. TOWNSEND, Adjutant-general."

"CONSULATE OF THE NORTH GERMAN CONFEDERATION
"IN BELGIUM, BRUSSELS, September 22, 1870.

"The American Colonel and Brevet Major-general W. B. Hazen has received permission from his Excellency, the Lord Chancellor Count Bismarck, to join the German armies, and will therefore be permitted to proceed unhindered through Sedan and Rheims to the royal head-quarters. So far as circumstances will allow, he will be assisted to reach his destination with celerity.

"The Royal Prussian Privy Councilor
"Of the North German Confederation,
"BALLOU."

"GRAND HEAD-QUARTERS, FERRIERES, FRANCE,
"September 29, 1870.

"Colonel Hazen, Brevet Major-general of the Free States of North America, is hereby authorized to follow the allied German armies to the seat of war, and remain with them.
"The Minister of War and Marine,
"VON ROON."

"VERSAILLES, November 11, 1870.

"SIR,—I am directed by Count Bismarck to send you the inclosed introduction to a gentleman attached to the Foreign Office in Berlin, who will give you all the information you desire there.

"I am your obedient servant,
"L. BUCHER.

"To GENERAL HAZEN."

"VERSAILLES, March 4, 1871.

"SIR,—I have the honor to acknowledge the receipt of your letter of the 2d of February, asking my consent to the publication of the conversation we had at Ferrieres toward the end of September last. Owing to the great number of interviews I have had during the war, I can not recall to my mind all particulars of that conversation; but, trusting to your discretion that with respect to persons you will observe the limits between confidential talk and public utterance, I have much pleasure in acceding to your request.

"I am, with great regard,
"V. BISMARCK.

"To COLONEL W. B. HAZEN,
"Fort Gibson, Indian Territory, U. S."

BISMARCK.

Sept. 27*th*, 1870.—I have just visited Count Bismarck with General Burnside. We found him quartered at Ferrieres, the country-seat of the Paris branch of the Rothschilds, where the king at present has his head-quarters. On our arrival Count Bismarck was engaged with one of the French legitimate princes, who was urging upon the Premier the claims of his House. On being shown in, we found Count Bismarck busily engaged in copying, with a lead-pencil as thick as one's thumb, some very rough draft of a document. He came forward and received us with warmth and a smile of genuine amiability and kindness, and, after a few remarks upon the latest war news, begged to be permitted to finish his copy, which would take but a moment. He occupied a small room, in which were a few chairs and a writing-desk. He is something over six feet in height, with a large frame, well filled out, but not gross; hair quite gray, and clear blue eyes. In conversation, the usual sternness of his countenance changes to kindness, with a manner of open frankness that can not fail to win the listener. On finishing and dispatching his copy, he turned to us, and, scarcely waiting for a fresh cigarette, began a very interesting talk of at least two hours' duration, in which he was the uninterrupted speaker.

He said, "The German people were astonished to find themselves involved in a general war. After a long and laborious season of duties at Berlin, I had gone down to my place in Pomerania, and was engaged in laying out my grounds and planting my gardens, with my wife and all my children about me, happy in the belief that I should have an uninterrupted summer, without the distraction of official work. Some time in May dispatches began to reach me, sometimes in cipher, indicating that there might be trouble with France; but I gave little heed to them, and continued the rural work of which I am so fond and which my health seemed to require. My place is not directly on the line of communication, so that my letters and papers did not reach me very regularly, and I had almost forgotten the events made possible by previous dispatches.

"The subject of the young Hohenzollern's pretensions to the throne of Spain had already been brought to the notice of the king, who had opposed them on the ground of the unfitness of German princes to rule Latin subjects, as shown by the experiment in Mexico. I had not been officially consulted on the subject, but it appeared to me a pity for a young man who desired a kingly career, and had the position at his disposal, not to take it; and, as he was married to an exemplary, good woman, and was himself a man of uprightness and correct life, his religion also being that of Spain, I thought that his example, with that of his wife, together with the management of Spain promised by his scholarly habits, might be advantageous to the Spanish people, and his reign successful. The matter had the year before been brought to the notice of the young man, who visited Paris soon after, and acquainted the emperor with the scheme, as a matter which his sovereign character gave him a right to know. The prince's acceptance, if the matter should be at last favorably considered, was still to be subject to a vote of the Spanish people. On his mentioning to me casually that the Spanish throne had been offered him, I remarked that a crown was not offered a lieutenant of hussars every day, and urged him to make sure of it, promising that I would see that the king consented.

"The king at last reluctantly gave his assent, not as sovereign, for the matter had not advanced so far as to be discussed in that light, but as the head of the army of Prussia, in which the young man held a commission. The king had grave doubts as to the propriety of Prussia's favoring the scheme, for the political reason that Prince Leopold would be too strongly in favor of the French idea and against Prussia. He was a blood relative of the emperor; his father had projected for the emperor his Strasbourg fiasco, and had always been the bosom friend of Napoleon; and it was he, in fact, and not the son, who was arranging the Spanish throne business. The thought that it could in any way be distasteful to the French sovereign never occurred to any member of the Prussian Government.

"It was at this juncture that the note came from the French Government requiring the renunciation of the young man's ambition. Seeing that it was likely to make serious trouble between the two countries, he had, by the advice of his father, made personal renunciation before the matter had been fairly brought to the notice of the Prussian Government; and coming himself to Berlin, found, as he supposed, every thing settled, and next morning went back to his country home, and the king went to his summer resort at Ems.

"Imagine the surprise of all Prussia, on learning in a few days that France was not satisfied, but required that the Prussian Government should disclaim all future intention of placing a German prince upon the Spanish throne. Instructions were at once given the Prussian ambassador at Paris, to see to it that the dignity of his Government was fully sustained, but he did not quite seem to comprehend the character of the business he was dealing with. The Government at Berlin now wrote me that it seemed inexpedient for the king to remain longer at Ems, unaccompanied by his ministers. The king abhors war, and our military system is such as to bring into the ranks the very best of our men. He seemed ready to make great concessions rather than bring sacrifices upon the country, and wrote a dispatch to the emperor virtually making the disclaimer asked. This dispatch was sent to me, his minister, for revision, and its tone somewhat altered to better suit the emergency. I now telegraphed again to our minister to sustain the dignity of Prussia. The king was not offended by the conduct of Benedetti, but saw fit to treat him with consideration. The ambassador at Paris was still unequal to his work, and wrote the king a letter urging the withdrawal of his dispatch and full compliance with the wishes of the emperor. The king, to save war, was inclined to do so, but the sentiment of Germany, and the advice of his ministers, prevented him; and, upon his refusal to withdraw his dispatch, set out for Berlin, where the ministry were summoned to meet him. By accident, we all met at the railway station in Berlin, were joined by the crown prince, and had set out for the Assembly Chamber, when our attention was attracted by the newsboys crying out that war had been declared by the French. We sought the papers, and the king, believing that war had been declared, put up his hands to his head, and said, 'Must I, in my old age, again go to war!' and tears ran down his cheeks. Upon examining the papers, it was found to be quite uncertain whether war had been declared or not. There was no actual declaration, but a telegram saying that a declaration had been made. But the time for action had arrived, and the crown prince, just behind me, whispered in my ear, 'Radical or nothing.' I then said to the king that there was no impediment to mobilizing the whole army, and that no occasion had ever been so favorable. He at once replied that he would mobilize the whole army. Fearing that he would retract, I spoke out quickly, and in a loud voice, so that forty persons could hear me, 'The king has declared that he will mobilize the whole army,' and the war minister, who was present, said, 'I have heard it, and will at once give the necessary orders.' The work was now beyond recall, and what followed you all know. Germany is a peaceful nation. We have a nearly perfect military system, but it is for defense and not for aggression, and is rendered necessary by our geographical position.

"France has within two hundred years invaded Germany twenty times, and has for a long time past crowded us, and we have swallowed the insult until now, when we feel like a man in his strength with his family about him, who has been pushed and jostled all his life by some one wishing to quarrel with him, until at last he has turned and said, 'Now let us have it out; let us have it out for good, and make that the end of it.' Ever since the war of 1866, a war necessary to clear the political skies of Germany, a purely family affair, having nothing to do with the outside world; and ever since the scheme of German unity commended itself as a scheme of strength and good to the German people, France has been jealous of our prosperity, and has wished to humble us. That idea could only end in war; the sooner over the better; but it must end with substantial guarantees of peace in future, and Germany would be untrue to herself and civilization if she stopped short of this.

"The future of France no one can foresee. There is no intention upon our part to interfere in any way with her internal affairs. The great trouble is, and will be, to find a government strong enough, or representing a sufficient component of French sentiment to deal with.

"Only a day or two since, a delegate visited me in the interest of the emperor's government, proposing that the French fleet gain some point on the coast of France under direction of the empress, and that we recognize the regency. And this evening a gentleman from one of the Legitimist families, who kept you waiting so long, desired recognition, with large representations of power and influence. To all these I have to say that, whenever any considerable portion of the French people express a wish that their claims be represented here, or whenever evidence of any sort is brought that such a wish is indulged by any considerable number of Frenchmen, the subject will be given attention proportionate to the extent of that sentiment. The same trouble is experienced with the Paris Republic. As yet it represents only the streets of that city, while many portions of France have denounced it, and it is well known that to the common people Republicanism is distasteful. I have wished, and so expressed myself to Jules Favre, that the sentiment of the people of France be taken as soon as possible upon this subject, that we may know with whom to deal, and this brings me to the subject of the Jules Favre interview of the 21st inst.

"He came three times to see me. The first visit was little else than a declamation, in true school-boy style, I being the listener; and the second was about to be like it, when I intimated the necessity of bringing our ideas into working order, to see if we could not agree on something practical. His whole topic of conversation was an armistice, which should continue not less than six weeks, to give time for holding elections and for the meeting of the delegates in Paris.

"The conditions of a peace were to be left for future consideration. He also wished the military status to remain as it was at that time, except that all the roads leading to Paris should be opened, giving free transit with the world; and proposed, as compensation, that the garrisons of Tours and Strasbourg should march out with the honors of war, and that we should be allowed free opportunity to bring up food and clothing for our armies. Metz, not being on the line of communication, was not considered. I replied that an armistice was always detrimental to a victorious army, and that, as our certain victory over Paris depended upon our shutting off the food supply, he must, in return for our granting free ingress, give us some commanding positions about Paris, like Mount Valerien; and added, that the garrisons of Tours and Strasbourg should surrender as prisoners of war, as they would be compelled to do in a few days, from advantages already in our hands. This, he replied, could never be done, as it would humiliate the proud people of France. I told him that I was not the advocate of the dignity of France, but of the interests of the German army and nation; and the interviews closed without seriously touching upon the eventual conditions of peace.

"The French people are anomalous—being neither like the Spaniard nor the Italian, but more like the Chinese. A Frenchman is content to be a servant, provided some one is servant to him, and never aspires to advance from his position. The American or German does not wish to be a servant, nor does he wish others to be servants to him, if there are ways to better their condition. They have within themselves elements of independent character, and always seek to improve their fortunes, and see their own prosperity in the prosperity of those surrounding them. They both possess the elements of manhood which constitute Republicanism. It is doubtful if the French people do; but this is not our business, as we have not come here to meddle with such things. The French people have been taught errors about their country and themselves from their infancy, until they are quite unable to comprehend their true position in the scale of humanity. From having a Bureau of the Government, I have often, during the campaign, been quartered in school-houses to give room to my numerous clerks, and have thus seen much of the character of French instruction from the text-books I have found in them. The elementary reading-books for the tenderest children are made up of the glories of France, and represent her as the birthplace of all the great men, the discoverer of all countries, the victor in all battles; in fact, the invincible centre of all that is good and powerful, and all other countries as, in a sense, her dependencies. This self-laudation extends through the entire life of a Frenchman; and, in believing it to be true, the nation have neglected the means of making it so.

"The terms of peace were casually mentioned in my conversation with M. Favre, when he remarked that the fortresses were the gates of the frontier; to which I replied, that France held the keys of these gates, and the German people had decided that for the security of Europe it was necessary to keep them on our side. He said that France might agree to the dismantling of the border fortresses, and would give all the money she had, but never agree to the cession of territory. I replied, that money was no compensation for the loss of life; that what were needed and would be insisted on, were material guarantees of a nature that would secure Germany from the necessity of sacrificing life in the future; that it seemed as if France, after choosing the arbitrament of war, was now seeking to escape the natural penalties of defeat; that she now had our terms, which might not be our terms six months hence, and that if she compelled us to protract the war ten years, we might annex France and crown our kings at Rheims.

"We are glad to have military men from other countries see our operations, although our generals have made some objections on the ground that they encumber our army; but we have told them to come among us, taking their chances for comforts. We have nothing, and do nothing, but what we are willing the whole world should see and know; and we have told the French people everywhere, that every body may write to any body and we will forward their letters, only stipulating that letters passing through our lines shall, for military reasons, be left unsealed."

As we took our leave, Count Bismarck said to us that during our sojourn with the German forces we might call upon him whenever we needed any thing. The whole manner of this remarkable man impresses one with his open, frank good-nature, and his conversation reveals a mind thoroughly trained in the highest school of German philosophy and liberality. He speaks English perfectly, and possesses to a singular degree the power of presenting subjects clearly and forcibly. The idea of Bismarck's personal appearance generally accepted in the United States is incorrect, as it makes him ten years too young, and too precise in dress. His brow is heavy, and his mustache shaggy at the ends, like his hair. There is a remarkable fullness under the eyes, and he has that blonde complexion peculiar to the Germans. His military rank is that of major-general, and he is also *chef* of a cuirassier regiment, of which he wears the uniform. He was born at the ancestral residence known as "*Schönhausen*," on the first day of April, 1815, and is descended from an old family of the better class, who took their name from the little town of Bismark, originally "*Bischofsmark*." His father was a retired officer of the Prussian horse guards, and married a daughter of one of the king's ministers. Young Bismarck passed his early days on the paternal estate, and was afterward sent to one of the private schools at Berlin, and, later, continued his studies at the "*Gris Cloître.*" Even at this period he gave proof of unusual energy, and indicated a preference for historical investigations. He studied both at Berlin and Göttingen, and during his student life was wild and impetuous, but graduated very creditably in 1835. In the following year he went into the practice of law, and took the position of Government referee, or commissioner, at Aachen and Potsdam. He then joined one of the battalions of riflemen as volunteer, and after serving his year, visited the Agricultural School at Edua. The paternal estates, now very much reduced, urgently demanded the attention of Bismarck, and were by his father turned over to his two sons. The death of their mother in 1839, however, somewhat disarranged their plans. Their father lived until 1845, during which time the management of the estates was shared by the two brothers, by whose extraordinary circumspection and care the property was soon brought up from desolation to fruitfulness. Bismarck's formerly active life unfitted him for the monotony of the country, and his thirst for greater activity gave him no rest. Whole days would be passed in woodland rambles, or in convivial sports with the young men of the neighborhood, among whom he was known as the "mad Bismarck." During all this time, however, he never neglected study, but devoted himself closely to history, theology, and philosophy, and it was at this epoch of his life that he amassed that fund of knowledge which distinguishes the present statesman. He also at this time traveled in England and France. Upon the decease of his father, a distribution of the estate took place, and Schönhausen fell to Otto. Here he afterward made his home, and thence he commenced his public career. He was elected deputy to several of the minor German Diets during the following years, till 1851, when he was appointed by the Prussian Government secretary of legation at Frankfort, with the title of Privy Councilor. He made himself well known in Germany in these six years, and the experience then gained was a valuable preparation for his subsequent diplomatic duties.

In August, 1851, he was nominated as representative of Prussia at the Federal German Diet, which position he held until 1859, when he was appointed ambassador to St. Petersburg. On his return to Berlin, he was offered a place in the ministry, but preferred the embassy at Paris, which was also at his disposal. He was speedily recalled, to take the Presidency of the Prussian Ministry, which position he still holds. With a firm hand, unmoved by the machinations of those around him, Otto von Bismarck worked from that moment to make Prussia the leading power of Germany, politically, as it was already in liberality, native character, and learning. The conclusion of the Gastein Convention, in the fall of 1865, brought him the title of count, as well as the satisfaction of seeing the settlement of all existing conflicts in Germany. Count Bismarck became at once the most popular man in Prussia, and after the establishment of the North German Alliance in 1867, was elected federal chancellor. His management of foreign politics has in recent years been no less a triumph to the man than to his country and to civilization, while his disclosures of the plans of Louis Napoleon have shown how far superior were his talents to those of the people with whom he dealt. He not only refused all offers made him by the French Government, but turned them to account in terminating the protective alliance with the South German States.

Count Bismarck is highly favored in his domestic life. In 1847 he married a woman of rare excellence and purity, and of a high order of intellectual endowment. His two sons have already borne a distinguished part in the present war. At the successful close of the Austrian war, the Prussian Government voted to Count Bismarck a sufficient sum of money to enable him to purchase in Pomerania an estate named Varzin, more in keeping with his tastes and dignity than his former home. It is here that his happy family reside, and here that the count himself takes refuge whenever a lull in his laborious life permits. He is reputed to be a careful and judicious manager of his financial affairs. He is unfortunately afflicted from time to time with a nervous malady which drives him from his labors and greatly alarms his friends. Count Bismarck is one of the few men who in their own lives see their names celebrated in all lands, and has in the present war taken the foremost place in the most memorable epoch of modern German history.*

FERRIERES.

Sept. 28th.—Ferrieres, where the king and his ministers have established their head-quarters, is the country-seat of the Paris representative of the Rothschilds. It is owned by the aged widow of a son of the founder of the family. The building is square, and without courts or turrets, hav-

---

* At the close of the war of 1866, Prussia voted each of her most conspicuous generals and statesmen a donation in money as a reward for extraordinary services to the state. This is done in England, Prussia, and nearly all the countries of Europe, and is only an expression, through the executive or legislative power, of the generosity of the nation. We see the same thing in our own country, where, since it is not compatible with our republican theory to make it a legislative act, the impulse of the people manifests itself through private channels. It is, however, in essence the same thing, and in every case comes from a natural and proper desire to make gratitude for great services felt in a substantial manner. In Europe no one thinks of refusing what is considered a proper reward, and I do not see why we should do differently. In refusing, one is neither just to himself, nor kind to those who would honor him.

ing four similar and highly wrought façades, each about two hundred feet long, is built of a drab-colored stone, and has two high stories and a basement. The grounds, some three hundred acres in area, are laid out with roads, drives, and walks, and contain deer-parks, and lakes alive with fishes, and covered with hundreds of swans and other aquatic birds. There are aviaries unequaled by any state collection I have ever seen, and every kind of rare specimen of the animal world. The grounds immediately surrounding the house are wrought in the usual English style of landscape gardening, and the whole forms the most beautiful work of the kind in France; none of the royal residences in all respects comparing with it. The interior is in keeping, and rivals royalty itself. The entire place cost six million dollars. Here it is that the king, who commands this great German army, resides, and from here he will go to Versailles.

SEDAN.

I will here record what I saw at Sedan, and on the neighboring battle-fields, six days ago, and the impressions gained there.

Sept. 22*d.*—Twenty days have made great changes here. We see the farmers at their ordinary work. The plough is doing its part to hide the scars of war, and already nearly all the hill-sides where the great battles raged are ready for the seed, and show only occasional fresh graves to remind one of the great tragedy. The town itself seems to the ordinary observer unchanged, and one would be compelled to spend some time in search before any shot-marks could be found. It is a comfortably built town of some seventeen thousand inhabitants, celebrated as the birthplace of Turenne. There is a German garrison here of about three thousand men, and near the fortifications are two or three acres of captured artillery, and at least a hundred cords of chassepot muskets.

In going over the field of battle, one is not greatly impressed with the fact that the engagement was sanguinary, for there are no long trenches of the dead—only an occasional grave, and sometimes two or three together; while in our war on every battle-field would be dug long trenches, sometimes several near each other, in which the dead were buried. We were, however, in the habit of moving near the enemy, and then halting and fighting in fixed positions, so that heavy losses occurred in small spaces, while these people seem to move forward until the enemy runs away or they themselves turn back. At all events, the graves are not numerous. On the road toward Bazeilles there are indications of sharp work. The numerous trees and farm buildings show scars everywhere, while knapsacks, canteens, and Bavarian hats, many of them with shots through them, cumber the ground at almost every step.

On approaching the village, I first find a huddle of paupers receiving rations at a country house. I learn that they are the very poor of Bazeilles, receiving their daily charity from the German authorities. A little farther on is the Franco-American Ambulance, or more properly, hospital. Only twenty patients, too badly wounded for removal, remain here. Nearly every house in Bazeilles was burned, and the smoke still issues from the ruins. It was a compact little village of some fifteen hundred inhabitants. The houses were all of stone, and stuccoed—the ordinary method here. The former residents are a low, ignorant class of farming peasants, few of whom can read. In the narrow streets, in front of each door, and not more than a yard from it, was the compost heap for each farm. These are still smoking, and the stench from them makes it difficult to move along the streets. One who has not been in France can not realize how near to barbarism this class of the French people have fallen.

The burning of this place has been severely criticised. I find that it was within the theatre of the battle, and, after it was carried, was made a place for the wounded, or rather a temporary field hospital, such as always affords the first relief and attention to the wounded in all engagements. The surgeons were fired upon from the houses, and some killed and wounded. This being reported to the nearest commander, a force was sent out to suppress it and arrest the guilty parties, but the perpetrators could not be found. The patrol was recalled, when the attack upon the surgeons was renewed, and orders were then given to burn the place. I doubt whether any commander under like provocation would have acted differently.

I hear and read much about the cruelty shown French prisoners, and the barbarity of burning this place. It is well to remember that these accounts are generally written by people who follow the war in the interests of humanity, and see and write of these things from their special humanitarian point of view, not modified by a true sense of what war means, and are apt to take individual cases as examples of general conduct. That among all the acts of every individual of a gigantic army some will be harsh and unjust, is as true as that human nature is imperfect, but it is unjust to hold the army responsible.

The guarding, care, and feeding of the French at Sedan have been a fruitful theme for sensational literature of this character. The condition of a prisoner is never acceptable to him, and he easily conceives it to be much worse than it is. It is charged that the French army, after being disarmed, were huddled together on a wet island, without shelter, with insufficient food, and that many perished. I find this, in the main, true; but the period of that battle was one of continued rains, and all places and fields were wet and muddy. That there was any neglect in providing food was not the fact; but as the French had not, before the surrender, sufficient supplies in Sedan for themselves, and as the Prussian army were compelled to live upon the country—a difficult task at best—and as organization in the French army was broken up, the supply was, of necessity, scant and difficult to distribute.

The Prussian army did not carry tents for themselves, and of course had none for the prisoners. A hundred thousand men deprived of their organization, without arms or equipments, but forming an immense herd, and covered with mud and rain, impressed the observer very much as an immense herd of cattle would, and naturally suggested the idea of cruelty and inhumanity.

And further, among so large a number of men there are very many sown full of the seeds of disease, only waiting the depression of such a humiliating defeat, with its attendant discomforts, or any sufficient cause, to bring death to them. And this is called starvation. I can learn of no well-grounded reason for the accusation made against the Germans here. The place is already perfectly clean, and I see nothing offensive anywhere in the neighborhood of the battle-field or the town.

Sedan has many points of interest, and to me none more than the fact that it is a specimen fortification upon the Vauban plan, the half front of which the cadets at West Point have been made to construct, and draw, as their model in military engineering, for many years. We are taught that it will take forty days to reduce a fort built on this plan, yet Sedan, with all its surroundings, has just been taken in three days. I find here every face, ditch, salient, covered way, traverse, and glacis just as I drew them sixteen years ago.

VERSAILLES.

Oct. 4th.—Versailles is a city of sixty thousand inhabitants, and is built in the old French style of architecture. The palace, which has taken its name from the city, is situated on an elevated plateau on the western border of the municipality, and is what is generally understood by the term Versailles.

The city is the model from which Washington was planned. The palace, like our Capitol, stands upon an elevated piece of ground, and faces away from the city. At its rear, instead of trees, is a large court-yard paved with granite blocks eight inches square, and beyond this the avenues of the city radiate, as at Washington. These radiating streets were cut through the old city by Louis XIV., and on each side, for a mile, are shaded by double rows of lindens, or, as we call them, bass-wood. The court-yard contains many colossal marble statues of the marshals of France prior to the present century, and a bronze equestrian figure of the great Louis. A small palace was built by Louis XIII., and extensive additions were made by his three successors; but the main plan was due to Louis XIV. Looking up the paved yard, you see fourteen gables of various heights, and two deep re-entering courts, which give the impression of a richly-built, compact village, rather than a grand palace. On two of these gables which face on one of the courts, you read, "To all the glories of France."

The other side of the palace presents an almost unbroken front of five hundred paces, three stories high, and, excepting that it has no cupola, not very unlike our Capitol. The material, however, is a dirty brown stone, and owing to the effect of florid statuary and bas-reliefs, the quiet grandeur of our Capitol is entirely wanting. The palace was at first the principal royal residence; but after the Revolution the people required the sovereign to reside at Paris. Since this the palace has been devoted to other purposes. From the Revolution to the reign of Louis Philippe it was occupied mostly by peasants, who in some of the grand halls erected as many as three flats of apartments, and made forty comfortable rooms out of one. It was in this condition when Louis Philippe conceived the idea of converting it into a grand museum of civilization, commemorating all the great events of French history from the earliest period. This project has been so far carried out that the collection now numbers a thousand pieces of statuary, and no less than four thousand paintings. Looking inside, we see a phase of life new to the place — the long rows of cots, each with its occupant, pale from exhaustion or flushed with fever, and white-hooded sisters flitting noiselessly about. The palace is one grand hospital for the wounded. The pictures are never wantonly injured, and where there is danger of defacement are carefully boarded over.

KING WILLIAM.

Oct. 5th.—To-day the king, with his ministers, came over from Ferrieres and established the royal head-quarters here. Some time before the hour for his arrival, four regiments of infantry were drawn up on the various streets leading from the City Hall, where the king was to take up his residence. In front of it, on the broad Avenue de Paris, was a guarded open space, within which were the various officers of rank on duty in the city, and some fifty or sixty princes, dukes, and counts, nearly all members of the crown prince's staff, waiting to receive the king. I join the party, and being with some citizen friends whom the guards will not let in, remain near the line of sentinels to keep my companions in countenance. Soon the leading carriages begin to arrive, and most of the ministers precede the king, all in the uniform of general officers. Then a little unusual commotion, but no shouting, announces the approach of the king, who comes accompanied by the crown prince. The royal carriages, ordinary barouches, are each drawn by four black horses. On arriving near the gate of the court-yard, they quickly stop, and the king, covered and begrimed with dust, jumps out with a quick, manly effort, and, with a pleasant word for each, takes by the hand those waiting to meet him. He then rapidly proceeds along the front of some regiment drawn up before the building, recognizing and speaking to many of the men. The whole air of the king is that of paternal kindness and good-nature, sometimes amounting almost to fondness. He speaks in a quick, eager style, often accompanying his words with rapid jerks of the head and hand.

The reception is soon over, and the king is shown his new quarters by the crown prince, who has just vacated them for his father. Considering his age, the king is wonderfully vigorous. It is evident that he bestows great care upon his bodily health and dress. He is about six feet in height, large without being corpulent, and steps with firmness and ease. He often rides twenty or thirty miles a day on horseback without inconvenience. Until his ascent to the throne of Prussia, he was a soldier in active command, distinguished by his exact and punctilious performance of duty, and by his strictness in requiring the same of others. He never appears with a button out of place, or a single decoration appropriate to the occasion neglected. He is known to have wisely said that a kingdom may be lost by one neglected button, as this may be the beginning of negligence which will end in disaster.

His popularity with the people of Germany is unparalleled. This popularity is, of course, personal, and does not militate against the republican views of a large class of the German people. Were they to institute a republic, it is very probable that he would be the successful candidate for the presidency.

The branch of the Hohenzollern family now reigning in Prussia bought the electorate of Brandenburg of the German Emperor Sigismund in 1415. The family from that moment to the present have been controlled by a traditional sentiment looking directly to the aggrandizement of their house, and making it the centre toward which all Germany must finally gravitate; and well have they worked for the accomplishment of this purpose. By embracing a liberal religion; by compelling universal intellectual culture; by promoting popular liberty, and increasing the material prosperity of their subjects; by counseling prudence and economy, and practicing those virtues themselves; by organizing and perfecting the best military establishments; by a regimen, both moral and physical, calculated to develop strength and form character, they have postponed the degeneracy that naturally follows in the train of riches and luxury.

King William was the second son of King Frederick William III. and of Queen Louisa, a daughter of the Grand Duke of Mecklenburg Strelitz, and was born on the 23d day of March, 1797. The hard fate of Prussia during his early years left indestructible impressions upon his mind, and the depth of her humiliation fired his heart to a life effort to elevate his country. The prince took an active part in the campaigns of 1813 and 1814, for which he received the iron cross. Following the tradition of his family, he devoted himself to the study of military science. In June, 1829, he married the Princess Augusta, daughter of the Grand Duke of Saxe Weimar. Two children were born to this alliance—the present crown prince and the Princess Louise, now wife of the Grand Duke of Baden. Holding military rank of various grades, and performing the routine duties of his position, he lived an easy, uneventful life till 1840, when his brother, King Frederick William, conferred upon him the title of Prince of Prussia, and appointed him governor of Pomerania and president of the state ministry. In the fall of the same year he was appointed general of infantry. In the year 1848, a plan for the reorganization of the Prussian army was first brought forward. It was a favorite project of the crown prince, and so fervently did he press the measure, then unpopular, that public indignation compelled him to flee for safety to England, where he remained six weeks. In the following year we again find him in command of the army corps at first assigned him. He was then designated to suppress the insurrection in the Palatinate, and successfully discharged the duty. In 1854 Prince William celebrated his silver wedding, and was on that occasion gazetted lieutenant-general of the infantry. In 1857 he celebrated his fiftieth year of military service, and in 1867 his sixtieth. During the dangerous illness of King Frederick William in 1858, Prince William undertook the regency, and, after the death of the king, ascended the throne of Prussia. The coronation took place at Königsberg on the 18th of October, 1861. It is related that the king himself took the crown and placed it upon his head with his own hands, exclaiming, "God gives it."

The character of King William has been much discussed by the German people, public sentiment changing considerably from time to time, but tending, upon the whole, in his favor. Upon his succession to the regency, he became very popular by reason of his supposed liberal views, but this favorable disposition of his subjects was entirely changed a few years later, when he carried through his reorganization scheme for the army against the people's representatives. But the unparalleled successes in the wars with Austria and France, which were made possible only by this reorganization, have justified his policy, and made him a popular favorite.

Much has been said of the king's belief in his divine right to rule. There is no difficulty in reconciling with common sense his views on this subject. To comprehend them clearly, it is better to call the right of kings to rule a natural right, which in this case is synonymous with divine right, and is the true foundation of authority as understood by all liberally educated believers in hereditary government. The right of the parent to rule his child is certainly a natural one up to a certain age, when the child can manage better for itself than the parent can for it. *When* this time arrives is entirely a matter of opinion, not susceptible of exact determination, but is fixed arbitrarily by the state. With us it is at maturity. With many people, particularly the barbarous ones, this arbitrary period is never fixed at all, and the right of the parent never ceases. For instance, this is the case with our own Indians, among whom the parental right extends over all descendants. Thus the patriarchal system springs up; and so long as its members agree to it, and have not resolved to terminate parental rule, the right to govern the fourth generation is as natural as the right to exact obedience from the infants of the first. To prevent confusion, it becomes necessary to fix the succession of patriarchal rule, which, as the community grows, runs naturally into the monarchy; and so long as this remains the acknowledged system, the right of the regular succession to govern is claimed to be as natural and clear as that of the parent to rule his offspring. It is in this sense that the King of Prussia believes his right to rule his subjects a natural one, and, if you so see fit to call it, a divine one.

As a community becomes enlightened, and the individual knows more of what is necessary for his best development and interests, he claims to be master of his own acts after arriving at maturity. Just so a people, when sufficiently enlightened to appreciate clearly their best interests, and know the value of individual and general liberty, throw off or terminate this right of kings which before was natural and adequate.

How much longer the ruling classes in Germany will be able to hold on to this claim of right, already a theory rather than an actual power, no one can foretell. That it will ultimately disappear, and without bloodshed, no one who knows Germany can doubt. It is but sixty-two years since the German people really gained their personal liberties, and their sentiment of reverence for kings and princes is still strong. That King William believes that he holds power to rule the people of Prussia by the interposition of a divine miracle, or by any other tenure than that by which Bismarck manages his children, except by virtue of certain conventions, I have never found any intelligent man in Germany bold enough to maintain. He is a sincere believer in the Christian religion, and has absolute faith in the special character of the rulings of divine Providence. I can in no way better give a correct impression of the character of the man than by quoting his address to the German Parliament on calling it together at the beginning of the present war.

"HONORED GENTLEMEN OF THE NORTH GERMAN REICHSTAG,—When I bade you welcome, the last time you assembled in this place, in the name of the Federal Government, I expressed my cheerful thanks that my sincere efforts to realize the wishes of the nation, and satisfy the necessities of civilization by preserving unbroken peace in Europe, had, under God's blessing, been crowned with success. If, notwithstanding, the menace of war and impending danger have imposed the duty on the North German Governments of summoning you in an extraordinary session, you will fully share our conviction that the Confederation has not sought to develop the power of the German people with a view to endanger, but to powerfully protect, the interests of general peace; and if we are now obliged to invoke the national strength to shield our independence, we are only obeying the demands of honor and the requirements of duty. The consideration of the question of the Spanish succession of a German prince, the appearance of this prince on the scene, and his subsequent withdrawal, are all matters with which the Federal Governments had equally little to do, the principal interest of the affair for the North German Confederation being limited to the fact that a friendly but much tried country saw in this candidature the guaranty of a peaceful and orderly government in Spain. Notwithstanding, the Government of the Emperor of the French has made the circumstance a pretext, in manner long unknown to diplomacy, for declaring war with Germany; and in this resolution the emperor persists, even after the original pretense has been removed, with that contempt for the just right of nations to enjoy the blessings of peace, of which we may find analogous examples in the history of former rulers of France. If Germany in former centuries silently bore such outrages upon her rights and honor, she only did so because, disunited as she was, she did not know her strength. Now when the ties of an intellectual and judicial union, which were first knit by the war of liberation, are drawing the races of Germany more closely together the longer they last—now when the defenses of our country leave no loop-hole for a foreign foe—Germany has both the will and the power to repel the renewed insults of France. It is no vainglorious feeling which induces me to speak thus. The Federal Governments, and I myself, act in the full conviction that victory and defeat lie in the hand of the God of battles. We have carefully weighed the responsibility which, before the judgment-seat of God and man, must fall upon his head who drives two peaceable nations in the very heart of Europe into a destructive war.

"The peoples of Germany and France, who both equally enjoy and desire the blessings of Christian civilization and an increasing prosperity, are called to a nobler emulation than the bloody rivalry of arms. Those who bear rule in France, however, by carefully misleading the great nation which is our neighbor, have found out a way to use the justifiable but sensitive patriotism of the country for their own personal interests and passions. The more deeply the Federal Governments feel that they have done every thing their honor and dignity permitted to preserve to Europe the blessings of peace; the more apparent it is to all that the sword has been forced into our hands; the more confidently do we, supported by the unanimous approbation of all the

Governments of Germany, of the South as well as the North, appeal to the patriotism and willing self-sacrifice of the people of Germany, and summon them to defend her honor and independence. We follow the example of our fathers in fighting for our freedom and our rights, against the violence of foreign invaders; and, as in this war we have no other aim than to secure the lasting peace of Europe, God will be with us, as he was with our fathers."

COST AND MANAGEMENT OF VERSAILLES.

The whole cost of Versailles was about one hundred and eighty millions of dollars, or four times as much as that of all our public buildings at Washington, and at a rate of pay for labor four times as small; so it can be said to have cost the bone and sinew of the French people sixteen times as much as our boasted Capitol.

The place requires the constant care of two thousand men, who are divided into three departments—the department of the palace, of the grounds, and of the waters—all under the control of the governor. They have a regular organization, are uniformed, and receive as compensation their clothing, quarters, fuel, medical attendance, schooling for two children, food for their families to the extent of wife and two children, ten *sous* a day, and a pension in old age. This is one of the many forms in which nearly all the French people seem to be put; gliding easily through life on a dead level, without an incentive, entirely content, and only hoping to be let alone.

GENERAL BURNSIDE'S MISSION IN PARIS.

Oct. 10th.—General Burnside has returned from his second visit to Paris. As he was the bearer of a diplomatic mail-bag, he has been the mail-carrier for all nationalities; and, as Versailles has no banking facilities available to foreigners, has acted as banking agent to many needy Americans and Englishmen, and in it all has done a kind, amiable service that will be remembered for a lifetime.

The true history of his going into Paris is that, happening to be in London on private business, he became desirous to see something of the war. Our minister accordingly got for him authority to visit the German armies, and then asked him to become a bearer of dispatches from our Government to Mr. Washburne, the American minister in Paris. He readily assented, and upon calling on Count Bismarck to make known his wishes and ask authority to pass the German lines under a flag of truce, a long conversation sprang up on the subject of the war. At the conclusion, the count remarked that no flags had been granted to any one for a long time, as several flag-bearers had been shot; but that in view of the great services rendered the German residents in Paris by Mr. Washburne, he would gladly grant the flag, and all possible facilities for making it available, and then asked General Burnside to convey a note to Jules Favre. General Burnside inquired if Count Bismarck would authorize him to repeat the conversation of the evening to Jules Favre, as it seemed perfectly reasonable that peace should be made upon terms which had been spoken of with approbation by Count Bismarck. After a little reflection, Count Bismarck remarked that General Burnside, being a man of high character and distinction, and of a neutral country friendly to both belligerents, was a person eminently suited to act in the manner proposed; that good might come of it, and that he would himself write out a brief synopsis of what had been said, which General Burnside could use in the interests of peace in such manner as he should find expedient.

I accompanied General Burnside on the thirtieth day of September to Creteil, a small place between forts Charenton and Vincennes, thinking we could pass here; but a sortie was going on; and as there was no chance to use the flag, we went on to Versailles, some eighteen miles farther. On the first and second days of October some unsuccessful attempts were made to pass the lines, but on the third the general got through at Sevres; and, after first reporting to General Trochu, proceeded with his dispatches to Mr. Washburne's residence, where General Trochu and Jules Favre soon after called upon him. After talking over the whole matter at great length in the presence of Mr. Washburne, Jules Favre said that Bismarck and himself could not quite agree, but that he desired General Burnside to report to Bismarck, on his return to Versailles, all that had been said. Count Bismarck proposed that there should be a partial armistice of about ten days, so as to give free ingress and egress to French officials for the purpose of making necessary arrangements for holding elections, then an actual armistice of two days for holding elections, and then another period of partial armistice for the meeting of the Assembly, and a reasonable time for deliberations. General Burnside, on reporting his interview to Count Bismarck, supposed his mission ended, and was upon the point of taking his departure, when Count Bismarck requested him to wait a few days and take in further propositions. He went in the second time, and held several interviews with Trochu and Favre, but there was not the remotest chance of the two belligerents agreeing. The French claimed from the first the revictualing of Paris as a condition precedent to any arrangement. As the consumption of food in Paris would lead to its certain capitulation, and as the supply was already controlled by the Germans, and as an armistice might result in nothing, the proposition was inadmissible, unless the Germans were given, as an equivalent, one of the commanding forts, and this the French refused to do. To the direct question by Burnside whether, if he were on the German side, he would permit the revictualing of Paris, Trochu replied that he would not. Any one can see that the Germans were asked to give up without any equivalent a great advantage already gained. The fact is, that the government of defense dared not risk the result of an election. General Burnside has now ended his negotiations, receiving the gratitude of at least the Prussian Government, and deserving that of the French, for an honest and zealous effort in the interests of peace. He has also gained from Count Bismarck authority for Americans and others to come out of Paris, in cases approved by Mr. Washburne.

PEASANTS EATING ROYAL GAME.

Oct. 16th.—In driving over the grounds of Versailles to-day, the freshness of the lawns and neatness of the walks are very noticeable. The Germans require the servants of the establishment to keep on with their regular duties, and the result is that one could not tell, except for an occasional foreign uniform, that a hostile army is quartered here. The usual care is taken of every thing, except that the Germans will ride over the lawns; but not a tree or shrub is marred, and not a statue touched. The former restriction that only royal carriages can drive in the grounds is, of course, removed, and the German officers, and, in fact, any one, may ride and hunt in the royal forests. The consequence is that one always sees deer and pheasants in the market, while the peasantry have lived on royal game for a month past. They have also driven a good business by fishing in the lakes and ponds of the grounds, and gathering fagots from the public woods. The Orangery, one of the oldest in France, was removed before the arrival of the Germans, and many of the well-known fishes of the lakes carried away to places of safety in the south of France. Strange as it may seem to Americans, there were fishes in the basins of the fountains that date back to the time of Charles X. Many of the ladies of Paris had their pet fishes, and would bring food here from home for their favorites. We saw a solitary swan swimming sadly about, and asked our coachman if it was still cared for. He said that it took very little to keep it, and its supplies were still furnished, but that the poor fishes had not tasted their rations since the Prussians arrived. One is filled with conflicting feelings in going through these grounds. Their beauty interests, but the evidences of almost superhuman toil for purposes essentially trivial tinge every thing with sadness. There were at one time thirty-six thousand soldiers at work on one aqueduct, which was never finished nor used. The outlay upon the palace and grounds was so great that Louis XIV. burned all the papers, that the world might not know the amount.

Oct. 20th.—VILLE D'AURAY is a small village situated just outside the Park of St. Cloud, and in it are quartered the 5th battalion of Jägers, or riflemen, which garrison the grounds of St. Cloud. At the burning of the palace, they rescued many beautiful articles from the flames. Since the fire the men of this battalion have been exceedingly popular, as their friends hope to obtain through them some small relic of the palace. The officers are all agreeable gentlemen, and always serve you a cup of coffee and a glass of wine. The men, seeing foreign guests at headquarters, at once divine their wishes, and soon one will bring in a goblet, wine-glass, plate, or creamer, of the most beautiful Sevres, with the golden crest and imperial arms, and "N" in old English text, for which a yellow coin is quietly exchanged, and two people are made happy. Going across the street, by invitation, to hear some music, we find five private soldiers quartered in a room about ten feet square. Much of the furniture of the house, including the piano, remains unmoved. The pictures hang untouched; the bedstead, with its mattress, is covered with blankets supplied by the men; the floor is scrupulously neat; and these five men in their shirt-sleeves are reading newspapers. They rise as we enter, and, giving us seats, order coffee, which comes immediately, and, opening a drawer of the bureau, set wine before us. One of the men goes to the piano, a miserable, little, upright affair, and plays for us admirably, and from the best masters. When he tires, another takes his place; and I was told that if I would stay long enough they would all play for me. As we were preparing to return to Versailles, they inquired how else they could entertain us, making a special request that we permit ourselves to be shaved, as one of their number understood it thoroughly. This my friend General Duff, of the *New York Herald*, gladly assented to, and soon appeared, renewed. We went into many houses, and found the men pleasantly quartered, clean and cheerful, and seeming as little concerned about the enemy as if they were leagues away. Wherever I have been, the men are quartered in this way. While at the front, they watch as their turn may come, and the rest are unconcerned. When they are in the rear, they have no care, but wait to be turned out, not in fear of a surprise, but quietly to march somewhere and confront the enemy. Much is gained by thus keeping the men cool and at rest. As we started to return, we were saluted by a shell bursting in the street next us, and then followed some sharp firing, both of artillery and musketry. The troops were rapidly put in line, and every thing about the village was hushed in breathless stillness. The effect was remarkable; and as we passed along, we were compelled to move at the slowest and stillest walk, while profound attention and watchfulness seemed to pervade the very atmosphere. The alarm was soon over, and the day has been uneventful.

SORTIE FROM MOUNT VALERIEN.

Oct. 21st.—In driving out to-day my course lay through the forest of Fausses Repasés, a long stretch of imperial forest between Versailles and St. Cloud, with drives and roads in all directions. When nearing the outskirts of St. Cloud, a cannonade set in, about three miles away, in the direction of Mount Valerien. I had last heard that sound at Bentonville, in North Carolina. Feeling certain that a sortie was being made, I hurried on, and soon found myself at a country place occupied by a divisional train hospital. The horses were already hitched up, and the men waiting orders. Soon musketry could be heard, and then mitrailleuses. They make a noise prolonged about three seconds, which, when heard at a distance, resembles the sound of a circular saw in cutting wood. The noise is produced by the successive firing through that period of time of twenty-five shots from a $\frac{58}{100}$ inch bore; and although no two barrels are discharged simultaneously, the reports almost blend, and are unlike any other sound in battle. Moving farther to the front, we came to an elaborate place, called Chateau Stein, owned by a Paris merchant of that name. We went into the house, and found it occupied by servants, who readily gave us permission to go to the top, and from the observatory we got a fine view of Paris, but not of the battle, which now became severe. We soon gained a position from which we could distinctly see the bursting of the French shells, but the fighting on our flank was covered by dense woods, and little could be made out.

Moving on through the little town of Marne, and near Gousche, we came upon the line in reserve, with several battalions in mass ready to re-enforce any portion of the line in front. It was plain enough, however, that they would not be needed. The troops were thoroughly in hand, and manœuvred with facility and precision. Except the occasional *chug* into the earth of a heavy shot, fired at high elevation from some battery within Paris, and the bursting of shells far in the air from the field-guns about Valerien, we even here could see nothing. We accordingly turned back toward Versailles, but stopped at a respectable house by the way-side for something to eat. A bottle of red wine and a loaf of brown bread were soon set before us, and a little cheese, of which we gratefully partook. The price was not greater than would have been charged before the war. This house may be taken as a fair sample of the houses of the peasantry. It was a story and a half rubble-stone house, plastered or stuccoed, with two good-sized rooms below, and several small ones above. The floors of the lower rooms seemed never to have been scrubbed. Each room had one table, covered with black oil-cloth, two or three old hide-bottomed chairs, and one or two benches, but not a book nor a paper; and every thing had an old, greasy, worn-out look. Neither parents nor children could read. They learned that we were Americans, and seemed to think that we had come to bring them help in some way.

On returning to Versailles, the peasantry all along the route, taking us for Prussian officers of rank, rise, as we pass, and lift their caps. This I have noticed everywhere. Servility is so strong a feature in the French character as to show itself toward their enemies. The ambulances in a long line are moving out slowly to bring in the wounded, and the streets are filled with people anxiously looking for the approach of the French battalions, which they confidently but vainly expect.

CHATEAU BEAUREGARD.

Oct. 22d.—I rode out to-day to the little town of Roquencourt, about two miles to the north of Versailles, where is situated the villa of M. Fould, late finance minister of Napoleon III. Like most French villas, it is destitute of architectural beauty—having a plain façade about 200 feet long, two and a half stories high, built of rough stone, stuccoed and painted glaringly white, and surrounded with groves of evergreens, oak, and chestnut, and straight beds of brilliant flowers. Driving a quarter of a mile farther, we reach the Chateau Beauregard, a place notorious as having been given by Napoleon III. to his mistress, Miss Howard, for money advanced him while Prince Napoleon.

After settling with the emperor, Miss Howard, or the Countess de Beauregard, married a Mr. Trelawney, and a month after died, when the chateau was sold to the Duchesse de Beaufremont, who now owns, and, at the commencement of the war, occupied it. This woman was the daughter of a banker, and widow of a wealthy Parisian merchant. Desiring title, she married the Duc de Beaufremont, a man very much her senior, wrecked in means and character, and greatly in need of money. She at once settled 80,000 francs a year upon him, and their entire relations end when she signs the check for the year, and he the receipt, while she lives with an Englishman, who is the father of her children.

After passing through a heavy iron gate-way with gilded points, we drove several hundred yards along a straight graveled road through the grounds, which comprise several hundred acres, laid out in gardens, parks, and lawns, and arrived at the house, which has a front of about one hundred and fifty feet, and is three stories high, with two nearly similar façades, the one to the north giving a beautiful view of the Seine over Beauguil, Malmaison, and toward St. Denis and Enghien. A great number of neatly-cut sandstone steps, curved to correspond with the handsomely swelling fronts, nearly surround the house. The place is the work of the late emperor. It is now occupied by a Prussian lieutenant-general, who, on satisfying himself as to our identity, at once placed himself at our disposal, and, with the geniality and kindness which we meet everywhere, proceeded to show us the house. We passed through a circular marble hall to the dining-room, which was filled with fruits and flowers, and then entered a large parlor eighty feet long, with mirrors covering half the sides, cabinets inlaid with Sevres, and curtains of Gobelin. Here were collected for safe-keeping, toilet articles, furniture, pictures, books, tapestries, china, music, and a thousand odds and ends of home life, piled, one upon the other, without order. A vast wardrobe was filled with every imaginable article of ladies' dress, of the richest material. Gloves of every color, laces, embroideries, playing-cards, rosaries, necklaces, fans, cosmetics, whist-counters, and toilet slippers, were heaped together without order. These articles, although shown to visitors, were not allowed to be disturbed, and a young Englishman, belonging to the household of the duchess, was charged with their custody.

We were next shown the second story, where simple camp-beds were fitted up and apartments prepared for the general and his staff. We also visited the bed-chamber of the duchess, a large room on the ground-floor, with an immense alcove at one end, and in it, shut off by a massive balustrade like an altar-rail, the largest imaginable bed, in blue and white, surmounted by a ducal coronet and ostrich feathers. To the right, and within reach of the occupant of the bed, were fourteen white and blue silk bell-cords, terminating in egg-shaped ivory balls, on each of which was engraved the name of a department of the household. The furniture of this apartment, with its adjoining dressing-room, was of precious woods, inlaid with gold, silver, and mother-of-pearl. Next to this was the nursery, filled with toys and books for children, nearly all of the books being in English, such as "Puss in Boots," "Mother Goose," and "Little Jack Horner." Marbles and dolls without number went to make up the collection.

Just as we were leaving, the king, with a portion of his suite, came, like us, to see the chateau of the emperor's mistress, and after saying pleasant things to each of us, passed on to inspect the premises.

CHATEAU BALZAC.

On the 29th of September, at Villeneuve St. George, a village on the Seine fifteen miles from Paris, we stopped to rest and feed our animals, and, while waiting, discovered the country home of Mme. Balzac, the former wife of the author Honoré Balzac. This is one of the many towns where the people fired from their houses upon the Prussians at their approach. When the town was occupied, the inhabitants fled, leaving every thing behind, so that we found it a barrack for soldiers.

This country house, known as Chateau Balzac, was bought by the Countess Balzac several years ago for about a hundred thousand francs. The grounds, which contain only a few acres, are beautifully situated on the right bank of the Seine. The house is of rough stone, without the usual plastering, and of ample proportions. We found a large number of books in different languages scattered about the lawn, and in the chateau an indescribable mélange of costly laces, handsome dresses, pictures, statuary, books, and china, strewn and piled upon the floors. Many of the pictures, and some of the frescoes and bas-reliefs, would not be tolerated in America; but the general character of the works of art indicated high culture.

The history of the owner of this property is not less singular than that of the Duchesse de Beaufremont. A Polish countess of rare beauty, she married a man of wealth, who was greatly her senior, and had a daughter (now Countess Meneschak, a highly respectable woman, living at Villeneuve St. George). She afterward left her husband to live with Balzac, and, on becoming a widow, married him. Afterward she lived with another man, whom, on the death of Balzac, she also married, but still bears the name of the author, and resides either at Chateau Balzac or in Paris. The story of these two chateaux is of itself a commentary on French civilization; and when I was told that nearly every one of the many thousand villas in the environs of Paris had a history almost equally notorious, another cause of the hard fate and degeneracy of France dawned upon me.

PRUSSIAN MILITARY BURIAL.

Oct. 23d.—While standing in the court-yard of the palace this evening, waiting to hear the band that seemed ready to play, it put itself in motion to a dirge. It was followed by a Lutheran clergyman; then came five coffins, one behind the other, borne by soldiers. The leading coffin was draped in black, and the others in white. Upon the black drapery was the iron cross, and among the mourners were many distinguished officers. I took my place in the procession, and moved on to the resting-place of the dead. A great number of French people followed to hear the music. I noticed a number of officers of rank occupying retired places along the route of the procession, and watching with tearful eyes as one more of their brave comrades was carried to the grave. They lower him into a grave made broad and deep, so that a half-dozen coffins can be placed side by side. The clergyman speaks of the young man's life; a dirge is played, then each one present drops a piece of earth upon the coffin, and the ceremony is ended. An officer seeing that I am a stranger, comes over and explains that the youth just buried was a brave and much-respected lieutenant, and was detailed for duty in one of the divisional ambulances, but, at the sortie of the 21st, asked and received permission to go with his regiment, and received his death-wound. The iron cross had been awarded him for conspicuous service in one of the early battles. The lieutenant-general in the procession was the commander of the Sixth Army Corps, to which the deceased belonged.

HÔTEL DU RÉSERVOIR.

The Hôtel du Reservoir is named from its proximity to a reservoir built of cut stone by Louis XIV., at an enormous expense, as a provision for the safety of the adjacent buildings in case of fire. The hotel is a three-story stone building, about one hundred and fifty feet long, with a carriage-way through the centre, and a court-yard and outbuildings in the rear. It was built by Louis XIV. for Madame Pompadour, and is connected with the palace, which is about one hundred yards away, by a secret passage through the stone-work of the reservoir. This building she occupied until her death. It is now fitted up as a hotel of some fifty rooms, and is the best in Versailles. It shows little of its original use except in one little side dining-room, where I sometimes sit. This room retains its richly-frescoed ceiling, the figures of which reveal plainly enough the moral atmosphere of the times when they were painted. This was the breakfast-room of Madame Pompadour and her royal lover.

GERMAN PRINCES.

On entering the main *salle a manger* at the ordinary dining hour, one sees an array of hereditary civic rank not often met with. The highest nobility of Germany here, representing all of the minor German States, are attached to the staff of the crown prince. They hold military rank from captains to major-generals, but receive no pay for military service. This can hardly be considered a hardship, as they in most cases do very little duty, only occasionally carrying dispatches home, or under flags of truce, and turning out in full-dress on grand occasions. These gentlemen are entirely ornamental, the crown prince having a really able and hard-working staff of army officers, who live with him at his own quarters, and do all the work. Among the officers at table are the Prince of Hohenzollern, the innocent cause of the war, the Grand Duke of Coburg, brother of Prince Albert, the Crown Prince of Saxony, and princes and grand dukes from nearly all the German States. Of these we will notice only two.

Prince Leopold Hohenzollern holds the rank of lieutenant-colonel in the Prussian army. He is slightly built, has blue eyes, light complexion, is about five feet seven inches in height, and thirty-five years of age. He speaks good English, has a bright, winning, intelligent face, and captivating manners. He is no exception to the other princes in the non-performance of duty. He is a thorough student, and almost any morning until eleven o'clock may be found in his room, in a common flannel blouse, reading or writing. He is highly respected by every one, is thoroughly moral and upright in his life, a consistent Catholic, highly educated, and perfectly amiable, but of no great force of character. He belongs to the senior line of the family of Hohenzollern, who reside in Sigmaringen, in Southern Germany, on the borders of Baden and Würtemberg.

As a kingdom, Prussia is of recent origin, and composed of several ancient states. Without mentioning the smaller provinces, it may be considered as comprehending four large divisions—viz., the Electorate of Brandenburg, the Kingdom of Prussia proper, the large province of Silesia, acquired by Frederick the Great from Austria, and one-third part of the ancient Kingdom of Poland. The ruling family was originally the electoral House of Brandenburg, an elector having the right to represent his electorate, or province, in choosing the German emperor. This family trace their origin to one Count Thassilo, who lived in the ninth century, and derived his title from an old castle called Hohen, or High Zollern, one of several eminences near Hechingen, in Suabia, situated on the beautiful heights known as the Zollern Hills. The domain contains a territory of about twenty miles square, and a population of about sixty thousand inhabitants. Here is found some of the most picturesque scenery in all Europe. The estate is still held by the father of Leopold, the head of the senior branch of the family.

Brandenburg, which was originally inhabited by a Sclavonic race, was first raised to importance by Sigafred, a Saxon count, appointed margrave, or marquis, in 927. In 1373 the Emperor Charles IV. assigned Brandenburg to his second son, Sigismund, who in 1415, being then himself Emperor of Germany, sold this Margraviate of Brandenburg to Frederick of Hohenzollern (then margrave, or imperial commissioner, of the town of Nuremberg) for the sum of four hundred thousand ducats. This first Frederick separated himself from his family, and, taking possession of his new purchase, showed many of the marked characteristics of the great men of his line who have succeeded him. This new branch of the Brandenburg Hohenzollerns, in 1530, embraced the Lutheran religion, which has ever since been the prevailing faith of Prussia, while the senior Suabian, or main family, retained, and still hold, their original Roman Catholic creed. It is this senior branch that the father of Prince Leopold Hohenzollern now represents. They have no resemblance, and no near relationship to the Brandenburg family, and, being very wealthy, lead a life of ease and scholarship. Not until 1851 did they surrender their rights of sovereignty to their tenth cousin, the King of Prussia.

Leopold is the eldest son of Prince Charles Anton and Princess Josephine, and therefore doubly related to the dynasty of Bonaparte, his father being a son of Princess Antoinette Murat, and his mother, Princess Josephine of Baden, a daughter of Stephanie de Beauharnais, who was an adopted daughter of Napoleon I. It is not surprising that the Government of Madrid should expect these ties of relationship to recommend their candidate at the Tuileries. Prince Charles Anton has been always an intimate friend and adviser, as well as relative, of Napoleon III., and was the manager of the affair of his son's candidature.

In 1861, Prince Leopold was married to the sister of the King of Portugal, which also gave him character in that portion of Europe. The father, Prince Charles Anton, with his family, generally lives at his chateau in Sigmaringen, built by the present King of Prussia for the head of the House of Hohenzollern. It was here that the preliminary negotiations with the Spanish Government were discussed.

In the contracts of December, 1851, between Prussia and the Princes of Hohenzollern (Anton's line), by which the latter ceded their rights of sovereignty to the crown of Prussia, it is expressly stipulated that, in case of extinction of male representatives, the crown of Prussia shall not claim proprietary rights to the principalities of the senior or Anton line, and that the princes of Hohenzollern shall not inherit the rights of the Prussian branch. The head of the family is, therefore, not the King of Prussia, but Prince Charles Anton, who by royal order received the title of "highness," and, later, "royal highness," but with the distinct specification that it changed in no manner the relation of the House of Hohenzollern to the throne of Prussia. It will, therefore, be clearly seen that the Prussian throne was in no manner interested in or profited by the possible occupancy of the Spanish throne by a representative of that House. No better expression of the motives of the Spanish Government in choosing Prince Leopold for their regent can be given than by quoting a paper of the distinguished Spanish statesman, Señor Salazar. He says:

"In the first place, Prince Leopold belongs to that branch of the Hohenzollern family which has for centuries kept aloof from Protestantism, now predominant at Berlin. He would be the present heir of the Prussian crown, had his ancestors, possessing the right of primogeniture, been willing to forswear the Catholic for the Protestant religion."

In the second place, Salazar puts the question:

"Can a parliamentary king involve his land in a foreign war? Is Portugal dependent on Spain because their thrones are occupied by members of the same family? To what profit, in 1866, was the relationship of the dethroned King of Hanover to Queen Victoria? Gratitude is an empty word in politics, and, aside from this, upon what ground of interest is Prince Leopold bound to Prussia? His attachments would all be to the Spanish Cortes. The Prussian Government had no part in this transaction, and King William was greatly surprised when the prince, who is of full age, came to Ems to communicate to him, as a matter of courtesy, his renunciation of the candidature. The only control which the king exercised over him arose from the fact that Prince Leopold was an officer of the Prussian army. The prince's own motives for this action were entirely personal. One reason, which he has authorized to be published in his own language, is that, without knowing what the people of Spain thought about it, every body in Germany versed in foreign politics was of the opinion that the Peninsula, on account of its geographical position and peculiar constitution, would have nothing to gain and much to lose by entanglements with European politics, and that therefore their sovereigns should be strong neutrals."

THE GRAND DUKE OF COBURG is a large, awkward-looking man of about fifty, with a heavy, sensuous face. He holds the military rank of major-general, is the nominal commander of the little force from his duchy, and *chef* to a regiment of cuirassiers belonging to his contingent. Although he commanded his troops in the field in 1866, and his regiment at Sedan—the papers say, at a safe distance—he is not looked upon as a soldier of any merit, and I have known him to perform only the duty of appearing well dressed and well mounted on grand days, and even in this he is untrustworthy, as he rides wretchedly. I am informed that he is anxious for a command, which he is not in the least likely to get. He speaks English well, and is especially polite to Americans.

The duke is a sovereign member of the North German Confederation, a ruler over one hundred and sixty-nine thousand people—a population a little larger than one of our Congressional districts—and dispenses a budget of about one thousand dollars annually. His career has been curious. Setting out as an absolute monarch, he is now about as near the ranks of democracy as a liberal German can be. He has been a great traveler, and has strong dramatic and musical taste. At his beautiful country-seat may almost always be found either the theatre or opera in full force, largely supported by his private means. It is not uncommon for him to act as manager himself. He, of all the men of rank about Versailles, bears the reputation of bringing a mistress from Germany; and it is said that the propriety of sending him home for it has been seriously discussed by the Government. He has a very social nature, and his rooms are made a sort of club, where the members of his mess may win or lose spare cash.

Sitting at the long table are the princes of Würtemberg, Augustenburg, and many generals of high rank from minor states. These gentlemen are show-soldiers, and have been replaced pretty generally by Prussian officers of experience and ability. They are attached to the staff of the crown prince, as the easiest and least offensive way to dispose of them.

These noble persons rise at eight, or earlier if industrious, and take in their rooms a cup of coffee, with a roll and butter, then work at whatever they have to do until eleven or twelve, when they eat a hearty meal — their breakfast — which they prolong for one or two hours. They then ride, or read, or play at some game, but seldom do any work until after dinner. At eight they dine heavily, prolonging the meal until ten or eleven o'clock, when they are ready for as much of the night as they may find means of occupying, either at work or play. They afford a fine field for study to those who make humanity one of their subjects of investigation.

Although the noble class in Germany is very large, and titles are innumerable, from the fact that all the sons of a family take the title of their father, it does not monopolize any considerable portion of the soil. In Prussia only one-thirtieth of the land is held by the nobility, the rest being in the hands of the people. The nobility are, therefore, generally poor in money, although usually owning handsome landed estates. Many of them, however, comprehending the drift of events, have taken up the industries, and become thereby useful members of society. But the forty or fifty men at the table before us are of too high rank, and trace back too far their names and lineage, to stoop to labor. In viewing them critically, one is impressed with the lack of force and intellectual character expressed in their faces. They are less in stature than the common people, and, except that they are unexceptionably well bred, are not to be compared with the active officers of the army; nor are the officers of the regular army, although perfect as soldiers, equal to those I have seen of the landwehr regiments, which are officered largely from the common people. This class is gaining rapidly in wealth and influence, and must before long be recognized as the new, progressive, and dominant power in Germany. The regular army clings to the tradition of gentle blood, and the officer class is really a kind of nobility, having equal social privileges with the king himself. There is hardly a thoroughly good face at the table, but, with two exceptions, they bear no marks of dissipation.

CHAPTER II.

TYPES OF GERMAN PEOPLE.

Oct. 23d.—The Würtembergers are large, have short, straight noses, little blue eyes, high cheek-bones, broad faces, and light hair, and are, in fact, the ideal "Dutchmen" of America.

The Bavarians are small, have dark complexions, and womanly faces, and are slight in stature.

The Hanoverians and Saxons are perhaps the handsomest of the German people. They have good faces, well-developed figures, a manly bearing, and winning manners.

The Poles are tall, with light complexions, and have furnished some of the best officers for this war.

The Pomeranians are large, tall men, and make good soldiers.

Much of Prussia is peopled by a race akin to the Russians—a dark-bearded, black-eyed, tall, handsome people, having nothing about them but their language in common with the other races of Germany. The men in all the extreme North German states find their counterparts in the Northern United States, and, meeting them in a strange land, an American might easily mistake them for his own countrymen. The physical types in many of the German states have become thoroughly, and in many instances viciously fixed; and if the Confederation breaks this up, and makes the people more homogeneous, it will have done a great work. The finest body of men I have seen in this army is the second division of the landwehr of the Guard. The officers, as well as the men, in every thing

CHACTERISTICS OF PRINCES.

In view of the aimless lives led by the German princes, their inactivity and isolation from their fellows, all of which cuts them off from the sympathy of mankind, their condition seems in no way comparable to that of a cultivated American citizen of fortune whose home is the world, and before whom the whole field of industry, art, and knowledge lies open. The lives of princes are wrought in forms, and no matter how beautiful those forms may be, they cramp development, check many of the best impulses of humanity, and come far short of furnishing the best examples of manhood. The entire system of hereditary politics may be classed among things of the past, incompatible with the highest conditions of civilization, and destined to disappear before it.

RUSSIAN OFFICERS.

The few Russian officers attached to the head-quarters of the Prussian army seem to be on terms of the greatest intimacy with the Prussian Government; and whenever Russian generals have arrived as special ambassadors the utmost warmth has always been manifested. Two of the Russian officers have rooms next my own, and although we have a tough time at conversation, their hearts evidently warm toward Americans.

POSTING AND QUARTERING THE GERMAN ARMY ABOUT PARIS.

Oct. 24th.—I have to-day visited the line south of Paris, passing through Chatillon and Sieux, where Vinoy attacked the crown prince on the 19th of September, when the latter was approaching Versailles to close the investment. Judging from the marks upon the buildings, trees, and fences, the fighting must have been scattering and weak. On arriving at the front line, or rather position, for there are no lines, but only posts of observation, we find three companies holding a strong point, and are told by the commanding officer that the enemy, thirty thousand strong, are lying just below him. As he has to hold the point at all hazards, he prefers that we should not show ourselves to the enemy, as it might draw their fire. Nothing has struck me more forcibly than the perfect success of the Germans at concealment. It is a strong point in their tactics: Their sentinels are always out of sight, their bayonets and gun-barrels dimmed with grease and by withholding the burnisher, while their troops are always marched and posted behind cover, so that not a trace of them can be seen. The Parisians are greatly disappointed because they are never able to see a German. They have telescopes, mounted for hire by the minute, all about the city, and on fine days the ladies, with their children, go out to see the Prussians, but none are ever seen. They thought it due to the leaves on the trees, but these are now all fallen, and still their efforts meet with no better success.

The posting of the investing line is a novelty to an American officer, and yet there is wisdom displayed everywhere. There is, in fact, no investing line at all, but a zone of occupation about five miles in depth. When the Germans approached Paris, the French quickly retired within the circle of investing forts. The Prussians have approached this circle within about a mile, and have judiciously posted a picket-line around the city. These picket-posts, secure from needless exposure to the fire of the forts, are called advanced posts, and are so situated that from them can be seen all that occurs between them and the enemy, and between the adjacent posts. We find a single man at one of these points of observation, who watches every thing, peeping over a wall, through a window, or out from the bushes. Not far away from him, and also out of sight, are two or three comrades and a mounted picket; one or two hundred yards to the rear is a platoon, generally concealed in some garden or walled yard, and a half-mile farther back is the regiment, comfortably quartered in a little village. If we go on, we soon find larger bodies of troops, but the main force is stationed well toward the outer portion of the zone of investment. The regiments in the front are replaced by others from the rear every three days, while those in the rear are so disposed as to concentrate on any threatened point in their front on very short notice, and the posting is such that two army corps, or sixty thousand men, can be massed on any position before the French can reach it. The regiments in front keep their belts on, while those in the rear are comfortably established in the deserted villages and towns. So thorough is the discipline and complete the subordination, that no man wanders from his company rendezvous beyond the sound of his bugles. The regiments in front are always ready to move at a moment's notice, while those in the rear are easily available, and there seems no tendency to straggle away as with us. I imagine that the secret of this is a more absolute discipline, and a more quiet disposition. When the long roll is sounded, the regiments move out with full ranks in a very few minutes. In case of an advance of the French, the single advanced man calls the mounted trooper, who at once notifies the reserve platoon and the regiment, which concentrate at a predetermined rendezvous, to check the advance. Word is at once dispatched to the corps in the rear, which gets under arms and takes up a line already resolved upon and prepared, perhaps two or three miles in rear of the advanced regiment. In the mean time the regiment, by taking advantage of every accident of ground, or fence, or wood, harasses and checks the attack as far as possible, without risking much, and falls slowly back upon the line already posted.

The investing troops are not evenly disposed all around the city, but there are several main points of concentration commanding the avenues by which, from the nature of the country, a sallying force must necessarily advance. The most favorable lines across these *debouches* have been strengthened, and thoroughly prepared for defense. Sometimes these points of concentration are very near the front, and sometimes far to the rear; but never has any sortie broken or passed beyond the prepared line, and the attack of some twenty battalions from Mount Valerien on the 21st instant did not even reach the advanced posts at any point. Two mitrailleuses which were run down a little too near these posts were swept in by a company of German troops like crumbs from the table.

The French, like ourselves in the late war, preface and publish such a movement by a long cannonade, thereby greatly aiding their adversary to make ready to receive them. This use of artillery is one of the absurdities of modern warfare. It seems to owe its existence to the old custom of using breaching artillery in order to make a practicable opening in a permanent fort before sending forward the assaulting party, when musketry fire was effective only at short range, and permanent works were reduced by regular approaches. Since the introduction of long-range small-arms, with thin lines of troops posted behind slight earth-works, the practice has become vicious, for it hurts no one, and only advertises your intentions.

The French, in order to do this effectually, collected a large number of field-guns near the assaulting line on the 21st instant, and for two hours fired an average of more than a hundred guns to the minute. As they only use time-fuses, many of their shells burst thousands of feet in the air.

At the assault on Fort McAllister during our war (the only time I had full control of a storming-party), some artillery officers stood aghast when told that I had no use for artillery. By quietly pushing up sharp-shooters and driving every body into the bomb-proofs, and at the same time deploying an assaulting party just out of sight, I was able to send it quietly forward, so that it nearly reached the enemy's lines before they were aware of the presence of a large force. Had they known our intention, and begun to fire upon us when we first came within range, our loss would have been doubled.

Oct. 25th.—The zone of German investment embraces hundreds, and perhaps thousands, of villas, châteaux, farms, and gardens. In France, every thing of this kind, of however little pretense, is surrounded by a rubble-stone wall about eight feet high and two feet thick. This has simplified the military problem for the German, as a starving siege consists mainly in the defense of the besiegers. Different lines of these walls, occupying commanding positions, have been loop-holed for musketry, embrasures have been cut for artillery, banquettes thrown up, and sometimes staging built for two tiers of infantry. These strong positions naturally deflect an assaulting column to the right and left into the more open ways, where it is soon enfiladed by a strong fire from infantry, and often taken in reverse by a force securely posted in loop-holed houses or garden hedges. The Germans at once saw and availed themselves of the great advantage of these combinations for defensive purposes, and prepared covers and opened roads through farms and gardens for artillery and infantry, so that, with their reserves comfortably quartered in the rear, they could at any alarm speedily man these successive positions with thin lines and sweep the open roads with their batteries. A combination of defenses practicably impregnable has thus been formed. The advance positions are given up at the right moment, and the various covers prepared for retreat make it easy and safe. From this statement, it will be seen how utterly hopeless and mad a night sortie would be, as it could not overcome even the physical difficulties. None will ever be tried.

Oct. 26th.—The star that guided all these four hundred thousand French troops, including a numerous cavalry, into Paris, within this net-work of infantry defenses, was certainly an evil one; and it is difficult to understand how, among so many able men, no one should have seen the suicidal policy of such a step. The thirty thousand cavalry now there—where under no circumstances can they be used, except as the horses may serve for food—if free in France under a Wilson or an Upton, and divided into five or six detachments, would cut the German line of communication, check and harass all their advancing columns, and in many ways make themselves felt and dreaded. This must, in the future, in consequence of the employment of long-range and close-shooting small-arms, be the main use of cavalry. Two hundred thousand men are quite as effective to defend the city as a more numerous army. By the remarkable policy of depopulating the environs of Paris, and calling the people within the lines, the French have not only some hundred thousand more mouths to feed, but have left excellent quarters for their enemy. While engaging in impossible attempts to burn the green forests, the French have left thousands of cords of bundles of fagots for fuel, and the extensive forests of St. Cloud, Versailles, and St. Germain are full of small saplings just to the hand of the Germans for making gabions and fascines. The surrounding country, instead of being desolated, is left covered with stacks of grain and barns full of hay; the gardens are full of potatoes, turnips, beets, and vegetables of all kinds, abundantly raised for the Paris market. It seems that every thing of a military nature that France ought to have done she has neglected, while she has done all manner of things she ought not to have done.

THE OLD NOBLESSE.

The incidents which occur in a town occupied by a hostile army are sometimes very ludicrous. Every one knows that the old noblesse of France have always maintained their exclusiveness, not extending even a social recognition to the Bonapartists when in power. Versailles is the home of many of these families, who, shorn of their fortunes, support, by means of their pensions, and God knows what else, a solitary and threadbare magnificence. They usually own their own houses and grounds, and keep within their own social circle, sometimes admitting Americans, rarely Englishmen, but never the new order of Frenchmen. In the morning the master of the house can be found, in dressing-gown and slippers, hovering over the least possible fire, while the mistress prepares the frugal breakfast. From two to six in the evening a liveried servant may be found at the door, and occasionally the whole family drive out in a carriage of a style decidedly antiquated, attended by footmen powdered and liveried, and drawn by horses whose best exertions toward speed never take them beyond a funeral pace.

These people are as likely as any one to have German officers billeted upon them, and their extreme poverty makes it a great hardship. The Marquise du Grammont, one of my neighbors, had three officers assigned to her house. Their dinner was ready at the usual hour of eight, but military duties at the front, or a game of cards in town, kept them away until three o'clock in the morning. But the dinner must be ready, and imagine monsieur the marquis and madame shivering over the coals of a scanty fire, for they are too poor for servants, until three o'clock in the morning, waiting for their self-invited guests.

Madame, the Marquise of ——, has no servants, and entertains two officers. The first day she cooks them her best dinner, but there is no wine. They wish Champagne, and are told that she has none, when, believing her the maid, they mildly intimate that it is procurable at the moderate rate of six francs a bottle at the restaurant opposite. Not having that amount of ready-money, she retires in much confusion. Next day, seeing no other woman about the house, they inquire, and learn, to their utter dismay, that it is Madame the Marquise upon whom they made requisition for Champagne. The most ample apologies, and a consideration suited to her rank, follow.

Madame —— comes with dreadful complaints this morning: "These horrid Germans, they have treated me so shamefully!" As she stops to take breath, I prepare to hear something like the usual and true tale — so often told us in Georgia. "I was told," she continued, "they carried the Prayer-book, the Bible, and the Commandments, or at least one of these, in each knapsack. Surely their Bible does not contain the eighth commandment. The Duke de ——, on joining the French army in Paris, left with me his harness, his whips, and his carriages, except the wheels, which he carried to some stable on the opposite side of the city, that the Germans might not be able to use them. When these officers were billeted upon me, they had horses, but furnished their own forage, only asking of me stabling-room, and I of course had to give it. On going to the stable two days after, what was my horror on finding the whips gone; and when I told them I would have them reported to the king, they told me if I did not keep quiet they would take the harness also — the dreadful thieving Germans!" This is the first and only complaint of the kind that I have heard at Versailles, where the head-quarters of the largest army in the world, and all of its dependencies, have been established for more than a month. The kindest relations seem to exist between host and guest all over the city as soon as they understand each other. The soldiers are everywhere favorites when they become domesticated, doing all manner of little offices for the family, and going errands, caring for the children, and helping about the house.

CHAPTER III.

FALL OF METZ.—ITS EFFECT UPON THE WAR.

Oct. 28th.—Metz has fallen, and M. Thiers is here, invested with plenary powers. I doubt whether he is different from other Frenchmen, and capable of looking upon the military situation with cool and elevated reason. It has been astonishing from the first to see the inability of the French to understand their condition. The cry everywhere is, "Not a fortress, not a stone;" and on the margin of the proclamations of Jules Favre to this effect in Paris, the populace add, "And not one cent of money." There is much in this to remind one of the "last ditch" in our own war. The French have, in common with our former adversaries of the South, the faculty of disbelieving the successes of their enemies. They say that the Germans dressed their own soldiers in French uniforms at Sedan, and marched them through the streets, and called them prisoners. The French also talk of battalions of *Amazons*, to fight when the men are all killed, and I find a vague general belief that something will come from somewhere to help them at last. This condition of the national mind, this disregard of reason, is not encouraging. Whether the cowl and gown have caused it, or are only concomitant with it, I leave to others.

With the Prussian army of two hundred thousand men set free from before Metz to overrun France, her chance of military success is reduced to nothing. If she will see this and act upon it, she will save millions of money, thousands of lives, and gain better terms than can afterward be secured. Thiers went into Paris early this morning to gain authority from the members of the Government there such as he already has from Tours. He went too early to carry with him news of the result at Metz. Count Bismarck can not be seen. "Fritz" and all the ministers have been called in council with the king. The little German kings are coming in a day or two. It all looks as if King William were to be made emperor.

The French people obstinately refuse to credit the news that Metz has surrendered. They even believe that Bazaine has come out himself, leaving his army still besieged, and is now operating on the German lines of communication, and exacting large sums of money from King William for the permission to send his sick and wounded home to Germany. They even say and believe that the Germans are beleaguered at Versailles, and must soon surrender.

The Prussians, I am told, refuse to parole any of the Metz prisoners on account of the conduct of many of the officers paroled at Sedan, who afterward exchanged with officers serving in Algiers, and thus liberated the latter for active service against Germany. The Prussians allege also that several of the paroled officers have themselves again taken the field at home.

There has been no firing of guns nor demonstration of any kind over the wonderful success at Metz, except a delicious concert with stringed instruments at the king's head-quarters. The king was called out by a large crowd of soldiers for a speech, but merely acknowledged his own thankfulness and retired.

FORTIFICATIONS ABOUT PARIS.

Paris is surrounded by a strong work of earth, faced with cut stone, nearly twenty feet high, and arranged for flank defense. This is the real barrier of the city, and is, for the length of some fifteen miles, a regularly built first-class line of fortification, with a deep moat on the outside. About two miles distant is a line of detached fortresses: Bellaire, D'Issy, Bicêtre, Charenton, and a few others. They are independent of each other, and each is capable of giving shelter to a large number of troops. The French hold to the front of these forts about one mile, and then comes a space of about a mile between the armies before we reach the German advanced posts. This gives a front for the German army of about forty miles, and the exterior circumference of their zone of operations is of course much greater. The Germans have not far from two hundred thousand men here, allowing five thousand men to the mile, which, from their plan of posting troops in reserve, and prepared positions, is abundantly ample for their work. They have no lines of rifle-pits such as we made every day during the last two years of our war, though sometimes lines of picket-pits are prepared; but the great number of stone walls gives them ready-made defenses. Sometimes these are crenelated; sometimes the top is razeed; at others, a temporary banquette is used. Stockades are built, so as to give a fire down avenues and roads, and all commanding points are made ready for artillery. This, with the pickets of observation in front, and their supports, are all we find within some miles of the French lines.

To an American who has seen our war, this all seems insecure, and not the best disposition of the German forces. But when he waits and sees that by this means many lives are saved; that the average loss by French shots is less than one man a day; that three-fourths of the command are kept comfortably housed, with minds at rest, instead of being worn out with anxiety; and when he sees the alacrity with which full brigades and divisions of cheerful men move out to their assigned places at an alarm, with positive certainty of being in the right place when wanted, he is likely to change his opinion. The plan here is purely defensive, and therefore certain; and, in my opinion, if the number of good troops in Paris were doubled, it would not add to the chances of the French breaking the investing line. Any other plan upon the part of the Germans would be uncertain and faulty; for although the fortresses can be taken by regular approaches, or the *enceinte* of Paris itself might be reached, it is not likely that it could be carried without immense loss of life; while the French troops left under cover of the fortresses would sally out upon the rear of the attacking force and cut them off. Neither do I see why Paris should be bombarded. Some injury could be done, but the city would surrender no sooner. Cities surrender only when carried by assault, which is impracticable here, or from starvation. The latter is certain, and a bombardment would accomplish nothing, unless to show the Parisians that the city is at the mercy of the enemy, which they do not yet comprehend.

AMERICANS FROM PARIS.

Oct. 28th.—A large number of Americans came out of Paris yesterday. Those within do not yet know the fate of Metz, nor the defeat of the Army of the Loire. They are rationed by the Government on meat, mostly horseflesh, but have their own bread, without butter or cheese. The death-rate among infants and invalids is already doubled. The Parisians are blind to their situation, and persist in remaining in darkness. These Americans are all French sympathizers, and remained in Paris, believing in French prowess, but now come out when food gets short. Among them is George Sanders, who, with General Ripley, of Charleston fame, has been endeavoring to impart to the French Government useful strategical knowledge gained by experience in our late war. I have not yet learned whether he has again suggested small-pox.

These people pass current over here as genuine Americans, while, in some way or other, they continually prejudice us. In coming through the lines, they were compelled to make a long detour, the point of passing having been changed from Sevres to Creteil. This delayed their arrival at Versailles until one o'clock in the morning. Every place was closed, and, being tired and dry, a party of half a dozen went to the Hôtel du France and rapped loudly, but gained no response. They then kicked vigorously against the shutters. This brought to the door an image in night-clothes, who asked them, in no tender accents, what they wanted, and they told him, "Something to drink." They were informed that they could go to the river for it, and, after taking their measure by moonlight, the supposed landlord closed the door, whereupon, in true rowdy style, they told him he could go to ——, and went away. The authority to pass the German lines gives no permission to loiter within them. Next morning the same party, thinking Versailles a pretty good place to halt for a time, betook themselves to the office of the major-general commanding the place, to apply for the much-coveted authority. They were somewhat abashed when informed that head-quarters were in the Hôtel du France, and entirely nonplused when shown the commandant, for they then discovered that they were face to face with the white-robed image of their last night's adventure, who, without waiting to receive their application, politely informed them that they must leave the town forthwith. Still clinging to the idea of having things their own way, they provokingly asked him how it would be if they gained authority to stay from Count Bismarck, and were informed that not Count Bismarck, but he, commanded the post of Versailles. The party will leave this evening.

Everywhere in Europe, and nowhere more than in Germany, Americans are received and treated with the utmost courtesy, their nationality being a passport better than nobility. Yet scenes like this are not of uncommon occurrence. If wars continue—and there is no reason to suppose that they will cease—humane people can employ themselves in no better way than by convincing non-combatants to keep away from the vicinity of military operations. Paris is filled with women and children who can not get away. There are tens of thousands of people who fled for safety to that city—the most dangerous place in France; but they were so advised, and no Frenchman seems to have an opinion of his own. This does not apply to the American families there and at Versailles, and their supposed good sense leaves them no excuse for so foolish a step. In war and in battle, any house or city is liable to be burned, and the passions of men at such times know no limits. These Americans seem not to understand what war is.

MITRAILLEUSE.

Oct. 29th.—The French mitrailleuse bears no resemblance whatever to the Gatling gun, except that it is mounted on a six-pounder carriage, and may be fired by turning a crank. It is merely a twenty-five barreled rifle, each barrel being loaded separately, and all, by a simple arrangement, fired almost simultaneously. To construct it, they have taken an ordinary brass field-piece, say a six-pounder, and enlarged or cut out the bore into a five-inch square chamber three feet long. Into this chamber is fitted and soldered a core, made of solid steel, bored quite through from end to end into twenty-five rifled barrels, in five rows each way, of a calibre of about sixty-one hundredths of an inch.

Although there are other sizes and calibres, it will be sufficient to describe but one. At the rear of this core the gun is cut down square across two-thirds through toward the bottom, and there is a similar cut one foot in rear of the first. The intervening metal is removed, leaving an open space of one feet in rear of the core. The cascabel of the piece is cut off, and through the breech in the direction of the bore is fitted a two-inch hand-screw. To the front end of this hand-screw is attached a heavy steel plate, with a smooth face on the side toward the muzzle of the piece. This plate can be strongly brought forward to the rear end of the rifled barrels by means of the hand-screw. The cartridge is composed of a pointed leaden bolt, two inches long, fitting into the end of a pasteboard case, in which is a three-inch charge of rifle powder, and is closed at the rear end by a brass cup, three-fourths of an inch long, with a central fire arrangement of fulminate.

These cartridges are put up in cases of twenty-five each, just corresponding in arrangement to the rifled barrels, so constructed that the top and bottom of the cases can be removed. To load the piece, the case, after its two lids have been taken off, is put in juxtaposition with the rear of the barrels, and an arrangement like a coarse flax hackle, with twenty-five fingers, each as long as the cartridge, and arranged in rows corresponding to the cartridges in their cases, is so placed that each finger-tip touches a cartridge. The screw is then run up, and all of the twenty-five cartridges are shoved home at once. The screw is then eased just enough for this loading apparatus and empty case to slip out, when the plate is run down closely against the rear of the barrels, and the piece is ready for firing.

The usual way of firing the mitrailleuse is to run the

plate well back, and introduce, in place of the cartridge-case, a "firing-block." This is a strong frame, having within it a lock and pin for each cartridge, and also a cylinder with an arrangement of pins like a hand-organ, which, when the cylinder is turned by a crank, strike successively the triggers of the locks just as in an organ they strike the keys. As the barrels are all parallel, the effect must be all at one point, giving rise to the expression of the sergeant, that he "would as soon be killed by twenty-five balls as by one."

As the fire is so nearly simultaneous, the recoil accumulates; and although great results were looked for from this engine, experience has not shown that it is of much use. The Germans hold it in great contempt, and it will hardly become a permanent military arm. The Gatling gun, which may be aimed between each separate discharge, and in which the recoil does not accumulate, seems to possess many and decided advantages over the mitrailleuse.

ROADS IN EUROPE.

Oct. 29th.—The roads in Europe, so far as I have seen, are all paved with stone, or macadamized, after being reduced to low grades; so that transportation is hindered by no such difficulties as we had to contend with in our war. It is common, after slight rains, to hear the most decided condemnation of roads which to us would have been models of excellence.

FOOD ABOUT PARIS.

The earth about Paris is literally filled with food. A belt of twenty or thirty miles about the city was a kitchen-garden for the Paris market, and under the highest state of cultivation. Potatoes, cabbages, beets, turnips, carrots, and cauliflowers cumber the ground. Mushrooms are as common as apples, and nearly as cheap. The humane efforts that I see are being made at home for feeding the destitute in France, as a kind of safety-valve for the humanity of our people, are unnecessary, and appear here highly absurd; for I can learn of no portion of France where want exists, or is likely to, in the future. There are, of course, villas, and villages, and towns bare of every thing, but they are all near neighborhoods full of the best food. The published stories of want are made up from the wails of the indigent, which one always hears in every Catholic country of Europe.

Balloons are very often seen moving in the direction of Tours. They have proved of real use as means of communication; but for reconnoitring purposes they appear valueless, being so unstable as to admit of no accurate observations, and the view most needed being usually cut off by trees. Neither are they useful for communicating in more than one direction, as one might as well try to shoot a bullet back into a rifle as send a balloon back into Paris.

CONTUMACY OF THE FRENCH PEOPLE.

Oct. 30th.—The French people in the streets look sullen, and ready to shoot any one wearing a uniform. That they would do it soon enough, I can easily believe from the many cases in which soldiers have been fired upon from windows. At Bauginal, a village only four miles away, on the 21st, at the sortie from Valerien, the peasants, when the French approached, began to fire upon the German soldiers. The penalty was a fine of fifty thousand francs, and ten men hung. The poor creatures, without newspapers or means of enlightenment, are ready to believe every thing, and in fact do believe all this war a kind of grand mistake which the people in Paris will soon rectify. The men of Versailles upon the street, on the 21st, would say to each other, with the greatest French enthusiasm, that the French soldiers were just outside the gates, and in a few minutes would appear *en masse.* Had there been the least show of French success, they also would have fired upon the Germans in the streets. An order was issued next morning that, in case of another alarm, all citizens should retire to their houses, and keep within-doors.

Considerable apprehension of a sortie in this direction has been felt here for the past few days. The information leading to this was gathered from a captured French spy; besides, it is the only thing to be reasonably looked for. If there are a hundred thousand men in Paris that can be manœuvred, and the leaders fail to use them in a determined effort before surrender, they will forfeit the sympathy of the world.

ALARM AND RE-ENFORCEMENTS.

As these are the general head-quarters of the king and his ministry, it is natural to expect the sortie in this direction; and such was the alarm about it two nights ago, that word was sent round to all the ministry, and all non-combatants attached to head-quarters, to keep their retainers well in hand, and at the sound of the bugle to hitch up their teams, assemble at the *place d'armes* of the chateau, and place themselves under the direction of the quartermaster-general. Word was telegraphed to a column of the Strasbourg troops then approaching to hasten up; the artillery horses were kept harnessed, and many a poor fellow's sleep was broken. The French did not come, while the Strasbourg troops did, eight thousand strong, with three batteries of artillery. We shall all sleep easier now, for this re-enforcement sets at rest all apprehension of a sortie ever reaching Versailles.

This is the second detachment of the landwehr that has

reached here. These are the men who the French said would come on canes and crutches. They are the finest body of troops I ever saw, excepting our own army after the Georgia campaign. They are all mature men, averaging about thirty-two years, and are stronger, larger, and wear fuller beards than the soldiers of the regular army. They march with a firm, military, yet easy, swinging step, and all have intelligent, pleasant faces—just like our Northern men about the region of the lakes. The king, and most of the princes and officers of rank, were out in their brightest uniforms to receive them.

It is marvelous how troops just at the close of a long march, without change of clothing, can, after a halt for the night, make themselves so trim and clean. These fellows are all ready for the closest inspection, and their uniforms look neat and fresh. This is due to the great excellence of the material, and their thorough means of cleaning. I notice this morning that, for the first time, the princes of the confederated German states wear the Prussian helmet and sash.

PROMOTION OF ROYAL PRINCES.

Yesterday was a notable day here, and its doings have raised a tumult in matters of German politics. As far back as the reign of the father of Frederick the Great, it was prescribed that no prince of the royal house should ever be created field-marshal — probably to remove from the throne the risk of military predominance. But yesterday the law was set aside by the king himself, and "Fritz" and the "Red Prince" were made field-marshals, and Moltke a count. The king made an appropriate speech, upon conferring the title upon the crown prince, saying that it was a proper occasion to bestow the highest military honors upon those most conspicuous in the late successes. This movement will in a measure strengthen royalty, and the fear is that the crown prince may be moved from his liberal instincts. His face, however, expresses so much that is good, as to preclude the fear that he will ever be unjust. I can not help believing that under his reign the great German Confederation will achieve all necessary civil liberty.

M. Thiers did not go into Paris until this morning. He saw the arrival of the landwehr, and will have much to tell his friends there: the fall of Metz, the tardiness of French army organization in the South, the loose and unreliable character of the Army of the Loire, the attitude of great compassion but inaction of the neutral states of Europe, and the failure of the French loan among their own people. He returns to-morrow. Any sensible people would say, "Get for us cessation of hostilities, and the best terms you can;" but no one can hope for this from the French. One hears on the streets everywhere from the French that the landwehr were some reserves posted near here, and brought in for effect on M. Thiers, to give him the impression that re-enforcements were arriving. Thiers is a little, short, white-haired, square-faced Frenchman of seventy-four, who scarcely looks his age, and not at all his character.

MOLTKE.

Oct. 30th.—This is Sunday; and, while going to church, I noticed near me, in a new uniform of a general officer, some one who at first impressed me as the youngest, blondest, and slenderest general officer I ever saw, and I tried to divine how promotion could have been so rapid in an army where every thing is regular. I looked again, and the quick, elastic step, the slender, almost womanly waist, contrasted strangely with his rank, which I now noticed to be that of full general. On looking into his face, I was still more surprised to recognize General Von Moltke. We continued on the remaining hundred yards to the chapel-door together.

He is a man of few words, of a singularly youthful expression of countenance and eye; and although one knows that he is seventy years of age, and heavy time-lines mark his face, it is hard to shake off the idea that he is a boy. He has a light and nearly transparent complexion, a clear-blue eye, flaxen hair, white eyebrows, and no beard. He speaks good English, and, on calling at his room, I found him very affable, and full of sagacity and accurate knowledge. In his room were a few chairs, a desk, on which was displayed a map of France, and not another scrap of any thing to be seen.

He was born in 1800, at his father's noble manor of Gnawitz, in Mecklenburg. After residing here a few years, his parents removed to Holstein, and, at the age of eleven, young Moltke was sent to the cadet school at Copenhagen. In 1822 he entered the Prussian service as second lieutenant of the 8th Regiment of Infantry. The parental estates had become much involved, and all the young life of Moltke was greatly straitened. This roused him, however, only to greater efforts to become accomplished in his profession, and he labored with indefatigable diligence to carry out this purpose. In 1823 he was sent to the Military Academy at Berlin for three years, was next detailed for two years as professor in the Fifth Division School of the army, then for two years attached to the Topographical Bureau of the general staff, and for the two years following to the general staff-itself. In 1833 he was promoted to a first lieutenancy, and appointed to the general staff. He previously, like all who eventually enter this corps, was only attached to the staff on a sort of probation. Two years later he was promoted to a captaincy, and in 1836 sent to Turkey to organize and instruct the troops of the sultan. He acted in that capacity till 1839, and became distinguished for his talents, and devotion to duty. He at one time took part in a campaign made by the sultan against the Viceroy of Egypt, and was decorated for distinguished services at the battle of Hisili. He was recalled soon after, and in 1841 assigned to the general staff of the Fourth Army Corps, and in 1842 became major. He continued on this duty till 1845, when he was assigned as adjutant to Prince Henry of Prussia, who died during the next year, when Moltke was permanently attached to the staff of the Eighth Army Corps, where he served until 1848. He was then made chief of staff of a division, and in the same year chief of staff of the Fourth Corps. In 1850 he became lieutenant-colonel, and in 1851 full colonel. He continued on staff duty with troops until 1855, when he was appointed major-general, there being no grade of brigadier-general in the Prussian army, and assigned as adjutant to Prince Frederick William of Prussia, the present king. In 1856 he was appointed chief general of staff of the armies of Prussia, which position he still holds. In May, 1859, he was made lieutenant-general, and in April of the same year ordered to the general command of the armies in Holstein, the operations of which he conducted in the most satisfactory manner. In 1864 decorations of three of the most honorable orders of Germany were conferred upon him. Moltke was appointed full general of infantry in 1866, and then proceeded to carry out that admirable plan of campaign in Austria, familiar to all as the "Seven Weeks War," which he had elaborated with much thought in advance.

The brilliancy of the campaign was unparalleled, while the sacrifice of life was marvelously small. The active fighting campaign embraced but seven days, with an effective force in line of 437,262 men and officers, and 120,892 horses. There were killed in battle and died from wounds but 262 officers and 4093 men, and died from other causes 53 officers and 6734 men; while the whole loss in horses from all causes was but 4750. Whatever credit is due for the wonderful success of this campaign and its speedy termination, largely belongs to General Moltke. The present excellent condition of the German armies, their rapid mobilization and transportation to the field of operations, and subsequent grand manœuvres, culminating in the victories at Woerth, Gravelotte, and Sedan, have resulted from his silent thought. There is still work for him, and who can doubt its final perfect accomplishment?

FRANCE UNABLE TO COMPREHEND HER REAL SITUATION.

Oct. 31st. — Dispatches from Tours indicate that the French Government still hold to terms of "No cession of territory," which confirms my opinion that there can be no peace even with the fall of Paris. It is incomprehensible to any one but a Frenchman how two and two give any other result than four, but these people are certainly deluding themselves in the belief that they arrive at other solutions. The quiet, determined, unboasting ways of the Germans inspire perfect confidence in their complete success, and indications are not wanting that all their demands will finally be granted. There can be hardly a doubt that they look upon their foe contemptuously, but there is no braggadocio in it. The cry of France, "Dishonor by cession of territory," is difficult to understand. There is no dishonor in the inevitable, in submission to facts and force greater than we can oppose. The loss of honor comes with the loss of character, which has led to this humiliation. Nothing is gained by refusing to acknowledge an accomplished fact, but in this case much is lost by refusal, and the penalty grows greater daily. That the Latin races lose by it is not true, for the loss to them has already come from loss of manly character and failure to educate. This defeat is merely declaratory of existing facts.

No one of discernment can travel through the Latin countries, even the Spanish countries in America, without being deeply and sadly impressed with unmistakable evidences of the decline that comes to all nations in the stage next after their greatest elevation. It is plainly traceable in the features and mental attitude of the people, but is still more manifest in their moral condition. Their religion prevents progress and checks learning, by giving supposed security in the future, and requiring no effort except to sustain existence. This war will serve to show the world, what many have been slow to learn and recognize, the immense preponderance of the Northern races, where religion calls for inquiry, and the people have learned the advantages of free thought.

THE AMERICAN PRESS.

Nov. 2d.—I have just received a number of the *New York Herald* of October 16th, the first I have seen since leaving America. It is painful to one who loves his country and people to see a widely-circulated and influential American paper containing whole columns of French dispatches, without one grain of truth, and fraught with mischief—for their publication can but assist to prolong a hopeless struggle, and, in respect to this war, is inexcusable and dishonest. The *New York Tribune* is a happy exception. Its dispatches and accounts have been always accurate, and except that they are old, would be valuable, even in the theatre of operations, as a reliable record of events.

CONDUCT OF THE GERMANS.

The humane and considerate conduct of the Germans toward their enemies, particularly to the non-combatants, seems to be no less due to the kind and generous natures of the men themselves than to their thorough discipline. I have never heard of unkindness to women, and during my sojourn at these head-quarters have never seen one drunken soldier. One great lesson of this war must be the power of popular education as an element of strength and virtue, and a disproval of the old idea that the greatest brute makes the best soldier.

When I passed over the line from Sedan to near Paris, which had been traversed by the armies, no traces of the march could be seen excepting an occasional field strewn with straw, where a division had bivouacked. The farmers were pursuing their usual avocations, and the women and children were at their homes, leading their usual quiet lives. The stacks of grain and barns of hay were undisturbed, while the vineyards of ripened fruit, extending to the road, hung full of clusters that could be gathered from the carriage windows. Bazeilles was burned, and men have been shot, and towns have been laid under contribution, but under similar circumstances we should have done the same.

To make war controllable, and at all compatible with civilization, it is positively necessary to confine it within rules, and to regularly organized and recognizable forces. In order to do this, and prevent what is known as bushwhacking and free-shooting—nearly akin to robbery and pillage—the Prussians have from the first refused to recognize irregular warfare, and have been compelled to resort to harsh means to carry out this policy.

CHAPTER IV.

GUARD-MOUNTING.

Nov. 2d.—Guard-mounting takes place at two o'clock in the afternoon, on the parade-ground in front of the chateau. This is an open paved space of six or eight acres, corresponding to the gardens extending from our Capitol toward Pennsylvania Avenue.

The whole guard of Versailles, made up of a dozen smaller guards, from a relief of three men to one of twenty posts, requiring, in all, about six hundred men, with a full complement of officers, is mounted at this hour. The soldiers are not inspected, as their officers are responsible for their fitness before bringing them out; but the line is formed, and the officers and sergeants are brought to the front and given their orders by the adjutant of the commandant, who then faces them about and orders them to their posts. So accurate has been their drill, that although there is no music to mark the cadence, and their routes carry them several hundred yards asunder, not one loses the step. The different guards seem to have been arranged before coming to the parade-ground; for, on breaking into column to march in review, each one wheels by itself, and is commanded by its own officers; and on passing the reviewing officer, who is the commandant of Versailles, each breaks into its own direction, and takes its proper street. The field-officer of the day now receives a few general instructions from the commandant, and the ceremony is finished.

On being relieved, the old guard repairs at once to its quarters. While passing the reviewing-officer, all march with a ludicrous degree of stiffness, reminding one of the stories of the soldiers of old Frederick. The small of the back is several inches in advance of the shoulders, and the head is held with an erectness which puts to shame our Plebes at West Point, while the foot is raised nearly as high as the knee, and considerably in advance of where it will rest, and is brought down with a spanking ring that makes the whole body shake. This, however, is kept up only a short time, and seems to be a kind of review-step. The men soon settle into an easy, graceful, swinging stride, the perfection of marching, and not unlike the gait of our own Army of the West at the close of the war.

Although the marching turned my face into a broad laugh, which I was not able to check for some time, and the same effect was produced upon several English officers near me, yet I have seen nothing which has more impressed me with the perfection of Prussian tactics and drill. The ceremony itself, without one unnecessary movement; the perfect equipment and arrangement of the men, requiring no inspection; the bright and intelligent directions of the adjutant to the commandants of the posts; the review of all by the major-general in command of the place; his own personal instructions to the higher officers; and the smart, active ways of the young ones, all showed that perfection of military detail so essential, and so rarely found.

SMALL-ARMS.

Nov. 3d.—The appearance of the needle-gun is not much in its favor. It resembles the Belgian musket used so freely by us in the beginning of our war, and for which we soon learned to feel great contempt. It is generally stocked with light-colored wood, with brass rings, guards, and butt-pieces. The main features which give it value are the breech-loading mechanism, and the arrangement for firing the front end of the cartridge, so as to prevent the blowing out of a portion of the powder before ignition.

The first needle-gun was invented by an Englishman, in 1831; but no government could be induced to use it, and the principle was never made available till 1849, when Prussia adopted the present weapon. The barrel has four rifling grooves, one twist to a length and a quarter, a calibre of fifty-eight and a half one hundredth inches, and an adjusting breech-sight for 200, 400, 600, 800, and 1000 yards. The metal of the gun seems too light for the bullet, and I have no doubt that the calibre will be reduced, and the barrel thickened. The breech-loading apparatus consists of a hollow cylinder or shell, working freely in another outer shell, to which the barrel is attached. By rotating the inner one out of a notch through about sixty degrees, by means of a knob two and a half inches long, it can be slid back like a door-bolt to admit the cartridge, and, if desired, taken out altogether. Within this inner shell is a solid cylinder of iron half an inch thick, which slides easily backward and forward. Attached to its front end is a needle, the size and half the length of a knitting-needle. Coiled about this cylinder is a spiral spring, which is brought to the rear by a small knob. The spring, on being released by drawing the trigger, carries the bolt, or cylinder, and needle forward with sufficient force to pierce through the powder of the cartridge, striking the point against the fulminate situated in the rear of a little sabot that separates the bullet from the charge, the natural tension or recoil of the spring at once withdrawing the needle from the chamber. The cartridge has a paper case, and the ball is seven-eighths of an inch in length, of an elongated egg shape, the butt-end toward the front. It is separated from the powder by a papier-maché sabot, or cup, three-quarters of an inch in length, in which the bullet rests, and in the rear end of which is the little capsule, or hardened drop of fulminate. Against this is the powder, and the paper case at the rear end is drawn, or puckered, together, leaving in the centre a small opening not large enough for the escape of the powder, but into which the needle plunges, and passes through the powder against the sabot in front. The knob, as with the chassepot, is used at a corporal's carry, or support, to sustain the gun. The arm is capable of about the same rapidity of firing as our own breech-loader, and in the hands of a perfectly-trained soldier is a very effective weapon. As the needle is within the explosion, it soon corrodes, or burns out, and must be frequently replaced.

The close working upon each other of such extended surfaces of bright metal as we find in the rotating shell and sliding cylinder, makes more care necessary to keep the piece in order than volunteers will give. In fact, out of a large number standing idle in officers' quarters and adjutants' offices that have been shown to me to explain their action, not one has proved serviceable, and only those taken direct from the hand of the soldier have I ever seen work freely. Such an arm at Shiloh during the rainy, dirty 9th and 10th of April, 1862, would have proved our ruin.

The chassepot is considered a very much superior arm, and resembles both the new altered Springfield and Enfield rifle. The barrel is three inches shorter than that of the needle-gun, which is three feet in length, and the breech-loading apparatus is three inches shorter also—making a perceptible difference in the length of the piece. The chassepot has a calibre of only $\frac{42}{100}$ inches, and weighs but eight and a half pounds, while the needle-gun weighs ten pounds. It is usually stocked in walnut, and its whole mechanical make-up is superior to that of the needle-gun.

The breech-sight can be adjusted to a range 400 yards greater than that of the needle-gun; and as the calibre is less, with a proportionally stronger barrel, a larger charge can be used, and greater range secured. This arm is in many respects similar to the needle-gun. It is fired by a needle-pin, which strikes a percussion-cap situated in the rear of the cartridge, and the force is communicated by an ordinary steel spring.

It has also an arrangement of hollow cylinders in the loading apparatus, with bright, closely-fitting surfaces, which easily become unserviceable from rust. The cartridge has a paper case, and a light covering of linen about the bullet, to keep it firmly in place. The powder comes against the bullet, and back of the powder is a common percussion-cap, with its open end to the rear, which is covered by a gutta-percha flap, and held in place by two papier-maché washers fitting over it. The paper case is gathered down closely on the cap. When fired, the pin of the lock plunges through the flap of gutta-percha against the fulminate in the cap, the impact of the blow being taken up by the papier-maché washers resting against the powder. The bullet is a leaden bolt three-fourths of an inch long, with a plain face in the rear and a blunt point in front. The chassepot has a short ring of gutta-percha just in rear of the cylinder to which the needle is attached, that expands from the blast when the piece is fired, and completely shuts off the escape of gas. The Prussians were about to make the same improvement in their own arms when the war began.

The powder used by the French is of a dull brown color, very dirty to the touch, and without glaze; while the Prussian is jet-black, with glazed grains, and admits of handling without soiling the fingers.

I am free to give my impression of these weapons, and

I do not consider them comparable to our altered Springfield, Remington, Spencer, or a half-dozen other arms used in our country. It is very doubtful whether, in the hands of troops imperfectly disciplined, either the needle-gun or the chassepot could be kept in a serviceable condition.

PRUSSIAN UNIFORM.

Nov. 4th.—The prevailing color of the Prussian uniform is blue, and the coat is much like that of our own troops. For infantry, artillery, the staff, and administration, the coat is a dark-blue frock, with a single row of eight buttons, with facings of collar and cuffs indicative of the arm of service, and dark pantaloons. The facings of the infantry are red, and for artillery black. The pantaloons are of very dark gray — almost black — with a red cord down the seam. The boot has tops about six inches high. The cap for ordinary undress is of blue cloth, neat and flat-topped, with patent-leather visor, and red band, one inch and a half wide. The helmet is of glazed leather, with a front and rear visor, a brass-scaled chin strap, a brass Prussian eagle displayed in front, and terminates at the top in a brass spike about two inches in height. For infantry, this spike is pointed; for artillery, it ends in a ball; and for cavalry, it is fluted.

All arms of the service use a long overcoat, coming near the ground, sometimes with a short cape, but usually without it. This coat is made full, and of the same color and material as the pantaloons. All the garments are of excellent, strong, all-wool cloth, and fit neatly. In addition, the men have for drill and fatigue common cotton pantaloons and a short cloth jacket, and sometimes a light forage-cap without visor.

The uniform of the mounted troops is still very fanciful and beautiful, and not quite out of the old order of chivalry and armor. The principal colors are white, light blue, green, scarlet, and brown. The pantaloons are re-enforced, and the coat has a very short skirt, and is elaborately ornamented with braid. The dress of these troops is too varied and complicated for description here. The Prussian button is a plain gilt oval; and upon the shoulder-lap worn by the men, the color of which indicates their army corps, is a single button bearing the letter of their company.

General officers, officers of the general staff, officers of the king's and crown prince's staff, and of the king's household, wear a broad scarlet stripe down the leg of the pantaloon; but otherwise the uniform of all grades is very similar, and, without close observation, the lieutenant-general can not be distinguished from the lieutenant. A neat sword, like the cavalry sabre of our service, is worn, and the belt fastens underneath the coat, the scabbard passing through and under the skirt of the coat by a slit cut for it. The sash is of white silver braid, with tassels of the same. To mark the rank of officers, there is a system of braids and shoulder-straps. For a second lieutenant, a plain rectangular piece of thick silver braid, about four inches long and one and a half wide, is worn from the collar of the coat to the shoulder; for a first lieutenant, the same as for a second lieutenant, with the addition of one star; for a captain, the same strap, with two stars; for a major, lieutenant-colonel, and colonel, the same as for the three grades of line officers, except that the braid is gold instead of silver, the stars being the same. There is no grade of brigadier, but for major-general, lieutenant-general, and general, instead of the braid, is a plait of heavy gold and silver bullion of the same dimensions as for the former officers, and the same arrangement of stars as for the lower grades.

The care taken of soldiers' clothing is remarkable. The suit is made of the best material, and is not owned by the soldier as with us, but kept in stock by the regiment. There are three suits for each soldier. The suit for every day he turns in when he has permission to go to town, and dresses neatly for his holiday. He turns in his common suit on Saturday, and is given the one for Sunday. He has still another, brought out only on great occasions, such as reviews before the king. The clothing is kept by the first sergeant, and although, on the average, a suit lasts only a year, each of the old suits being degraded one degree in importance when a new one is issued, it is not uncommon to find suits in stock that have been in service twenty years.

The foregoing arrangement applies, of course, only to garrison life; and when the army takes the field only one suit is worn; but a marvelous faculty for brushing up enables the men to come out on occasions of ceremony as neat and glittering as though just from the wardrobe of the barrack.

The soldier is besides allowed annually two pairs of cotton drawers, two shirts of the same, and two pairs of boots. The latter must be topped after the first three months' use. He also has each year one cotton suit for drilling, and two black-cloth stocks. The stock is worn by all grades, no one using white collars.

The officers receive a tolerable pay, and clothe themselves, and the most scrupulous care of their personal appearance is exacted. Their dress is so like that of the privates, that but for its texture, and the shoulder-straps and swords, one can scarcely distinguish them from the common soldiers. The have three distinct dresses. Full dress is a single-breasted frock-coat with one row of buttons, sword, sash, and helmet, and corded black pantaloons. Dress nearly full, corresponding to the dress-coat and black cravat of a civilian, is a coat like the first, except that it is double-breasted, and has two rows of buttons, with the same pantaloons, sword, sash, and helmet. The fatigue-dress is the last-described coat and pantaloons, with the forage-cap in place of the helmet. This corresponds to the morning-dress of a civilian. There is, besides this, the working-suit, answering to the drill-jacket and pantaloons of the men. The most scrupulous deference is always paid to superiors in rank; and many regulations seem, to unmilitary people, quite absurd. For example, officers are not allowed to carry an umbrella or bundles. If walking with a lady while shopping, an officer could not carry her parcel.

Most ample provisions are made for officers' servants. Soldiers are designated by law for this purpose, which is considered a part of their duty, and not menial service. The Prussians recognize the fact that the relations between an officer and his men is of such a nature as at times to make this service indispensable. It is natural, and inseparable from despotic life, and military service is necessarily despotic. It is doubtful if prohibitory legislation has any other effect than to compel officers to commit breaches of the law. This fact becomes most clearly apparent with detachments serving in distant and isolated localities, where servants can nowhere else be obtained. Under such circumstances, no officer can maintain his position among his men without having certain services performed for him.

THE IRON CROSS.

For several days the officers stationed on this portion of the line have had all their effects packed, ready to move out at the shortest notice, and rendezvous have been appointed for the Government personages and all attachés, in case of alarm. This is merely a precautionary measure; and so perfect is every preparation that a half-hour's notice is sufficient to make ready to move from the rendezvous in traveling column.

The crown prince to-day reviewed the three regiments of mounted troops stationed here—one of lancers (Uhlans), one of dragoons, and one of cuirassiers (the Grand Duke of Coburg's)—and presented, as rewards for special acts of gallantry, the decoration of the Iron Cross. This order was created by the King of Prussia in 1813 for conspicuous services against France; and from the fall of Napoleon I. until now has been discontinued. It has been lately revived, and is given exclusively for gallantry in battle. There are two grades of the order: the first is given for the greatest services to the state, and is worn on the left breast, without a ribbon. Only about twenty of these have been given. The second is more common, and is worn on the left breast with a ribbon. It is a Maltese cross, about two inches from point to point, of black iron, with a burnished silver border. It is given without respect to rank—many more privates than officers receiving it.

The parade and presentation took place on the lawn just in front of the Petit Trianon. Those on whom the order was to be conferred moved to the front, and, closing to the right, formed according to rank, the adjutants calling the roll. The crown prince, still mounted, took his place in front of them, with a staff officer on foot carrying the medals. The officer or man on the right, upon an intimation to that effect, rode near the prince, who shook him heartily by the hand, placing in it by the same motion his medal, and, while holding the hand, said some pleasant words of recognition and congratulation. There is no doubt the system gives *esprit*, and strengthens the Government by gaining the personal devotion of the bravest and best men—a result especially important, since promotion is not attainable by all classes.

THE CROWN PRINCE.

Frederick William, Crown Prince of Prussia, was born in October, 1831. His youth was guided by a watchful, careful mother, now Queen Augusta, under whose eye he received an excellent education. He inherited from his father strength of mind and will, and from his mother brightness of intellect, and a high regard for, and interest in, the arts and sciences. In his youth, his openness of character, unassuming simplicity, earnest manner, and thirst for knowledge, gained for him, while a school-boy at Bonn, the love and esteem of his professors and fellow-students. He began his military life in the lower grades, serving as a captain of infantry with his company. Upon his marriage to the Princess Royal of England, he at once gathered about him the most eminent savants of all professions, and, although twenty-seven years of age, did not relax his studies, but devoted a portion of each day to books, and free social intercourse with the learned men who composed his household. Science, politics, and military studies received at this time full and careful attention, Moltke being his instructor in the latter.

His life remained purely domestic and scholarly up to the war with Denmark, when he applied for active service, which was given him in a secondary position, as no one dreamed that he was suited to a high command. In fact, his life had been so entirely domestic, as to give him no opportunity to display military aptitude.

In this war he won the devotion of the entire army by his humane character and fidelity to duty. Still, a large military command was never thought of for him; and not until Königgrätz, in 1866, did he attract attention as a military genius. I have reason to know that the movement which at that battle brought his troops to the right spot at the right time was greatly due to his own suggestions and efforts. From that time his reputation has steadily increased; and though entirely subordinate to the orders of General Moltke, he is considered a general of the first order of ability.

At the beginning of the present war he was assigned to the command of the Third Army Corps, made up of the contingents of the South German States, which has so nobly followed him in nearly all the great engagements. His expressions of sympathy for the suffering, and regret at the stern necessities of his duty, have reached the hearts of good people, while his simplicity and courtesy gain the esteem and confidence of all who meet him. His face is that of the highest type of the cultivated European, and speaks of good-breeding, physical health, happiness, and honesty. There is not a trace of the generally accepted German face in it. At his table, the excellent custom of never repeating the wine is followed. What is suitable and ample is on the table when the party sits down, and none is added afterward.

ARMY-POLICE.

Nov. 5th.—To each corps are attached forty picked men, who serve as gens d'armes, or army-police. They are mounted, armed with sabres and revolvers, and uniformed much like cavalry, only that the color of the coat is green. Each man wears about his neck a metal chain with a plate in front, on which is his number. They are a very superior and useful body of men. They receive orders only from general officers, and in their own proper sphere are obeyed by all below that grade.

Each division has its police judge. The force never meddles with military matters, but has charge of all secret service, and exercises surveillance over every one.

They look out for the personal safety of all general officers and personages of importance, prevent pillage in the army, compel payment for all purchases by soldiers, make the way clear for marching columns not in presence of the enemy, attend to executing all sentences of courts-martial, and are expected to know all that happens. The troops affect a great contempt for them.

AMERICANS.

In the last batch of Americans who came from Paris were the three proprietors of the *Democratic Review*, of New York, a publication which ceased to exist at the beginning of our war. Its founder was Chevalier Wykoff, who sold it to Mr. O'Sullivan, who parted with it to George Sanders. The Chevalier is in the interest of the *New York Herald*. O'Sullivan was Mr. Buchanan's minister to Portugal, and, during Mr. Lincoln's administration, became a rebel adviser and agent in Paris. He has not been in America since. George Sanders is perhaps best known as the advocate, during our war, of introducing small-pox into our armies and cities. These three men are now figuring in Versailles as distinguished American citizens.

The Franco-American Ambulance, with one or two worthy exceptions, I find made up of Southern sympathizers. It was formed at Paris by Dr. Sims, under the auspices of the emperor, for aiding the French, but, after Sedan, found itself with the Germans, and has come here and almost demanded to be let into Paris again. This request is of course denied, and the ambulance-men are in turn told that they can go anywhere else but into Paris, and that they must get away from Versailles without delay. They are not only in full sympathy with the French, but by their loud-mouthed denunciation of the Germans, who keep themselves thoroughly informed of the sayings and doings of every body, have become thoroughly obnoxious not only at Sedan, but afterward at Metz, and now here. It is this class of impertinent people who, everywhere they go, gain interviews with high officials as Americans, while they in no sense represent our country.

THIERS IN PARIS.

Nov. 6th.—Within the past forty-eight hours the firing from Paris has greatly increased. Nothing whatever is known outside of the king's government of the doings and results of M. Thiers's visit and mission. The story on the street is, that the leaders in Paris received him coolly, almost uncivilly, regarding his statement of the true condition of affairs in France as colored and influenced by the people he has for the past six weeks been thrown with. He has now been here four days, has had several audiences with Count Bismarck, dined with the king, and been treated with many marks of distinction.

CHURCH AT VERSAILLES.

Go with me this bright Sabbath morning to divine service at the chapel of the palace, a beautiful piece of architecture by the younger Mansard. Within we find room for five hundred people, and an interior of great richness and beauty. Upon the ceiling are two excellent frescoed groups, copies from the old masters, and above the altar a golden effulgence. The marble floor is richly inlaid with porphyry of various colors, in devices of monograms, harps, crowns, and other insignia of royalty; and all over the beautiful columns are blotches, where emblems of the different reigning houses of France have been effaced as those families have been superseded. There are two rows of narrow benches, covered with red plush, with very narrow ribbon-backs.

As these seats are not fastened to the floor, one must sit bolt upright for fear of accident. The service soon commences with the music of a military band of a hundred pieces. A Lutheran chaplain conducts the service, which does not differ materially from that in an American Congregational Church. There are, however, four candles burning, and the minister occasionally turns round to bow to the cross. In the great chair in front is King William; on the right, the crown prince; not far away is Moltke; then the Russian general, Kutersoff, and scores of generals and officers of the staff and line of all grades. Every nook and corner is filled with private soldiers, in their trim, clean uniforms. The king is in the full dress of a general; and among the whole assembly there is not a button out of place, nor an evidence of carelessness in the minutest particular. When church closes, the king remains for some time in the open court outside, receiving and talking with a crowd of officers, who wait for his departure before dispersing.

FRANCE CLAIMS THE REVICTUALING OF PARIS.

Nov. 7th.—M. Thiers left for Tours at six o'clock this morning, in great distress at his failure to effect any thing for France, or, as he expressed it, "after failing to gain for my unfortunate country an armistice acceptable to it, and unable to stop the effusion of blood that every honest and generous heart must deprecate."

The Germans offered an armistice of twenty-eight days for holding elections and calling together the delegates, but required the maintenance of the military status, while the French required the revictualing of Paris.

CAPTURE OF METZ.

The spectacle of one hundred and fifty thousand well-armed and officered troops, held captive three months by a force only one-fourth greater, and then surrendering, is new in warfare. The books, experience, and received opinions upon such matters make it necessary for the surrounding force to be three to one. There will naturally be many theories advanced to account for this surrender, as it subverts our preconceived ideas. There is one fundamental reason for it; the greater moral power arising from the superior intelligence of the German people. It is the compulsory education of children which makes the German army so effective.

The world has been led astray as to the character of the common people of France. It has taken the academicians, the statesmen, and the generals as national types, than which nothing could be more erroneous. In France more than in any civilized country, the few have had many privileges, and the many few. The result is, that the great peasant class is little removed from barbarism; and hence her weakness. There is another purely military reason—the advantage of the side that awaits the attack—provided it is prepared, the troops are thoroughly in hand, and the enemy can be made to attack in front. These conditions were all fulfilled at Metz.

This situation with troops armed with the long-range and accurate rifle, and so confident of their power as to exercise it fully, gives an advantage not realized except by those who have observed it. Our own officers who served in the field during the last year of our war will readily understand it. The attacks upon our forces by Hood in front of Atlanta, where we were always ready and confident, are cases in point. The most conspicuous is that of the 28th of July, 1864, when he attacked our right in position. A single brigade, commanded by General Charles R. Woods, received the attack coolly and confidently in their prepared position, losing but fifteen men; while Hood lost in killed, buried by us, long trenches of men, and his number of wounded must have been great in proportion.

At Jonesboro' my depleted division numbered but twenty-two hundred muskets, but every one could be counted on. We took up our position just at evening of the 29th of August, 1864, and on the morning of the 30th it became necessary, from the nature of the ground on my left, to occupy a line half a mile long. This made a single rank the whole length, and not one man in reserve. This was positively necessary, on account of commanding heights which could in no other way be controlled. The division of General Osterhaus lay on my right, but not on ground that the enemy coveted. After feigning a movement against him, the entire corps of S. D. Lee attacked my thin line, and received so severe a repulse that the same night, on receipt of the intelligence, Atlanta was given up.

We were enabled to do this through perfect confidence, resulting from a slight work we had thrown up under fire, giving each man six or eight deliberate shots after the enemy came within range, while his own person was comparatively safe. This inspired each man with such a feeling of security as to afford him collected use of all his faculties; and the result was, that so many of the enemy were struck that they began to give way a hundred yards from my line, and the few — about one hundred — who came over the works were at once made prisoners. I give these two illustrations, in which the attack received at least ten times the damage it inflicted, to show how a very small force may repulse, and even defeat, a very large one. If several of these positions are prepared one behind the other, I can scarcely see any limit to the power of the defense, provided the *morale* of the troops be perfect.

This new strength of the defense is mostly due to the late improvements in fire-arms, by which their range, rapidity, and accuracy of fire are greatly augmented. I think it may be safely said that a single line in two ranks, composed of thoroughly good troops, with the new style of breech-loading arms, and protected by some slight work, can defy any sort of attack that can be devised, provided it be made in front, and over ground affording no cover. This comes from the fact that there is a moral limit to the capacity of men to face danger.

This limit may be increased by discipline, but one in three put *hors du combat* is about the highest in fair fight. At Shiloh my brigade lost thirty-six per centum; but it may be safely laid down, that when every third or even fourth man is struck, the body of troops of which they are components is neutralized, until it is reorganized and recovers its confidence, impaired by the presence of death.

PRUSSIAN SOLDIERS.

Nov. 8th. — The Prussian soldier ready for marching looks very much like our own under the same circumstances, the uniform being similar, and the equipments not differing materially. His overcoat is made into a long slender roll, and hung on the left shoulder, the two ends coming together, and being fastened on the right hip. His haversack of coarse white linen, and glass canteen covered with leather, are slung from the right shoulder. Around the flask are buckled two broad straps, used in peace to cover the sights of the gun. He wears no shoulder-belts, but a pipe-clayed waist-belt, on which are slipped two cartridge-boxes of black leather, carried on either side, each box holding twenty cartridges.

The knapsack is of calf-skin, tanned with the hair on, and is slung by two pipe-clayed leather straps hooked to the waist-belt in front, and then passing over the shoulders. Two short straps attached to these in front pass back under the armpits, and are fastened to the knapsack. The knapsack is made to keep its shape by a light wooden frame, and the leather is flint-tanned, or stretched over this frame while green. On each end outside is a deep box, in which is carried a case of twenty cartridges. Within are one shirt of white flannel, one pair of drawers, one pair of drill trowsers, a short jacket, one pair of boots, and the cleaning and toilet kit, consisting of four or five brushes for the clothes, hair, teeth, gun, blacking and polishing; then a box of pumice-stone, a bottle of sweet-oil, and the usual quantity of old greasy rags for cleaning.

In addition to this, the soldier carries writing material and a roll of bandages. On top of his knapsack is strapped a galvanized iron pot, holding about three quarts, with a tight-fitting cover, which is used separately for cooking. Within the knapsack, slipped into little loops, are a spoon, knife, fork, comb, and small mirror. The latter does not seem to be required, but is permitted. In his haversack is carried whatever may be the food for the day. He wears a single-breasted frock-coat of blue cloth with red facings, very dark gray pantaloons, short top-boots, and no stockings. He wears on his waist-belt a strong sword fifteen inches long, which he can use for defense, and for cutting wood, or material for fascines or gabions. His gun is unburnished, so that it may not attract the enemy by flashing in the sun, and is pretty well coated with grease. He carries no blanket, but hopes at night to find some straw for his bed. He wears on his head either a flat forage-cap with red band, or the peaked helmet. Carrying the inspection farther, you find that the soldier answers to the question "When did you bathe last?" "When at home, I bathe daily from May till September, but I have not bathed at all since leaving Germany;" and his under-clothing is saturated with the exhalations of his body.

His equipments have much to recommend them. The knapsack is made so that it retains its shape, and never becomes baggy like our own, nor is it filled with an undue quantity of articles. It is so slung as to fit closely to the person, and is not a burden to the soldier. In fact, the men appear greatly attached to their knapsacks, and are always careful of them, instead of throwing them away, as is invariably done by our troops on long marches. The flask canteen, in which is usually carried a little brandy, is liable to break, holds less than ours, and, I should think, is not so desirable; while their haversack is like ours, except that it is never painted.

The use of the waist-belt for supporting the cartridges is without doubt correct, as our troops on long marches throw away the shoulder-belts, and sling the cartridge-box on the waist-belt. The plan of placing one-half the weight of the cartridges on either side is too great an advantage over our own method to need comment. A leather pouch for money is hung about the neck, and also a zinc plate attached to a card, on which are engraved the soldier's regiment, company, and number. The whole weight of the soldier's arms and equipments is fifty pounds. His mess is entirely different from the messes of our troops, and the cost of it, on a peace-footing, comes out of his daily pay, which is three and one-half silver groschen, or about eight cents. He is allowed, besides, a pound and a half of rye bread.

Excepting the bread, the ration is not fixed in kind, but is determined by a board of officers, and varies with the products and prices of localities. The companies are divided into messes of about twenty men, each of which is under the charge of a non-commissioned officer. Each company has its mess-board, composed of the captain, a lieutenant, a non-commissioned officer, and some privates, who decide all questions pertaining to themselves, regulate the bills of fare, and determine the daily cost to each soldier, and the hours of meals. The bill of fare varies greatly with localities.

Usually, in Germany, the breakfast consists of a thin flour soup, with some slices of bread; the dinner, of meat, generally mutton, or beef and vegetables; the supper, of what happens to remain over. Coffee or tea is usually had once a day, although not considered a part of the ration. But while in active service, each man receives a good ration of bread and meat, with coffee and wine, or whatever the country supplies. The daily cost rarely exceeds two silver groschen, and with this an abundance of vegetables is provided, in addition to meat and bread. At stated intervals, say once in two or three days, the cost of messes is collected, and the little leather bag suspended about the neck is inspected, to see if the money has been foolishly expended.

The soldiers receive their pay every ten days; and those who spend it, and have nothing left for their messing, are paid daily. Then, if they fail to save for their mess, the pay is given to a non-commissioned officer, who uses enough for this purpose, and hands the remainder to the soldier. Each soldier is allowed six cigars a day, which cost him but one silver groschen. He is responsible for his arms and equipments; and if any are lost by his fault, the loss is made up by the company, if he has previously borne a good character; otherwise he must pay.

A broad line of demarkation exists between the officer and soldier—broader, perhaps, than in any service in Christendom, and more accurately defined by law; but I have seen only kindness at all times in the relations between officers and soldiers. The men expect, and receive, justice, knowing their duties and the laws that control them, and never seem for a moment to question them. On examining the accoutrements of a soldier sent to me for that purpose, I desired him to give me a needle-gun cartridge, that I might examine it at my leisure. He at once handed it to me, but the next moment, remembering the orders against parting with his cartridges, required it back again; and I do not believe that any bribe could have then obtained it.

HOW THE SOLDIER IS BROUGHT INTO SERVICE.

The soldier is easily brought into service, as military duty is exacted from all, and no one thinks of evading it. A list of all the young men is kept by the parochial magistrate; and as each arrives at the age of twenty, he is summoned to appear for medical examination; and if he passes, which he always desires to do, is sent at once to the head-quarters of the landwehr battalion of the district, and from thence to his regiment. For the first six weeks he is taught the position of the soldier, honors due to superiors, the distinctions and insignia of rank, and generally the first principles of military duty. He is then given his gun, and, while the former instructions continue, is trained for six months in the manual of arms, and then put in the ranks of his company. For the first year, his drills occupy four hours each morning and evening, varying somewhat in summer with the weather, but being pretty closely kept up. During the second year, his drills are lighter, but their range is extended to manœuvring in the battalion; and some instruction is given in riding, the drill of the piece in light artillery, and in making siege materials—such as gabions, fascines, sap-rollers, mantlets, etc. Those who show special aptitude are now assigned to different branches of the service. During the third year, those who go to the cavalry, artillery, and engineers have special instructions in their particular branch; while those who are permanently assigned to the infantry have little to do but guard duty and some theoretical exercises in the schools. At the end of this year, all receive their furlough for the next four years, holding themselves always in readiness to be called out for annual exercise, or to rejoin their commands in time of war. During much of the three years, schools are held for swimming, gymnastics, duties in quarters, duties as sentinels, in garrison and on outposts, in target practice, the care of arms, the duties of soldiers toward their officers, reading and writing for the few who need instruction in these branches, and such higher studies as the commandant may direct. Military service is popular in Germany; and, on filling up the army for the present war, many of those who assembled at the dépôts and were not required, went away with heavy hearts.

When on campaigns, the men are forbidden to bathe, for fear of taking colds from immersion when the body is not in a condition to bear it. The Germans all seem singularly careful about changes of weather and exposures to draughts, and especially after exercise. I have seen the king, with his whole suite, change position to get away from the draught through a sally-port; and Bismarck often excuses himself for keeping on his hat and overcoat in his room after returning from his daily ride. This special care is required of the men, and seems to us Americans excessive.

RATIONS IN KIND.

There are two clearly defined and distinct conditions of the Prussian army, known as the peace and war footing. Whenever the latter is declared, every officer and soldier is entitled to receive one ration in kind, and no more, daily. Under certain circumstances this may be commuted in money. Its value is about twenty-one cents. It consists of one and a half pounds of bread; twelve ounces of meat; four ounces of rice, or barley, or beans; or it may be eight ounces of flour and three pounds of potatoes. Four ounces of salt and four ounces of coffee are also allowed. This may be varied by the commanding general, who may add whisky, brandy, wine, or beer, with dried fruit, *sauerkraut*, butter, and tobacco. Considerable discretion is allowed commanding officers in regulating the ration in kind, and a slight additional money allowance is given men when traveling on railways or steamboats for extra cost of living.

The regular forage ration is eleven and a quarter pounds of oats, three pounds of hay, and three and a half pounds of straw. This, also, may, be varied. Any portion of the fixed ration not drawn is commuted.

EXTRA ALLOWANCES.

There are also many changes of pay and allowances under various circumstances. An officer promoted from cadet or sergeant receives an equipment fund of from twenty to forty dollars in peace; and in war, if promoted for service, of one hundred and fifty dollars. When a man is captured his pay ceases; but prisoners of war of the enemy receive, if officers, from twelve to twenty-five dollars monthly; while private soldiers receive only food and clothing. For the loss of clothing and equipment in war an officer is allowed seventy dollars. If he furnishes his own horse, he is allowed one hundred dollars for it; if sick, and not in a public hospital, he is allowed an amount daily, not exceeding in the aggregate one hundred and fifty dollars during any one term of absence. A premium of eighteen dollars is given for every useful animal captured from the enemy. Nurses in hospital receive nine dollars a month. All civilians brought into service as military officials receive three months' advanced pay. A soldier in the field may assign one-half his pay to his family. The reserves and garrison troops are, in respect to pay, on a peace footing. The daily pay of non-combatant officers and officials ranges from one dollar for an assistant paymaster, to three dollars and fifty cents for a corps surgeon. A chaplain receives two dollars, a staff surgeon the same, and a paymaster one dollar and eighty cents. The general average is about two dollars per day. A certain allowance is given for horses and equipments. Combatant officers receive a monthly rate of pay, from thirty dollars for a second lieutenant, to one hundred and fifty dollars for a colonel; while general officers get considerably more. The equipment fund for mounted officers ranges from twenty dollars yearly for a lieutenant, to forty dollars for a colonel.

ANNUAL COST OF EACH SOLDIER.

The pay and allowances of the Prussian army would seem to us paltry and absurd. Two hundred and twenty-five thalers, equal to about one hundred and sixty dollars gold, is appropriated for the annual cost of each soldier; and this must pay all his expenses, and, if he be mounted, the blanketing and trappings of his horse. This money includes the pay of the man, amounting to forty-three thalers a year, out of which must come his messing, his pocket-money, and his necessary personal kit, brushes, etc. The remainder is administered by a regimental board of officers, to provide arms, clothing, equipments, and repairs. The ordinary pay is three and one-half silver groschen per day; but the regimental board of control may increase or reduce this by an amount not exceeding one and one-half silver groschen, according to the cost of living. The arms, clothing, and equipments are the property of the regiment, and are administered by its own board of control, according to fixed regulations. Even with this system, large savings are often made by regiments, by which the men are benefited in many ways.

During war, officers receive about one-third more than in peace. They also have an allowance for servants, but must feed and clothe them from their pay. Mounted officers receive thirty thalers a year for harness, or a new horse furnished by the Government every five years. The higher grades receive better pay than mere difference of rank would indicate. The princes serve gratuitously. Although army pay seems ridiculously small, the cheapness of living renders it sufficient. A captain told me that at his station at home he lived comfortably, supported and clothed his family, consisting of a wife and two children, educated the latter, and kept his carriage, and all without difficulty, on his army pay. There are many allowances in kind—such as fuel, lights, quarters, medical attendance, forage and stabling for horses, or, in their stead, commutation in money.

RETIRING UNWORTHY OFFICERS.

Whenever a Prussian officer is deemed, from his immoral life, improvidence, or any cause not military, unworthy to continue longer in service, he is permitted to remain on the rolls until he arrives at promotion by seniority, when his junior is put over him. He then usually seeks a board of officers to recommend him for retiring. Failing to do this, he is dropped in orders. In time of war, liberal authority to remove incompetent officers is given to commanders in the field.

BILLETING.

When on campaigns, the army is billeted, as far as possible, in the houses on the line of march. When any branch of the army—as the king's head-quarters, for instance—approaches a city or town, an officer of the administration is sent forward carrying an abstract of the wants he is to supply, and at once calls upon the mayor and makes requisition for the various quarters required; as, for instance, for the king and his personal household, the best establishment in the town, or city, entire; for General Von Roon, a house, with capacity for himself, his various adjutants, clerks, secretaries, and servants, and so on for the entire command. The mayor at once designates houses of the various capacities required, and sends an official with the officer to point them out. Upon the gates or doors of each house, the officer writes with chalk the name of the official, or the number of men assigned to that establishment, and at once sends an orderly back to meet and conduct the intended occupants to their designated quarters. Every corps, division, brigade, or regimental commander, on approaching his destination, in like manner sends an officer of his personal staff forward, provided with a piece of chalk for a like purpose. The arrangements can not, of course, be made in the presence of the enemy.

To the question, "How do you sleep at night without tents or blankets?" Adjutant Tresscott answered, "We usually sleep in the mud, without straw or wood; and for sixteen hours before Woerth we had not tasted food. An officer may consider himself fortunate to get a little straw for a pillow."

When men or officers are billeted, the family is required to provide soldiers with the equivalent of the ration, for which two groschen a day are paid; and for officers such a prescribed wholesome meal, including wine, as is usual in their own messes, for which payment is made, regulated by the market price.

The higher officers and the king carry their own household establishments. Each minister has his own traveling outfit, made on purpose for campaigning. Billeting is made to fall as lightly as possible upon the inhabitants of a city, and the mayor is directed to apportion the burdens according to the wealth of the citizens. The mayors, policemen, and all civil functionaries who have not run away, are commanded to administer their trusts as if there were no war; and great advantages have been gained by this course.

REGIMENTAL BANDS.

Each regiment in the Prussian army has a band of twenty members; or, if the officers are able and desire it, there may be more. Most of the expense for instruments, music, extra compensation of first-class musicians, and in fact almost the entire cost of the bands, is borne by the officers. Each company has two fifers and two drummers.

BRIGADE COMMANDERS.

There is no grade of brigadier-general. Brigades are usually commanded by colonels, sometimes by major-generals and lieutenant-generals.

CHIEFS OF REGIMENTS.

There is a custom here of naming individuals of rank as chiefs of regiments—probably a relic of feudal times, when regiments of serfs were commanded by their own lords, and given away by them. Bismarck is chief of the 9th Cuirassiers. Moltke was made chief of a regiment for distinguished service in Denmark; and nearly all the higher princes have the same distinction. It is, however, only a compliment, as it confers no command. It is usual, as a mark of courtesy, to gain the assent of the chief, which he never withholds, to the appointment of new officers. On occasions of ceremony the chief usually rides at the head of his regiment. The obligation often rests on the other side; and the presents of plate, *fêtes*, and dinners looked for from the chief are onerous unless he possesses large revenues, which is not the case with many German princes.

AMBULANCE.

Nov. 9th.—The field-hospital train of a division I find, by inspection to-day, to be a complete hospital ready for service in the field, and easily convertible into a permanent hospital.

Each division has a light hospital train, composed of thirteen surgeons, seventy-four men, fifty-six horses, and ten carriages, and accommodations for two hundred men, or about two per cent. of the command. The ten carriages are made up as follows: There are two medicine-wagons for four horses each, and about the size of the telegraphic operating-wagon. These are fitted up with combination cases, in which seems to be packed every thing in the way of medicines and surgical instruments and appliances ever required in a field-hospital—bandages, splints, surgical cases in perfect order, and all kinds of drugs, with large quantities of narcotics and anæsthetics, each in its place. There is an assortment of placards or tags, used in action by the chief surgeon, who writes on them what is to be done with the patient, whom he leaves for others to attend, while he passes quickly on. There are blankets, a few simple articles of hospital dress, a large quantity of food and spirits; and on the top, folded in two parts, amputating-tables. The economy of space, by which so much is stored in so small a carriage, is marvelous. There are, besides, three large six-horse wagons, filled with cooking utensils, tents, cots, bedding, food, and in fact every thing necessary for establishing a field-hospital.

This leaves five ambulances proper for carrying the wounded. These are somewhat lower than our Rucker ambulances, and set on smaller wheels, but are much better made, being all of seasoned timber and smoother workmanship, and seem perfectly firm and strong. They are made for two or four horses. They have no seats, and are intended to carry two men at a time, placed on stretchers side by side. The body of the ambulance, which is like our own, is set on six springs, of best quality, while ours is put on four, of inferior quality. Iron axle-trees are used; the body of the carriage is covered with canvas, and a slight railing goes round the top, to carry the knapsacks of the wounded. Except that the style of the carriage for carrying the wounded is antiquated, the ambulance-trains are admirable.

We were received with the greatest courtesy by the medical officers; and on our displaying authority for inspecting their train, they at once afforded us every facility, and seemed to take great pleasure in serving us.

Although the medical department is very complete, and the surgeons accomplished, it has, in a measure, failed to meet the full requirements of service. Whenever American medical men have assisted, as has often been the case, I hear the highest praises of their facility and skill.

There is a prevailing impression that the Prussian medical service was considerably behind ours in the late war—a fact due to the superior enterprise and adaptability of the American character. In Germany, where lives are regular, and follow fixed rules and theories, and where there are few great prizes to strive for, there is much less to develop the faculties than with us. Moreover, our people were unaccustomed to military affairs, and so the war reached deeper into the sympathies of all classes. Besides, our war, by its duration and extent, gave great impetus to the study of surgery.

Every thing here used as a hospital is called an ambulance. The Franco-American ambulance, of which we often hear, means an immense traveling hospital, or train. The Germans have fallen into the same error that we committed—that of using buildings for hospitals instead of tents, or field-hospitals; and there is scarcely a doubt that the French will do likewise. It is unaccountable that scientific and practical medical men do not appreciate and advocate the advantages of outdoor over indoor hospitals. It is a matter of the gravest importance, and the humane societies of Christendom can, in no way, do more good than by thoroughly investigating and making generally known the facts relating to permanent hospitals in time of war. The seeds of disease seem to cling to the walls, ceilings, and floors, and the death-rate of the wounded is often greatly increased by putting them in these places. So strongly was I impressed with this in our war, that, as far as was in my power, I kept my wounded out of them.

At the battle of Mission Ridge, the colonel of the 41st Ohio lost his leg above the knee by a musket-shot. I forbade his going to the hospital, and caused him to be treated in his rude split-shingle cabin, and his recovery was remarkably rapid. Officers of my command who were grazed by musket-shot upon the arms were put into the hospital, and died from gangrene. At that battle, the wounded of General Thomas's army were treated in fixed hospitals, or buildings fitted up beforehand, at Chattanooga, with many comforts and great care. The proportion of deaths among the wounded was frightful; and we were told that it was due to the low vital condition of our men, resulting from short rations. The fact was that they died from hospital diseases. General Sherman's army, just arrived from Mississippi, without hospitals, treated their wounded in the field, and the proportion of recoveries was astonishingly great. They were cured by fresh air.

At the battle of Peach-tree Creek, a very worthy staff-officer of mine was seriously, although not dangerously, wounded in the abdomen. The medical rules were very strict; but by sending messengers all night, I got authority to send him home to the North without his going into the hospital. Arriving at Nashville, and being unable to proceed without further medical authority, he was taken charge of and put into one of their comfortable hospitals. In a few days he became terribly afflicted with gangrene, and only escaped with his life after a perilous and racking illness.

With all the facts before them, our medical officers went on building and furnishing the most expensive hospitals, on the most approved plans, until the end of the war.

FIELD TELEGRAPH.

Nov. 9th.—The progressive character of the Prussian army is shown in nothing more clearly than in the application of the electric telegraph to field purposes. Morse's system is used. Each head-quarters of an army and each army corps has a telegraphic division of three officers, one hundred and thirty-seven men, seventy-three horses, and ten wagons. Two of the latter are fitted up as operating-rooms, and the other eight are used for carrying poles and other material, including five miles of wire to each wagon, which can be reeled off by the moving of the vehicle. Of the whole forty miles, five are insulated, and can be run along the ground.

It will be seen that each army corps can put out forty miles of line without recourse to other wires, but use is always made of lines found in the country, in case they will answer. Single poles of light material are used, without joints, and about ten feet long, and only every third pole is put in the ground. The *personnel* is brought into the army from the civil telegraphic service at home. While in the field, the operators assume military rank, and, like agents of the Post-office Department, are known as "military officials," not as "military officers." The men are on a footing with train-soldiers, and all wear a distinctive uniform. The carriages are painted of a dark olive-brown, and are each drawn by four horses. The operating-wagons are a little larger than the Rucker ambulances of our service, but much heavier. They are considerably better made, and are closed with thin matched pine. Just in rear of the driver is a partition shutting off the rear portion of the carriage. At his back, and under his seat, is a capacious box, in which are carried tools, and the material necessary in telegraphing. On one side of the rear closed portion is a neat table, with a compact operating instrument on it, and the battery under it; and on the opposite side is the operator's bench, the space underneath it being also economized. On the outside, near the table, are sockets, with thumb-screws connected with the battery, to receive the wires. Besides keeping the king in telegraphic communication with his ministers, lines are run from General Von Moltke's headquarters to all of the different corps in the field. The Germans seem to have but the simplest and most limited system of signals, not approximating to the dignity of an organized corps, and use, so far as I can see, only a mast, with flags displayed at different elevations. The telegraph corps always evinces admirable promptness in keeping the lines closely up as the army moves forward.

THE MAIL SERVICE is very complete. The *personnel* belonging to it is brought from the civil mail service at home, and is upon the same footing with the telegraph corps. Each brigade, division, corps, and army, as well as the king and his ministers, has its own special service, its own officers, and the principal personages have their own mail-sacks. The mails received daily at the terminus of the railway are delivered to officers of the postal service for the various parts of the army, and the greatest celerity is practiced in the distribution. Even the railway cars, constructed at home for this service, are brought directly through.

TRANSPORTATION.

The transportation of the army is excellent. Horses only are used. Two, four, and six-horse carriages are employed according to the needs of the service. The carriages are all well made of seasoned timber, as were our own before the war. They are not as expensive as ours, have fewer parts, and are more simply constructed. The body of the larger sizes is V shaped, and has a canvas cover over wooden bows, like our own. The lighter vehicles for the medical, telegraph, and postal corps are all of excellent make, like the Elliott work of Concord, or the Dougherty of St. Louis; while our own during the war became mere botches of green timber, with insufficient fastenings, fourth-rate springs, cheap machine-work, and rough finish.

EX-UNITED STATES MINISTER TO PORTUGAL.

Nov. 10*th*.—Mr. O'Sullivan, whose card reads, "ex-United States Minister to Portugal," and who, on its strength, gains interviews with Count Bismarck and the crown prince, was yesterday escorted out of Versailles by a file of men, as he had overstaid his permission. On meeting Count Bismarck, a short time ago, he was told that the balloon from Paris, captured the day before, compromised certain persons who little expected it. This is the last of the three editors of the *Democratic Review*. The war of the rebellion has scattered over Europe an immense amount of drift-wood—spurious Americans, who left their country in disappointment or anger, and curse it, or claim its protection, according to their needs and their company, while they at all times bring discredit upon it by their conduct and conversation.

The truth seems to be, that Mr. O'Sullivan, in associating with conspicuous people, sometimes made his conversation unwelcome; and that in this case he proposed to Count Bismarck a plan of settlement with the French people by giving Alsace and Lorraine to Belgium, and guaranteeing neutrality, so that from the English Channel to Italy there would be neutral territory between the belligerents. This advice caused the "ex-United States minister" to be looked upon as a meddlesome person, whose presence was not desirable.

The English who came from Paris to-day are even worse than the Americans who came a few days ago. The sinking ship has sent flying a lot of rats, American and English, of no credit to any country.

CHAPTER V.

VON ROON.

Nov. 10th.—The ministers of the king are seldom seen, with the exception of Bismarck, who nearly every day, from three to five, rides in the park or toward the outposts.

Von Roon drives when he goes out, which is not often. He is sixty-eight years old, and, though younger than the king or Von Moltke, shows age more than either. He has a serious, thoughtful face, and wears a long, drooping mustache. He was born in Mecklenburg, of titled parents, and at the age of thirteen entered a military institution, and, two years later, was transferred to the Cadet School at Berlin. In the year 1821 he was commissioned as a lieutenant in the army, and at twenty-four entered the war academy at Berlin, taking a two years' course, when he joined the 15th Infantry of the Line, where he served six years. During this time he published several military and scientific works of value. He then took a professorship in the Berlin Cadet School, but very soon after joined his regiment, to accompany his corps in its operations during the confusion then reigning in Belgium. There he first attracted attention to his brilliant administrative abilities, and, on returning to Prussia in 1835, was transferred to the general staff, and the next year promoted to a captaincy. He served in this capacity several years, without any fixed station, performing such useful service as was assigned him from time to time, when he was appointed major, and joined for a short time the staff of the Seventh Army Corps, but was soon retransferred to the general staff at Berlin, and given charge of the education of Prince Frederick Charles, whom he accompanied, in 1846, to the University at Bonn, and subsequently in his European travels. In 1848, Von Roon received the appointment of chief of staff to the Eighth Army Corps, and controlled its mobilization and subsequent operations in Baden. In 1850 he was made lieutenant-colonel; in 1856, colonel; and two years later, major-general, and assigned to the command of a division.

As many defects in the Prussian army system had been brought plainly to his notice during his thirty years of active service, he drew up and submitted to the ministry a plan of reform, which found such ready consideration, and was so heartily approved by the crown prince, now King William, that Von Roon was summoned to Berlin to assist in perfecting the plan. The reorganization proposed, and which failed at that time, contemplated such an enlargement of the regular army, that, although a large portion of the years of service would be spent on furlough, still, in case of mobilization for active service, all the battalions might be at once filled without calling recruits, sometimes imperfectly instructed, from the landwehr. The theory of Prussian service is, that every man, on arriving at maturity, owes certain years of military service to the state; and that the regular army shall be large enough, and this term of service short enough, to oblige every able-bodied citizen to serve, and to become a good soldier. But as the population of Prussia had nearly doubled since the size of the regular army was fixed, a large number escaped both service and instruction, and, when called on to expand the ranks of the battalions in war, were uninstructed, and often proved inefficient. The proposed reorganization was designed so to re-adjust the size of the army and the term of service, that all men should be disciplined, and, on mobilization, the regular army need not be dependent upon the landwehr. The Prince of Prussia espoused this plan of reorganization so zealously, and the measure, on account of increasing the military establishment, and thus adding to the burdens of the people, became so unpopular, as to make it necessary for him to flee the country.

On his return, he became regent, and soon after ascended the throne. Though he again pressed the measure, it was not until ten years later that he succeeded in carrying it. These circumstances made the king a warm friend of Von Roon, to whom, as the reward of his services, he gave the port-folio of war minister. Von Roon came in for his full share of public dislike; but the magnificent work of the army, both in 1866 and in the present war, which was made possible only by this plan, has changed entirely the public feeling toward him.

GENERAL BLUMENTHAL.

On the arrival of the king at Versailles, the crown prince gave up to him his splendid head-quarters, the *mairie*, or *hôtel de ville*, or, in plain English, the "town hall." Each town and city has its *hôtel de ville*, humble or pretentious, in proportion to the size and wealth of the city. It not only contains all the offices of the city government, but is the home of the mayor; and, in a place as large as Versailles, becomes a magnificent public establishment. The portions of the building set apart for the mayor are fitted up in a style little short of regal. The crown prince betook himself to a place known as the "*Aubrages*," in the outskirts of the city—a sort of villa in the English style, like many of our second-rate places upon the Hudson. Here one always finds one of the most meritorious and unostentatious officers of the Prussian army—Lieutenant-general Von Blumenthal. He is small, of unmistakable German face, and so full of open kindness, and with a mind so clear, direct, and comprehensive, that no one can know him without respecting and admiring him.

General Von Blumenthal is the chief of staff to the crown prince, and, next to General Von Moltke, may be looked upon as the leading strategist of the German army. He speaks English perfectly, and his intercourse with others is always frank, amiable, and unpretending. He is about fifty-five years of age, and is a Mecklenburger. He has spent his life in the army, was chief of staff to the crown prince in 1866, and for his splendid service in that campaign was made lieutenant-general. Just before the present war he was appointed general, and, upon the outbreak of hostilities, again assigned to the crown prince. His services in the present war have been most efficient, though not always conspicuous; and much of the credit for the remarkable victories of Weissenburg and Woerth, as well as the accurate tactics by which all portions of the crown prince's army came on the field at Sedan just where and when needed, is due to General Von Blumenthal. I thank him personally for many kindnesses.

PRUSSIAN ARTILLERY.

Nov. 11th.—The Prussian field-artillery now in use is of two calibres—four-pounders, adopted in 1864, and six-pounders, adopted in 1869. The guns are steel rifles, of the Krupp manufacture, and are long and slender, not materially differing from the Parrott gun, the breech-loading arrangement causing an enlargement not unlike that formed by the re-enforce band of the Parrott. On close inspection, they are found a much better finished gun, although I doubt whether, aside from the advantage of breech-loading, they will prove more serviceable. In accuracy, our Parrotts and Rodmans surpass them. They carry an elongated shell like the Parrott, except that it is a little shorter, and has a leaden jacket to take the grooves of the rifling. The breech-loading arrangement is the principal feature of these guns; and as this is the first really successful use in the field of this mode of construction, the subject deserves a special notice.

The four-pounder is five feet six inches long, with a fifteen-feet twist, and has twelve grooves. It is sighted like our Parrott guns, but arranged to work also horizontally by a thumb-screw, to correct for variation of the shot by wind, and from the veering caused by the twist. The four-pounders are very slender, with the bore of the piece passing through the gun from end to end. About ten inches of the breech is at least doubled in size, and made square; and horizontally, quite through the centre of this, perpendicular to the axis of the piece, is cut a square mortice, somewhat thicker than the bore of the gun, into which passes a closely-fitting key, or piece of steel. This is formed of two acute wedges, with faces working on each other, so that by the turn of a small hand-screw, fastened to the end of one and working against the other, the whole breech is made close. To load the piece, this hand-screw is turned loose, and the tenant drawn out so far as to leave the bore clear. The cartridge is then shoved in at the rear of the piece, past the key, which is pushed into place by a turn given the hand-screw, and the cartridge is pricked, and fired by a lanyard and friction-primer. Notwithstanding the remarkably close fitting of this mechanism, which has shown no apparent wearing or loosening after long use, there is a little escape of gas, which is obviated by fitting into the tenant, where the rear of the cartridge comes against it, a circular copper disk having a diameter a little greater than the bore of the piece, which is rimmed or bored out to the depth of a quarter of an inch, in the prolongation of the bore of the gun. Just in the rear portion of the circumference of this rim a deep groove is cut outward, so that at the explosion, the gas, acting in this groove, presses the thin rim of copper metal firmly against the piece, and effectually closes the joint.

The six-pounders differ from the four-pounders, in being closed at the rear by a plug fastened in place by a pin. They are very much like the four-pounders, the bore passing entirely through the piece. A close-fitting steel plug about eight inches long is shoved in, and closes the breech. This is attached to the breech of the piece by a swinging hinge, by which it is pushed in and drawn out, and, when in place, is held against the blast by a round steel pin about three inches in thickness, which passes horizontally quite through the breech of the piece and plug. To prevent any escape of gas around the point of the plug, a papier-maché cup fits on the rear of the cartridge, and, at the explosion, effectually closes the almost inappreciable space between the plug and the bore of the piece.

These guns are effectively served by four men: a gunner, who aims the piece, one to sponge and load, one to prick the cartridge and fire the piece, and one to bring up ammunition. As the piece is sponged and served at the breech, it is unattended with special danger. These arms, on account of the strength of the steel, are made very slender. They were originally more so, but two burst during the war of 1866; since which time they have been made stronger, and there have been no further accidents. The guns have neither fillets nor rings, but are plain, slightly tapering, hollow pieces of steel. The effective range of the four-pounders is about 1300 yards, and that of the six-pounders slightly greater. The full range, with high elevation, is of course more but the Germans do very little random firing.

Much has been said of the effectiveness of these guns, and with justice, although, as is always the case, something is ascribed to them as materially valuable which is merely so morally. The Prussian artillery has been of the greatest use in this war; and I am free to say that, as an accurately constructed rifled arm, admitting of light and easy manœuvre, and safe and rapid firing, these guns are far superior to any thing we have. The officers of artillery are greatly pleased with them, and say that they have nothing more to wish for; and each captain seems certain that his battery is better than any other.

I met in Versailles the commandant of the reserve artillery, Lieutenant-colonel Von Bories, an old comrade of General Willich, of our army, who was so glad to hear the good account I gave him of his old friend, that he seemed to redouble his attentions in showing me every thing connected with his arm of the service. He, with his officers, were quartered in the Royal Artillery Barracks, just in front of the Palais formerly built by Louis XIV. as a school for the boys of the poor noblesse, but converted by Napoleon I. into barracks. Each battery has six guns, each gun its caisson, and each battery two carriages for rations, two for smithies, carrying six extra wheels, and one for officers' baggage. The guns are mounted on carriages very much like our own, painted olive-brown or blue, but they have iron axle-trees, and some of the hubs are iron. The stock is in two pieces, bolted together, and on it is a small box for carrying implements or cartridges. The men are distributed on the limbers very much as with us. Two ride in basket-seats fitted up on the axle-tree of the gun-carriage. The knapsacks are generally packed on the rear box of the caisson, and with each gun-squad is carried, on the rear box of the limber, a pick, an axe, a spade, and a cooking-kit. Each carriage is built for six horses, but often only four are used. They are destitute of unnecessary flesh, but always in good serviceable condition, and of fair medium size. The harness is very similar to our own, except that flax rope is employed for traces, as is usual on the Continent for common work. The guns are well browned, and the batteries, without showing any particular care, always look serviceable and in good condition. Only percussion shells are used, not from any special partiality for them, but because the Government do not fully approve of the time-fuse, and are experimenting with the percussion shell.

The gunners carry a short sword, longer than that of the infantry, but no gun. The horse artillery carry pistols. The drivers and horse attendants are enlisted for that purpose, and have nothing to do with the service of the guns. They have no knapsacks, but their kits are carried on the middle horses in immense holsters. The siege-guns, to the number of nearly three hundred, I saw in park. They were from twelve to sixty pounders, mostly old, and call for no special remark.

I have had little opportunity of examining and judging of the French artillery, except the captured guns at Sedan, which covered about two acres. I saw nothing about them worthy of notice. They were plain four-pounder rifled guns, of brass, about a foot shorter than our field-guns, and were muzzle-loaders. We have much to learn about artillery. The application of the breech-loading mechanism to steel guns for field purposes, and rifling for heavy guns, are steps plainly necessary. It is manifest that the same desirable results which have been secured by rifling small guns will be obtained by rifling large ones also.

CAVALRY EQUIPMENTS.

Nov. 12*th.*—The general appearance of the German cavalry equipment is heavy. The horses are of medium size, never fat, like those in our service, but spare in flesh, like animals in training. They seem always in excellent service condition, and in perfect health. The saddle has a tree composed of two side pieces of wood like those in the M'Clellan saddle, attached at the ends by cast-iron forks made to form a decided pommel and cantle, the latter being very high, and terminating backward in a handle by which the saddle is seized; a strip of leather, drawn tightly, connects the two pieces of iron, and is laced across with leather thongs, supporting much of the weight of the rider. The seat is covered with a close-fitting, padded leather cushion. Several strong cords are fastened to the under portion of these side pieces, by which is firmly attached to the tree a temporary padding of straw, laid straight, and made to fit precisely to the shape of the horse. This can be changed in a few minutes, as the animal may alter in condition, or when the saddle is shifted to another horse.

The front portion of the padded leather cushion terminates in a thin bag, in which the trooper carries his under-clothing. The girth ends in three buckle-straps, and is made of some twenty or thirty small cords. A breast-strap and crupper, and a plain iron stirrup with ordinary straps, complete the saddle. A double wool blanket is carried underneath the saddle, to cover the horse when necessary. It is doubled into nine folds, and is, in this shape, somewhat larger than the single blanket used in our service, when doubled into six folds. Over the whole is a shabrack of green cloth lined with coarse linen. On each side of the cantle are iron rings, to which are attached spare shoes, which hang under the shabrack. The mantle of the trooper is fastened to the shabrack, and on top of it one ration of grain is carried in a small sack. Both mantle and sack are so elongated as to lie across the cantle and hang down each side of it.

On the right side of the pommel is a coiled picket-rope, and on the left a simple cooking-kit. A surcingle of leather is now put on, and a narrow leather strap is fastened under the thighs of the rider, and passes around the pack in rear and holster in front, under the cantle and pommel, holding every thing firmly in place. In the left-hand holster are carried brushes and a personal kit, while in the other is an old smooth-bore horse-pistol like those used by our dragoons twenty years ago. A cotton stable-frock is thrown over the front of the saddle. The bridle is double, with a powerful curb-bit and a light snaffle-rein buckling on to the bottoms of the single cheek-pieces. The weight of this rather remarkable equipment is from seventy to eighty pounds. All mounted troops have curved sabres like our own, while, in addition, the Uhlans carry pistols and lances, the cuirassiers, pistols, and the dragoons and heavy cavalry, carbines.

Each year a board of officers condemns such horses as are unfit for service. These are sold, and an equal number of two-year old geldings or mare-colts are bought, and reared to take the place of those that will be condemned two years later. They are put in service when four years of age.

The pack seems unnecessarily heavy, as it does in the infantry, and, to keep pace with every thing else, must soon be greatly lightened. We too try to make the soldier pack these heavy weights, but, following his natural instinct, he throws them away.

For more than a hundred years great attention has been

paid in Germany by many families, in different provinces, to the rearing of a stock of horses especially suited to the wants of cavalry, and the result has produced an abundance of horses of excellent quality, and admirably adapted to cavalry purposes.

NO STRAGGLERS.

The streets are free from stragglers, and, although officers and soldiers are seen, they move along with an air of business. The theatres are closed; the restaurants are conducted under restrictions; and, while every body is cheerful, there is no trifling, and nobody out of place. This results from having a regular organization for every thing, previously perfected, where every man fits easily into his place and quietly does his work. How different from Nashville during our war, a city of nearly the same number of inhabitants, and also a great head-quarters! There we had special details for every thing—courts, boards, staff duty, hospital and prison service, and for a thousand other quasi civil employments, to the prejudice of the effective fighting strength, and of good discipline. This rabble of military out of place supported several theatres and other places of amusement, while the streets were filled with men in uniform, not always orderly, and with the air of people without much to do. Here every body has work. A minister of the king, or the general-in-chief, going to a meeting of the Government, carries his portfolio under his arm, and is attended by a single orderly. The crown prince rides to the front accompanied by two aids and as many orderlies, and generals of divisions and army corps are usually attended by one staff officer and an orderly; while the king himself drives with a less guard than escorted the commanders of our small armies. I never see here the spectacle, so common in the first two years of our war, of a general thundering along the street with a whole cavalcade at his heels, making the dust fly and every body run for life.

Nothing is more remarkable than the perfect unanimity manifest everywhere. There is no bickering of any kind, or questioning of orders, and, from the king to the last recruit, a single purpose prevails—to secure the success of the German arms. Some questions have arisen as to the consideration due the minor states, especially Baden, for their greater hardships and losses in battle, but nothing that in any way impairs friendly feeling, or breaks the harmony of military operations.

KERATRY'S SUCCESS.

Nov. 13th.—The partial success of Keratry toward Orleans has closed another period of the war, and what remains is scarcely more than German occupation, interspersed with considerable sharp fighting. This affair has awakened the Germans from a little torpor and over-security, resulting from a long series of successes. The Metz army is already disposed so as greatly to strengthen the besieging force about Paris, making the fall of that city certain, while leaving detachments, under Prince Frederick Charles, to overcome the Army of the Loire, and occupy, if necessary, other portions of France.

Having seen every phase of this army—its organization, composition, system of supply, drill, discipline, conduct in battle, and methods of living on the march, in the field, and in cantonment—I will proceed to Berlin, carrying ample authority from the Prussian Government for gaining from the bureaux there all the information that I may desire. The siege is becoming monotonous beyond expression. Even I, who every day have my appointed work with some officer, who kindly gives me his attention, find the time weighing heavily. The newspaper people, who are recognized and given the first social place here, and are often English lords or generals of the army, find it a difficult task to spin out a few incidents into a column of matter for their papers. The members of the American ambulance, so fresh and manly, in marked contrast with the young Frenchmen in the streets, gather in knots about the hotel door, all waiting, like Wilkins Micawber, for something to turn up.

THE ENGLISH PRESS has taken a much higher stand than that of our own country. It lacks our enterprise, but employs better talent; is more careful, and is looked upon much more as a guide of public opinion. It is not so partisan, and gathers about it, as contributors, the brightest men of the land. Several of the leading papers have medical, military, and political representatives here.

WHO ARE HERE.

At evening, some one of the foreigners who enjoys the luxury of a convenient suite of rooms invites this element of the society of Versailles to pass the evening with him. No gatherings could be more agreeable. Our distinguished friend W. H. Russell, known as "Bull Run" Russell, whom we could not permit to speak the truth about ourselves, perhaps tells more and better stories than any living Englishman. Captain Kingston, an Englishman also, and a Rugby boy, now of the Austrian army, is remarkable in music. D. O. Home, the spiritualist, is good in recitation; and Sidney Hall, the well-known illustrator of the *Graphic*, a graduate of Oxford, contributes his quota to the enjoyment of the party. Coffee and cognac fill up the pauses of conversation, and the evening hours fly swiftly. These parties usually break up with arrangements for the next morning's breakfast, where friends arrange further programmes. Every body here has a calling which occupies most of the day. It was my good-fortune to meet this morning at the breakfast-table Mr. John Skinner, who will be remembered by many as of the suite of the Prince of Wales when in America, and Mr. J. Scott Russell, the builder of the *Great Eastern*, whose clear, broad views and well-stored mind make him an attractive and interesting companion. He has the high forehead, black eyes, and thin English face of Mr. Herbert Spencer, and is one of that important class of English thinkers who seek to unfold the hidden laws of nature, and apply them to the practical good of man. He expressed the opinion that in future the military strength of nations must be found, not in standing armies, but in the ability to always keep prepared material of war, ready to be put into the hands of men at the approach of hostilities. I replied that it might be found rather in the ability to produce material of war at the approach of hostilities, as in this age of rapid improvement we are at any time liable to find our work of to-day superseded and made comparatively valueless by the inventions of to-morrow.

An occasional dull boom from one of the forts about Paris is all of war we hear; and when we ride to the front, the same monotonous, quiet watching, and the same spry work at gabions and fascines, is all we see. The short sword, hung at the waist, is all that is used for this work, even to the cutting down of trees eight inches through.

WHAT THE TROOPS ARE DOING.

Nov. 14th.—I went to-day, by invitation of the chief of artillery, to the front, near Garches, where a good view of the city of Paris is had. It is about four miles from Versailles, and the first three are through the public forests of St. Cloud. The roads have been carefully made, and are well drained and macadamized. These forests are painfully silent—not a living thing but an occasional magpie breaking the death-like stillness. As we near the front, and pass the little village of Vauenessau, two light batteries are seen encamped in a neighboring field. It has rained considerably during the past three days, and their camp has the drowned appearance, with dirt bespattered on every thing, so easily recognized by all our officers of the late war. Nowhere have I seen so complete a duplicate of similar experiences in the South. As we go on, through the deserted grounds of a country-house, we pass a party, under a major, felling the timber, and trimming it into impassable abattis. This is the first time I have seen this about Paris, and it is only recently that it has been begun. But it is out of the question for these people to be idle, and so they work away, each day making the investment closer. I have seen no good axemen in Europe; and here they cut down the trees with crosscut saws. We proceed, and pass successively the battalion, the platoon, the guard, and at last arrive at the single sentinel, carefully concealed, peeping over a wall. We are cautioned not to show ourselves, but peep over also; and before us lies Paris.

PARIS FROM THE LINES.

The new opera-house, from its great height, and the abrupt offset, by which the upper story is made to seem set upon the tops of the other buildings, is the most prominent object in that portion of the city in which it is situated, while in the Latin Quarter the Pantheon overtops every thing. Between these comes Notre-Dame, with its two truncated towers, the Invalides, with its gilded dome, the Tuileries, the Palais d'Industrie, the Madeleine, besides many other well-known landmarks, and, beyond the whole,

Montmartre and Père la Chaise. This is my last view of Paris for many years, and very likely some of these grand and beautiful structures will crumble into dust and thin air before my next visit.

NO BATTERIES IN POSITION.

As I look about me all along this front, I see a slight epaulement thrown up in many places, to repel sorties, but I notice no batteries for large guns anywhere. I do not believe that there is a single gun in position about Paris, nor that any good could come from their use, nor that it has been the policy at any time to open a general bombardment. A few shots will probably be fired into the city, to let the citizens know how completely they are in the power of their adversaries, but nothing more will be done. In returning by another route, we found the entire woods of St. Cloud filled with stacks of gabions and fascines. Thousands of cords of them cumber the ground in every direction. It seems to be thought best to have an abundance of material on hand ready for any future use.

Nov. 15th.—After breakfasting with the crown prince, I took my leave of him, bearing many kind messages from him to Mr. Bancroft at Berlin, of whom he spoke in the most flattering terms. He expressed many regrets at not being able to visit America, which he said he ought to have done in earlier life, but that he was now too old to think of it, referring of course to his increasing political responsibilities, due to the age of his father, which make his presence near the seat of Government at all times imperative.

LEAVING VERSAILLES.

Nov. 19th.—I left Versailles on the 17th, in company with an officer of the East India service, coming to Nautem, the terminus of the Strasbourg Railroad, a distance of fifty miles, in two days. The route is desolate, as the people have left the neighborhood of the line of communications. It is here that the French destroyed a tunnel half a mile in length. The Germans, after a month spent in repairing it, abandoned the work, and are now laying a temporary track around the hill. In improving and repairing railroads and bridges, the Germans have done nothing worthy to be compared with our own work during our war, but this may be due to want of time necessary to gain experience in such matters. I do not remember that we performed in the first three months of the war any achievement in this direction equal to those of later date.

RAILWAY TERMINUS SUPPLIES.

This is the railway terminus, from which is supplied an army of two hundred thousand men; and what do the supplies consist of? Acres upon acres of ammunition, shot, shell, and cartridges, and such articles of necessary food as the country does not afford, the newly arriving mail, and nothing else. Whoever has seen the stores for our armies during our war can not have forgotten the numberless kinds of merchandise, of all possible descriptions and uses, brought together and known by the general term, "quartermaster's property." They embraced every thing, from a cambric needle to a complete set of quarters ready to put up. The accumulation at Nashville and Chattanooga in the last year of the war, when the advent of peace was plain to every one, is past belief. There were thousands of tons of property, having but the remotest relation to military matters. It is true, that our troops required to be re-clad in the field, while the Germans will take home most of the clothing they wore to this country; but this is due largely to the superiority of their all-wool, well-made clothes over our *shoddy*.

A NIGHT AMONG THE SOLDIERS.

On arriving at Nautem, the captain in charge told us that the train would leave for Strasbourg in half an hour. We waited vainly until after dark, when the rain began to fall. We were then told that the train would not get off until next morning. The quandary about the night would have been serious enough, as there was not a public-house in the place, had not a soldier standing near at once recognized our dilemma and asked us to accompany him into the town, where he would provide for our comfort overnight. Calling to some comrades to assist with the baggage, he led the way in the pitch darkness along the paved street, then covered with an inch of almost fluid mud, to his quarters some half a mile away. He took us to the second story of a house of very respectable appearance, in the two front rooms of which were quartered himself and five comrades. There were in the room a stove, a washstand, and upon the floor beds of common mattresses, with blankets for six men. The men all instantly comprehended the situation, and in the shortest possible time made one of the rooms unexceptionably comfortable; while one began to prepare our supper, and another went out to bring us some bottles of wine.

SOUP SAUSAGE.

In a few minutes a pot of excellent soup was made from their prepared soup sausage, composed of ground peas and finely chopped ham, flavored with garlic, and closely pressed and dried. With the soup they gave us bread and butter, and thin slices of fat pork. This they call *speck*. It is very excellently-cured side-pork, which, instead of being fried to a scrap, and three-fourths of it thrown away as fat, as is done by our troops, is cut in thin slices and eaten cold with bread. Their bread, which I have often tasted, is not light and sweet like ours, but is always clammy and sour. The meal was soon discussed, and a more satisfactory one I never partook of. We slept excellently, and in the morning, after having coffee and handsomely remunerating our hosts, were assisted by them to the cars, where they took leave of us, with many hearty good wishes for America.

CHAPTER VI.

THE PRUSSIAN ARMY.

THE origin and growth of Prussia are similar in many particulars to those of the United States. We colonized, while they crystallized. We created a nation by the voluntary accretion of individuals; they, by attaching whole communities, with their lands and fortunes, and not always with their consent. The work was done in each case within nearly the same limits of time, and with the same fostering care of the moral and material interests of the people. While both nations equally promoted general education, the United States neglected the science of arms, and Prussia made of it a leading duty. The result is that, as their general civilization is higher, so their military system is more efficient than that of other European states. How much of all this is the work of rulers, and how much is due to the natural evolution of human character and sentiment, it is unnecessary to discuss.

THE GREAT ELECTOR.

The Great Elector of Brandenburg, Frederick William, was the real founder of the Prussian nationality, and gave the civilized world an example of military organization and tactics which, until within a few years, it has closely copied. Under the able but despotic rule of the elector, from 1640 to 1688, his little electorate received the addition of the Dukedom of Prussia. The aim of this first great Hohenzollern was to advance the bounds of his dominion, and to elevate the condition of his subjects. Prussian policy has ever since been directed to the same results. Some credit is due a family of almost absolute rulers, who for generations have labored for the public good, always fostering the best civilization, and winning the confidence of neighboring states, till all of North Germany has for many years clung to Prussia for protection, when intrigue threatened within, or invasion from without. The little dominion of the great elector soon came to be looked upon as a rallying-point for those who believed in the coming unity of the Fatherland; and thus, while the German Empire was dissolving, Prussia was inaugurating a new life. She also became, like our own beloved land, the home of the oppressed; and no less than two hundred thousand Protestant Christians, driven from their homes by the Inquisition, found here liberty of conscience, and, from their skilled knowledge, became the teachers of the Prussian people in the arts and practical conduct of life.

The successor of the great elector devoted his reign exclusively to the moral and material elevation of his people. He was followed by Frederick William, first King of Prussia, who perfected the military art; and, although attaching an absurd importance to the size of his men, nevertheless left to his son the finest army in the world. His method of instructing recruits one at a time, called by us "setting up," and known by others as "swallowing the ramrod," is to this day the system employed by all civilized nations. He also, in 1733, by parceling his dominions into cantons, and assigning to each the duty of keeping up a regiment to its effective strength from its own limits, laid the foundation for the magnificent Prussian military system of to-day. It is difficult to overestimate the importance of this geographical distribution. It connects the army with the very framework of society, enlists local pride in its support, and, by diffusing responsibility, simplifies the administration of affairs.

FREDERICK THE GREAT.

It was left for Frederick the Great to raise Prussia to the rank of a first-class power. The times favored his ambition; for the year of his accession saw the decease of the last direct male descendant of the line of Hapsburg, and a young and inexperienced woman had just ascended the Austrian throne. The ten years which followed the seizure of Silesia were occupied by Frederick in consolidating his scattered realm, and making all his resources available for the struggle which he already foresaw. The real cause of the Seven Years' War, which now followed, was the resolve of Austria to check the further growth of the power of its new rival, Prussia. Various were the changes of fortune which befell Frederick for the next six years. He wrote, in 1762, "Success alternated from one side to the other. The victories of Rossbach, Prague, and Leuthen were overshadowed by the disasters of Kolin, Hochkirch, and Kunersdorf." He seemed at times to despair of any issue but death for himself and desolation for his realm. Yet his boldness as a general and readiness as a tactician remained unimpaired by defeat. These qualities, with the excellent training of his troops, his great good-fortune in possessing two of the best cavalry officers ever known, Ziethen and Seidlitz, and the moral support of Great Britain, at last saved the struggling kingdom from the ruin that at times seemed inevitable.

Nothing can better illustrate the condition of Prussia at this period than the words of Frederick himself: "The peace awakens universal joy. For my own part, being but a poor old man, I return to a city where I know nothing but its walls; where unmeasured toil awaits me; and where I must soon lay me down to rest in that place in which there is no more unquiet, nor war, nor misery, nor man's deceit. The nobility is in the last stage of exhaustion; the poor man is ruined; countless villages are burned, and many towns destroyed. Prussia is like a man covered with wounds, who, weakened by severe loss of blood, is on the point of succumbing to the excess of his suffering."

The position of Prussia was now assured, and the policy, steadily followed for three generations, had attained its first great result. The obscure electorate was to hold a solid place among the nations of the earth, and thenceforth to contend with Austria for German pre-eminence. A long season of peace, which now followed, gave Frederick the much-needed opportunity to foster the internal improvements of his kingdom; but he did not for a moment neglect to put his army again on the most perfect war-footing. The standing forces which he maintained, and handed over to his successor, were little less than those which Prussia, with resources more than three times as great, kept in pay before the late war with Austria. The standing army numbered then three per centum of the population of Prussia—a proportion large enough to supply now the whole of her peace army, the additions required for war-footing, all of the first call of the landwehr, and most of the second call. Frederick never lost sight of the two grand principles of his policy — to extend Prussian influence in Germany, and to humble the pretensions of Austria.

In his advanced years, the opportunity again occurred to take up arms against Austria, as the apparent protector of the lesser German states against her encroachments. In 1777, an elector of one of the small principalities died without heirs, and left a complication as to the succession. The Emperor of Austria, by virtue of some collateral connection with the deceased prince, asserted a claim to it, and prepared to defend his right by force of arms. Frederick, either unwilling, from growing infirmity, to enter into a new war, or seeking to preserve the appearance of moderation, prolonged negotiations, but not the less diligently prepared for hostilities.

In July of that year, he suddenly took the field, after it became apparent that Austria would yield to nothing else. The campaign which followed is remarkable for two things—his moderation, in contrast with the reckless strategy for which he was so justly famed, and the striking parallel which its opening affords to the tactics of 1866. Its scene lay on the very ground where Benedek was called to oppose the recent invasion of Bohemia. In 1778, Frederick entered that country suddenly, as his descendants did eighty-eight years later. Like them, he had an army too large for a single movement over difficult mountain roads. His commissariat, although a masterpiece of organization for that age, could not safely be relied on for so large a force, and consequently one-half of his army was distributed on the frontier before the movement began. Half of his force, led by himself, moved into Bohemia from Glatz, through Nachod and Skalitz, while the remainder entered by the line of the Elbe. They found the roads open through the mountain passes, as the Prussian army did in 1866, and moved to within one day's march of the junction near Gitschin, important then, as now, as the crossing of the two roads. That last day's march, however, was destined never to be made. Austria, sufficiently apprised of the movement, had cleverly posted an army of two hundred and fifty thousand men in a strong defensive position, well chosen to prevent the Prussian concentration, and had already prepared a rough line of intrenchments of such strength as to deter attack. The forces of the kaiser occupied a line about seventy miles in length, formed in the general direction of a semicircle, using as their front the Elbe, the Iser, and some hills which were strengthened, wherever necessary, by double and treble lines of palisades, escarpments, and redoubts. Frederick thoroughly reconnoitred the entire length of this line, and withdrew after a single weak attempt upon one point. There are many theories to account for this failure, but no view is more satisfactory than that the king had undertaken a campaign which required the separation of his forces, without first providing adequately for their junction. The enemy took advantage of this fatal weakness in his plan of campaign, and defeated the effort. The next six weeks were spent in gathering meagre supplies, which consisted mostly of potatoes, from the thin belt of country between the enemy and the mountains in the Prussian rear, which gave the campaign the historic name of the "Potato War." Frederick now retreated, finding great difficulty in carrying away his immense trains, which, however, Austria did not disturb, fearing to push any success which might be within her grasp, for the reason that Prussia appeared now as the champion of the smaller German states. Negotiations for peace were at once entered into, and ended in the renunciation by Austria of claims on Bavaria, and a money indemnity to the minor states, while Prussia was satisfied with the position of protector of the lesser German states, and the practical admission by Austria that her political acts, outside of her own limits, must in future depend upon the consent of Prussia.

BLUCHER.

The successors of Frederick used the magnificent military force bequeathed to them, until the wars with the first Napoleon, to strengthen Prussia's influence with the neighboring states. A personage destined long after to render to his country valuable service now begins to be heard of.

Dismissed from the army fifteen years before for questioning the justice of a promotion over him, Blucher had retired to his home in Pomerania, when his case was brought to the notice of King Frederick William II., who restored him to the army with the rank of major. Perhaps a better cavalry officer never held a rein.

A mighty tempest was now gathering in the West. The ancient empire of the kaiser was to be laid prostrate by French republican armies, and the strong Northern kingdom, got together with such care and energy by Hohenzollerns, was to be brought lower still, and for years to wear the chains of the conqueror. A new general, with a new system of warfare, was to eclipse the achievements of Frederick, and confound the armies he had trained. A bolder and more unscrupulous diplomacy than the great elector's was to change the whole map of Europe. The revolution and Napoleon came, and the shadow went back on the dial of Prussian progress. Prussia, with scarcely eight millions of people, was for a long time unwilling to take any decided step against the new order of things in France. Not until the sacred right of kings was attacked in the person of Louis XVI., after his flight to Varenne, did the king move to the rescue. He then roused himself from an almost indolent life, mingled freely in diplomacy, and proposed to join the Austrian emperor in an armed intervention.

The influence of Frederick the Great in those days almost surpasses belief. His instructions were considered the perfection of military precepts; his administration was copied in its minutest details, though its spirit had passed away with the author; and his generals, however old, were deemed necessarily masters of their art. The troops of the empire for the first time moved to the order of Prussian commanders; and the force which entered Champagne in 1792, was thought by friend and foe irresistible, because made up largely of Prussian battalions. An easy march to the French capital was considered certain. Boastful proclamations were issued; contempt was expressed for their foe; and a careless, ill-directed advance soon met at Valmy the fate so often dealt out to overconfident, proclaiming commanders.

The Prussian staff, relying too much on the promised support which they nowhere met, threw aside the prudent but cumbrous arrangement of magazines, by which Frederick had always prepared for his offensive movements, and led their troops into an inhospitable country in bad weather, where they perished by thousands for lack of supplies. On meeting the enemy, the vacillation of the commanders proved the ruin of the expedition and the turning-point of the revolution. Henceforth the republican armies increased rapidly in *morale* and numbers, and a new system of tactics was formed, destined, under Napoleon's master-hand, to replace that which Frederick had bequeathed to Europe, and to overthrow the army of each great power in turn. The failure of the Prussian troops was as great a surprise to Europe as was the collapse of Austria in 1866. Goethe, who was on the battle-field, discerned at once, with his keen, intuitive sagacity, the change which had occurred in the forces of the world.

In 1794, the insurrection of the Poles, under Kosciusko, gave opportunity for withdrawing from an alliance in which Prussia had no heart, and she gladly seized it. The treaty of Basle soon followed, and the great German powers were compelled to admit the claim of the republic to advance her borders to the Rhine. Prussia, still mindful of her rivalry with Austria, offered the guaranty of neutrality to any of the smaller German states which would withdraw from the alliance, and many of them were thus induced to retire from the contest. During this war, so inglorious to Prussia, where, excepting the part taken by Colonel Blucher, disasters befell her everywhere, her influence and power both rapidly sank. With the exception of the officer just named, every Prussian commander seemed weak and imbecile. The men also appeared to have lost all the qualities of the soldiers of Frederick except stiffness. In spite of the severe system of conscription, enforced by heavy penalties, a trade in permits of absence had long been established as a perquisite of captains. Those who would pay well were exempted from service, the bribes received being used in part to attract an inferior class of recruits into the ranks of an army made thoroughly distasteful in time of peace by an iron discipline maintained in every detail. Inferior troops, thus brought together by a corrupt system of exemption substitutes, were commanded by officers without youth, hope, or love of their profession—commonplace veterans who had served with Frederick, and to whom war was a mere trade, or the scions of princely houses of the smaller states which Prussia wished to propitiate. So enlisted, trained, and commanded, the army, once acknowledged the best in Europe, was now the least fit for vigorous war.

The growing enthusiasm in republican France, springing from a political fanaticism, and sustained through the sternest want by hope of promotion and riches, was fast preparing her army to sweep away the proud battalions of Prussia. Frederick William III. succeeded to the throne in 1797. For ten years he continued a selfish policy of neutrality, viewing complacently the repeated humiliations of Austria in the belief that he saw in them gain for Prussia, till at last the time came when it was necessary to take sides. Russia combined with Austria to check the growing power of Napoleon, and each party sought a passage through Prussian territory. This right of transit, which was refused to the czar, Napoleon seized without asking. The march of Bernadotte through Anspach, on his way to Ulm and Austerlitz, produced such indignation in Prussia as to shake the royal power, and showed plainly the tendencies of popular feeling.

The visit of the czar to Berlin was at once followed by the withdrawal of the French minister, Duroc. Napoleon had reason to expect the Prussians on his line of communications, but the sword of Brandenburg proved rusty in its scabbard, and the maintenance of an overgrown standing army had overtaxed the nation's strength without fitting it for ready defense. Before the needful preparations were made for taking the field, and the last vestige of the king's vacillation removed, the great venture of Austerlitz had been made and lost by those who could wait no longer for Prussia.

On the 15th of December, the day Frederick William had fixed for declaring war against Napoleon, his ambassador accepted at the latter's hand the much-coveted prize of Hanover. The offer of this bribe at first staggered the conscience of the king; but he soon yielded to the urgency of Napoleon, and decided to take it. This degrading acquisition soon proved to be no free gift. Bavaria was enlarged at the expense of Prussia, and other provinces were seized to make a new duchy for one of Napoleon's brothers-in-law. Humiliations were heaped upon her, and from the rank of a great power she suddenly found herself fallen to the condition of an appanage, and her monarch treated as a vassal. Yet she had made no struggle and suffered no defeat, had looked on unscathed while her neighbors bled, and, without one honorable wound, now found herself isolated, exposed, humbled, and unpitied. The people would endure this no longer. Noble, burgher, and peasant alike felt the thrill of patriotism, and a tempest of passion swept over the nation. Without counting the cost or the odds, Frederick William was forced into the struggle he dreaded; and Prussia, single-handed, faced Napoleon with his devoted and well-tried army. Planted already, by Bavarian permission, within easy distance of the decisive points, armed with superior numbers, and flushed with victory, the French rushed on the flank exposed by the rash advance of their enemy; and the battle of Jena was fought and won almost within sight of the little hill of Rossbach, which had given name to French defeat half a century before. With a rapidity almost incredible, the kingdom was overrun, the remainder of its army annihilated, and its cities occupied. Blucher, though surrounded by imbecility and cowardice, fought fiercely to the last.

The servile worship of Prussian models was changed to an unreasoning contempt for them. Reduced as Frederick was to a single city and a few square miles of territory, he refused, while a gleam of hope was left, to submit to the harsh terms required of him. His troops gave valiant and hearty support to their allies on the bloody field of Eylau, but the fearful mistake at Friedland sufficed to bring about the abandonment of the unhappy kingdom, which followed on the celebrated armistice of Tilsit. Stripped of half her territory, the rest a field for French tax-gatherers and parade-ground for French troops, the history of Prussia for the next six years was a record of submission to a master whose chains she had no power to shake off. Her revenues were swallowed up by foreign exactions; her army reduced to a mere corps by decree of Napoleon; her means of rising against the oppressor to all appearance hopelessly gone.

I have been thus particular in sketching the outline of

Prussian history up to the conquest by Napoleon, in order to introduce the account of those subsequent measures which laid the foundation of her present military strength, and to show the folly of dependence upon any system of the past, however effective it may have been in its day. Our own army at the commencement of the rebellion, and the present army of the French, content as it has been for half a century to rest upon its fame with the first Napoleon, are cases in point. An army, to be of value, must possess the true national spirit of its time, and be allied in sympathy to the people; otherwise the profession of arms is reduced to a mere trade, and becomes an incubus and a danger, because it induces a false security.

THE BEGINNING OF THE PRESENT GREATNESS OF PRUSSIA.

During the degradation of Prussia there were those among her statesmen who, knowing her past history and inherent qualities, never despaired of her better destiny, and set to work with unremitting toil to accomplish it. Stein, her best minister, sought to elevate the peasantry, by improving their legal status, fostering a higher morality, and effecting domestic reforms.

SHORT TERMS OF SERVICE.

Schoenhurst, the war minister, did a no less effective work, by devising a system of short terms of service in the regular army, with a constant supply and discharge of recruits, on which the present organization of the Prussian army rests, and which gave such splendid results in 1813, '14. Patiently these great men bided their time, unmoved by the presence of calamity or the untimely ardor of such men as Blucher, who fretted himself into illness at his enforced inaction. They observed grimly the exactions of Duroc and the brutal violence of Davoust, and watched among their countrymen the growth of that heroic type of character which is bred in the school of adversity.

The hour of French defeat and Prussia's opportunity finally came. At first the king was inclined to temporize, but a torrent of popular feeling swept him on. He then put himself boldly at the head of the movement, and directed it with wisdom. Blucher was summoned from retirement, the command of the chief army committed to his hands, and a staff formed, skillful to guide, and moderate to control, the ardor which might expose his force to too great dangers. Disaster and suffering had been no less useful in schooling Prussia's army than her people, and had effaced all minor differences. Her infantry had been trained to a light system of tactics, their weapons modernized, her staff and leading officers selected solely for their efficiency, while England engaged to supply all the material needs of the soldiery. After a long year of struggle and victory, the Prussian ensigns were carried in triumph into Paris.

Another year had scarcely passed when Prussia was seen in the van of Europe, striking a second time at the throne of the common enemy; and history will always record as one of the most timely and complete of military movements the work of Blucher upon the flank of the French at Waterloo. It now became necessary for Prussia to reform her military establishment. The foundation of the system had been laid by Schoenhurst during the years of Prussia's subjugation. Napoleon had decreed that Prussia should have an army of but forty thousand men, but nothing was said as to length of service. By limiting the term of enlistment to six months, Prussia was enabled during each year to return to their homes eighty thousand well-disciplined and instructed soldiers, which in the final struggle gave her five times as many veterans as were counted on by the allies, and enabled her to take the lead in their operations. This, with the plan laid down by the father of the great Frederick, by which each regiment was furnished by a particular district, gave the key to the future organization of her army.

LOCAL DISTRIBUTION OF ARMY CORPS.

To this, on which the landwehr system is still based, Frederick now added many improvements, one of which was to distribute the various branches of the service in due proportion over the respective districts, so as to enable him to make the troops of each province an independent army corps complete within itself, and to prohibit entirely the procuring of recruits from abroad. This gave the Prussian army a distinctive national character, which has been strictly maintained ever since. The materials which Stein and Schoenhurst got together were ready to the hands of the Government, and patriotism did the rest. The bonds of paternal government had been greatly loosened, and confidence much impaired by the presence of foreign armies in the country, holding and controlling every thing; and the great minister Stein had taken advantage of this feeling to inculcate a spirit of national and individual sacrifice. Great political reforms had been introduced, the last remains of serfdom abolished, the peasant enabled to inherit and hold land in his own right, and the towns given enlarged municipal privileges. Taxation was equalized, civil offices were thrown open to free competition, and privileges of the nobility abolished; so that during this period of apparently hopeless prostration, Prussia made immense advances in her inner political life. The immediate effect of these reforms was a vast increase of national spirit, strength, and prosperity. The burden of military service, imposed on all classes with an impartial hand, was accepted as a matter of course; and, at the close of the struggle of 1814, there was a general desire to perpetuate a system which had restored glory and freedom to the country. The foundation of the permanent constitution of the national army was laid by the remarkable law of 1814, which for more than forty years continued in force, and which in its preamble declares the public sentiment to be that, "In a lawfully administered armament of the nation lies the best security of lasting peace." All former exceptions in favor of the noblesse were at this time abolished, and every native of the state, on completing his twentieth year, was held bound to enroll himself in her defensive force. With a view to avoid inconvenient pressure upon the professional and industrial classes, the armed force was to consist of sections, whose service should lessen in severity with length of service. The whole system comprised, first, a standing army; second, a landwehr of the first call; third, a landwehr of the second call; fourth, a landsturm. Although changed in some minor particulars, this arrangement of forces is still adhered to. The standing army was composed of young men from twenty to twenty-five years of age. Three years of the term of service was spent with the colors; then two years at home on furlough, the men pursuing their usual avocations, but ready at the first sound of war to join their standards. A most important provision was, that young men of the educated classes, who could clothe and arm themselves for one year, might spend that period in the rifle corps or light-infantry, and then at once enter the landwehr. This clause was introduced to save the wealthy and well-born from the degradation which, in a country essentially aristocratic, the association in the barrack-room with the recruits from the lowest classes would be felt to occasion. There has been built upon this a very extensive and remarkable feature in the Prussian service, known as one-year volunteerage, which has solved, without difficulty, two important questions. The universality of the conscription law has been maintained, without opposition from the better middle order, which has grown rapidly in wealth and influence, and, notwithstanding its strong claims, is excluded from the higher posts of the army; and, besides, a body of efficient officers, trained in all the duties of the line, is provided for the landwehr, without expense to the state.

The landwehr of the first call was intended as a reserve support to the regular army in case of war, liable to serve at home or abroad, but in time of peace only to be called out, like militia, for instruction and drill. It was formed of all the young men, between twenty-one and twenty-six years, not in the regular army; all the one-year's volunteers after their year of service, and the rest of the male population up to their thirty-third year, excepting only such as had already served twelve years in the army.

The second call of the landwehr was intended for garrison troops, and, in case the first two classes were all required in the field, might be summoned to re-enforce the regular army. This call embraced all members who had passed through the regular army and first call, and all other males up to their fortieth year. Their drill was only by company, for occasional instruction in their own neighborhoods; and provision was made, in case of a change of residence, for enrollment in the regiment nearest to the new domicile.

The landsturm was composed of all male inhabitants, between seventeen and fifty, not included in the three other classes. It could be called out only in provinces actually invaded, and not there except by royal decree. It could, however, be used for civil purposes, such as for *posses* to marshals; but no provisions were made for its drills, and it existed only as a paper organization. The priesthood only were exempt from service. Even the sons of the king served as one-year volunteers. These volunteers might choose their arm of service, were encouraged to live in respectability, and allowed to wear plain clothes when not on duty, and employ servants to clean their equipments. The law allowed an alteration of the term of service in the various classes in time of war, if desirable. Soldiers who desired to re-enlist for a second term were permitted to do so after serving three years, and then wore a distinguishing badge; and, after a second re-enlistment, received a higher rate of pay, and the right of pension if invalided. The same rule held good in the landwehr, continuance in service entitling the soldier to promotion if his qualifications justified it. A special committee, composed of one military officer, one civil magistrate, and one landed proprietor, was created for each regimental district, to administer the recruiting law. Such were the outlines of the enactment which the war of independence established. For more than forty years this compact between government and people was fairly maintained, although the other portions of the wise legislation of the Stein ministry suffered at the hands of the reactionary party, which rioted in all the courts of Europe after the final overthrow of Napoleon. The people were contented with a military administration which fell evenly upon all, and imposed a moderate tax on their resources. One hundred and thirty battalions of infantry, one hundred and fifty-two squadrons of cavalry, one hundred and two companies of artillery, and a few battalions of engineers, comprised the regular army. The landwehr of the first call consisted of one hundred and sixteen battalions of infantry, having each, permanently, a commander and an adjutant, the one-year volunteers furnishing the remaining officers. They were superficially drilled, and only occasionally called together. The one-year volunteer clause probably saved the law through the long years of peace that followed. Without this, it would have been insufferable to the people, after the miseries of their subjugation had been forgotten and the keen sense of the need of a good army blunted. But a system that gives service and education in place of a conscript's fine needs no defense.

The workings of a law so radical and universal developed some phenomena worthy of notice. The law made no provision for officering the regular army. The original exemption of the nobility from conscription by Frederick almost implied that they would enter the service as officers. Practically, until the war of independence, no one else was made eligible to these positions, and, although this exclusive privilege was then abolished, yet, by a rule which required all candidates for a commission to be accepted or rejected by the votes of the officers of the regiment itself, the army has retained to the present day this distinctive characteristic. The officers, although generally poor, do not thereby lose their social standing. Any young man may enter as a one-year volunteer, before the end of the year pass all the necessary examinations, and, upon exhibiting university degrees, will have the legal right to apply for an ensign's commission. Here his prospects will end, unless he be of aristocratic birth; for, although the commission is nominally given by the Government, he must appear before the committee of his regiment, whom he must satisfy not only as to his professional qualifications, but as to his means, his freedom from debt, and his parentage and general morality. The result has been to make of the Prussian service the closest corporation ever known, and it can not in this form last much longer. After the war of 1866, a few promotions were made from the ranks, in the manner practiced by us, but the officers so appointed did not find their positions endurable, and have since all been transferred to various branches of the civil service. Many of the noble families are almost without means, except what they receive from the Government; and, since the civil service has been thrown open to all classes, the aristocracy are all the more tenacious of their supposed hereditary right to officer the army. There is a single exception to this plan of officering the regular forces. The graduates of the royal cadet schools, which furnish about one-twelfth of the officers required, are commissioned by the king, and the regiments have no right to reject them; but as these men are the elite of the military schools, say one in five, and enjoy the special favor of the king, they are as far separated from the people as the hereditary aristocracy, with whom they are at once admitted upon a social equality. The present king and his predecessor have leaned upon the aristocracy as against the trading classes, and this has given the nobility increased importance. These needy people, dependent entirely upon the king for preferment, with no income but their scanty pay for military service, and separated from the people by birth, habits, and profession, are apt to widen, by offensive personal bearing, the distance which in Prussia more than in any other country separates the soldier from the civilian. This may be looked upon as the most dangerous question now existing in German politics, and one which must soon bring about strife, as the people will not much longer consent to fill a secondary place. Such a military caste can be endured only while external strife makes readiness for service the paramount consideration; but in the long and prosperous peace which must follow the unification of Germany, this question will surely be reached, and the claims of the people must be admitted. The common assumption, that predominance of monarchical and aristocratic ideas is a necessary corollary of the present war is founded neither on fact nor reason.

True democracy has taken such root in Germany as to be certain of final success and vindication, and at no time has the sentiment grown more rapidly than in war. Observation of other countries, unless it be our own under like circumstances, affords us no criterion, for never before have we seen a nation at war where the people were all enlightened, and indoctrinated with sentiments of liberty. Republican Germans have often told me, "The war of 1866 and the present one are doing our work more rapidly than we could do it ourselves. When unity is established the shell of aristocracy must break up." The three strong points of the Prussian system are universal service, suffrage, and education. This trio is carrying the nation on with a momentum that an effete system of aristocracy can no longer resist.

OFFICERING THE ARMY.

For the past fifty years, there has been no opening for a military career to the people, except in the landwehr. Promotion from the ranks, as understood by us, is unknown. Excepting this special feature, the plan of officering the Prussian army is, without doubt, the best yet devised. By far the greater number of officers enlist and serve six months in the ranks of a regiment, not as common soldiers, but as admitted candidates for commissions, as will be shown in the discussion of military schools. A reformed scamp, by entering the ranks, as in the English service, or a decently intelligent conscript who shows brute courage in battle, as in the French, can make no claim for promotion to a position for which he is unfit. Nor, as in the American service, is a law which was intended to encourage enlistment and elevate the service, by giving a portion of the commissions as second lieutenants to men in the ranks, defeated by enlisting young gentlemen, not to be soldiers, but to fulfill the letter of the law and become officers.

OFFICERING THE LANDWEHR AND ONE-YEAR VOLUNTEER-AGE.

In the landwehr promotions in the lower grades are freely thrown open to the people, but in time of war the battalions are placed under command of regular officers. The Government has done much to render attractive this one-year system of volunteering, by which the landwehr is officered, and is thereby enabled without expense to train up a large body of well-instructed and available men. For a long time the one-year volunteer course has been considered a part of the education of the sons of every manufacturer, proprietor, professional man, and well-to-do shop-keeper. Only those, however, who show great industry and special fitness are selected and prepared for commissions. A board sits twice in each year to receive the credentials of candidates, and issue the necessary warrants. They require certificates of birth, evidence of good character, bond of parent or guardian to pay the necessary costs, and certificates of teachers showing the behavior of the candidate at school. Evidence of any dishonorable conduct is fatal to the application. If these papers are satisfactory the certificate is granted, after the applicant has passed a medical examination. In the case of candidates from the universities, first-class royal schools, and some other schools specially designated, a personal appearance may be dispensed with, but with respect to applicants who have not enjoyed such advantages an actual examination is required. A knowledge of German, French, mathematics, geography, and history, and the elements of natural history and physics, is necessary; but the commission has wide discretion in varying these requirements according to the intended occupation of the candidate. Those designed for trade are excused in Latin, while young men who elect to serve in the cavalry and are good horsemen, are passed lightly in scientific subjects. In fact, there is no great difficulty in getting permission to serve the state at one's own expense.

It is a rule, in matters both civil and military, to take advantage of fitness for special pursuits. Young men in garrison towns, if competent, find no difficulty in gaining their warrants, and commandants are directed to accept all who present themselves with warrants; but at all other places only four cadets are allowed to each company. The candidate is a cadet attached to a company for instruction. He is required to attend all parades and drills, and study such lessons as may be assigned him; but otherwise his life is easy enough. He wears a simple distinctive badge, and may have his uniform of fine fabric, and live according to his circumstances. His military duties are generally finished by twelve o'clock, and he can, if he desires, devote the remainder of the day to his civil education, and continue his university course, or preparation for a profession, just as if he were not in the service. If a young man of birth and fashion, he gains admittance to all the gayeties of the place, like an officer or citizen of his own class. There are a few who desire to know more of the profession of arms, and to these every encouragement is given to prepare themselves to become the future officers of the landwehr. They are formed into classes of twenty, each under the instruction of a competent officer. At the end of the year the candidate is examined, and, if he passes satisfactorily, becomes a corporal; and the higher grades are then open to him, under regulations governing promotion in the landwehr, provided he is acceptable, in conduct and attainments, to the officers of his corps.

A WEAK POINT IN THE MILITARY SYSTEM.

Many of the young nobility, who do not wish to follow a military career all their lives, qualify for officers of the landwehr; but most of these commissions go to the sons of manufacturers, proprietors, and professional men, often citizens of large means and local influence, but outside of the "well-born" class. It has followed, as a matter of course, that the growing wealth and increased influence of the middle classes have given a political character to the landwehr, which completely divides it from the regular army, and at times makes it distasteful to the crown.

The landwehr, officered, in comparison with the regular army, by men of more substance and often more talent, its ranks filled with veteran soldiers of equal position, riper age, and greater influence, becomes naturally the more popular branch of the service, and threatens at some future day to become a power in the state. At one time a jealousy sprang up on either side, which, although of little consequence in peace, seemed likely to paralyze the military power in the emergencies of active service. The tactical system of 1814 contemplated that the one hundred and sixteen battalions of the landwehr of the first call should be formed into brigades, each of which was to be joined by a brigade of regulars, and thus constitute a division. These troops, with the reserve men of the regular battalions, gave at once a field army of three hundred thousand combatants. The ardent spirit of patriotism, caused by the rigor of French exactions, had at that era wiped away all class differences, and rendered the system in the highest degree effective. The landwehr regiments long after enjoyed a proud reputation, gained in the French campaigns, which made commissions in them objects of ambition to the large and highly respectable classes from which the one-year volunteers were supplied. But the growing political differences between the people and the crown caused the king to distrust the landwehr, which was in consequence made secondary to the regular army. The nation had again outgrown its military system, and found itself carrying an immense military mechanism, no longer entirely available for purposes of defense or aggression. The patriotism which made the system adequate in 1814 was replaced by forgetfulness of its causes, and a desire for domestic ease and industrial pursuits. Three different times an attempt was made to use the old system — once to anticipate difficulties likely to arise with the Elector of Hesse Cassel; again, in 1854, to preserve neutrality with the Western powers; and in 1859, when French encroachments seemed to make war imminent. Although actual hostilities did not follow in these cases, the unsuitableness of the old system became each time more plainly apparent. The landwehr officers showed jealousy, both of the regular officers, who affected superiority, and of the staff placed over them. Thoroughly educated themselves in their profession, often superior in every thing except the accident of birth, commanding veterans and endowed by the laws of the land with an actual equality with the regulars, they showed dissatisfaction and impatience in being called out, and particularly in cases where the object was not thoroughly supported by national sentiment. The Government saw clearly that the army could not be relied upon to win the prize of Prussian supremacy. Austria must be dispossessed of her influence in the German Bund, in order that the lesser states might gravitate toward strong Prussia. To effect this, a powerful and ready force was indispensable.

ARMY REFORM.

As early as 1848, Major Von Roon, seeing the imperfections of the existing system, laid before the ministry a plan, since adopted, adapting the military force to the new condition of Prussian politics. During the next ten years the question of army reform was the chief subject of contention between the liberal and aristocratic factions, until, in 1859, the trouble encountered in mobilizing that portion of the army placed upon the Rhine as a menace to France gave an excuse for carrying a reform measure through, in spite of the constitutional objections made in the Lower House. This movement was distasteful to the representatives of the people, because it was carried in open disregard of their right of granting or withholding supplies, and lowered the status of the landwehr; while it gave importance to the regular force by adding to their years of service, and enlarging the number of battalions. This was, of course, in keeping with the views of the aristocracy, as it gave them promotion, created new offices, and greatly increased their power and influence, already on the wane. During the next year the national force received, by the will of the executive, the long-wished-for changes; and, notwithstanding the next six years of remonstrance from the House of Deputies, the new system was perfected, and maintained in every particular.

When these long years of preparation had put every man in his place, and a map of the ground to be passed over into the pockets of every staff and general officer, and when every bridge along the line of operations had its exact duplicate on the frontier, the war of 1866 came, and in seven weeks was successfully closed, having effectually broken the last weak tie attaching to Austria the states of Southern Germany. Not until now were the king and his cabinet justified by the people in their unconstitutional acts. The first grand scene in the drama of German unification was successfully closed, and Bismarck, the mouthpiece of German destiny, became the virtual ruler of his country.

DETAILS OF THE LAW.

We will now notice how this important change of organization was effected. The annual supply of recruits drafted into the line of the army was changed from forty thousand to sixty-three thousand. The standing army was augmented by one hundred and seventeen battalions, seventy-two squadrons of cavalry, thirty-one batteries of artillery, eighteen companies of engineers, and nine battalions of train troops. A far more serious innovation was the addition of two years to the soldier's term of reserve service. The reserves are so subject to calls by the Government, so liable to drills and inspections, that they are but one step more free than the men in the ranks. The unpopularity of this measure was complete when it was learned that the landwehr were in future to form no part of the field forces, but to stay at home as garrison troops. In peace, the standing army was now as large as before it would have been with the whole of the first call. In war, the new plan was to give about three hundred thousand infantry, one hundred thousand cavalry and artillery, and the first call one hundred thousand more. The term of service in the first call was shortened three years, and in the second call two years, as compensation for the additional years in the reserves.

WAR OF 1866.

It is not necessary to narrate the constitutional struggle which followed the promulgation of these orders. The popular party failed to shake the position taken by the Cabinet; the only effect of their efforts was to precipitate a foreign policy intended to bring about the open rupture with Austria, for which the change was expressly made. The war incident to the Schleswig-Holstein question, although really fought for the same general purpose of confederation under Prussian lead, had little significance, except as a training-school for the coming campaign in Austria. The army was now officered entirely by men devoted to the crown, who were counted upon to lead forward the admirably disciplined masses of the regular army, as boldly and steadily as if the whole nation had urged the war; while the landwehr in the second line could effect little by their disapproval, and, in case the field army was successful, would be influenced by their natural military instinct to support their victorious brethren. The Austrian infantry was conceded to be better drilled, but their *personnel* and arms were inferior. It was believed, also, that her generals were superior in experience and activity.

Prussia's system of promotion by seniority had placed in her highest grades men past the age when a general leads his troops with vigor; and many, from their campaigns against the first Napoleon, enjoyed chief commands who otherwise would have been long before retired. Among these were Herworth, Steinmetz, and Vogel. On the contrary, Austria's wars in Italy and Hungary had supplied her with experienced generals in the prime of life. This difficulty Prussia quickly overcame. The tradition which for generations had made soldiers of her princes, was now of great service. The king himself, an active soldier all his life, had learned to recognize merit, and gathered round him a staff of the highest intellectual order; while the crown prince and Frederick

Charles, both in vigorous manhood, had already, in addition to careful military training, shown qualities eminently fitting them for high command. Prince Frederick Charles, next to the king himself and Von Roon, who formed the plan, had been the most earnest advocate of the army reorganization and, by several military publications, had evinced such devotion to his profession, and such insight into military affairs, as to point to him at once as the chief leader in the field. The troops in the front line were divided into two grand armies, each under command of one of the royal princes.

The intention of seizing Saxony made it necessary to detach a sufficient force to control matters in that direction, and this was given to General Herworth, whose admirable management kept him in this independent command until the close of the war. This triple division of force was opposed to the well-known principles of war; but the use of the magnetic telegraph made the plan safe, and the whole was given in charge of General Von Moltke, who conducted the manœuvres of this army with a regularity and certainty which, without the aid of electricity, could only have been secured by keeping the parts together, and thus rendering the army so unwieldy as to make celerity impossible.

THE FIRST TRIAL OF THE BREECH-LOADER.

The breech-loading musket was now to have its decisive trial. It had been used in the small affairs of Baden and Schleswig-Holstein, but there were many who decried it, because of its wastefulness of ammunition—the precise argument so often used in our country by incompetent judges, who fail to recognize that their objection relates to the discipline of the men, and not at all to the qualities of the arm. There were those, however, like Prince Frederick

Charles, who at once saw its decided advantage, and by writing and practical experiments proved clearly its wonderful superiority. A few things should be borne in mind in the use of these arms. The rapidity of fire is so great that, in receiving an enemy, a command can with perfect safety reserve its fire until they are within five hundred paces. The attacking force should be made to approach over ground where they can not take advantage of cover. With these conditions, well-trained troops, with the energy and tact to cover their front with a slight epaulement, such as we were accustomed to make during the last year of our war every night before the troops rested, may await the assault of an adversary, no matter in what formation, with as little concern as the approach of a picket-line. It is safe to estimate the advantages of the breech over the muzzle loader as three to one. In its use troops must be well controlled, and not permitted the same liberty of firing on their own impulse as with muzzle-loaders.

I have taken the liberty of digressing in this matter, as there are still officers of our service who croak about the waste of ammunition with the new arm. Its use secures such decided advantages as should forever close the mouths of all who now oppose it. There are two requisites to its employment—that the officers should control the fire of their men, and themselves have the intelligence to know when to order it. There can hardly be a doubt, however, that more ammunition will be used in every engagement than we have been accustomed to use with the old style of arms. This makes it necessary to consider carefully the subject of supplying the line with cartridges from the ammunition-trains a little distance in the rear of the engagement. Our previous want of any system in this matter might, unless remedied, result in disaster with the new arm.

The Prussians scarcely used their arm for skirmishing, or random shooting, either in 1866 or in the present war, but reserved their fire for close quarters; and about Paris there was no exchanging of shots on the picket-line; nor was their attack, made by Prince Frederick Charles upon the very slightly intrenched position of the Austrians at Sadowa previous to the arrival of the crown prince upon the enemy's flank, of any avail. It is scarcely possible to hope for success in attacking an intrenched position in future, defended by firm men armed with the new breech-loaders.

THE GERMAN ARMY ENGAGED IN OPERATIONS AGAINST FRANCE.

I have endeavored to trace the historical growth of the military power of Prussia, and will now give a succinct sketch of her army as we find it to-day. We have seen how the father of the great Frederick laid the foundation of the present system by dividing his domain into regimental districts; how, in a later day, the different arms of the service were so apportioned to the provinces as to give each its distinct and complete army corps; how French domination suggested expedients; and how, the country having outgrown that system, the reorganization of 1859 came about, and introduced many changes and improvements.*

As the entire North German Confederation is engaged in the war with France, the Prussian army is only one element of the force under arms. Every young man in North Germany who is twenty years of age and physically qualified, is a soldier, without distinction of rank or wealth,

---

* In this discussion I have followed Colonel Chesney somewhat closely, and have also referred frequently to the "Seven Weeks' War," by Captain Hozier, of the Royal Horse Guards.

and without reference to the number or size of regiments in service or rated size of the army. He serves with the colors three years, and is then furloughed for five years, unless needed in time of war. These furloughed men are the reserves, and are called out during war whenever required. They serve in the landwehr for eleven years.

On a peace-footing the army numbers three hundred and nineteen thousand three hundred and fifty-eight men, and on a war-footing nine hundred and eighty-three thousand three hundred and twelve. In the latter case, it is composed of five hundred and eleven thousand eight hundred and seventy-six field troops; one hundred and eighty-six thousand six hundred and seventy-two dépôt troops; two hundred and sixty-five thousand and eighty-two garrison troops; and nineteen thousand six hundred and eighty-two men upon staff duty and in military schools. This force is augmented by the armies of the South German states not yet absorbed in the confederation, as follows: Bavarian army, eighty thousand; Würtemberg, thirty-four thousand four hundred and five; Baden army, twenty thousand seven hundred and twenty-two. This is the German army that assailed France; making a grand aggregate of one million one hundred and eighteen thousand four hundred and thirty-nine.

The field army is composed of twelve army corps of the line, numbered from one to twelve, and one of the guard, the twelfth corps being the Army of Saxony entire. Each corps, with slight variations, has two divisions of infantry, one of cavalry, sixteen batteries of artillery, and a military train. Each division has two brigades, and each brigade two regiments. Each regiment has a colonel, lieutenant-colonel, and adjutant, and is composed of three battalions, each of which has a major, an adjutant, a surgeon, an assistant-surgeon, a paymaster, a quarter-master, two non-commissioned staff officers, and four companies. Each company is composed of one captain, one first and one second lieutenant, and two hundred and fifty enlisted men. A cavalry regiment is composed of twenty-three officers, six hundred and fifty-nine enlisted men, seven hundred and thirteen horses, and seven carriages, and is divided into four squadrons. Each division of cavalry has two brigades, of two regiments respectively, and to it are attached four batteries of artillery. It is usual, also, to attach a regiment of cavalry to each infantry division.

The artillery of each corps forms a regiment. As it is the duty of this branch of service to provide arms and ammunition for the army, thus taking the place of our Ordnance Department, it has at home its artillery dépôt for this purpose. On mobilization, each regiment forms nine ammunition trains—each train being complete, and composed of two officers, one hundred and twenty men, one hundred and seventy horses, and twenty-five wagons. It has a reserve ammunition park of two divisions. Each has one hundred and ninety-five men, and two hundred and sixty-four carriages. These divisions are again divided into eight trains of thirty-three carriages. These are brought to the field of operations by water or railway transportation.

In the field the ammunition wagons follow directly in rear of the field army, but are kept entirely separate from the field batteries. The duty of these wagons is to bring up ammunition from the reserve trains. Siege trains are made up for their special purpose, and brought on the field in the same manner as the divisions of the reserve ammunition park, and both rely on procuring animals in the country to haul them. The nine light ammunition trains march directly in rear of the corps, while the two reserve trains follow two days later. They are so organized as, if detached, to form two divisions, composed of one heavy and four light trains, leaving one light train for the cavalry. To each corps is attached a battalion of riflemen and one of engineers, which takes with it a train loaded with intrenching and construction tools, a heavy pontoon train, and a light bridge train.

The peace establishment consists of about three hundred and twenty thousand men, one hundred and six thousand horses, twenty thousand of which belong to the cavalry and artillery, and nine thousand carriages. It is formed of army corps assigned to provinces, and each composed of two divisions belonging to the two halves of a province. The divisions are divided into brigades, and these again subdivided into regiments, which are further divided into battalions formed each of four companies, as already explained, each drawn from its own locality. We see how this organization rests on the very foundation of society. The commissariat of this vast army is decentralized, subsistence for each corps being drawn from its own province; and thus, with ample railroad transportation, it becomes as simple a problem to feed a million men as a thousand. It should be borne in mind that the capacity of railways for carrying freight under a perfect organization, and by running trains in convoys, is almost unlimited.

MOBILIZATION OF THE ARMY.

With these facilities in peace, every thing is kept ready for the mobilization of the army for war. Every officer and every civil official knows what will be his part when mobilization is determined upon; and the moment this information is flashed over the wires, each springs to his work without further orders or explanation, but in so quiet and regular a way as to be scarcely noticeable. The Government may decree either that the whole or a certain number of the army corps shall be mobilized, and the fact is at once announced in the provinces or province where mobilization is to take place. The general commanding each corps at once mobilizes it. The commandants of the fortresses take immediately proper steps to complete their armaments, and the heads of administration supply their needs for a war footing. The necessary steps are exactly defined and thoroughly understood, and each officer is held responsible for the proper performance of his duty. It is essential to the smooth working of this mechanism that all its parts be perfect; hence great pains is taken in the selection of officers, no one ever receiving a commission until he is positively known to be fitted for his work and acquainted with its details. Then, with a centralized power and a decentralized administration, wonderful results are accomplished.

In 1866, the whole field army, the first call of the landwehr and a portion of the second call, were mobilized, and six hundred thousand men put under arms in about two weeks, and this in a cause so unpopular, that, outside of the field army, "The One Man's War," as it was called, was the theme of constant criticism and denunciation; and, had the expedition failed, the crown would have been in great jeopardy.

In the present war, within four days from the decree of mobilization, forty trains daily began running toward the Rhine frontier; and in a fortnight every part of the army, even to the grave-diggers, was in its place. A large number of horses are required on mobilization. Of these Germany has no lack. The Department of Supply may at first buy them of contractors; but in case this means fails to secure the proper number, mixed boards, composed of officers and civilians, are empowered to take them at a just valuation.

The army is mobilized in the following manner: All orders are sent by telegraph to the main stations, and the civil magistrates are required to serve notices upon the necessary reserves at their homes in the respective magistracies. The reserves at once assemble at the head-quarters of the landwehr of the district, where they undergo a medical examination, and are then forwarded to their proper regiments. The process may be classified as follows: 1st. The filling up of the field army to its war strength; 2d. The formation of dépôt troops; 3d. The formation of garrison troops, and arming the fortresses; 4th. The mobilization of the field administration; 5th. The formation of an extensive staff, which performs home duties, while the regular field staff goes with the field army.

To complete the field army, a portion of the reserve soldiers is called in. There is usually an abundance of them, and the battalions and squadrons are easily filled up. Each regiment of artillery forms its nine ammunition columns, and two heavy reserve trains, as before explained. Each regiment of engineers forms its trains of pontoons, tools, and bridges. Arms and ammunition are drawn from the artillery dépôts; and every captain of a company secures horses, as he is required to be mounted in war. Regimental trains are also made up. They are, more properly speaking, battalion trains, each battalion having one of its own—consisting of officers' servants, the drivers, one six-horse ammunition wagon, one four-horse wagon, carrying the money-chest, paymasters' books, and material for repairing arms and clothing, a hospital cart, drawn by two horses, a four-horse officers' baggage-wagon, and four led horses, packed with the books of the four companies. The men of these trains are mustered as train-soldiers. The train of a regiment of cavalry is not very different from that of a battalion of infantry.

DÉPÔT TROOPS.

In this way the army is made ready to take the field, and we find in its ranks only men who pull a trigger, or lanyard, or draw a sabre. These amount to more than one-half of those who receive pay and wear uniform. The other half do a different, but equally necessary duty. These latter work for the one purpose of keeping the ranks of the fighting-men always filled. Not a day passes, after mobilization is complete, that men do not drop out of those ranks. Fatigue, illness, exposure, and a thousand causes at once commence the work of depletion. The first skirmish sends many men to the hospital, and in the first battle many are lost forever, and many more so badly injured that the army can not wait for their recovery. Adequate means are taken to fill their places as soon as possible, and restore the force expended in overcoming the first obstacles in the campaign.

Accurate statistics have shown that, at the close of the first year, forty per cent. of the infantry, twenty of the cavalry, artillery, and engineers, and twelve of the train troops will have been lost. To provide for this waste, dépôt troops are collected as soon as it is determined to mobilize the army. Each infantry regiment has a dépôt battalion, each rifle battalion a dépôt company, each regiment of artillery three light and one heavy dépôt batteries, every cavalry regiment a squadron, every engineer battalion a company, and every train-battalion two companies, all of the full regulation strength. These all recruit at home, and replace those who fall at the front. One-half of the dépôt men must be old soldiers of the reserves, the other half recruits just coming into service, or men already with their colors, but not sufficiently instructed to take the field. The dépôt troops are usually officered by those who, from wounds or other causes, are not able to go to the field. Four weeks after the field army has marched, one-eighth of the calculated yearly loss is forwarded; and on the first day of each succeeding month another proportionate installment leaves for the scene of active operations. If the command has been engaged in a sanguinary battle, a supply of men estimated to be necessary to fill the ranks is at once furnished. These men all go from the dépôt completely armed and equipped, those for the cavalry taking their horses, and their places are at once filled by calling in other reserves or landwehr.

GARRISON TROOPS.

We have seen how the field army is made up, and how dépôts are employed to keep it filled; but there are still domestic fortresses to be manned, long lines of communication to be kept open and guarded, convoys to be protected, dépôts of supplies watched, prisoners held, and positions in the enemy's country garrisoned after they are captured or occupied. To make detachments for these purposes would waste much of the effective force of the army, and unfit it for the accomplishment of its main object. To obviate this garrison troops are organized from the landwehr, to whom are assigned all these duties, and who may, in case of need, be brought forward to support the field army. They are all veteran soldiers, thoroughly drilled, and in the prime of life. They represent the average public sentiment of the country, and, if the cause is popular, or the front line flushed with victory, are a formidable organization.

FIELD ADMINISTRATION.

We have now seen the army in complete readiness to fight, assured that its ranks will be kept full, and its rear protected, but we have used an immense number of men for this, and they must be fed every day, or they are at once helpless; and, more than this, this food must be furnished them as they move forward. Then there must be provided medicines, and attendance for the sick, appliances for the wounded, and means of conveying the disabled from the places where they fall, to some safe spot where they may receive care and be healed. The feeding alone is a work of almost inconceivable magnitude. The field army that entered France contained more than half a million of men—more than half as many as the population of New York City; as many as the population of Chicago and St. Louis combined; as many as the entire population of Georgia or Maine. This community moves twenty miles farther away each day, and their food must follow them, and be ready for distribution when it arrives.

The transportation which follows a German army in the field, exclusive of the wagons of each battalion, and the artillery, engineer, and field-telegraph trains heretofore described, is divided under two heads. The first and principal portion is attached to the commissariat, and is solely for the purpose of supplying food to men and horses. The second portion belongs to the Medical Department, and carries medicines, hospital stores, and means for the transportation of the sick and wounded. The first portion consists, in time of peace, of a certain number of wagons, which, on the mobilization of the army, are provided with men and horses from the military train, each corps having a battalion of train troops, who are not combatants. These are under the entire control of a principal commissariat officer, with the rank of captain, who is attached to the head-quarters of each corps. Each army has a principal commissariat officer, who is a member of the staff.

The commissariat columns of each army corps are five in number, each of which has two officers, twenty-eight men, one hundred and sixty-one horses, and thirty-two wagons. These one hundred and sixty wagons carry three days' provisions for every man in the corps. As soon as the wagons which carry the first day's supply are emptied they are sent to the magazines in the rear, and must be again with the troops, to give them their fourth day's food. By this arrangement no army can move more than one and a half day's journey from its dépôts. Each army corps takes with it a field bakery, as flour can be more easily carried than bread. This bakery consists of ten officers, one hundred and eighteen men, twenty-seven horses, and five wagons. A small dépôt of men and horses accompany it. This force is distributed among the troops as is most convenient. These provision trains do nothing in the way of gathering food, but merely bring it from the dépôts to the troops. These magazines must move as the army moves, and means must be provided for gathering food into the dépôts. So long as railways are unbroken, and trains follow the troops, no difficulty is experienced; but as this is not always the case, it becomes necessary to gather supplies. For this, as well as to carry hay and corn from the dépôts to the horses of the cavalry and artillery at the front, an immense number of carts and wagons are hired in the country. The people are compelled to do this service, but a fair compensation is paid them in cash. This, as well as service on the roads, was first paid for in scrip, to be settled at the close of the war; but at the instance of the crown prince, these people, who are mostly needy, and have families to support, are now regularly paid in money. There seems to have been no difficulty in procuring an unlimited quantity of this rough but efficient transportation.

Although the requisition system has proved immensely useful, especially in France, where the army sometimes moved sixty or seventy miles from its communications, it is considered only an auxiliary means of supply. Requisitions alone could not long subsist an army, as it would soon eat up every thing in the country, leaving among the people starvation and disease, which would be quickly communicated to the troops. The medical train which accompanies an army corps consists of three heavy hospital trains, each of fourteen wagons, one hundred and fourteen men, sixty-nine horses, and eleven surgeons, and three light divisional trains for hospitals, elsewhere described. Each train carries every thing necessary for treating men in the field, and for establishing field hospitals. Every corps has also a company of sick-bearers, who on the day of battle are divided among the troops. Each battalion has also ten sick-bearers, and no men are allowed to leave the ranks under fire. The sick-bearers convey the wounded but a short distance to the rear, under some cover from shots, where they are received by the hospital men.

OBSERVATIONS.

The foregoing is a sketch of the general system upon which the German army is organized for war. What such an army will accomplish in the field depends very much upon the general who commands it. What it can accomplish when guided by a skillful hand was seen in 1866, and in the recent war with France. Every European state has a bureau for the purpose of gathering, during peace, statistics of all foreign armies. When war is declared, information as to the movements of the enemy is obtained by means of spies. Although many persons undertook this service in the French and Austrian wars, this system had not a tenth of the importance ascribed to it by those who saw a spy in every stranger, and treachery in every officer who was unsuccessful. Considerable information is gathered from deserters, but the great reliance is upon scouts and reconnaissances in the presence of the enemy. This service has been done remarkably well, the Uhlans often reaching a point fifty or sixty miles in advance of the column. The telegraph has been of wonderful aid in transmitting intelligence. This was partially employed in 1866; and during the present war its use has been systematized and extended.

One can scarcely comprehend the grandeur and completeness of the German army. There has been no parallel to it; and no nation, unless favored by distance, can hope to cope successfully with it in war. On the fifteenth of July war was declared by France. On the seventeenth of the same month, Moltke said, "Give me until the third of August, and we are safe." Just three days later, on the sixth of August, the French army was driven back, and the Germans began their march into the very heart of France; and so complete was the mechanism of the entire army, that during this period of preparation Moltke never missed his daily drive in the "Thier Garten;" and, although every body was active, there was no confusion. The Prussians have taken lessons from every modern war, and have constantly sought improvement, never foolishly thinking that they had nothing more to learn. Their tactics have changed with the requirements of service, until now very little remains of the system employed by Frederick the Great. Attacks are made by skirmish lines supported by small columns, covered as much as possible by accidents of the ground. These thin, long lines usually overlap the flanks of the enemy, and make those flank and rear attacks which have proved so effective in this and the Austrian war. The columns are brought forward and deployed whenever the skirmish lines need re-enforcements, or concentrate to resist a counter attack. This is an application of the same principle upon which the siege of Paris is conducted. In this organization every thing is foreseen and provided for. We see an army formed to fight, and adjuncts adapted to keep that fighting army in full strength. No details are ever made from it for any purpose whatever, but its efficiency is wisely considered the first and paramount object, and to this end every thing is subordinated. The best men are put in it, not taken away from it; all of its wants are anticipated, and all gaps in its ranks are filled as soon as they occur.

How different was the case in our war, where, no sooner was a regiment formed, than it began to waste away from every imaginable cause. We had no system of recruiting, but preferred to have new regiments formed, in hope that the desire of gaining commissions would promote volunteering. As soon as our regiments arrived at their posts, details began to be made for all the uses of administration—details in the trains, in the hospitals, at head-quarters, for engineers, for telegraph corps, for the post-office, for ordnance duty, for permanent hospitals, for store-houses, for bake-houses, as clerks, as mechanics, as sick-bearers. Then came that greatest of all enemies of "fighting-strength reports," a quarter-master's department, well described as intended to do all manner of things not prescribed for the other branches of the service. It performed its part effectually. Its greed for men knew no limits. We even detailed men from the infantry regiments to serve with batteries. The worst of all this was, that so-called staff officers, at the head of these departments, would by some means learn the names of the best men in the regiments, who, by their character, gave tone to all about them, and these men would be detailed by name, until a regiment would be left at the end of six months with a full complement of officers, a thousand men on its rolls, and about three hundred in its ranks, and these the miserable remainder after subtracting its best components. This result was sometimes ingeniously effected. Just before the battle of Stone River, General Rosecrans issued an order for each regimental commander in the Army of the Cumberland to form for his regiment a pioneer corps of twenty men, two from each company, of the best mechanics in it, to be put under the command of a civil engineer, if the regiment were fortunate enough to have one among its officers. Every colonel was pleased with this, and in good faith detailed twenty of the very best men in his regiment—men upon whom he was dependent, as every colonel is, for a thousand good services in crossing his command over bad roads and streams, and in other emergencies. This being done, the commanding general ordered them to his own head-quarters, formed them into companies and regiments, and finally brigaded them under a captain of engineers, where they remained, never again to see their regiments. By doing this, he not only deprived every regiment in his command of a great part of its leaven, but made every colonel feel, either rightly or wrongly, that a trick had been played upon him.

When these endless details were in a measure filled, and our army moved forward, every town, every railway station, every train, every bridge, must have its guard, and every city its garrison, and all were subtracted from our fighting force. The wonder is, how we ever accomplished any thing; and it can only be explained by the fact that the enemy practiced the same suicidal policy. How long would our war have lasted had there been two field armies, one in the East, and another in the West, each of a hundred thousand men, with their ranks kept full? After every battle, we were six months in gathering up our shattered forces to advance again. At Sedan, the Germans moved out of camp for Paris the morning after the surrender. We were compelled to establish and sustain by everlasting details all the various departments which the Germans maintain in regularly organized corps; and it took nearly twice as many men with us, because we had no perfected system. The Germans manage to keep at least half of their force in front, with muskets in their hands.

At the close of our war, our rolls bore a million names, while the combined armies of Grant, Sherman, and Thomas, who commanded the fighting-men, amounted to less than a third, and not much more than a quarter of that number. In the ranks the Germans have many more highly educated men than we, while our ranks contained men of more self-reliance and versatility. From their system of universal service, their troops are all better drilled and instructed than our best regiments; while their landwehr, which is the German militia, are their finest troops. Their officers are technically vastly superior to our own, and the landwehr officers are as good as those of the regular army. This is due to the great care used in educating and selecting them; while we commissioned whoever could control a certain number of troops, without imposing a single condition as to fitness. An exception should be made in favor of the officers of our regular army, and some volunteer officers whose great personal character made up for their want of technical knowledge. But I have commanded regiments of volunteers with not a commissioned officer in them equal to some of the non-commissioned officers in every German regiment; while I have seen many sergeants there who in our service would have been given colonels' commissions. Their system makes every man a soldier, while our officers of high grades were often third-rate men who happened to have smelled powder in Mexico, had been in some plundering expedition on the Isthmus, or commanded at a militia muster. Nothing was more common than to give commissions as majors, lieutenant-colonels, and even colonels, on the recommendation of persons who would not have trusted the appointees with any considerable civil responsibility, but acted upon an impression that a man would make a good soldier who was fit for nothing else.

The patronage of royalty and the nobility has made war so important and respectable as to enlist the best talent of Germany; while a system of schools and practical exercises, with prizes as the reward of conspicuous merit, keep officers improving during their whole lives. With us, when the officer is commissioned he drops his books, if he prefers to, and often retrogrades from that moment; while there are few, if any, tangible advantages held out in our service as inducements to industry. We also attach a false value to places in our administrative departments, because they offer a life of comparative ease and luxury. Our specially promising young officers are rewarded by appointments in these branches, where they become clerks or civil officials, rather than soldiers. Many of our best soldiers are thus unfitted for active command. These positions in the German army are not given to, nor sought by, active officers; but enlisted men, who show excellent business capacity, are trained for the purpose, passing many examinations in various grades, and finally receiving commissions as pay-masters, commissariats, and quarter-masters.

The Germans have nothing corresponding to our Quarter-master's Department, which has such unlimited liberty to buy and issue all manner of merchandise, and do all manner of things. Supplies of a purely military kind are specified and given to particular departments, and there the matter stops. They have a quarter-master general—Lieutenant-general Padleidski—who is a kind of vice-minister of war, whose business it is to say how and by what routes troops shall move, but who has nothing to do with supplies.

Subordinate officers of a like character are attached to all the lower organizations. Their duties are military. The engineers of the army are also a purely military body of men, having the arms and organization of battalions of infantry. Their duties are those of military engineers, and do not embrace map-making or light-houses. Their system is so completely decentralized, and every officer in it is held to such strict and close accountability, and duties are made so clear in every detail, that failure is never heard of. In reply to my inquiry of a captain and commissariat in charge of the supply department of a division, as to what would become of him if his food trains should fail to reach his division, he looked up as if such a thing were impossible, and coolly replied that he would be hung. This system worked without failure in France, while the French centralized intendance, responsible only to the Minister of War, failed continually. The Germans have no Ordnance Department, all the duties relating to this branch of service being performed by the artillery. The artillery and engineers bear a close relation to each other. Their field duties run together, and their school in Berlin is one and the same.

The army comprises another and most important department—that of the staff of the *etat major*, or the Grand Staff. At the head of this is General Von Moltke; and here is gathered the intellect of the army, which guides and controls it. The staff officers are purely soldiers.

Though much of their duty is done in an office, still it is all of a military character. They gather military information at home and abroad, make military maps, have charge of military archives, become chiefs of staff to the divisions, corps, and armies, and are generally fitted for high commands themselves. The adjutants of the various organizations are little more than clerks. The staff is managed with economy, and in that particular is vastly superior to our own.

The Prussian army has a minimum of high-pay soldiers, while ours has a maximum. Their regiments of infantry, always full, have three thousand men in the ranks, with four field officers, twelve captains, twenty-five lieutenants, and three administration officers—in all, forty-four commissioned officers. Their companies are as large as our regiments after a year's service and the subtractions already described. Their battalions are as large as our brigades, and their regiments as large as our divisions. My division, composed of three brigades, carried, in front of Atlanta, but twenty-two hundred muskets, and after that, until the close of the war, never numbered more than three thousand, or the equivalent of a German regiment. It contained twelve regiments. Its complement of officers was, one major-general, three brigadier-generals, thirty-six field officers, one hundred and twenty captains, two hundred and sixty-four lieutenants, and fifty-six administrative officers—in all, four hundred and eighty. The regiments were not always fully officered, and the commanding officers of brigades and divisions did not always have the full rank of their commands; but it is safe to say that two-thirds of this organization was in full commission, giving us three hundred and twenty officers against forty-three for the same number of muskets in the German service. This state of things was generally known to exist;

but still our Government saw fit to organize new regiments, rather than to avail itself of the services and experience of officers already in commission and under pay.

The German department of justice seems to be very complete and convenient. Every commissioned officer may punish to an extent precisely specified by law and graduated by the officer's rank. Each division has a judge, whose jurisdiction extends to certain classes of cases; while others come before a court-martial, where, when private soldiers are on trial, enlisted men form a portion of the court. No officer can be dismissed unless by sentence of court-martial and the approval of the king. Promotions and appointments are all regulated by law. A certain number of appointments from the cadet schools are made arbitrarily by the crown; but in every other case the candidates must come up regularly recommended by their commanders through a great number of checks and tests. Political influence is unknown, and the king never interferes.

Except in the cases of the royal princes, it may be said that not a case of appointment by favor exists in the army. Absolute discipline prevails, and any man who deserts or quits his post is certain of death. Any young officer who, by close application and industry, makes himself in any degree more worthy than his fellows, is sure of recognition, and there are ways left open for his advancement. The administration has succeeded in a remarkable degree in discovering the fitness of officers for special services, and seeks always to employ talent in its peculiar field.

The arms are not remarkable, except the field-pieces, which I believe to be far superior to our own; but the Germans, like ourselves, attach an exaggerated value to this arm. Their heavy guns about Paris were mostly old, and common enough. Their small-arms are inferior to many patterns in our own country. Their accoutrements are no better, and perhaps not so good as our own. They have discarded the shoulder-belt, and sling two small pouches upon the waist-belt, one on either side, for cartridges, which is a great relief to the soldier. Our shoulder-belt is all on one side, and suspended from a point two feet above the centre of gravity. Their knapsack is better than ours, because it has a frame that keeps its form. Ours, with the present pack, can not be worn, and the men invariably throw them away. The belts of the regular army are still chalked, but the landwehr wear black belts like our own. Much of the arming and equipments of the cavalry is still old-fashioned; such as the old horse-pistol, lance, fancy dress, cuirass, and metal helmet, and the heavy packs. These will probably soon give place to a plain, sensible dress for the men, lighter weights for the horse, and the revolver or repeating carbine for all mounted troops.

Their clothing is excellent, and vastly superior to our own, excepting their boots, with a short leg and small heel, which I consider greatly inferior to our shoes. Their coats and trowsers are of excellent all-wool stuff, and very durable, saving immense cost in transportation.

Their wagons are much less expensive, and not nearly as good as our own. They have vehicles of different capacities, from a one-horse cart to a six-horse wagon, while we have only the heavy wagon for six animals; but in model and general excellence, I doubt if any army wagon equals our own, as made before the war, of seasoned timber; and as for teams, I have never seen any comparable with our six-mule teams in their best condition. In going to war without tents or blankets, they show a military instinct superior to our own. These articles are comforts adding indefinitely to the labor of moving an army, and nothing whatever to its health and efficiency, notwithstanding the popular belief to the contrary. The sanitary reports of their armies in the present and in the Danish war, and that of the rebel commands in our own war, and my own experience, prove this.

Their bravery and endurance under fire is unquestioned, and the mortality in battle has been very great. Captain Trescott, the adjutant of the commandant of Versailles, told me that at Toul his regiment buried on the field twenty-two officers, and his orderly showed me his fifth gun since the opening of the campaign, the other four having been disabled by shot. The soldiers marching in the streets showed in every few files a pierced helmet. Of the nine commandants of the guards regiments who left Berlin, all have been killed. The last, Colonel Vanvalzah, the author of the plan adopted for this campaign, fell at Les Bourget in the early part of November.

If called upon to give a summary of the special characteristics which make the Prussian army pre-eminent, I should enumerate the absence of exemptions and substitutes, which secures for the army the best men, and makes service even and acceptable; a thorough knowledge of duty; general education of soldiers and officers; high character of non-commissioned officers; an effective system of keeping the ranks full; superior training, and careful selection for merit alone of the higher staff; a decentralized administration; impartial justice; the certainty of recognition and reward for enterprise and industry, and intolerance of sloth and indolence; a strict but not harsh discipline throughout all grades, and a rigid economy in all things. The peculiar character of the French mind, which knows no settlement of a dispute but victory, or revenge for defeat, will make it necessary for Germany to maintain, and even increase, her present army for many years to come; and this need not be taken as presaging aggression upon her part.

CHAPTER VII.

THE FRENCH ARMY.

SINCE the misfortunes of the French army in the present war with Germany, our principal interest in it is to discover wherein lay its defects, and how it was that we have for so long made the mistake of supposing it worthy to serve as a model for our own. With this in view, its details will be noticed only far enough to ascertain its faults.

At the beginning of the war, foreign officers, by imperial direction, were refused authority to accompany the French army, and but little information as to its real condition is available beyond the published criticisms of its own officers, made after Sadowa, with direct reference to the inability of France to cope with Prussia in a war then plainly in prospect. The astonishing results of the war of 1866 awakened doubts where before there was perfect confidence, and resulted in a series of discussions which engrossed the attention of all the best officers of France. The Prussian system was regarded by officials in France as a school of militia, imperfect for defense, and of little value for offensive warfare. But after Sadowa it became at once evident that France had been resting upon her past glories, while Prussia had employed the intervening years in industrious progressive study and labor upon every thing that pertained to the science of war, and had adjusted her military burdens, so that, while availing herself of the full military power of the nation, she did not impose depressing exactions upon her people. Among the essays brought out by this startling revelation are those by the Duc d'Aumale, General Trochu, and General Changarnier. Whatever appears in this notice of the French army, beyond a mere sketch of its history and organization (in which I am aided by the writings of the Intendant-general of the French army, and of Colonel Chesney of the Royal Engineers), will be in the words of these essays, not mine—words of which results have proved the truth. So severe were their criticisms, as to bring down upon the heads of the writers the ill-concealed displeasure of the Imperial Government, which continued until the fall of the empire, and had much to do with raising one of the number to the supreme control of the succeeding defense of Paris.

EARLY HISTORY.

The history of the organization of the regular armies of all civilized countries, including that of France, dates from about two hundred years ago. Prior to the reign of Louis XIV., war was carried on by loosely organized bodies of men, generally independent corps, recruited, commanded and almost owned by noblemen of various grades. The soldiers were often foreigners, kidnapped and forcibly impressed, or induced to join the ranks by trickery and false representations. Once enlisted, they remained soldiers, without hope of again seeing their homes, until, from wounds or old age, they were no longer useful, when they became beggars in the streets. Notwithstanding their many celebrated achievements, these unorganized forces bore little resemblance to an army of to-day; could not be easily controlled by their sovereign, and were actually a menace to him.

Louvais, the War Minister of Louis XIV., was the first great master of military organization in France, and contributed more to the success of French arms than Turenne and Luxembourg, who led the troops to victory. He instituted uniformity of arms and dress, regular promotion, a graduated pay, stricter and more just conditions of service, and more certain methods of subsistence. With his world-renowned inspector-general, Colonel Martinet, whose name still survives to indicate military precision, he wrought out of the discordant military elements of France her first modern army, which gave her some of her best successes, and which survived until the great storm of the revolution of 1789. Many of the fatal defects of its ingredients were unavoidably incorporated into this force. It was a royal and aristocratic body, officered almost entirely by the nobility. It was never an institution of the people, and was always known as "the King's Army," a sort of chattel, and had no real influence upon, or sympathy with, the masses. How different now, when every family has its representative in the ranks, and the army occupies an equal place with the first civil institutions of France!

The expatriation of the nobility at the revolution destroyed that old army, and rightly, for its loyalty was personal, not national. Such an army is a snare and a delusion. To be efficient and trustworthy, an army must represent the popular sentiment, and without this it is unsafe to give it the national support.

In some instances in our own war, personal devotion assumed such proportions as to predominate over all else, and made it necessary to relieve from their commands some of our best soldiers, to the great detriment of military operations. In other cases this devotion was so associated with the leading political sentiments of the country as to make it necessary to deal with it cautiously, although it neutralized large bodies of troops. This sentiment of personal fidelity, while it may serve the nation in battle, is always dangerous, because it makes an end of a means.

ORIGIN OF ITS TACTICS.

In 1791 the French army consisted of one hundred and sixty-six regiments of foot and horse, and the regulations promulgated at that time still form the basis of the drills and manœuvres of the troops, although overlaid with an enormous mass of subsequent matter. It will be interesting to trace the origin of these manœuvres, as they have been copied *in extenso* by ourselves, and form the basis of all our subsequent tactics. They were adopted throughout Europe at about the same time, and are the work of Frederick the Great and his father, reduced to practice at Potsdam by Leopold von Dessau.

The French at Rossbach were greatly impressed by the steady and rapid manœuvres of the Prussian troops, and were not slow to adopt the new tactics. To the present day we, as well as the French, employ the same manœuvres, and designate them by the same phrases. The position, as given in our tactics, of the soldier without arms; the movement of the eyes to the right and left; the quick and common step; and, in fact, nearly every thing known as "the school of the soldier," is almost directly translated from the rules of Potsdam. Rossbach was to France the beginning of military greatness, as Jena afterward was to Prussia—proving the old maxim, that "the teachings of defeat, which subvert old ideas and establish facts, better serve the military institutions of the future than victories." The first teach modesty and self-reliance, and are the nurse of progress. The second create pride and unlimited self-confidence, which fail in the crises of battle. How strikingly has this been true of France, which has rested content with the tactics of Frederick, while the Prussians themselves have never been satisfied, but, since Jena, have steadily advanced. How true the proverb, that "Tradition serves as an excuse for carelessness, and has lost more battles than it has saved." The French army has existed for fifty years upon the traditions of the first empire.

The adoption of skirmishing tactics, which have come to play so important a *role* in all battles, is due more to General Morand, one of General Bonaparte's best division commanders, than to any one else. This, with many other modifications and some new principles of formation, were introduced early in this century.

THE EARLY ARMIES OF THE REVOLUTION.

The French army of 1791, although well trained, was numerically weak, and the political agitations of the times had shaken its unity and self-reliance. Its first operations were disastrous, but the enthusiasm of the great volunteer movement of 1792 and 1793 restored France, and defeated Prussia and Austria. A year later, when it was opposed to regular troops, the army of France was driven back, and it became difficult for her to raise men to protect herself, the eight armies of France not numbering more than one hundred and fifty thousand men. Upon this subject the Duc D'Aumale wisely says: "It is of the essence of special volunteer corps not to renew their strength, although the very existence of these corps seriously interferes with and may arrest regular enlistments."

We found this true in our war, when regiments, once formed, scarcely ever received any renewal, and were suffered to die out, while new ones were constantly raised. So the patriots of France who enlisted for one year, as our own did for ninety days, took their discharge at the end of their engagement, although they might be in front of the enemy and on the eve of battle.

The Convention called out three hundred thousand National Guards, but the measure failed. On the 15th of

July, 1793, the statements show that the French army was composed of four hundred and ninety-seven thousand men, but it is generally believed that it did not amount to a third of that number. When Carnot joined the Committee of Public Safety, the *levée en masse* was decreed by the Convention, and then the national army of France sprang to life.

"This measure differed essentially from the requisition which had preceded it. More harsh in appearance, it was less vexatious and oppressive in reality. It confined itself to men of from eighteen to twenty-six, but within those limits it took all. In six months all the pressure of the reign of terror had failed to raise three hundred thousand men under the former law. In three months the general levy was effected, without serious opposition, under the latter law. Let it not be said that it was the guillotine that saved France. On the 1st of January, 1794, the strength of the army had risen to seven hundred and seventy-one thousand men."—Duc D'Aumale.

This was easy, because it was just. There was no discrimination, and no one tried to escape on the plea that others were not called. This vast army was consolidated by the genius of Carnot into one uniform mass. All distinctions of corps, and even grades of non-commissioned officers, were abolished. All provincial designations and appellations were obliterated, and the regiments numbered instead. The uniform of the whole army was made alike, and the blue tunic of the Republic adopted. From this homogeneous mass the wonderful hand of Carnot wrought the great and immortal armies of France, that won twenty-seven victories in one year, captured three thousand eight hundred guns, and dissolved the coalition. The demi-brigades, or regiments, were given an organization of three battalions of nine companies each, which has never been materially changed.

"But what was beyond all praise was the noble and manly bearing of this victorious army. Carnot, by his example, and by the spirit which dictated his measures, had infused civic and military virtues into its ranks. To borrow the elevated phraseology of the time, which was not always false, 'he had placed courage, self-sacrifice, and disinterestedness on the order of the day.' The discipline of the army had ceased to be vexatious and galling, but was firm and even severe in the unfrequent cases in which repression was necessary. Even the German inhabitants were struck with surprise and admiration at the demeanor of these republicans. They saw these dreaded soldiers enter their towns in ragged clothes, often in wooden shoes, but with a martial air, halt in the market-place amidst a terror-stricken people, eat their black bread beside their stacked arms, and await in the ranks the orders of their officers.

"Contributions of war were levied, but they were levied by the commissariat, who followed the army, and did not share its self-denial. Sometimes the neglect of the commissariat caused the men to maraud, but not to pillage. In the sharp winter of 1794–'5, which the army passed before Mayence, the troops, reduced to the utmost necessity, stole bread, and bread alone. At the time of sowing seed, they watched the peasants by day, and at night dug up the seed-corn with their bayonets. It is recorded by those who were in both campaigns, that the hardships endured by them in 1812 were not more severe. Many died of cold and hunger, but those who survived remained faithful to their colors. If they dispersed in search of food—and what food!—wild fruits and poisonous bulbs—they were in the ranks again at the first cannon-shot. The officers shared the penury and destitution of the men. All led the same frugal life, all were bound by the same lot."—Duc D'Aumale.

Such were the early troops of the Republic; but the Army of Italy, under a different chief, was animated by a different spirit. Bonaparte promised his soldiers glory and riches. He kept his word, but at what a cost to France! The revolutionary spirit of the Army of Italy was but the instrument of the future master; and Carnot, the real creator of the armies of the Republic, was himself proscribed. It is remarkable that Napoleon, the greatest master of modern warfare, did nothing to improve the organic constitution of the army. He employed the military resources of the country with consummate ability and with insatiable rapacity, but consumed everything that he created. The permanent military strength of France could not keep pace with his extravagant demands upon it, and the termination of the empire was the annihilation of the force by which it had been raised to the highest pinnacle of power and glory.

ORIGIN OF THE CONSCRIPTION.

The law of conscription was first established in France in 1798. From that time to the present, the youth of France, just entering manhood, has been gathered by law, as tracts in the forest are set apart for annual felling. The first act of the first consul was to demand, not an installment, but the whole class of the year, amounting to two hundred thousand men, and the strictest precautions were taken against every evasion of the law. These demands and the measures for their enforcement increased in enormity and intensity during his entire reign. The whole strength of the forces thus brought together was four hundred and fifty thousand. It was this army that threatened England, marched to Austerlitz, and perished in Spain. These old corps wasted away, and were replaced by hastily organized detachments, who were formed into fourth and fifth battalions, to conceal the fact that the other three had perished. The armies of the later empire had, by these expedients, been raised to enormous numbers, but the result was that described by Marshal Macdonald: "The men are as brave as ever, but they don't hang together."

It is good men who make good troops, and no number of bad men can make a good army. We lost sight of this in our own war, when States thought only of filling their quotas, and the vicious clause allowing exemptions and substitutes was incorporated into the law of conscription. This impaired the value of an otherwise most meritorious step. It gave us a great crowd of worthless men to take the place of soldiers, from whom we were expected to exact military service. To do this was an impossibility, for substitutes and bounty-bought men never served a nation, but are positively in the way. The policy of bringing the whole virile population into the field can not be too strongly condemned, on the ground of its weakening the vital powers of a people.

General Changarnier says, in his pamphlet, page 24:

"Let us not attempt to raise the number of our soldiers to that of our possible adversaries, even if at the risk of exhaustion we should be able to accomplish it. If it is very difficult for three thousand men, to oppose successfully five thousand, it is much less difficult for sixty thousand to beat one hundred thousand. The more the proportion rises, the less is numerical inferiority to be feared. It may be compensated by the skill of the general, or by the superior character of the troops. Beyond a certain number, there is no good army, and no army whose supplies can be secured and whose movements can be directed. The army which invaded Russia in 1812 was reduced by one-half before it reached Moscow. When that gigantic and lamentable expedition had completed the ruin of our veteran legions, already exhausted by incessant wars, Napoleon succeeded in rallying large masses of recruits, and led them now and then to victory. Unhappily, those young troops, always gallant, always brave, but incapable of taking care of themselves, suffered more from the bivouac, from long marches, and from sickness, than they had done on the fields of battle which bore the names of Lutzen, Bautzen, Dresden, Leipsic, and Hanau."

How these words recall the experience of our own war, where, instead of encouraging the old regiments by filling their ranks, young and tender regiments were continually brought out, to lose half their numbers in learning how to take care of themselves!

REORGANIZATION OF THE ARMY AT THE RESTORATION.

For three years after the battle of Waterloo, France had no army; and the Allied forces were not all withdrawn from her territory when Marshal Gouvion Saint-Cyr, Minister of War, undertook, in 1818, under the Restoration, the difficult task of reorganizing the military institutions of the kingdom. The peace establishment was fixed at two hundred and forty thousand men, to be raised by an annual conscription of forty thousand. It does not seem essential to follow all of the modifications of the army from that time to the present, but the subject of conscription may well claim attention. The annual call was increased successively to sixty thousand and eighty thousand men, by Louis Philippe; and during the Second Empire it has never been less than one hundred thousand, rising to one hundred and forty thousand during the Crimean War.

Notwithstanding this enormous drain upon the country, the result has not been to increase the army as much as was expected; and at the first surprise and alarm, which succeeded the battle of Sadowa, the French nation was startled at the declaration that the Government must have the means of raising the army, in the event of war, to eight hundred thousand men. The proposition met with little favor in the Legislature, and spread dismay among the peasantry.

It may be well to examine some stubborn facts connected with this matter, and which have vital relations to national prosperity. The measure of a nation's military strength must be its population. No more men of a given age can be pressed into its ranks than the country produces in a given time, and it is frightful to discover how very nearly in France the number of conscripts, even in peace, reaches this limit. The population in France increases more slowly than in any other country—indeed, it hardly increases at all; and one of the obvious causes of this is, that one hundred thousand stout and able-bodied young men of twenty years are marched off every year to the barrack, or the camp, that for six or seven years at least they are unable to contract marriage, and that those who stay at home, cultivate the fields, marry and rear children, are precisely those who are rejected from the conscription by reason of their diminutive size, feeble constitutions, or other physical infirmities. The effect of this upon a nation is readily appreciated. The normal annual increase in France has been accurately determined to be but one hundred and fifty thousand, or about $2\frac{5}{10}$ per centum; and it has also not only been incontestably shown that the conscription directly affects this increase, but the extent of it has been ascertained. When the conscription was forty thousand, the increase was rapid; when it was sixty thousand, it was slower; when eighty thousand, slower still; at one hundred thousand, it was arrested altogether; and with one hundred and forty thousand during the Crimean War, the population positively decreased. Is it possible to demonstrate more clearly the fatal effects of vast military establishments upon the vital powers of France, or that the conscription is a depressing, saddening weight upon the entire industrial population of the nation?

The loss of the vigorous, active men as fathers of the succeeding generations, while those who take their places are feeble and those least adequate to perpetuate a strong people, with the great loss in money from the neutralization of their industries—a sum not less than fifty millions of dollars annually—are the immediate practical results of large standing armies upon wealth and population, while their indirect consequences are incalculable. It is a system based upon fear, and allied to barbarism. That state is not the strongest which keeps in time of peace the largest number of men under arms, but rather that which avails itself of the industry of the greatest number, and at the approach of war is able to employ most of its active energies for military purposes.

France is weakened by the immense loss of the industries of the active years of all her young men, and, when war approaches, is not then prepared to meet it, but must still call for extraordinary additions to her army, which she can little afford.

FRENCH ARMY IN 1867.

The efficient strength of the French army in 1867, including the staff, *gendarmerie*, and military train, was three hundred and eighty-nine thousand one hundred and four men—of whom twenty-three thousand were officers, seventy-one thousand non-commissioned officers, twenty-six thousand musicians and unclassed troops, and two hundred and sixty-nine thousand private soldiers. Deducting eighty thousand as the least possible figure for home garrisons, dépôts, and troops serving in Africa, we have not far from one hundred and eighty-nine thousand men in line. Another considerable deduction should be made for newly-called conscripts, and men entitled to their discharge, and we have left a very small army. This, in theory, could be raised to about six hundred thousand men by calling in all of the reserves—that is, men who had served a number of years in the army, but were still liable to be called out for war; but as these men, as well as all the conscripts, were allowed to commute, or buy off their service by paying a certain amount of money, a large allowance must still be made.

In peace times, about one-fifth bought themselves free from service for about eleven hundred francs each, and in time of war about one-third. The best military men agree that the system is a vicious one. When a nation's vital want is men, it receives a bank-note instead. It was, however, a pet scheme of the French emperor, who expected with commutation money to buy the re-enlistment of old soldiers; but it was found that these old soldiers were apt to be dodgers, and often drunkards, and the system was abandoned in 1868. The provision for reserves was at that time practically inoperative.

General Trochu has clearly pointed out that, with all these sources of subtraction, in the Crimean and the last Italian war, France could send to the field, and maintain by re-enforcements, only one army, not much exceeding one-fourth of her nominal effective strength.

This corresponds very closely with our own experience in our war, resulting from the same subtractions, and a loose and inefficient way of bringing men into the field. Careful examination shows the fact that, at the close of our war, we had at the front, as belligerents, only about two hundred and fifty thousand men, while the Secretary of War's Report shows an army under pay of a million. How different all this from the army of Prussia, where more than half of all the men under pay fought in the front line!

It is not strange that the emperor, and all the leading military men of France, should have arrived at the conclusion that her military establishment was not adequate to meet on an equal footing the armies of Prussia. In the absence of a free Parliament and an independent press, it is possible only by the publication of books and pamphlets to reach and enlighten public sense in France.

Among the multitude of pamphlets which appeared upon this subject was that of General Trochu, of which Colonel Chesney says:

"Among all these publications the one by General Trochu is the most remarkable. It is the result of the reflections and observations of a life. It embodies a good deal of the blunt wisdom and keen sense of Marshal Bugeaud, on whose staff General Trochu learned the art of war. We have seldom read a book so succinct and so wise. There is not a page in it which does not contain some principle one would wish to fix forever in his memory; and we do not remember that any modern writer has treated the art of war, as it now is, with so much practical sagacity and elevated feeling. In it they will find a brave and unsparing exposure of many defects in the French army, but which are certainly not peculiar to that army alone, and they may learn much from it that is applicable to all armies in all countries."

GENERAL TROCHU.

General Trochu was born in 1815, at Palais, in one of the sea-coast departments of France, and was educated at Saint Cyr. He joined the infantry, has been all his life in active service, and was for a long time on the staff in Algiers. He was on the staff in the Crimea, or rather was sent there by the emperor as his confidential observer and informer, until St. Arnaud's death, when he took command of a brigade. He also commanded a brigade, and afterward a division, in Italy, and was subsequently in the war-office at Paris. His career has been singularly faultless and distinguished; and never, except after his failure in the defense of Paris, and in his speeches before the Deputies in which he endeavored to account for his failure, has he ever shown lack of cool wisdom or of high and cultivated reason. In his pamphlet he says, most truly, that there is no remedy but publicity for imperfections and abuses.

The confidential appeals previously made by him to the War Department had failed to produce any effect. It was in view of the transition-state of the army at that time that he pointed out the weakness and infirmities of a service to which he was greatly attached, sparing no one, and calling down upon himself unpopularity and even hostility, as all men do who tell unwelcome truths. He says that the strength of all armies lies in their motive force and mechanical power. The motive force is a moral principle, and is formed of the great sentiments of national pride, love of country, and the spirit of self-sacrificing devotion to duty, to discipline, and to good order. The mechanical power is entirely material, and consists of the different parts of an army and its organization, by which parts are so related as to work easily and freely. Some armies excel in one, and some in the other; but one that combines both in a high degree would be almost invincible in war. The first relates to the people; and when the relation between the army and people is strongest, this moral element will be most powerful. The second relates to the army alone; but whatever tends to weaken the first, weakens the force of the army in the same degree. An army must be strongly in sympathy with the people, and, when severed entirely from them, is useless, and even dangerous. Every army and every people have their own peculiarities; and each army must, therefore, be organized on principles adapted to its particular case. Yet there are certain rules applicable to all armies, under all conditions.

General Trochu traces with a masterly hand the various characteristics of the French army, in details too extended for notice here. He urges short terms of service, sending the men back with their military acquirements to the people, before they become fixed in military habits not suited to civil life. He most truly says that the best soldiers are young men who know their business; and combats the policy of the emperor, which would set apart an army of men to the military calling for their whole lives, severing their relations with the people and their homes. He says that all the systems adopted in France for the past fifty years have been peace systems, influenced by political motives, bearing on the domestic interests of the country, and contain no adequate provision for a competent reserve in war.

The following remarks are of universal application, and are well worth attention:

"Discoveries made in sciences which are the handmaids of industry and the arts of peace have always been used with advantage by armies. One of the most important of all, the invention of gunpowder, determined the forms of modern warfare. Formerly these inventions appeared from time to time in the lapse of ages. They were slowly tried, and perfected by generations. In our time, Science is no longer content to be the auxiliary of war, she aspires to be its principal agent. Discovery succeeds discovery with a rapidity which bewilders the mind, throws governments into perplexities, and their budgets into confusion, and which will throw families into mourning; for all these inventions have invariably the same object, which is, to kill the maximum of human beings in a minimum of time. An opinion is gaining ground that these irresistible mechanical improvements will reduce armies in the field to mere masses, employing engines of destruction which are to slay the enemy. The composure which permits of observation and reflection, that glance which chooses the decisive moment, that bravery which executes a movement and overcomes an obstacle, would then be out of date. Just the reverse is true. All these faculties must be multiplied, all these qualities must be augmented, to work on fields of battle the same problems as of old, now rendered more difficult and more perilous. It is essential to purge the minds of our troops of these notions and paradoxes, which lower the part they have to play. Do not allow them to relax in the exercise of those virtues which are the soul of great efforts. Let them be persuaded that the greater and more painful are the sacrifices required of them by this improved art of slaughter—an unexpected result of superior civilization—the louder must be the call of honor and patriotism in the soldier's ear."

From the foregoing passage it may be inferred that the first requisite of a good army, in the opinion of General Trochu, is a high moral and intellectual standard. It is idle to inflame the minds of troops with a fanciful conceit of their own superiority, which delusion may be rudely dispelled by the resistance of a superior army; for the qualities on which an army has to rely are those which can be found in its own ranks. As has been wisely said:

"It matters little to find the enemy weaker than was expected, but it becomes a very dangerous matter to find him stronger." . . . "France is full of proud military traditions, reaching back to her earliest history; yet she has as many that are mournful as that are glorious. But we have a wonderful way of excusing and justifying our reverses, and console ourselves through their memories from age to age. For the contemporary French mass, the day of Waterloo is embodied in these words: 'The guard dies, but does not surrender,' as for our fathers the day of Fontenoy was, 'You first, gentlemen of England;' and for our grandfathers, all the disaster of Pavia had been in the beautiful words of the vanquished king: 'All is lost save honor.' It is the memory of French victories and honor which live in our thoughts, and make us a warlike people. We are, in fact, more a warlike than a military people, for we have not the calm temperament, the constant preoccupation, the exactitude and punctuality, and the steadiness of habits, which forms the people of the North into obedience to law and discipline, and finally makes them accept cheerfully the exigencies of arms.

"In Prussia and Russia the soldier obeys immediately and silently, no matter what his ideas are in regard to the order. A remark, or even a stifled murmur, would be an unheard-of enormity, and result in punishment. The French soldier will also execute the order, but the question of its propriety occupies his mind, and his bad humor shows itself in some way, and, when executing it, if a word escapes him, it is overlooked. The nature of our soldier is not disciplinary, and he must at all times be kept under surveillance. A military obedience is not one of his traits, but, on the contrary, he is negligent and very unmilitary, requiring constant efforts at correction."

Still General Trochu says that the French soldiers readily submit to sacrifices and the sufferings of the camp; that they have strong attachments, which give them great cohesion; that they have powerful traditions, and their leaders great energy; and that the greatest military force France can boast of lies in the relation of its army with the masses of the people. They have also great enthusiasm, and come quickly forward for hopeless duty. He gives the following example, which is the relation of an actual event in his own command at Sebastopol:

"Desiring to make an attack, he assembles his command, already reduced one-half in eleven months, the officers and colors in the centre, and addresses them as follows: 'I have something of interest to tell you. To-morrow we make the attack. The head of the column will be destroyed, but I have a firm belief that the rear will surmount the obstacle. To form the head of the column, your general demands two hundred men of superior courage and devotion. I have never deceived you, and I can not promise those brave men who survive decorations or grades of promotion, but I promise you they shall receive the highest recompense that can be given to such soldiers. The staff will to-day receive the list, and inscribe their names upon the rolls as "Volunteers in the attack of Sebastopol;" and when these heroes return to their homes bringing with them this title of honor, I rest assured that they will be respected by their friends and countrymen.' At the end of this address, the troops expressed the highest enthusiasm; and there is not a doubt that every man would have willingly sacrificed himself for the hope of such reward. After some hours of reflection, five hundred and sixty officers and men enrolled themselves for this deadly service.

"It is by such scenes impressed upon the country by the army, which receives again its impetus from the people, that French military character is distinguished. Yet general comparisons made with other European armies are seldom satisfactory, and I repeat that I am far from asserting our absolute superiority in arms, although I have had the most exalted ideas in this particular during all my life."

In respect to discipline, General Trochu says:

"The great dispersion of troops over the entire country, by which colonels seldom see their companies, and generals never know their officers and men, makes the situation critical in actual service. Each tries to excel the other, and chance does the rest. As soon as danger commences, the military habitude is abandoned, military learning is forgotten, and the ranks become broken; officers, and often generals, are seen passing in the midst of soldiers, even of their own commands, without receiving the customary salute, and often without being noticed. We have been greatly surprised, in our late wars, to notice the contrast between our own and the foreign troops with whom we were allied. The latter were generally better disciplined, well instructed, silent, and calm, and, when under arms, performed their duty with promptness and exactitude. They showed themselves respectful to French officers, and in a way altogether in accordance with military forms. How could we expect those tokens of respect toward strange officers from our soldiers, when we could not obtain them ourselves. Generals also of great experience complain of the peculiar temperament of our soldiers, and the insufficiency of their military instruction; and to that cause is assigned the loss of many good opportunities and positions in war."

This want of knowledge of each other necessarily results in want of that unity of action so essential in armies, as well as in all the other affairs of life. The moral tone of the army has been greatly impaired by the temptation to convert it into a political instrument. Many a worthless officer has had his debts paid from the privy purse, and got his promotion, because, whatever his vices might be, they only served to make him a more devoted and subservient tool to the Imperial Government. But promotion gained in that way costs a man the respect of his comrades and the confidence of his men. Those who have most closely studied the formation of the Prussian armies are strongly of the opinion that they contain all the moral qualities to a much higher degree than other armies of Europe, owing, in great part, to their general education, peculiar local organization, and thorough military training, whereby every one is made to know his exact place and keep it. Although the Prussian army comprises a large democratic element, it is commanded and officered on aristocratic principles, and has none of that spirit of equality which in France has so largely entered into the officering of the army, and which has, without doubt, greatly weakened authority.

Every good officer in our service knows the immense harm to discipline and efficiency arising from any species of familiarity between officers and men. The officer gains no respect by it, but contempt is always engendered. The low moral standard which France has applied in her selection of officers has had its effect also. Another wonderful advantage of the Prussian system is, that its organization permits mobilization for war without agitating the people, while in France the entire nation is shaken. This, in Prussia, is due to the fact that in peace whole organizations remain together, each and every part knowing its exact place in war; while in France the different parts, being widely separated, come together unknown to each other; and when war breaks out, the concentration and necessary preparation must be done in the presence of the enemy, with endless perplexity and confusion, which are fatal to coolness and cohesion. The truth of this is made clear by the following letter of the emperor:

"WILHELMSHOHE, October 29, 1870.

"MY DEAR SIR JOHN,—I have just received your letter, which has given me very great pleasure, especially because it is a touching proof of your sympathy for me, and also because your name reminds me of the happy and glorious time when our two armies fought together for the same cause. You, who are the English Moltke, have understood that all our disasters arose from the circumstance that the Prussians were *more ready* than we were—that is to say, they surprised us in the very act of formation.

"The offensive having become an impossibility for me, I resolved on the defensive; but hampered by political considerations, the retreat was delayed till it became impossible. Having fallen back on Chalons, I wished to march on Paris with the last army left me, but at that juncture also, political considerations forced us to make that very imprudent and unstrategic march which finished with the disaster of Sedan. There, in a few words, is the unhappy campaign of 1870. I rely on you to afford this explanation, for I rely on your esteem.

"In thanking you for your kind remembrance, I renew the assurance of my affectionate regard.   NAPOLEON.

"SIR JOHN BURGOYNE, Field-marshal."

ADMINISTRATION.

We now come to the *administration*, which means the whole subject of supply and hospitals; and were there space, the whole chapter by General Trochu could be advantageously introduced:

"The splendid retreat of Moreau, who, fighting every day, and sleeping every night on the battle-field, supported his army through an active and farseeing administration; the army of Suchet in Spain, living in abundance, and returning to France with treasures; the immortal winter campaign of Napoleon at Eylau and Friedland; the camp at Finkenstein, in the midst of glaciers and the northern solitudes of Europe; and the re-organization of the army in 1813—these marches and battles in all directions, and the prodigious efforts necessary to maintain them, all had their lessons, but these lessons are lost to us. Yet we find in the memoirs of Napoleon, as well as in those of Prince Charles, of Jomini, Suchet, and St. Cyr, documents which may serve in some slight way to elucidate these great problems."

THE INTENDANT-GENERAL OF FRANCE.

Trochu says:

"The rules and arrangements which can satisfactorily supply armies in time of peace are not difficult, and may be said to be nearly complete. Here every thing is regulated and foreseen, and delivery is perfectly simple, regular, and easy. In war, every thing — time, place, and demand — is urgent, difficult, and irregular. We are compelled to trust in native ideas, common-sense, activity, and, above all, great experience. In fact, the only way to deal with so many unforeseen contingencies is not by military routine, but by a ready and complete knowledge of business. At present, all the officers of the French Intendance are officers of the army, most of whom have served many years; who know nothing of the laws of trade, by which alone supply can adjust itself to demand, while the heads of departments are superannuated generals of the line. The French military administration is, throughout, honorable, and we owe full justice to their zeal and effort, but it has not been established on war principles, and is in many ways contradictory. In the great operations of the First Empire, where all the departments worked without interference or the least confusion, the directors, controllers, and executors were business men, who had been so all their lives, and were ready and competent to do their duty under all circumstances. During our campaign in Italy, our divisions often suffered for want of bread in a country that was full of it. From this lack, our men were given corn-bread, which they would not eat, and sometimes, being surrounded by the enemy, we were for days near starvation. We have lost sight of the great principle taught us by so many years of successful warfare—that the division is the great administrative unit, as well as the great unit of conflict. The army should supply itself in a country where resources are ample; and it is a lack of good sense, and against all rules of experience, to provision an army through its administration in a country full of rich villages and teeming with products. When the responsible officers were accustomed to control these transactions, and where they were in intercourse with the producers and holders, the divisions, which now sometimes suffer greatly, were able to live economically and in plenty."

There is a lesson in all this for ourselves, and nearly every officer of rank in our war can remember some instance when his command, left to his own resources, was better and more cheaply fed than at any other time during the four years. In East Tennessee, during the winter of 1863–'64, after the battle of Mission Ridge, when we were sent to the relief of General Burnside at Knoxville, to a country where supplies were supposed to be exhausted, we took, on leaving Chattanooga, seven days' rations and no tents, and those rations were the last the "*administration*" issued us for seven weeks. Each division and brigade was required to provide for itself. Each commander detailed an officer and a few men to gather grain, and grind it at the mills; others to collect forage, cattle, and small rations. The men built little houses of fence-rails and straw, and the officers made themselves comfortable in the houses and barns within their lines, or improvised log huts. During the entire war I never knew men better fed, and at less cost, or more contented, or so few on the sick report, and this in the middle of winter.

General Trochu, says:

"I do not hesitate to think that, under analogous circumstances and during a long war, the same administrative errors would be repeated, and it would become necessary to employ commercial agents to supply by contract the various wants of the army. This was the case in the Crimea, where, when the administration became complicated, and the problem of supply difficult, and the troops were famishing, a mercantile house in Marseilles came to the rescue on its own responsibility, and undertook the subsistence of the army, and actually did furnish it abundantly."

What is here predicted really took place in the recent war. The French administration broke down completely and everywhere. It was one of the causes of M'Mahon's tardy movements from Chalons, by which he was sandwiched against the Belgian frontier; and when finally captured at Sedan, his troops were literally destitute. Trochu says:

"All the military functionaries have the welfare of the army at heart, and watch over its interests with great devotion and professional pride. They have numbers of troops under their control, and with these they should study, in times of peace, those principles which in time of war would secure efficient military service."

Nothing is more characteristic of vulgar ignorance than prejudice against contractors, who are said to enrich themselves at the cost of the public. No doubt they enrich themselves, and they ought, if they succeed in a critical and complicated service; for riches are the great and only incentives in commercial life, and, unless money should be made, commerce would die. While making money for themselves, they save the army and state from far greater expense and imminent peril. That we were furnished with shoddy coats and trowsers, stationery that was a sham, hats that sell for a penny apiece, and are considered dear at that, and blankets made of cows' hair, so coarse and heavy that they conducted away all the heat of the body instead of retaining it, and made our bones ache with their weight, was due to a controlling organization, with many of the defects of the French Intendance, whose duty it was to keep all these articles up to the standard, but who never performed it. If a second-rate article will be accepted as first-rate, no contractor will be so absurd as to furnish the better quality.

General Trochu is strongly opposed to exclusive military establishments, and in that evinces remarkable wisdom; for any nation that shuts out from the really commercial part of its administration the active life and widely-gained experience of its progressive people hedges itself about with forms and routine, without vitality, and soon finds itself behind the age, and unable to cope with the new order of things. He says:

"The Intendance is composed of a great number of distinguished persons, who have been for the most part members of the Polytechnic and military schools. It is a superior corps, and holds a position of high esteem and regard. I think, however, that I have shown that the method of selection of members of this corps has not all the strictness desirable; and as concerns the great movements in time of war, which depend upon the Intendance, there is much to wish for. To fulfill its functions usefully, the Intendance has properly claimed that its position in the army should be one of extraordinary rank, and has sought to gain for its officers grades from generals of division to captains of companies, with the honors and special privileges incident to those grades, but by this arrangement the Intendance has to a certain degree deteriorated, and with it the whole military administration, direction, execution, and control. The administrative officers charged with the execution of their service have become purely unmilitary agents—their entire duty being that of store-keepers, distributors, and accountants, and thus fail of proper experience in military affairs. They are absorbed in their routine, and, when their duty is done, their whole energies are concentrated in gaining distinction, advancement, promotion, rank. These innovations, which have so greatly changed the administration, date back to a period even before Louis XIII.; and the few well-informed at that time predicted accurately the damage that would result from such a course, particularly in time of war. The direction and administration of armies must depend upon commanders, because it is their duty to conduct the war, and they alone are responsible for success or failure. It is to be regretted, and it is greatly against the public interests, that the commander of the army has allowed it, step by step, to sink, and deviate from the public interest in the matter of its administration. These transactions should be placed in the hands of civil agents interested in their execution, who will furnish guaranties for their ability to properly perform their trusts. These agents should be real business men of true commercial experience, and, if you please, under the surveillance of the Intendance. Administrative control is a high and necessary mission, which the Intendance holds directly from the state, and which it fulfills with an absolute independence. It is in the efficient discharge of this mission that they should have sought the distinction to which they have a right, but they have demanded military rank and prerogatives—prerogatives to which the law has contested their right, and which experience has proved calamitous."

INFANTRY.

Of the infantry he says:

"Infantry is the principal agent in battle, as well as the principal support to all other corps. When it advances, forcing back the opposing lines, and occupying the positions so obtained, the victory is gained. When it holds its own ground, standing firm, and wrestling with the enemy without looking back, the victory is perhaps uncertain, but may be gained by fortunate manœuvres or a last effort. When, governed by events, it retreats farther and farther, without being able to obtain strongholds which the battle-field offers, or to advance and take the offensive, defeat is at hand. The position of infantry also regulates the advancement, and controls the *morale* and hopes of the entire mass, and when its mission is fulfilled, it resumes its permanent duty of marching day after day in a heavy equipment. It executes all great works, and watches night and day over the safety of all. It is the instrument of strength and endurance."

We will now see how the infantry is made up, and notice the faults common to the French and our own army. The conscription is first made. The artillery and engineers have the first choice, as they require men of physical strength and superior intelligence. The large men are then taken for the heavy cavalry, and the agile and hardy for the select light-infantry. The regiments of the line now receive the remainder, when the Imperial Guards are selected, and two companies from each battalion as riflemen; and as these, from their greater exposure as skirmishers, lose men rapidly, they are kept full from the battalion. What remains is the mere dregs of the whole mass, or, as has been pointedly said, "the residuum of the conscription." This plan of fostering picked corps has been a favorite one with the late emperor, and in this he has committed the most fatal of errors. It is continually weakening the body, to unduly strengthen the members, until the body is so enervated as to be no longer able to support the members.

The infantry is, by common consent the world over, the most essential and important element of an army; and we, as well as the French, have lost sight of this, and have weakened this branch — more for personal convenience than from any real necessity of the service. General Trochu would do away with all these fancy corps, and throw back into the line all these strong and effective men, more particularly now, since the introduction of the rifle has rendered the carbine no longer useful in war. He would select two platoons of picked sharp-shooters from each battalion, and nothing more. There can be no question that the infantry—the great trunk which supports all—should be made as powerful as possible; and this fact has been recognized by Prussia, while forgotten by France and ourselves. French service in Africa has had the effect to greatly increase individual resource and self-reliance, and taught the inestimable advantage in war of the light, elastic movement of select parties—skirmishers and sharpshooters. This has been secured, however, at great cost to that steady, shoulder to shoulder, deliberate movement and compact order which is indispensable in all great operations. The latter had come to be viewed in France, as well as in our own country, as a sort of mistake, and quite unnecessary, than which no greater error is possible. In no other way can troops be brought under that perfect control necessary to make them available under all conditions.

General Trochu appreciates the immense advantage of cover for infantry. He says that in no other way can we have accurate firing, and that otherwise the men fire at random, omitting aim entirely, and many not even bringing the gun to the shoulder. To render accuracy possible, the soldier should be in a place of security, behind a wall, a tree, or, far better, in hastily-made rifle-pits, such as were used by us in the last years of the war. The soldier then is not disturbed by a sense of his own danger, his mind is clear, and he will invariably carefully aim his piece. General Trochu also recognizes the vital importance of the men becoming thoroughly acquainted with their arm, and advises that the best shots of the regiment should be posted under charge of select officers, either singly or in small groups, so that they may, by their superior skill, accuracy, and persistency of fire, pick off artillerymen, cause troublesome bodies of troops to withdraw, annoy mounted men and officers, and generally harass the enemy. The great effectiveness and importance of sharpshooting we never fully appreciated or availed ourselves of, while systematic target-practice in many commands was entirely neglected.

CAVALRY.

General Trochu says that the invention of the new and more effective small arm has entirely changed the part cavalry must play in war, and that to attack infantry in position while in full strength and courage would be but destruction to the cavalry, and that cavalry must recognize the altered conditions of the age and adapt itself to them. Its true mission in war is that of swiftness, and, to give to it its full usefulness, we must make it as light and active as possible. These observations apply to all cavalry. In France the horse is compelled to carry from two hundred and eighty to three hundred pounds, while the regulation pack of a mule is but two hundred pounds. General Trochu recommends the entire abolition of the heavy cavalry; that the helmet, cuirass, and shako be abolished; that light, active men only be recruited in the cavalry service; that there be but one kind of cavalry, and one of infantry; and that the musketoon be abolished altogether, and the revolver substituted. These recommendations are all full of good sense, and must soon be adopted.

Cavalry does not, as is popularly supposed, actually perform great things; but it can produce great moral results in proportion as it moves swiftly, and consequently is found unexpectedly in the midst of a retreating and disorganized enemy, confronting his carelessly-advancing columns, breaking up his trains, interrupting his lines of communication, cutting off his isolated detachments, dashing in where least expected, and getting out of harm's way before resistance can be organized. The wonderful moral force over and above the merely material efficiency of this arm of the service did not seem to be comprehended by the French in the late war. They permitted their cavalry to operate compactly with their infantry, to be enveloped at Sedan, and even to charge lines of the investing Prussian infantry, of course only to their own destruction. They drew their cavalry in after them at Metz and Paris, where it could by no possibility be of the least service. The Prussians are not much better off than the French in the matter of the heavy packs of their cavalry, and even we are not quite up to the modern requirements. The sabre as well as the lance is no longer useful, and is always left in camp when our troops go on active service. How to reduce weights so as to give to cavalry the greatest attainable speed, must in future be the problem to be solved.

WANT OF SIMPLICITY.

General Trochu deplores the great complexity of army regulations and manœuvres, that the army is no longer governed by rules which are easily comprehended and observed by all, and quotes the maxim of Frederick the Great, that "any thing not simple is useless in war." This is so true that every soldier would do well to remember it. Armies are made for war, and the great law of simplicity must, by a natural necessity, regulate the existence and action of troops in the field. Here all that is not simple is impossible. The most ingenious and brilliant inventions adequate to all requirements of peace fail miserably in war. The exercises in peace should conform to the inevitable necessities of war. Yet who in front of the enemy ever had occasion for a tenth part of the complicated tactics with which we burden the mind of our troops. The present manœuvres are those of a time when the small range of fire-arms permitted battalions to be brought with deliberation and accuracy into the near presence of the enemy. The tactics should be reduced to a few pages easily comprehended, and so simple as to admit of rapid application under all circumstances and conditions.

General Morand, an officer of the First Empire, says.

"Our present manœuvres can not, without great danger, be executed in the presence of the enemy. If employed, the consequence would be, as the consequence has been, the massacre of whole battalions. These manœuvres are also injurious, because the study of them diverts the mind of an officer from the true object of war. Generals have been beaten because their heads were full of nothing but these nonsensical forms."

In the last years of our war I used only a single manœuvre, and that not mentioned in our tactics (yet while in camp I carefully instructed my troops in the whole three books)—a movement by wings of regiments, a sort of folding up of the regiments into two folds. This was so simple and so rapid, susceptible of the speediest formation, fronting the men in any direction, and shortening the column one-half while marching by flank in narrow roads, that it answered for all purposes, and enabled me to put my command on any portion of the line before those about me comprehended what was required of them.

POPULAR ENTHUSIASM IN WAR.

General Trochu has a low opinion of popular enthusiasm as an element of military success. The eagerness of the start counts but little during the heat and burden of the day, and far less when Fortune ceases to smile and reverses have to be borne. In support of this opinion, he quotes the following graphic passage from "Marshal Bugeaud's Reminiscences," which is worthy of introduction here:

"I served in the Peninsula," says the marshal, "for seven years. I sometimes beat the English in isolated movements and in detached operations, which, with the rank I then held, I was able to prepare and direct; but during this long warfare, I am sorry to say there were but few general operations in which the British army had not the best of it. The reason was obvious. We almost invariably attacked our adversaries, without the slightest reference to past experience, in a manner which generally succeeded against the Spanish, and which generally failed against the English. They habitually occupied a well-chosen, defensive position, with a certain elevation of ground, showing only a portion of their strength. The cannonade began. Then, in hot haste, without waiting to study the position, or see how it could be turned, on we rushed to 'take the bull by the horns.' At about a thousand yards from the British lines our soldiers began to talk, and hurried forward with a slight degree of confusion. The English, silent, arms grounded, looked like a long red wall, which had a good deal of effect on our youngsters. The distance became less. The troops began to cry, '*Vive l'Empereur*,' '*En avant a la baionnette*,' and to wave their caps on their muskets. The march became a run, the ranks were somewhat broken, the agitation swelled to a tumult, and a good many shots were fired. The British line, still silent, still immovable, though we were but three hundred yards away, seemed not to perceive the storm about to reach it. The contrast was striking. More than one of our fellows began to think that the enemy was very slow in firing, and that his firing, when it came, would shortly be very unpleasant. We felt less ardent. The moral influence, irresistible in war, of the composure which seems to be undisturbed, even when it is not so, over disorder intoxicated with noise, weighed upon us. At a moment of painful suspense the English 'wall' presented arms. An impression they could not define riveted to the spot many of our men, who were beginning to open a dropping fire. The fire of the enemy, in perfect unity and precision, mowed us down. Struck back, we receded to recover our balance. Then three formidable hurrahs broke the silence of our adversaries. At the third cheer they were upon us, driving in our disorderly retreat, but, to our great surprise, they did not urge their advantage beyond a hundred yards, but fell back upon their line to await a second attack. The second attack, with reenforcements, was generally made, but with similar results and fresh losses."

The marshal has given us here a very fair idea of the French soldier of to-day, the wars in Africa having had a tendency to increase rather than to diminish this style of behavior in presence of the enemy. I have a clear recollection of a few occasions in our war where our own troops attacked under like circumstances, and with precisely similar results. These impetuous movements are ill-timed, and very inconvenient. They anticipate and embarrass the operations of war, and, in the event of a check inflicted by an enemy under better discipline and control, the men, if broken, can be no longer readily manœuvred, and the most disastrous results may follow.

ORGANIZATION OF THE FRENCH ARMY AT THE COMMENCEMENT OF HOSTILITIES.

The agitation in France caused by the Prussian success at Sadowa resulted in a law, passed February, 1868, which extended the period of the conscript's service from six to nine years—five in the ranks with the colors, and four at home, as a member of the reserves—creating the "*Grande Nationale Mobile*," which is a sort of militia, or landwehr, available for the defense of France. This law, in fact, placed at the disposal of the state all of the available male population from twenty to twenty-five years of age; but very little progress has been made under it in organization or instruction, and only companies here and there were armed and uniformed.

The infantry of the regular army of France embraces one hundred regiments, of three battalions each, all of precisely similar organization. Each battalion has eight companies, but in time of war two companies of each battalion are taken out, after transferring their trained men to other companies, and form a dépôt battalion, for recruiting, under command of the lieutenant-colonel. These three battalions are commanded by "chiefs of battalion," corresponding to majors. A company consists of one captain, two lieutenants, four sergeants, eight corporals, and one hundred and eight privates, or an aggregate of one hundred and twenty-five. The battalion has then six companies, one chief, one adjutant, one under-adjutant (a non-commissioned officer), and twenty-five field musicians. The aggregate is seven hundred and seventy-eight for a battalion; and three of these, with a colonel and lieutenant-colonel, form a regiment, amounting, in the aggregate, to two thousand three hundred and thirty-six. To the regiment is attached, of non-combatants—medical officers, six; medical non-commissioned officers, fourteen; musicians, thirty-eight; and sick-bearers, seventy-five; or, in all, one hundred and thirty-three. Add to this the home battalion of seven hundred and seventy-eight, and we have a complete regimental organization of three thousand two hundred and forty-seven. In order to get the sum total of infantry of the army, or any of the above parts, we have only to add two ciphers to any of the foregoing numbers. This is the organization for war. In time of peace the companies are greatly reduced; and official papers say it is then one hundred and ninety thousand men, being fifty-six thousand less than the combatants of the war establishment, or one hundred and thirty-four thousand less than the complete war establishment. It is a pertinent question, Where did France get this vast number of men at the beginning of hostilities?

The law of 1868, before referred to, provided for a reserve of about four hundred thousand men; but as they only become reserves successively after their five years' service with the colors, it would take until 1876 before France could have a full reserve; and she could not have had in July, 1870, more than one hundred thousand reserve men available. It is very certain, then, that no battalion of the army went out with seven hundred and seventy-eight combatants; and if we deduct the sick and others out of place, which can not be less than ten per cent., we have battalions of not more than six hundred and fifty, or, at the utmost, regiments of not more than two thousand men. In fact, several battalions at Strasbourg on the 20th of July had only five hundred men each.

The brigade has two regiments, and a division two brigades. To one of the brigades is usually attached one battalion of chasseurs, and to the division two light batteries and a company of engineers. This gives about nine thousand men to the division.

All the cavalry regiments have six squadrons, of about one hundred and twenty-five horses each, giving a regiment seven hundred and fifty horses; but as two squadrons have to be left at home for dépôt purposes, a regiment goes into the field with five hundred and twenty-five horses. Two of these regiments form a brigade, and two brigades a division, which is attached to every army corps. The army corps has also a reserve of artillery, of from twenty-four to thirty guns, and an engineer train. It is easy to construct the entire army as it existed at the commencement of the war, from the following data, which are accurate:

	Guns.	Cavalry.	Infantry.	Total.
M'Mahon's 1st Corps	40	3,640	36,500	40,140
Froissard's 2d Corps	72	2,080	26,250	28,330
Bazaine's 3d Corps	90	3,640	35,000	38,640
L'Admirault's 4th Corps	72	2,080	26,250	28,330
De Failley's 5th Corps	72	2,080	26,250	28,330
Bourbaki's Imperial Guard Corps	60	3,600	16,450	20,050
Canrobert's 6th Corps	78	10,800	8,750	19,550
Total	...	27,920	175,450	203,370
Add to this for Artillerymen	...	....	....	17,000
" " Engineers	...	....	....	4,000
" " Train	...	....	....	5,000
" " Non-combatants	...	....	....	4,000
Total	...	....	....	233,370

Or an entire field army of two hundred and thirty-three thousand three hundred and seventy, which was the extent of the emperor's forces at the beginning of the war, and will be found to correspond very closely with the captures by the Prussians at the first battles, at Sedan and at Metz. M'Mahon got in many of the reserve battalions and some raw conscripts at Chalons, but the number of these did not vary much from the current losses from sources other than capture during these operations. This was substantially the Army of the Rhine, that marched early in July to the invasion of Prussia, the last of whom were captured at Metz. France had also then in formation the Seventh Army Corps, under Douay, from the troops in Africa and the division in Rome. There were also a few regiments in fortresses, and some ten thousand marine troops. The four battalions of the marching regiments were ordered to be filled up and employed as separate regiments. Some of these were collected by M'Mahon at Chalons, and others, with a portion of the marines, withdrew into Paris. Then comes the Garde Nationale Mobile. These were, theoretically, five hundred thousand strong, but had never been embodied. Some of these, as every one knows, came out in time to assist in the defense of Paris, and others formed provisional armies outside, and did some service.

The arms of these troops I have already described. The French were superior in small weapons, but greatly surpassed by the Prussians in light artillery. The mitrailleuse can hardly be said to have accomplished any thing.

OBSERVATIONS.

I have now traversed imperfectly the subject of the French army, giving a slight sketch of its history, as well as of its organization at the commencement of the war. I have endeavored further to give, from the mouths of its most able officers, such views of its different parts and general character, as to permit others to form their own estimate of its value. I think it will be readily seen by all fair military observers that it has fallen into many timeserving and vicious errors, resulting largely from political and personal causes, and somewhat from a kind of egotistical over-confidence in traditional systems. We have in many ways, and from our very existence as a nation, closely copied much that was found in the French army, the fact that we found it there being taken as a satisfactory guaranty that it was worthy of imitation. It may be well to ask if this fact alone is sufficient to warrant a continuance in this course, and if it is not possible that we are perpetuating errors copied from this model. Nearly all our tactics and military system we have received from France, second-hand from Germany. Will it not be as well in future, if we are still to borrow, to resort to original sources, and of the latest, most highly approved, and effective pattern? We have much yet to learn, particularly in administration and accounts. I have never failed to say, when there was occasion, that I believed our system in these particulars faulty in its very essence, and that there is but one remedy—to remove entirely, and rebuild from the foundation.

We have seen that the emperor thought it well to go to war with two hundred and thirty thousand men; that with this force he undertook the invasion of a country whose Government could oppose him on his own frontier, as soon as he could reach it, with nearly six hundred thousand men in the front line. This he knew, as did every military scholar in Europe. He was not deceived about the strength of his own army, as many have supposed; for the figures I have given were national property, and known to every officer in France—the same situation existing at the time of the Crimean War in 1855, and again with Italy in 1859. It is true, that a law creating the reserve and the Garde Mobile was passed in 1868, but sufficient time had elapsed for the creation of only about one hundred thousand of the former, and the latter had not been embodied at all. The fact that such an enterprise was undertaken can only be accounted for on the ground of inordinate French egotism, or as the desperate resort of a political gambler.

The German soldier is about one-fifth larger than the French, vastly superior in education, and better instructed in his duties. He is plodding and steady in every thing he does, thoroughly subordinate, has a tenacity of purpose that never flags, and a constitution that rises superior to all vicissitudes. He is as brave as the Frenchman, has less enthusiasm that wears out the will, marches lighter, has a more rigorous regimen, is more sturdy of purpose, and has a deeper respect for authority, and a more intense love of country. Had France been the equal of Germany in all these respects, twenty years of industrious preparation would have still been necessary to place her in a condition to challenge Prussia with an equal chance of success.

CHAPTER VIII.

COMPARATIVE OBSERVATIONS UPON THE UNITED STATES ARMY.

IN comparing our own with foreign armies, it is easy to be misunderstood; and I will here say that I believe no men are braver, more patriotic, self-sacrificing, and enduring of hardships and privations of all kinds than American soldiers. There are none susceptible of better discipline than they; although, from having led more independent lives than foreign troops, they do not so readily yield to it, and none can stand up more squarely and honestly in hard battle. No one should more readily, or can more heartily, say this than myself, for I served through our entire war in command of a body of troops which bore a conspicuous part in nearly all the great battles of the West, and I never had occasion to complain of the conduct in battle of any regiment or company. But, while all were praiseworthy, some regiments were worth twice as much as others; and when I compare the 41st Ohio Volunteers, a regiment raised and instructed by myself, which was in my command nearly all the war, and never hesitated or failed in any duty, with other regiments which worried the patience by their snail-like and uncertain movements—when I remember that I served twelve months under a corps commander, and eighteen months under a division commander, neither of whom during that time ever gave me a single direction respecting the instruction of my command—I am strongly impressed with the immense loss which our country sustained in consequence of the indolence, ignorance, and shiftlessness of its officers; and finding in the German army all this thoroughly corrected, I am the more inclined to make it known. I say not a word in disparagement of our men, but I do most fervently maintain that we lost incalculably by not employing the means in our hands for bringing our commands to their highest efficiency. This resulted principally from having men at the head of military affairs who, not being soldiers themselves, did not appreciate the necessity of discipline and instruction, nor understand the steps necessary to secure them. This was, in the main, true of our leading staff officers, who had much to do in regulating affairs, and on whose advice the civilians mainly rested. They had been office men so long, entirely separated from troops, that they had lost the spirit and character of soldiers. There were regiments in one of the divisions of the army corps which I commanded at the close of the war—veterans of '61, bearing a fair fighting record—in which the enlisted men felt but very slightly, if at all, the spirit of subordination, and manifested few soldierly qualities except courage. They were on the most intimate social terms with their officers, did not rise in the presence of officials, no matter what their rank, nor remove their hats on entering officers' tents, and scarcely knew how and when to salute. These may appear little things, but it is by them that all soldiers are known. The good these troops did us, which I have no doubt was great, was gratuitous, and not because their officers had the power, as they ought to have had, to compel it. They were earnest, patriotic men, but not soldiers.

The morale of the rank and file of our regular army is exceedingly unsatisfactory; and to no one is this discouraging condition so apparent as to officers serving with troops. There is no remedy for desertion, and one sees his authority quietly set aside, and a third of his force abandon the colors every year, without the power to prevent it, and without any apparent notice being taken of it, or any adequate remedy provided for it by those in authority. If we stop desertion, other matters will soon correct themselves. But there can be no military excellence where the worst military offense can be committed with impunity, and without remedy. To stop it, we must simply enlist good men. To do this, we do not need bounties, classifications, increased pay, or legislation of any sort, but merely the application of some simple common-sense rules which every good business man applies when he employs a servant. We must require proof of identity and character. There will be no trouble in obtaining this, as any men worthy to be enlisted can easily furnish such proof. I have applied this rule for the past year to my own regiment with perfect success. There have been scores of applicants who would fill all the requirements of our recruiting service, who, upon being asked as to their identity and character, have slunk away never to come back, and, upon inquiry, I have found them desperadoes, thieves, and deserters.

Our present system requires only physical qualifications for enlistment, and ignores moral character. The result is, that common thieves, discharged convicts, deserters, and vagabonds find an easy entrance in our army. No squad of recruits enlisted in New York leaves that city without containing many faces familiar to the old city detectives, while all the worthless men who were discharged at the reorganization and reduction of the army in July last are getting back into the service again; and no two regiments approach each other without there being many desertions from each by men who have previously deserted from the other, and fear detection. A party of five New York thieves within the past year enlisted, and were assigned to one of the companies now forming my garrison. They have all, at different times since, "made their raise" and deserted; the last one but a few days since garroted a discharged soldier, and robbed him of some three hundred dollars.

We enlist men, and make them our debtors to the amount of about two hundred dollars before we receive any recompense, without knowing their names, residences, or any thing whatever about them. Is it strange that a third of our army desert every year?

The plan here proposed is perfectly feasible; for as about one-third of our men would re-enlist at the end of their term, we should need but about four thousand recruits a year, or three hundred and fifty a month, and it is absurd to say that a nation of forty million people will not yield this number of good men for its army. But our system has never sought them. This change may require more than the ten minutes' daily time usually devoted to his duties by an officer on recruiting service, and a few more branch rendezvous; but there will be no difficulty if it is intelligently made. The prevention of desertion will then be the fear of disgrace, and almost certain detection and rendition; the present trouble being that, in nine cases out of ten, when a man deserts, his name on the rolls is an alias, and his residence fictitious.

A thorough application of this plan would save the Government a million dollars annually now lost by desertion, and besides secure an incalculable advantage, in the moral character, respectability, and efficiency of our army. It is absurd to reject a thoroughly well-tried, good man because he has lost an eye, a tooth, or an ear, perhaps in battle, and to receive a recruit who, for all that is known of him, may not possess one attribute that makes him better than a beast.

A peculiarity of German military organization is the plan by which the fighting army is made paramount, and every thing else required to minister to it, so that a general always knows his exact force; while with us every thing necessary for the administration of the army is drawn back out of the fighting material in the most objectionable way, by selecting its best officers and men, thereby doubly weakening it, instead of constantly drawing up to it elements of strength. In our war the administrative and the fighting organizations were blended, so as to continually deceive the commander and the Government as to the force available for active operations, while victories were expected corresponding to the strength of both.

The German staff and administration are models of efficiency and economy. The former contains one hundred and fifteen officers, headed by General Von Moltke, and is composed of the very best men of the army, selected with the utmost care, after every possible trial by service with troops, and courses of training at the best schools. The officers are purely soldiers, and have nothing to do with administration, except in the highest military sense as chiefs of staff. The administration which pays, feeds, clothes, and supplies the army, is made up of men who have risen from the ranks, and shown special fitness for that mercantile style of work.

Our army is 30,000 strong, being one or two thousand under the strength of a Prussian army corps in time of war. We find the troops of one of their army corps commanded by seven general officers: one for the corps, two for the divisions, and four for the brigades. This does not materially differ from the number of general officers allowed for the line of our army, when the present incumbents have passed out of the positions that expire with their retiracy.

The Prussians have fourteen staff officers in all at the seven head-quarters, from a second lieutenant, who is adjutant of a brigade, to a colonel, who is chief of staff of the corps; six field officers, who are quarter-masters and commissariats, at corps and divisional head-quarters; ten commissariats, who are captains and lieutenants with the train; twenty-four pay-masters, who are second lieutenants with battalions; three officers with the telegraph division; one with the bakery; eighteen with the battalion of engineers, which is armed and drilled like infantry; and eighty-one medical officers, none above the rank of captain; in all, one hundred and forty-three.

Our army register shows of the officers we vaguely term "staff" five hundred and forty-two. Of these, two hundred and ninety-four are captains and lieutenants; one hundred and eighty-five, majors; thirty-six, lieutenant-colonels; twenty-three, colonels; and eight, brigadier-generals; while our entire line will have but nine general officers, and has but forty colonels, forty lieutenant-colonels, and seventy majors. It is true that our engineer corps performs many duties done in the Prussian service by civilians, and that our extended domain and great number of separate posts require a larger force of medical officers, and add also to the labor and difficulty of administration, while our ordnance corps performs excellently a work which the Prussian artillery regiments do equally well in addition to their other duties. But a glance shows that we have an immense preponderance of "staff" both in numbers, and, more especially, in rank.

We have in the line of our army sixteen hundred officers; and in the staff, including acting assistant surgeons, six hundred. If to these we add the persons who, numbering about six hundred, are employed by the staff as their assistants and receive about as much pay as officers—

say one hundred dollars monthly—we have twelve hundred, without including the officers of the line detailed as quarter-masters and commissaries. If these are added, it will be found that we employ with our present system as many officers, or their equivalents, to administer the army as we have fighting officers in it. This fact is its own commentary, and shows how much is required to administer the administration. This works injuriously to the public service in many ways. The high rank of the staff gives them extravagant pay, with which their service is not commensurate, and unfits them for the petty duties incident to a small establishment. They, for a like reason, habitually seek to exalt their duties and stations, and call for increased establishments of officers, clerks, superintendents, masters, store-keepers, and chief men, who do no labor, but rate on the pay-roll with lieutenants.

By their numbers and rank, and the fact that the chief of each branch, with several of his higher officers, is always stationed in Washington, they become a strong social power, and are enabled largely to influence legislation and executive action in their own favor and against the line. For example, in our late war nearly all the high officers of the staff department gained brevets for office duty ante-dating brevets of a like grade given to officers who commanded armies in the field. They also, in nearly all cases, received brevets one, two, or three grades above any real rank they ever held, while a rule was made to brevet officers of the line up to within one grade of that they fought with. The staff managed to hold, after the war closed, nearly all the rank they had gained in the war, and to secure the enlargement of their departments disproportionately to the enlargement of the army. One department succeeded by a special act in gaining one grade for all ranks. In another, the officers became captains in three years after their first entry into service, thus getting an advantage over the lieutenants of the line, who might have seen four or five times as much service. As the staff have charge of the army archives and records, Congress is largely dependent upon them for information, while their social relations and settled lives in Washington add to their influence. Their duties group them about the general officers of the army, with whom close relations of friendship spring up, gaining them the favor and influence of these high officers in all questions affecting their status. So strong a power is this, that we see its influence in nearly every appointment to the staff, or advantageous transfer, in which the law leaves discretion to the President. By their superior rank, when on duty with officers of the line, they take precedence in choice of quarters and in other ways. It can be readily seen how the tendency of things is to elevate the administration—a mere adjunct of the army—over the army itself, which thus becomes subordinate to its own servants.

The staff officers also, from their rank, numbers, and nearness to the executive, habitually, and by almost insensible degrees, arrogate to themselves powers and privileges which belong only to the commander-in-chief, until the heads of staff departments have nearly all gained independence of army control, and bear the same relation to the Secretary of War as the commander-in-chief himself—becoming, in fact, independent commanders of their own branches. This is destructive of military organization, and fatal to the harmonious and economical administration of military affairs. The staff departments are now substantially independent bodies, instead of connected links of a great chain of military administration.

With so many sources of power, there can be no unity of action, and this leads to waste and extravagance. As one of many examples of this, I will mention that at Fort Gibson, which had been without a suitable hospital since the war, one was constructed in the spring of 1871, by order of the surgeon-general of the army, at an expense of about twelve thousand dollars, when the commander knew that the post would be broken up, as it was, a few months later.

A major-general commanding a department may at any time find a second lieutenant of ordnance or engineers at his own post holding correlative power with himself, flying his own flag, and controlling his own resources. The commander of the department in which New York is situated finds within his command no less than a dozen military establishments, controlling perhaps all the sinews and appliances of war, over which he has no authority. Such a system fosters insubordination, and is rapidly destroying that kindness, respect, and fraternity so essential to an army, and for which ours has been distinguished.

I have heard a captain of one of these departments make his boast publicly that he waited in Washington two days for the return of the Secretary of War, as he was not under the control of the commander-in-chief; and that although the latter was in town, and could have given him his orders, he would not report to him. I heard another staff officer express his indignation that he had been placed upon the staff rolls of his department, whereas he claimed that he should be mustered with the military division staff.

The members of the engineer corps of our army are in no sense soldiers, being separated entirely from troops, performing no military duties, but holding military rank, and wearing the uniform of the army; and the same can be said of the ordnance, whose sympathy with the army springs mainly from the associations of a common Alma Mater. Our system virtually deprives the army of our most talented men, by placing them in these branches of the service which are not in the least military. This separate administration of each branch tends to magnify its importance in the eyes of its own officers, who expand and amplify their methods and systems, without commensurate good to the service, and sometimes to its positive detriment. Since the war the United States have been divided, for purposes of military administration, into military divisions, departments, districts, and posts. The posts each have a quarter-master—generally an officer of the regiment stationed there—who does the actual work of the department, and usually with enlisted men. Then at each separate district, department, and military division head-quarters is a quarter-master of the regular establishment, almost always of high rank, with a small army of clerks and other civilian employés about him at high pay, who do an amount of compiling reports and writing letters beyond all calculation. These officers require from the post quarter-masters a great number of reports upon all possible subjects; and as the post quarter-masters are usually allowed only one, and often no clerk, most of their time is occupied in this kind of work, greatly to the detriment of their proper duties. These officers at higher head-quarters always surround themselves with a large administrative establishment, and a great part of the funds appropriated for the department is thus consumed in keeping up its own cumbrous machinery.

The advantage of all this is not obvious, as these intermediate officers have no power whatever to do any final act. The only purpose of all this machinery seems to be to make places for a superabundance of officers, with so much rank as to unfit them for their legitimate duties. It can not be said that it is necessary to keep up this organization for use in war, for it then at once fails, and each army and corps commander is compelled to organize his own departments, as these officers have been found to be unfitted by their routine lives for service in the field. Any one who knew the working staff of Grant, Sherman, and Sheridan, remembers that they were made up of young, active civilians. The busy commercial life and experience of the nation is its strongest arm, and is what it must inevitably depend upon in time of war to supply the wants of its armies. In peace, while the line of the army is rusting out for want of occupation, it is an open question whether the regimental organization, with well-chosen dépôts in the hands of business men, and an able corps of inspectors, is not ample for all purposes. Indolence, the bane of our army, is due mainly to the want of defined duty.

The general efficiency of the system itself is open to grave question, and the experience of the world has been that these centralized organizations have failed in great emergencies. Ours may be said to have done so in our late war, as such success as we had in this direction was won only by lavish expenditure.

The quality of nearly every thing which the centralized departments pretended to furnish, excepting food, arms, and ammunition, was several grades below the standard, and lower than was paid for, the blankets and stationery being detestable cheats, and the clothing the vilest quality of swindling "shoddy." Only a few months since several hundred uninjured hats were sold at Fort Smith for five cents apiece, and it was considered a high rate. The Prussian Government has open accounts only with the colonel of a regiment, who is made responsible for the funds by which it is maintained, and supplied with food, clothing, arms, and all other requisite articles; while we open in Washington a book account with every man, from the colonel to the last recruit. The Germans have also with the army a corps of auditors, officers of the treasury, who close these accounts on the spot.

What has been said of our Quarter-master's Department is in a measure true of all the rest, and in nothing more than in the bepapering they all treat us to. By a little calculation it can be proven that, unless this system is corrected, there will, in a short time, be too few public buildings in Washington to contain the army archives. For instance: every colonel is made superintendent of the recruiting service for his regiment. To report at the end of a month that he has recruited one man requires five square feet of the best folio-post paper, and the same if he has recruited no one. At the end of each quarter, for a post-commander to satisfy the Ordnance Department as to the disposition of a few cartridges, requires three duodecimo books of thirty-six pages each. These absurdities are all avoided in the German system.

The officers of our administrative departments, from complete official separation from the line, become also entirely divided from it in heart and sympathy, and their peculiar relations to the Government and civil life always enable them to succeed whenever their interests run counter to those of the army itself. This is sometimes made still easier by the influence of the higher officers of the army, with whom, from the nature of their duties, staff officers are always associated. For example: at the close of the war, the line-officers found that their pay amounted to even less than it was before the war, as, though nominally the same, it was lessened by the income tax and the discount on paper money, while the cost of living had increased about thirty-three per cent. The staff, in consequence of receiving a large amount of additional money-pay as commutation of fuel and quarters, which had advanced largely during the war, did not feel this reduction; while all the other branches of the Government, except the Supreme Court, had been additionally paid to correspond with the increased cost of living. Many of us who had commanded divisions, army corps, and armies in the field, with the rank of major-generals, found ourselves, as field officers in the line of the army, with a less pay than field officers received before the war; while a few of the highest officers had their pay greatly increased, from additional rank given them, with new rates of pay, after the war closed. It was natural that we should be neither satisfied nor silent under such a state of things. As early as 1866, efforts were made to bring the matter before Congress, with a general petition for relief, and "Schenck's Salary Bill" was the result. This bill was greatly to the advantage of the line, as it gave a uniform and increased rate of monthly pay. This failed to become a law, but was each year brought forward, passing sometimes one branch, with certain defeat in the other, owing to the opposition it received from members of the staff residing in Washington, and from the higher officers whose pay had been already raised. In July, 1870, all field officers of the army felt that they could not much longer keep out of the poor-house, and the bill was again brought before Congress. When it had passed the House and gone to the Senate, I wrote to every senator whom I knew, stating what I have said here, and urging the positive necessity of the passage of the bill. The following is one of six replies which I received, and is a sample of them all:

"U. S. SENATE CHAMBER,
"WASHINGTON, D. C., July —, 1870.

"Gen. W. B. HAZEN, etc., etc.,—Your letter from Fort Scott, Kansas, is just received, and I regret it did not come yesterday. The 'Army Pay Bill' came up last night, and was lost by three votes. Legislation upon the army is all under the whip and spur of the people here, and your letter is the first word we have had from the line of the army.

"Yours, very truly, ———— ————, U. S. S."

A few days later this bill was attached to the "Army Reorganization Bill," and passed both Houses, but not until a clause had been added by which the staff gets it commutation as before, in addition to the increase given the line.

At the close of our war, an effort was made by officers of the line, who realized the evils of the system of exclusive sutlers, to have it abolished altogether. The practice of the sutlers had been to bribe the officer and rob the soldier, by selling at cost to the former, and making it up by overcharging the latter. This system was finally abolished, and a law passed making it the duty of the Subsistence Department to furnish the articles formerly sold by the sutler, to both officers and men, at cost. This was very advantageous to the line, but the law was disliked by the Subsistence Department, because it added to their duties, and was considered by many degrading. A deliberate intention not to execute the law was soon manifested. The first excuse for not carrying it out was that Congress had made no special appropriation, and the adjutant-general published an order excusing the Subsistence Department from compliance with the law, although the general appropriation for that department was so large that none was asked for during the following year. This was the entering wedge to kill the law. Then the adjutant-general authorized department commanders to appoint as many traders at posts as should desire to trade, only requiring evidence of fitness. This was an admirable arrangement, as it gave troops the advantage of competition; but the law was still evaded by the Subsistence Department, as these traders kept all articles that the troops wanted. Not content to let matters rest here, a clause was incorporated in the new law of 1870, at the instance of some special interest, providing that the Secretary of War might appoint one trader at each post for the benefit of the traveling public. This was ingeniously worded, but the practical result is to provide one sutler, whose schedule of prices is not supervised as before, but who is free to make his own terms, while the commanding officer must protect him in his exclusive trade-rights, and the post council has no voice in his nomination, or right to assess him for the benefit of the post. Besides, the sutlers could not formerly farm out their privileges as they now do. I have reliable information of one trader who pays twelve thousand dollars, and of another who pays five thousand dollars per annum for his monopoly. These sums must of course be made up from extra charges to troops. These are some of the evils which result to the line of the army, from the failure of the Subsistence Department to perform its legal duty.

It has been a custom, since our service began, for some of the more careful men of each company to deposit their savings with their captains, often greatly to his annoyance, as he has nothing but his trunk in which to keep money. Sometimes these savings accumulate through twenty years of service, and during all this time the soldier's bag of money lies in the captain's trunk, or in the bureau of the captain's wife, receiving its little accretions each pay-day, but earning nothing. Some two years ago I prepared the draft of a law, enacting that a soldier might leave undrawn with the pay-master such sums as he saw fit, and that at each monthly statement the pay-master should forward to the pay-master-general an abstract of these sums, and the latter invest the amount in United States securities, and deposit them in a safe, to be known as the "Soldier's Safe Deposit," so that at the end of his term of service the enlisted man, instead of his little bag of twenty years' idle money, might have a large capital that had been compounding for twenty years. I submitted this to the Chairman of the House Military Committee, who heartily approved it. I then presented it to the pay-master-general of the army. He wrote me a short note, in which he expressed his heartiest disapproval, as it would "add to his duties," and closed by saying that, if presented to Congress, he should consider it his duty to appear before that body and exercise the weight of his influence to defeat it. As he had previously carried all his points before Congress, I did not think it worth while to urge the project.

I cite these examples, that it may be seen how our system fosters special interests. Whenever questions arise between line and staff, as is frequently the case, they are referred to the chief of that branch of the staff which they affect, and his decision is usually final. In other words, a party to the question is made the final umpire, and he is invariably of the staff.

The funds appropriated for the general benefit of the army are not so expended as to be equally beneficial to staff and line. At a department head-quarters, as far from Washington as staff officers ever get, is found every luxury in quarters, grounds, and appliances of living, while distant posts go year after year without even comforts. Fort Leavenworth and the posts of the same department are examples of this. I have known distant posts denied the authority to employ a blacksmith or carpenter, who was almost indispensably necessary, "as the number of civilian employés authorized would not allow it," while the chief of the department, who made this decision, was then employing half a dozen civilians to sod his grounds. This is but one instance of what takes place constantly.

UPON THE OFFICERING OF TROOPS.

Our plan of officering from a military school is excellent, as far as it goes. The additional officers who are required should be selected from the whole body of educated young men, with reference to a fixed standard of excellence. At West Point there is very little or no selection at first, as cadets are usually appointed by the caprice of individuals, and the subsequent winnowing is made by applying the single test of plodding labor.

Our present plan for supplying the remainder is perhaps even worse than the French—none could be worse than ours. We actually appoint men at the mere wish of influential persons, without any evidence of a single qualification; and it is not surprising that they sometimes possess none. There seems to be a prevalent idea that to be a good soldier requires some miraculous gift, differing from what ordinary men possess, and not susceptible of the same tests. My observation has been, that a man in the military profession, as in every other, is worthy in proportion as he is sensible, cultivated, industrious, and moral. The French promote men for bravery, although they may possess no other qualification. To be brave is essential, but not sufficient to make an officer. We did the same; and during the last years of the war, when men had been tried and estimated, one could look down a whole column of the names of brigadier-generals in the register without finding many holding commands in the front. It was most unfortunate that the General Government gave to governors of the respective states unrestricted authority to officer regiments. The opportunity of forming a well-officered volunteer army was thus thrown away. Many of the governors made a sort of barter of commissions by giving them as a reward for recruiting services, the rank conferred being graduated according to the number of men enlisted. This might do were it at the end, instead of the beginning, of a costly service. The Governor of Ohio made an arbitrary rule from which nothing could move him—namely, to promote by seniority, no matter what were the claims against it, and would even give lieutenants' commissions to sergeants who had been reduced for worthlessness. This in time of war is the most vicious system possible. None is so cruelly unjust and discouraging to brave, good officers, who are always in battle, and none so favorable to the cowardly shirks who are never there, but swarm around the executive. Such a policy discriminates against the most valuable military qualities. The governor also favored the plan of forming new regiments, instead of filling the ranks of the old ones. This course gave Ohio weak regiments of veterans, and inexperienced ones of recruits, while it drew away from the old organizations their best men, moved by the hope of higher rank in new regiments. The result was that Ohio, toward the close of the war, occupied a secondary place.

These are examples of executive acts, exceedingly detrimental to the service, which could have been arrested, and were not. The result was, that we had colonels who were not fit for captains, and it was often necessary to look through the list of subalterns of more than one regiment to find an officer competent to record the proceedings of a board of survey. Governors of states, always well-meaning, were often without experience with men, and seemed to view them like marbles—all of a size, all of the same material, all of equal soundness, weight, and value. Perhaps no place so clearly disproves this notion as an active army. Men are found there of silver, gold, and sometimes of pure diamond, and also many of brass and lead and some of unmixed dross.

Our selections of men were made by neglecting all the usual tests and checks which are usually resorted to by other armies and by civil corporations to secure efficiency. Governors of states had not the facilities for applying these tests, and some of our commanders were destitute of the capacity to appreciate their value. This was, happily, not the case with those generals who led our armies through to the final glorious close. Upon the intelligent exercise of this discriminating faculty, and upon the resolute determination that promotion be given to those who earned it, greatly depended their success. We lost immeasurably by making no appeal to noble minds. Our country was full of young men of culture—like Shaw, Bartlett, F. W. Ransom, Terry, Garfield, and Cox—who could have been had for the asking; but they were not sought, and their places were often filled by barbers, billiard-saloon keepers, and in a few cases by professional gamblers; while it was notoriously a matter of frequent occurrence to commission men of dissipated habits, who had failed all their lives, and would not be trusted with any civil responsibility. After costing us years of war, hundreds of millions of money, and thousands of precious lives, this plan had to be abandoned; and when we did adopt a compulsory system, we well-nigh made it nugatory by incorporating in it the vicious provision for hired substitutes.

In the German army it is made nearly impossible for an unworthy and inefficient man to become an officer. Bravery and patriotism are esteemed at their true worth, but they alone are thought to constitute no valid claim to a commission. Duties and responsibilities of such a character are imposed upon all officers, that no incompetent man can remain in service, while the poorest shirk with us may hold his commission all his life if he does no flagrant act and signs his pay accounts regularly. Justice as impartial as human fallibility can administer, regulates the appointment and defines the duties of Prussian officers, and neither woman, statesman, nor king ever interferes with the exact operations of the law.

The Prussians have also a just system of rewards for service. With us duty goes for little, compared with personal favor. An officer may shirk for years, and then claim, by virtue of his rank, and gain the best post of his grade in the service, to the exclusion of those who have all the while labored faithfully. The effect of any system that rewards alike those servants who do their duty and those who do not, can be readily imagined, and in the end will, as it should, destroy itself. In the Prussian army service is certain of due recognition and reward, and this is the strongest stimulus to its proper performance. With us, those who do honest, rough duty uncomplainingly are very likely to do it all their lives.

Our legislation discriminates against the regular army. At the close of our late war a law was passed reorganizing the army, and providing that half the field officers should be volunteers. There were twenty-seven officers of the regular army commanding military divisions, departments, armies in the field, and army corps, while there were but three others who held commands of like grade. The result of the law is, that some colonels of volunteer regiments in the war are now colonels of regular regiments, while their former army corps commanders are their lieutenant-colonels.

In 1870, a statute was passed requiring that all officers of the regular army should be officially addressed by their full rank, leaving in force the law requiring volunteer officers who are not in the regular army to be addressed by their highest brevet rank. Some volunteer officers are accordingly addressed as generals, while we of like brevet rank who are attached to the service, and have elected to give our lives to it, are known officially as colonels, lieutenant-colonels, and majors.

These evils will in time correct themselves by the inevitable working of the spirit of reform and progress. When this rectification begins, public opinion will be satisfied with nothing short of rigid and strict economy in all branches of the public service. But nowhere will this be so difficult to secure as in the administration of the army, for the evil to be dealt with is not "corruption," but want of business capacity. Numbers of our staff possess a high order of talent, for they are among the best graduates of the Military Academy. They are rigidly upright, have superior social qualities, and are in every way personally most worthy. It is the system, and its effects upon them and upon the army, of which I speak. The greatest fault in the system is, that these men, by being so widely separated from the army, lose the true character and spirit of soldiers, and gain no experience in business. At the breaking out of war, the nation finds that these departments, instead of being vigorous auxiliaries, are legal impediments to the administration of affairs. Before the evil can be removed, much time is lost, and vicious systems are inaugurated which are corrected afterward with difficulty.

This want of business experience leads to great extravagance. The waste, from want of care of property, needless transportation of troops on public conveyances, the unlimited purchase and use of stores not strictly necessary, and the entire failure to hold officers to a cash responsibility for their carelessness or stupidity, are some of the evils that will at last certainly work their own cure. If these matters are reported, as they sometimes are, no especial notice is taken of them, and no one is held responsible. A board of officers is called to investigate and report, and if its action is not satisfactory to the party charged, he calls for another board, and so on, till at last a report is obtained in which the board relieves him by its recommendations. There is a disposition among staff officers to stand by each other, which is apt to be stronger than the wish to serve the Government.

The cost of the army may be divided into two parts: the specific, such as pay and allowances, fixed in amount by law, and the general costs, such as arms, equipments, quarters, transports, and general incidental wants not specified by law, but left to discretion. It is in the latter division that restriction is necessary. At present the storehouse of an army quarter-master will be found to contain almost every known article of merchandise, the connection of much of which with an army would puzzle the best soldier living to find out. These general supplies are issued on a requisition which requires only the approval of the commanding officer. There is no definite check or limit to the purchasing power, and no necessity for care, as new articles are readily procured to replace the old. Thus it is common to see an officer living under five times his allowance of tents, or going on a scout with many times his allowance of wagons.

In the spring of 1871, the quarter-master-general called upon the general of the army, who was about to inspect the posts in the Department of Texas, to say there were no carriages there suitable for him to travel in, and offered to send one there expressly for him. On his arrival at Indianola, he found there awaiting him an immense traveling carriage that took six mules to haul when empty, and so large as to be of no use whatever to the general. I am informed that it was ordered to be sold, and brought about one-fourth of its cost. In the first place, if we are to have an efficient and economical administration, the law should not allow such latitude; and, in the second place, it should hold an officer accountable for such a misapplication of money. If the head of a bureau can, at his own discretion, do this, he can buy a thousand worthless carts or Concord coaches.

It is a popular thing to advocate retrenchment in the army, and, to effect this, the army register is scanned, and the line of the army plucked here of a regiment, and there of a major, or adjutant, or quarter-master, or the pay of the soldier is reduced. The administration, which is the real source of expense, is never touched. The present Secretary of War ruled that but five thousand civil employés be kept in service, but nothing was said as to grade or amount of pay. The poorly-paid day-laborers were discharged, but the clerks, agents, store-keepers, and masters of all kinds who rank in pay with lieutenants of the army, were scarcely disturbed. There are of these, in the quarter-masters', commissaries', and pay departments, some seven or eight hundred—nearly as many as there are lieutenants in the army. These men form a sort of staff for these officers, often remaining with them for years, and finally carry on nearly all the business of their chiefs.

There are also a large number of forage-masters and warrant-officers appointed by the quarter-master-general, at nearly the same pay—a relic of the war—who seem to have been overlooked. Some of these men are necessary, but they should be enlisted as sergeants, at about one-fourth the pay now given, and rated as accountants, calculators, and store-keepers. These places should not be given to old soldiers as rewards, but, like the position of sergeants in the signal service, to the bright, educated young men of the country.

The grand fault of our army administration is, that it is too much centralized, every thing being directed from our central office in Washington. Such a plan can not be practically efficient, where the work is so far from the authority directing it. We saw this in the Indian Bureau, where the commissioner, no matter how pure, was never free from the influences of contractors, who always tried to use him for their own purposes. It was impossible for this to last after the authorized commission had visited the Indians, and studied their affairs on the spot. So apparent were the errors of the commissioner's administration from his Washington office, that their repeated reports appeared to him like persecution, and his resignation followed. Equally apparent are the errors of the centralized Washington administration to an observing officer upon the frontier. Effort is not exerted with sufficient directness, but loses its force in its passage through the tortuous channels of administration. I feel certain that all this will be corrected. The country will not remain content with any thing short of the best systems, even for our little army. Unless these reforms can be brought about, and the country satisfied that our army is earnest, capable, and, above all, economical, it will turn out that the staff has been and now is digging a grave in which the whole service must soon be buried.

Every nation that gives protection to its people has a right to call on its citizens to maintain it. It also has the right to prescribe its own systems, and it is its imperative duty to employ those methods that will be least burdensome to the people. It is common to hear that ours are good enough, and there is no need of their being better—that they carried us through the war—and many like sayings. This position is not tenable so long as our system is not the best. The waste of treasure and life in our war, as well as the noble sacrifices then made by a willing people, without respect to party, wealth, or station, are without a parallel. There never was a more sacred trust than rested with those whose duty it was to apply the resources of life and treasure placed at the disposal of the Government. It is natural to ask, Were they well applied? So far as the integrity of the heads of Government is concerned, they were; but in methods of administration they were not, unless it can be shown that we employed the best known methods. One of the purposes of this work is to ask, "Were they the best?"

It was common to hear that the state received no more than half the service it paid for, and it appears to be a settled sentiment that the state can not be served with the economy one finds in private affairs. This is an unfortunate misapprehension, but one that can not be corrected till we employ systems in which educated reason, and not political expediency and personal favor, shall govern. If our system required a million men on the rolls of the army, under the pay of the nation, which was losing their industries, to get two hundred and fifty thousand men in the front line with muskets in their hands, when we might have had the same number of muskets there with but half a million on its rolls, then our system was not the best. If we had seventy-five thousand officers under commission and pay, when we only required fifteen thousand, then our system was not the best. If we paid for the best quality of clothing, blankets, hats, stationery, and a long list of necessary articles, and received only shoddy and shams, then our system was not the best. If we lost half a million of lives, when by some other course we could have conducted the war as effectively, and lost but a hundred thousand, then our system was not the best. If our war cost six hundred millions of dollars, when it need not have cost more than two hundred millions, then our system was not the best.

CHAPTER IX.

PRUSSIAN MILITARY SCHOOLS.—PLAN OF OFFICERING THE PRUSSIAN ARMY.

The plan of officering the German army is nearly the same in all the states, and is founded upon the Prussian system, the superiority of which has been proved. Some trifling exceptions are made in deference to the wishes of the petty sovereigns, but the tendency is toward the Prussian plan, and soon the entire German military system will be uniform. The change has somewhat lowered the Prussian standard, but it is thought that more is gained than lost by uniformity, and, after peace, the standard of the whole will soon reach the Prussian mark.

In Prussia, military is based upon civil education, and these two systems are carefully made to act upon each other. A superior civil education makes military service easy, by affording facilities for gaining commissions, and by shortening the service in the ranks. Every man in Prussia, without regard to position, owes seven years' service to the state—three years in the active army, and four in the reserves. In time of peace, the reserves are called out only for occasional exercises, but are at all times prepared to march at once to the field, the men being at home engaged in their ordinary business, while their arms and equipments are kept at the dépôt.

A young man who can show a certificate of having passed some time in the higher public schools is permitted to join the army as a one-year volunteer, and serves wholly at his own expense, and is then transferred to the reserves for the other six years. The army requires about eight hundred officers each year, of whom about one-third are furnished by the military schools, and the remainder come from civil life, but not, as with us, without any preparation.

A young man who wishes to enter the army as an officer must first be nominated by a colonel of a regiment. He then serves as a private soldier with that regiment for six months, with the recognition that he is a candidate for commission, and is called an "advantageur." His treatment during this time depends upon the colonel, and differs in different regiments; but the rigor of discipline is generally moderated by the fact of his position. At the end of this time he must pass an examination on the subjects covered by a liberal civil education, and, if successful, becomes a "sword-knot ensign"—a rank between a sergeant and sergeant-major. If he can show a certificate from one of the recognized public schools that he has passed the required grade, this examination is dispensed with. He now goes to a war school, which will be described farther on, where he receives ten months' purely military instruction, and must pass a severe examination. He then returns to his regiment, and it is submitted to the officers whether, in view of his capacity and personal qualities, they will admit him among their number. If successful in this, his case goes up to the king for appointment as second lieutenant whenever there may be a vacancy for him. This method furnishes two-thirds of the Prussian officers. The other third come from the Cadet Schools. There are eight of these, situated in different parts of Prussia. They are intended for the education of the sons of officers of the army, and such civilians as have rendered signal service to the state, but are really open to all. Those who have no claim upon the Government pay their own expenses, and the others are assisted upon a scale graduated according to their means. These are schools for boys, the pupils being admitted at the age of ten years. The course usually covers six years.

A student is not obliged, on leaving the Cadet School, to enter the service, but the course generally leads to a military life, and does not excuse the pupil from the seven years' service due the state. Although these military schools serve a purpose, their course of education is purely civil, except in the two higher classes of the Berlin school. This is a high school, to which the best scholars from the other six are sent.

Fifty pupils each year, known as the select, form an advanced class, remain two additional years, pass their academic and military examinations, and at the end of that time receive full commissions from the king as second lieutenants, as our cadets are appointed directly by the President. These fifty do not come before the officers of the regiment for acceptance. All other cadets, on leaving the academy, must, like civilians, pass the academic examination, then join a regiment as advantageurs, serve six months as private soldiers, become sword-knot ensigns, go to a war school for ten months, be accepted by the officers of their regiment, and appointed by the king, subject to a vacancy. It thus appears that to become an officer requires, first, a good academic education, some military service, ten months' technical instruction, and, except in the cases of the fifty select, the nomination of a colonel, the acceptance by the officers of the regiment, and the appointment by the king. The fifty select are upon about the same footing as our cadets, and receive about the same style and amount of education. Officers of engineers and artillery come in under very similar conditions. The engineers are formed into battalions, and artillery into regimental organizations. The applicant comes in as an advantageur, or cadet, has the same service and examinations, and becomes a second lieutenant. He then attends the School for Engineers and Artillery at Berlin for two years. The landwehr are officered in two ways: first, by officers of the regular army, who leave it before completing their seven years' service; and secondly, from the one-year volunteers, who have served at their own expense.

We now come to the schools. They are of five classes; but, for want of space, only the first, which relates to the preparatory education, and later professional instruction of combatant officers, will be considered, the others being special, or for enlisted men. There are four schools, or kinds of schools, of this class: the Cadet Schools, which we have noticed, for boys; the War Schools, for advantageurs; the Engineer and Artillery School at Berlin, and the higher Academy, for officers of all arms, after they have seen several years' service with their regiments, and developed some special aptitude. This school has a general bearing on advanced instruction, professional and civil.

There are, besides these, a great number of schools for the general training of officers and non-commissioned officers already in service, two medical schools for the education of surgeons, one veterinary school, three schools for the preparation of young civilians for the grade of non-commissioned officers, regimental schools for the instruction of enlisted men, regimental music and swimming schools, and schools for the gratuitous education of the children of non-commissioned officers and soldiers. Only the first four named will be considered, beginning with the Cadet Schools.

CADET SCHOOLS.

These are divided in two classes — lower and upper. Each school forms a battalion, composed of companies, and all the battalions form the Royal Cadet Corps of Prussia, founded in 1717, and subsequently reorganized by Frederick the Great, who was a member of it himself. It has always been an object of special interest to the sovereigns of Prussia. It is composed of about fifteen hundred cadets, a hundred officers, a large number of civilian professors, and commanded by a major-general. The corps has a distinctive uniform, insignia, and standards, adopted by Frederick. The officers are detached from regiments for this duty, and changed every four or five years, but the civilian professors hold their positions during good behavior. The control of all military schools is vested in their immediate commandants, subject to a mixed board of military officers and civilians, under the superintendence of an inspector of military schools, who visits each institution every year.

At the six lower schools cadets enter from the age of ten until sixteen; and at the Berlin, or upper school, from fifteen to nineteen; and at the latter, either direct from civil life or from the lower schools.

The sons of non-commissioned officers who have served twenty-five years are eligible to these schools as free cadets. The sons of officers are partially free, according to the condition and pay of their fathers. The annual cost of the cadets, who all enter on the first of May, is from two hundred to three hundred thalers each. For purposes of instruction, the schools are divided into four classes, and each class into sections of from twenty-five to thirty cadets. The course of instruction in the six lower schools is the same, omitting Greek, as followed by the civil schools of like grade. Promotion to the next higher class usually takes place at the end of each year. The cadet, if not prepared to go on, is generally dismissed, and obliged to serve seven years as a private soldier, but sometimes special exceptions are made. All the junior schools have a similar organization, each being commanded by a field officer, assisted by ten or twelve captains and lieutenants, and a suitable staff of civil professors. Each school or battalion is composed of about two hundred cadets, and is divided into two companies. The subjects of instruction are Bible history, Latin, German, grammar, composition, French, arithmetic, elementary algebra, geometry, natural philosophy, drawing, and writing; also, during the whole four years, gymnastics, swimming, and dancing.

There are no examinations at the end of the course, but cadets who have been a year in the higher classes are transferred to the senior school at Berlin. The system of discipline, which is uniform throughout, will be spoken of in describing the Berlin school. In the junior schools, officers are required to exercise a moral influence, and trust more to admonition and reproof than to punishment. The power of inflicting punishment, however, rests with the commandant and captains of companies, and, as in every other case in the Prussian service, the extent and character of such authority are exactly defined by law. The most careful attention is paid to religious instruction. The officers seem devoted to their duties, and are always with the cadets, even sleeping in the same dormitory, separated from them only by a curtain.

BERLIN CADET SCHOOL.

The Senior, or Berlin Cadet School, was the only one I personally visited. Cadets enter here from fifteen to nineteen years of age. The course occupies two years, although the select, about fifty of each class, remain another year for higher instruction.

The staff, civil and military, is similar to, but larger

than for the other schools already described. It consists of thirty officers and twenty-eight civilians. There are, in addition, two chaplains, Protestant and Roman Catholic, three surgeons, and a staff of sixty-three subordinate employés and servants of all grades.

All officers and instructors are appointed by the king, upon the application of the commander of the cadet corps, after approval by the inspector of military education, and must be men of high attainments. The officers are usually sent to their regiments after a few years, but are brought back after short service, as their experience is considered valuable.

The civilians are first appointed on probation, and, if competent, are confirmed in their places. The officers receive a small addition to their regimental pay, and the civilians have salaries ranging from six hundred to fifteen hundred thalers a year. The building is situated on one of the principal streets in Berlin, and was originally built by Frederick the Great. Many additions have since been made, but the accommodations are still insufficient. A new edifice will soon be built, in keeping with the new position in which the country finds itself. The main building is a large quadrangle, in which are the quarters of cadets, officers, dining-hall, library, and large hall for examinations.

In another building are the class-rooms, and quarters of the commandant and professors. The cadet quarters consist of sets of large rooms and bedrooms, each suite accommodating about fifteen cadets. Each bedroom contains two iron bedsteads, and a narrow table running down the centre of the room, holding a wash-basin for each occupant. In the sitting-rooms each cadet has a cupboard, a table, a chair, and small desk, which complete the furniture. The dining-room is capable of seating five hundred cadets, and is a handsome apartment. They take three regular meals a day in common—breakfast, like the soldiers', merely of soup and bread; dinner at midday, of soup, a small quantity of meat, and an abundance of vegetables; and a light supper just before bed-time. In addition, bread and butter are sometimes served out to each cadet for lunch. The pupils are seated at small tables, each accommodating about twelve. No beer nor wine is permitted within the school building, but coffee and fruit can be bought at a specified place.

The cadets of each suite of rooms usually have a piano and music. Reading and gymnastics are the usual amusements. The daily routine is as follows: the cadets rise at five in summer and six in winter, and, twenty minutes after, turn out for parade and breakfast; then follows half an hour of private study in rooms; then a short time of cleaning arms, dress, and accoutrements; after this, a parade and minute inspection, and then prayers, which all attend. From eight o'clock till one, except twenty minutes for lunch, all cadets are in the lecture-rooms. At one o'clock companies are formed, daily orders read, and they are then marched off to dinner. From this time until five o'clock, the more general duties of fencing, gymnastics, singing, and dancing are attended to, and from five until eight o'clock, strict attention is given to studies in rooms; then supper and recreation until nine o'clock, and taps at ten.

There are four short vacations in each year—in all, about two months. The distinguishing feature with regard to discipline is a system of conduct-classes. These are four in number, and are entirely independent of the classes for instruction. They seem to carry out the principle of demerit-marks as at West Point, but much more completely. On entering, a cadet is assigned to the third or censor class, and some limited indulgences are granted him. For good conduct he is promoted to the second class, with additional privileges, and, if exemplary, goes to the first, in which he enjoys indulgences of a very ample kind, and, in fact, nearly every thing a careful student could wish. The fourth class is reserved for those guilty of serious misconduct and immoral offenses, and is considered degrading. Any cadet found in it at the end of his course would be promoted to the ranks as a private soldier. It is not usual for more than three or four from each class to get in it. At the end of each quarter, the professors and captains of companies make reports, under the three heads of behavior, diligence, and progress, which are sent to the parents, and upon which are founded the arrangement of conduct-classes. The results of this system, tempered with the kindness and sympathy always exercised in these schools, have been found to be extremely satisfactory.

The course of study for all below the "selects" is the same as in the civil public schools, and in the higher class the same as at the war schools of ensigns. Dancing is required of all military scholars, not only as an accomplishment, but as a suitable gymnastic exercise. The class-rooms accommodate about thirty, which is as large a number as one instructor is supposed capable of serving. The cadets are arranged on parallel benches, with desks, and the lessons are heard both *viva voce* and from the blackboard. Punishments are inflicted strictly in accordance with prescribed law, and range from forfeiture of holiday to dismissal. Smoking is strictly prohibited, both within and without school; and any immorality or association with improper characters when on leave results in dismissal if discovered. No watches, rings, nor other jewelry are permitted to be worn, and the amount of pocket-money allowed never exceeds about two and a half thalers per month.

The most scrupulous neatness is required, and, when on leave, cadets must at all times appear with belts and gloves.

Discipline, though severe, is not harsh. The officers mix freely with the cadets, and take great interest in their welfare. Insubordination is hardly ever known, and would result in dismissal. This is due partially to the national trait of tractability, partly to the system of censor classes, and greatly to the effect it has upon the question whether the cadet shall enter the army as an officer or as a private soldier. When he leaves the school, a full report is made upon the conduct of each cadet during his course, and forwarded, to be filed with his regiment, as a sort of chart indicating his future. The cadet is not examined, on passing from the second to the first class. This promotion is determined by the reports on each cadet's diligence, abilities, and progress, and on a general estimate of the character of the men, rather than by any fixed value given the exercises. The rules for arriving at a conclusion upon this question are remarkably full and exact. At the end of one year, after being examined by the school board, the pupils, if found competent, are handed over to the military examining commission, who are in no way connected with the school, and are subjected to an examination precisely like that of an advantageur. Those who pass, except the fifty who go to the "select" class for two years more, are transferred at once to the army, with the rank of ensign, admitted on the nomination of a colonel, serve six months, and then go to the War School, as before described, as advantageurs. We are now done with the Cadet Schools, except for the "fifty," who, after two years, get their commissions from the king direct.

The principle of competition is very little employed in Prussian schools, though, to a limited extent, the best pupils are known as the heads of the classes to which they belong, and have some additional privileges and authority. Also in the select, a few of the superior pupils are mentioned in a general report to the king, and are usually appointed in the Guards. There seems to be little lost, however, as other means are employed to stimulate industry, and no amount of "cramming" at the end of the year avails a cadet; for if he has been idle during the term, he is not allowed to present himself for examination, which is equivalent to failure. Although no system of marks is employed, there is a very correct plan of estimating the work done, and the system of universal service is a powerful incentive to good conduct and industry, for failure invariably sends one to the ranks to serve out his term.

It can not have escaped attention that the plan of keeping the candidates for the army as long a time as possible at purely civil studies is a distinguishing feature of Prussian military education. There is a strong feeling of antagonism to these schools, from their alleged tendency to confine the mind to narrow grooves; and notwithstanding the purely non-professional character of instruction in them, it is claimed that deleterious effects arise from keeping boys from a tender age to manhood in a military atmosphere. Another objection raised to them is, that they assist to keep up the peculiar class feeling, so manifest in the Prussian army. There is also a tendency to take all the officers from the well-educated and higher classes, which is beginning to be felt by the people.

The education given at these schools is said to be inferior to that of the civil schools, but the advantage claimed is, that it maintains military *esprit du corps*. Good soldiers are not confined to the schools, but seem quite as apt to come up through the other system, Moltke being an example of the latter course. Commandants of regiments are decidedly in favor of the advantageur system, and say that so long a course of training exclusively in a military atmosphere hampers free development of character. No one recommends that all officers should be educated at the Cadet Schools.

The Prussian cadets wear nearly the same uniform as the soldiers, and are remarkably smart and neat in their ways. Their hair is kept short, but not cropped. They always wear short swords, and can be at once recognized by their trim appearance. They are generally younger than our cadets, and at the preparatory schools have many more privileges. It is not uncommon to see two or three rows of seats across the parquet of the opera-house filled with them. They are a grave set of boys, but unusually courteous. From the more lenient system, less mature age of the pupils, and many other causes, the proficiency of cadets, except "the select," is much less than at West Point.

WAR SCHOOLS.

The War Schools, where the advantageurs and cadets not of the select gain their military instruction, were formerly attached to army corps in the different territorial districts, but have recently been detached from them. There are at present seven schools, with about one hundred pupils each, and the eighth will soon be established. These may be considered the great military academies of Prussia. Before entering, a young man must have acquired a good civil education, and had some six months' military service in the ranks. They are generally considered ensign schools, though privates, corporals, and sergeants may attend. The military aspirant, on entering, is usually nineteen or twenty years of age. He must receive ten months' instruction, then pass the "Royal Officers' Board of Examiners," and be accepted by the officers of his regiment. He usually knows, before coming to this ordeal, whether he will be accepted, for should he fail in this, he would pass through life a marked man. There is a general Board, which prescribes the studies, and the course is uniform for all the schools. Each is directed by a field officer, assisted by an adjutant, who is also librarian, two instructors for tactics and administration, two for the science of arms, two for fortifications, two for surveying and drawing, six inspectors, who act like commandants of cadet companies with us, and six officers for instruction in riding, gymnastics, drill, and musketry.

No civilians are employed in connection with these schools. Officers appointed to these duties have not the privilege of declining, and receive about one-fifth addition to their regular pay. They are changed every five years. The yearly expense of each student, besides the regular army pay, is about one hundred and fifty thalers, and is borne by the Government. The buildings differ in their arrangements in all the schools, but their general administration is similar. The officers have a mess like that of a regiment, and the pupils a separate one, where breakfast and supper are taken at pleasure, but their presence is required at dinner. This mess is under the management of two officers and six of the senior pupils, and, like all soldiers' messes in Prussia, is supported from the daily pay. There is a reading-room, a library, and lecture-room, where from twenty to twenty-five receive instruction at a time; model-rooms, and quarters very plainly furnished, where from two to six students live together; a gymnasium, riding-school, and drill-ground.

The course of instruction usually commences in October, and comprises a very large number of subjects, commencing with tactics of all the arms, and is carried through the highest grade of manœuvres for battle, the history of tactics, the defense of places, the transport of troops and post duty—in fact, every thing that comes under the head of tactics. The course embraces the science of arms, their history and uses, every thing about the history, manufacture, and care of gunpowder, manufacture of artillery and small-arms, gun-carriages, artillery ammunition, the theory of projectiles, effects of rifling, sieges and siege-guns, breech-loading arms of all kinds, fortifications, topography, military drawing and surveying, construction of places, perspective projections, bird's-eye views, horizontal and vertical projections and profiles, military surveying, military regulations and duties of service, army organization, how to mobilize it, the administration of the army, comprising its staff, medical department, intendance and manufacturing departments; military law, courts-martial, general regulations, duties connected with the interior of a company, squadron, and regiment, and the whole subject of military correspondence and accountability. This gives but a partial idea of the extent of the course.

For instruction, each school is divided into four sections, and, on entering, each pupil is examined as to his general abilities, which is usually done by requiring essays on given subjects, and the sections are arranged from this test. The course is precisely alike for all the sections.

No books are used at lectures, and the professor is not allowed to read his lecture. The pupils are forbidden to use in their notes the phrases of the teacher, but are required to submit briefs in their own language. The system aims not to task the mind with the details of knowledge, but to cultivate a habit of native reflection. As a check, the quarterly examinations are held by other instructors than those who serve at the lectures. Great importance is attached to *viva voce* examinations, for cultivating readiness of resource and rapidity of judgment. As in all German educational institutions, but little attention is paid to the private application of students, so long as they are prepared at the lectures. Special instruction in tactics is given to the ensigns of the different arms of service in their respective arms, and swimming is taught to all.

The daily routine does not differ materially from that of the Cadet Schools—lectures leaving about three hours' free time each day. About ten days are spent in reconnoitring on horseback and making sketches, without instruments, of the country passed over. Great importance is attached to these sketches, which are not required to be highly finished.

Discipline is secured principally through the inspectors, who live in the buildings, and have their quarters among the pupils. One of these is on duty each week, and is always with the pupils, even taking his meals with them; visits their quarters during study hours, and observes their attendance at all duty. The best pupils are given certain authority for purposes of discipline, and are also reported to their regiments, and entitled to be commissioned to fill the first vacancies.

Games of hazard are strictly forbidden, and outside of the school pupils are required to conduct themselves in every way like officers, and would be punished for unofficer-like conduct. Plain clothes are never allowed. The greatest neatness of dress and person is required, and getting in debt or getting drunk entails dismissal from the school. At the end of each quarter, the professors, after examining the marks, give each pupil his proper credit for progress.

The strange custom of dueling with swords, common in all Germany, is sanctioned in the schools, but serious results seldom follow. A board of honor, as it is called, is formed to investigate all quarrels, and decide which party is wrong, and whether a duel shall be fought; after which the original aggressor is punished. The classes of punishment are parole punishments, deprivation of leaves of absence, open arrest in quarters, close arrest in quarters, confinement in the guard-house, and dismissal; but dismissal of an ensign from the school only carries him back to his regiment, with a warrant to begin over again at the War School the next year. While the ensigns are, like our West Point cadets, treated very much as common soldiers, they are at the same time carefully made to feel the high character they are preparing to assume. Their *esprit du corps*, which is strong, is in every way fostered and encouraged by the Government.

The examinations are carried on by the "Royal Officers' Examining Board," which is entirely disconnected with the schools. The officers of the academies determine from the quarterly reports whether the pupil shall be allowed to appear at all for examination; if not, he goes back to his regiment; but if permitted to appear, he is turned over to the Officers' Board, whose examination continues some four days, and who look mainly to positive knowledge of subjects, and general capacity. Each ensign then returns to his regiment, and the report is soon forwarded, announcing to his colonel the result. The steps by which his commission is afterward gained have already been explained. An ensign who fails is not again admitted to a war school, but, if he sees fit to qualify himself while serving with his regiment, may again appear for examination. If he again fails, a third trial is given only by the express authority of the king.

The special feature of entire lack of competition characterizes all the military schools of Prussia. It is even discouraged, as apt to prevent application to those branches for which there is special aptness; and the aggregate of study is believed to be greater without than with it. But the great objection is, that no competitive examination can be made a practical test for all qualities, personal, practical, and intellectual, which go to form military capacity. A stimulant to industry seems to exist in the fact that failure would retard entry into the army with an officer's commission, and might finally lead to service in the ranks.

The greatest satisfaction is felt in Prussia with the results of these schools, which have been greatly improved within the past few years.

ARTILLERY AND ENGINEERING SCHOOL.

The Artillery and Engineering School, situated in Berlin, is a technical school for young men who have gained their commission in the usual way, and has a course of two years. Its management is so similar to that of the war schools, as to require no detailed notice. The officers are permitted to quarter themselves wherever they please.

THE WAR ACADEMY.

The highest military school is the War Academy, for officers, situated at Berlin, and intended for one hundred pupils—officers who have served three years or more, and is open to candidates of requisite service who are successful at a competitive examination, and who bring from their respective colonels a certificate that they are perfectly acquainted with regimental duty, and have at all times shown themselves thoroughly practical officers, that they have a disposition for, and ability to profit by, a high scientific education, that their health promises long service, and that they possess strength of character and firmness, and are not in pecuniary difficulties.

At the examinations it is not sufficient that the officer shall show learning, but it must also appear that he has kept up his professional knowledge, and that he has general ability and intelligence enough to profit by the course at the academy. Preference is given to those who have distinguished themselves in the field, or who, from special qualifications, give greatest promise of usefulness, or whose more advanced age makes it undesirable that they should wait to a later day for admission. About two-thirds of the officers who enter here are from the advantageur class, and an intellectual superiority is said to exist in their case over those who come from the Cadet Schools. This is easy to account for, on the theory that brains are born with men, and not given to them afterward. The cadets are taken in childhood, without competition, and shoved through the schools, where the standard is not high enough to sift them, while the advantageurs are taken from the whole class of cultivated people, and are such boys as have shown capacity at the civil schools.

Our own military academy would gain in a similar way by leaving the places to competition among the youth of the districts, instead of subjecting them to Congressional patronage. The same very marked result was seen near the close of our war, when military commanders of discernment were untrammeled in selecting for promotion the bright men trained by the war itself, who had come up through all the grades.

The course is of three years, takes a wide range of subjects, and is intended to give to a few of the finest intellects the best possible general education, both liberal and technical. It carries with it no promise of promotion; but an officer has of course the advantage of the positive knowledge gained, which will always be in his favor, and will always make itself felt. Regimental commanders object to the school, as it takes officers from their regiments, but its general usefulness is highly commended.

OBSERVATIONS.

I have now gone hastily through the subject of military education in Prussia, and nothing is more striking than the connection between the military and civil education of the country. The competitive system in the schools is almost universally objected to, and mathematics are thought to be worthy of attention up to the highest grades only by those of peculiar aptness, on account of time lost by the others in this pursuit. There can be no doubt of the great merit and usefulness of the Academy, which gives a superior education to the first men of the army, who will afterward become generals and staff officers, while it is a suitable and most encouraging reward to those who show industry and ability. The greatest possible care is bestowed upon methods of study and instruction, and every thing is distinctly defined.

The most remarkable feature of the system is the attention paid to forming and disciplining the mind, and encouraging habits of reflection. The regulations repeatedly assert that the object of education is not acquisition of positive knowledge, but to develop the intellectual faculties, and cultivate powers of thought and reasoning. The education is eminently practical, and frequent visits are made to manufactories and other places where actual work is carried on. At least one foreign language must be spoken by a Prussian officer, although some latitude is allowed as to which one he will learn.

CHAPTER X.

FRENCH MILITARY SCHOOLS.—PLAN OF OFFICERING THE FRENCH ARMY.

THE theory of officering the French army is, that one-third shall be furnished from the ranks, one-third by imperial dictation, and the remaining third from military schools. There are required annually in the line about six hundred new commissions, one hundred and twenty-five in the artillery and engineers, and twenty-five in the staff. In practice, nearly or quite two-thirds come from the ranks—the largest proportion going to the line; while less than one-third of this class are found in the artillery and engineers, and every officer in the Staff Corps is carefully educated. Six months' service is required of a private before he may be a corporal; after six months more he may be a sergeant, and at least two years must elapse before he may be a sub-lieutenant. In the military schools one may arrive at the last-mentioned grade in two years. Promotion afterward is, in times of peace, made partially by seniority, and partially by choice; but, in time of war, entirely by choice. Unless in war, however, one must serve in each of the grades as follows: as sub-lieutenant, two years; as lieutenant, two years; as captain, four years; as major, three years; as lieutenant-colonel, two years. Very few, however, coming from the ranks ever get above the grade of captain, as all promotion above that grade is made by choice. A careful system of confidential reports is carried on in the French service, by which the character and capacity of officers are judged, and upon which, it is supposed, promotion is largely based. The principal military schools in France are—

First. The Polytechnic School in Paris, where a thorough civil education, largely mathematical, is given. All who enter the artillery and engineers from the schools take their degree here before entering the military school at Metz, and most of the young men who enter the civil service are educated here.

Second. The School of Application at Metz, for Artillery and Engineers.

Third. The Military School of Saint-Cyr, for infantry and cavalry.

Fourth. The Staff School at Paris, where a number of the graduates of Saint-Cyr are educated for staff duty.

Fifth. The Military School at La Flêche, for the civil education of the children of indigent officers and non-commissioned officers.

Besides these, there are two schools for military, surgical, and medical education, riding-schools, schools of musketry, of gymnastics, and regimental schools—all at a cost to the empire of about 5,000,000 francs annually. Although the state requires that educational expenses be defrayed by scholars who are pecuniarily able to do so, yet it liberally assists all others.

IMPERIAL POLYTECHNIC SCHOOL.

The Imperial Polytechnic School, situated in Paris, has always played an important part in the educational system of France. It is a purely preparatory school, nearly civil in its character (the students wearing a plain uniform), and is under the direction of the Minister of War. Admission to the school is determined by competitive examinations, held by a board which first sits in Paris, and then travels through France for this purpose.

Youths are admitted between the ages of sixteen and twenty, and non-commissioned officers and soldiers of the army between the ages of twenty and twenty-five. About one hundred and fifty in all are admitted each year, and two years completes the course. About one-third of the students are in receipt of Government aid; but excepting the enlisted men (soldiers and non-commissioned officers), who receive their regular army-pay, the students are not under pay from the state, and the annual expense of each is about 1000 francs.

On graduating, those already in the service as soldiers go into the army as officers. Of the remainder, about three-fifths enter the army through the Staff and Metz Schools. Those graduates who prefer to do so may decline service altogether, or enter it in a civil capacity. The school is organized into a battalion of four companies; and although it is not under the penal code of the army, the discipline and punishments have a military character.

Besides its military staff, the school has thirty-nine professors and teachers; its examinations are conducted by ten eminent scientific men not connected with the institution, and it is controlled by four separate Boards of Management—viz.: Board of Administration, Board of Discipline, Board of Instruction, and Board of Improvement. Its military staff consists of a commandant, who is a general officer; an assistant, who is a colonel or lieutenant-colonel; six captains and six adjutants, who are non-commissioned officers of the army. At the entrance examination, which is conducted by a board of five, appointed by the Minister of War, two members of the board precede the other three, and partially examine all candidates, rejecting those who are clearly incompetent, and giving to the others certificates entitling them to appear for a final examination a few days later.

The subjects for examination are chosen with reference to the civil instruction at the lyceums, or ordinary civil high schools of France, and comprise arithmetic, plane and solid geometry, algebra, plane and spherical trigonometry, analytical and descriptive geometry, mechanics, hydrostatics, electricity, magnetism and chemistry, and German and French composition.

A system of marking is adopted for estimating the comparative merits of the candidates, and, in fact, is used in all the French military schools, and does not differ essentially from the plan employed at West Point. The relative importance of each subject is expressed by a number called the coefficient of importance. A few foreigners are admitted to the school, but not as boarders in the institution.

I visited this school in 1867. It stands near the Pantheon, and consists of two main buildings for students and professors, and smaller detached ones for chemical and mechanical laboratories, library, fencing and billiard rooms. The basements of the main building are used as kitchens and dining-rooms, and the first floor for two great lecture-rooms for the students of the separate years. The lecture-rooms are amphitheatres. A student's name is attached to each seat, and at the foot is the platform, with the lecturer's desk, a blackboard, and a chair for one of the captains, who is always present at lecture to maintain order. On the first floor are also models, machines, and instruments required in the lectures.

The whole of the second floor is occupied by a series of smaller lecture-rooms, called halls of interrogation, to be described hereafter. The third floor is occupied by study-rooms—perhaps more properly living-rooms—where most of the studying and drawing is done, and the greater part of the students' time is passed. Some seven or eight occupy one of these rooms. A long corridor, in which there is always an officer on duty, separates the rooms into two rows. The fourth floor is used entirely for dormitories, and the arrangement of rooms is much like that of the third floor. Non-commissioned officers lodge at each end of the corridor, and in the middle also, to keep order.

The hours for daily labor are from six A.M. until two P.M., with half an hour for breakfast, and from five P.M. to nine P.M.; but much of the spare time from two till five is occupied by drill. Students rise at six o'clock; at half-past six attend roll-call, and then for two hours are occupied, under charge of officers, in preparing for the mathematical lecture of the day. They breakfast at half-past eight o'clock, and from nine to ten there is for each class a lecture given in one of the great halls, when every student must take notes. From ten to eleven each student is occupied in the study-halls in completing his notes, and is aided in comprehending the subject of the lecture by a number of assistant professors, who go about through the rooms for that purpose. The remaining time, from eleven till two P.M., is given to light subjects. A lithographed summary of the subject of the lecture is always furnished the students. At two o'clock they dine; and, unless there is drill, they are then free until five o'clock, when the evening work commences. Until nine o'clock the time is spent in the study-halls, under the eye of assistant professors, upon German, history, drawing, composition, and general study, with frequent examinations and help on the morning's lecture. At nine o'clock there is supper, at half-past nine roll-call, and at ten lights are out.

The method of instruction is peculiar. One principal professor of high ability and character is secured for each subject. He gives the principal lecture in a free, unburdened way to the entire class, and is assisted by a large corps of teachers, who go over his work afresh, explain and elucidate it in every way—"whip in," so to speak, the stragglers, and hurry up the loiterers. By repeated interrogations in the halls for this purpose, each student being taken separately almost daily, and constant hammering and spurring by this numerous corps of assistant teachers, who thus fulfill the duty of private tutors, nearly all are brought up to the standard of proficiency.

The whole system is one of enforced labor, and such a thing as private study is unknown, no provision being made for it. Every thing is done under the eye of an instructor, and of an officer who enforces obedience. A powerful aid is recognized in the stimulus of sharp rivalry. The performance of each day is marked, and this determines the final class-standing of pupils to a greater extent than do the examinations. The spirit of *camaraderie* is exceedingly strong at this school, and has much to do in giving it character.

The course of instruction extends over a period of nine months in each year, and is solely scientific—the only military element of the course being a short series of lectures, which have no influence in making up the yearly standing of the classes. Indeed, although a degree of the Polytechnic is necessary for entering certain branches of the army, and the institution itself is under the direction of the Minister of War, it might, with equal propriety, be under the Minister of the Interior.

The course for the two years is fixed. That of the first embraces differential and integral calculus, descriptive geometry, geometrical drawing, mechanics, physics—including heat and electricity—chemistry, astronomy, and geodesy, French composition and literature, history, German, and figure and landscape drawing. The second year's course of study includes integral calculus, stereotomy, mechanics (extended from the first year), physics (extended from the first year), chemistry (continued), architecture, and building roads, canals, and railways, French composition and literature, history, German, military art, topography, and drawing. Great attention is paid to mechanical drawing, and, in fact, to practical instruction of all kinds—such as exercises in topography, sketching, and visits to machinery and manufacturing establishments, where much of the course can be practically illustrated. The students are drilled in company and battalion, but riding and swimming are not taught. The term begins in November, and ends in August. About three months are occupied in examinations, and in special preparations for them.

The educational and disciplinary departments of the school are entirely separated, professors having only the power to report to the military staff for dereliction of duty. Instead of any want of respect being shown the civil branch of the school on this account, its importance is rather increased. The adjutants, who are non-commissioned officers of the army detailed for duty here, have much to do with the discipline, and can administer punishment.

A few of the best scholars are made non-commissioned officers in their companies, but attend only to the routine of duty, and have no control over their comrades. Liquors are prohibited, and smoking is permitted only at special times and places. Billiards are allowed, but not dice or cards. The strictest surveillance is exercised over the pupils while in school, and exemplary conduct required when out of it. It has, however, been found impracticable to have much control over students out of school, although they are directed to wear their uniforms, and it is made the duty of all officers to arrest them for cause. Two officers are sent into the city as monitors whenever the pupils have leave to visit it. No books, magazines, or newspapers are allowed, not even such as bear upon the subjects of study.

Marks are given for good conduct, but they have no bearing upon final standing. Examinations are carried on by a board having no connection with the school, and who are not permitted to know any thing of the marks which the pupils have received. Not more than two per cent. fail to pass the examinations. On taking their degrees, the cadets have choice of service according to their place on the merit-roll, and those entitled to priority always select civil service, except in time of war. Here seems to be one of the great causes of the marked success of this school, as the large choice of honorable careers excites the keenest competition for the first places. The Director of Studies wisely says, that no institution, although it may imitate the details of the Polytechnic ever so closely, can secure similar results, unless it holds out similar inducements to its pupils. The remarkable success of our own military academy as an institution of learning is due very largely to the same cause. On leaving, those students who choose the military service receive the commission of sub-lieutenants, and enter the schools of special application. There seems to be a wide difference of opinion among the best men of France regarding the course of education at the Polytechnic, many urging that so exclusive a mathematical course makes men unpractical. The larger number, however, seem to think it the best possible foundation for the subsequent course at Metz and the Staff School, as it draws a higher order of talent than a more military course would do, is more liberalizing than a special training, and creates an intimacy between the civil and military branches of Government which is afterward exceedingly desirable.

It may not be unworthy of notice, that in France, which is believed to be the first military nation of the world, the best talent seeks civil pursuits, "showing," in the words of a Frenchman of ability, "that the military profession is not their natural vocation."

SCHOOL OF APPLICATION FOR ARTILLERY AND ENGINEERING AT METZ.

The School of Application for the Artillery and Engineers at Metz claims attention, as perhaps next in importance to the Polytechnic. The school was founded at Douay, by Louis XIV., in 1679, for the artillery alone, while the engineers had their own school at Mézières, a town of some importance, six miles from Sedan. Both schools passed through many vicissitudes and removals until 1802, when the two were combined at Metz, and have there been united ever since. Students destined for the army, on leaving the Polytechnic, after taking three months' leave from August to November, join the school at Metz as sub-lieutenants of artillery or engineers, and, having so chosen their arm of service, do not change it, although they go on in the same classes, and follow nearly the same course of study. Most of the students come from the Polytechnic, and are not examined for admission. A few officers of artillery and engineers, who have been promoted from the ranks, also enter the school. The course is two years in length, and is very full. On graduating, the students are commissioned as second lieutenants in their regiments, and for the purpose of decorations, retirement, and so forth, the two years at Metz count for four of ordinary service. The number of admissions each year is regulated by the wants of the service, but the average is about eighty.

The school occupies buildings erected on the site of a suppressed Benedictine monastery, and formed, in part, of the old ecclesiastical structure. Three sides of the cloistered monastic quadrangle are devoted to lecture-rooms, galleries, and halls of study. The fourth, formerly a church, is converted into the hall for manœuvres. Detached buildings form quarters for the students and officers of the school. The museums, laboratories, and instrument-room are very full and valuable. There is quite an extensive library to which students are admitted at certain hours of the day. The rooms in the barracks are grouped so that twenty are entered by a single stair-way, and one servant provides attendance for all who live on his stairway. There are usually two students in each room. They mess in the town at the various restaurants, where their food is regularly contracted for by the authorities of the school. There are no amusements furnished by the school, but students have considerable liberty in town.

The school is presided over by a commandant, who is a brigadier-general. He is assisted by one colonel, two majors, eight captains as military staff, eighteen officers of the army, and two civilians as instructors. The general control is under the management of several boards and councils. The whole annual cost is about 500,000 francs—more than half being for pay of students, who are all officers of the army. The course of study embraces artillery, fortification, military art, military legislation and administration, military topography and field-sketching, geodesy and trigonometrical surveying, physical science, applied mechanics and machinery, architectural construction, German, veterinary science, riding, drill, swimming, dancing, and photography. About two-thirds of the course is common to both arms of the service.

Considerable time is devoted to practical surveying and field-sketching, and many establishments of a military character are visited; but the construction of batteries and fortifications, except the tracing and profiling, is entirely theoretical, and the application of electricity to telegraphy is imperfectly taught. The subject of military bridges of all kinds is thoroughly studied. Careful instruction is given the students of both arms in drill, riding, and fencing. The officer acquires much of the practical part of his profession after he joins his regiment, but such exercises as may be sanitary in their character are regularly taught in the school.

The plan of delivering lectures to the entire class, who then go over and finish the subject in study-rooms, is followed here, as at all French schools. No text-books are used, but the school library is much frequented. Frequent examinations are held by the instructors, but the pupils are always notified when to expect them. In the daily routine, eight hours of study and attendance at the lecture-room are required, besides drill, riding, and fencing; but as these do not come every day, there is considerable free time. There is one vacation of three weeks during the three years. More freedom is allowed here than in any of the public schools of France. Excepting the manual exercises, the daily duties end at three P.M., when the students are permitted to go in town, and are generally treated as officers. Private study is expected, and provision to a small extent is made for it. Not much more is done, however, than the accomplishing of allotted tasks. The students' evenings are usually spent in the cafés and theatres of the town. As officers of the army, they are subject to military law, and it is not only the right, but the duty of every teacher to enforce military authority in cases of irregular conduct.

At all lectures an officer is present to require order, and the field officers on duty take weekly details as officers in charge, and, for the time being, severally become responsible for discipline. An officer is always on duty at the theatres, and considerable surveillance is exercised over the students when in town. Formerly the limits extended only two miles each way from the town; but the completion of railroads has given great facilities for going long distances, and provided a student is not absent from duty, no notice is taken of the extent of his excursions. There seems to be little or no moral control over the students. There is no chaplain, and it is not obligatory to attend religious service on Sunday. Marks are given to represent progress in all the studies. Conduct-marks are an important feature, and have a value of about one-sixth of all the marks given. They are awarded for general behavior, gentleman-like conduct, smartness, and military aptitude. Idleness, or neglect of any of the subjects of study, is followed by arrest; but no one is ever dismissed for it, or fails in his examination if he comes up to the low minimum of marks required during the course, or if he by his general proficiency impresses the Examining Board favorably. More weight is given to this general test than to the answering of special questions.

Examinations take place at the end of each year, and are thorough, yet few students are ever dismissed for inefficiency. They are either permitted to pass, or are reported to the Minister of War, with the recommendation that they be allowed to remain another year. If they then fail, they are dismissed; but this number never exceeds two per cent. The dismissal, however, seems to exclude them only from their chosen arm of the service, as they eventually get commissions in the cavalry and infantry. This, as might be expected, prevents actual competition, as the only incentive to stand well is the choice of regiments, and the seniority of rank that it gives. The class-list is very much changed, on leaving Metz, from what it was in coming from the Polytechnic, as practical sense is preferred to mere acquisitiveness.

Each of the regiments of artillery and engineers has a school where army officers, after joining, continue for one or two years the more practical parts of their professional studies, the real purpose being to instruct non-commissioned officers in actual construction. But in both arms several years of service with the regiment are required before any officer can be detached.

MILITARY SCHOOL OF SAINT-CYR, FOR CAVALRY AND INFANTRY.

The special Military School of Saint-Cyr, for the education of young men for the cavalry, infantry, and marines, is situated three miles west of Versailles. The first school of this nature in France was founded in 1759, and after being twice suppressed, frequently moved, and at times reduced to a camp of instruction, was in 1808 transferred to Saint-Cyr, where it has been successfully maintained ever since. The course of study occupies two years, and three hundred students enter each year. The institution is open to all, and is reached through competitive examinations, held throughout the country, upon the subjects taught in the schools of France. Although the payment of tuition is generally required, it is wholly or in part dispensed with in the case of pupils of insufficient means.

Saint-Cyr was originally founded for the sons of the *noblesse*, but gradually lost that character, until for many years the nobility would not send their sons there; but of late this feeling has died out, and now a socially higher class of young men are found at Saint-Cyr than at the Polytechnic. An effort was made at one time to make this exclusively a school for young officers promoted from the ranks, but it was believed impracticable, as such a plan would reduce the social character of the army by keeping out the well-born. There has been a tendency of late to give the course of instruction a more literary character, by endeavoring to elevate the taste, and cultivate polite accomplishments, such as music, singing, dancing, and modern languages.

Pupils appearing for examination must be between seventeen and twenty years of age, and must be graduates of some one of the French lycées. These examinations are conducted very much as they are at the Polytechnic. The subjects are — arithmetic, algebra, geometry (plane, solid, and descriptive), trigonometry, mechanics, physical science, physical and political geography, history, Latin, French composition, drawing, and modern languages—the students having the choice of nearly all the principal languages. The marks given, and co-efficients of importance for each subject, are about the same as at the Polytechnic. Non-commissioned officers between the ages of twenty and twenty-five years may enter, and a few foreigners are nearly always in attendance. Several of our own countrymen, officers of the army, after graduating at West Point, have gone to Saint-Cyr; but this was many years ago, before our academy had been brought up to its present state of thoroughness. It is doubtful if graduates from either of our national schools would now care to spend time at any of the preparatory schools abroad. The practical course might be found advantageous. The number who gain admission each year from the army is about twenty-five, but they are for the most part young men who have failed at an earlier age to enter direct, so that the real intention of the privilege is defeated. The same is true in our own service. Many who desired to join the army as officers, or who have failed to enter it from West Point, have enlisted, to gain commission through the channel for the promotion of non-commissioned officers. In fact, the entire system of officering an army from the ranks can be easily shown to be vicious, as it either becomes perverted to the advantage of those who wish to become officers, or debases the army itself. So well is this understood in Prussia, that the evil of the system is admitted, and the few officers promoted for gallantry in the war of '66 have been transferred to the civil service, in deference to the sentiment of the army.

The school is organized into a battalion of eight companies, each commanded by a lieutenant, and each two companies by a captain. To each company is attached an adjutant, who is a non-commissioned officer of the army, and has authority in matters of discipline.

The cadets, for that is their rank at this school, are divided between the cavalry and infantry, and are separated entirely for matters of drill. In every thing else, their course is the same. The school is under the charge of a brigadier-general, who is assisted by a lieutenant-colonel, two majors, six captains, seventeen lieutenants, three directors of studies, and seventeen professors and assistants. There are also seventy non-commissioned officers and soldiers, and one hundred and forty civil employés, as servants, instructors in fencing, gymnastics, artillery practice, and for taking care of the horses of the establishment used for instruction of cadets in riding and cavalry drill. The whole annual expense of the school is 1,300,000 francs, of which about one-half is paid by the cadets.

When I visited the school in October, the cadets had all been commissioned in the French army, and the buildings were used for a German hospital. I found, however, Major Duparq, the director of studies, who showed and explained the entire school to me with the utmost courtesy. The main building, which is three stories high, is a long parallelogram, divided into four courts, each about one hundred feet square, named Rivoli, Austerlitz, Marengo, and Wagram. It was originally built by Madame de Maintenon, for educating the daughters of the poor noblesse. It is of rough stone, stuccoed, and, although in good repair, looks rusty, and has not a trace of architectural beauty. On the north of it are a riding-school, gymnasium, parade-ground, stabling and yards for about four hundred horses, barracks for the men who attend them, artillery practice-grounds, and, as everywhere in France, extensive flower-gardens of great beauty. Beyond is seen the picturesque forest of Versailles.

In entering the building, you find on the first floor dining-rooms, kitchen, museums, model-rooms, and wash-rooms. The kitchens are very complete, with immense copper kettles for coffee, and soup, and vegetables. The bill of fare, as stated to me, was simple enough—meat, soup thickened with vegetables, coffee, bread and butter. At dinner, at twelve M., a bottle of wine is allowed among five cadets. The dining-rooms are neat, with short marble-topped tables on either side. In the museum and model-rooms, which are not extensive, but choice, I found many of the models, charts, and cuts, the copies of which I had studied so hard at West Point eighteen years before, and I could hardly take a step without seeing some plan, sketch, or method that carried me back to my own cadet life. The wash-room was certainly unique. It was nothing but a long stone trough, waist high. Above it, and about eighteen inches apart, were zinc faucets to let on the water. To this the young men are marched, or go themselves, and all wash in a common trough. There seemed to be no provision for bathing.

On the second floor are found the large lecture-rooms, one for each class—furnished with seats without backs, and no desks. No officer is necessary here to preserve order, for cadet officers, as at West Point, are given authority in matters of discipline, and held responsible for its maintenance. The system of lectures to large classes is employed. There are no facilities for private study, and none is expected. No text-books are used, and the library, which contains 24,000 volumes, many of which are rare and valuable, is allowed to be visited by only thirty cadets a day.

In the third story are the dormitories, which are nothing more than ordinary barrack-rooms. The entire furniture of these rooms consists of two long lines of iron bedsteads, thirty in each row, head to head, and with a gun-rack at the foot of each; over the head a deep shelf, and near the bed a small box or locker. Above the barrack-rooms are store-rooms, and a great number of prison-rooms, which seem to have been well used. Besides the two large lecture-rooms, there are four study-rooms, where the students are marched after the lecture. Here, under the direction of assistant professors, they complete their notes, and in these rooms all their work is done. Adjoining the study-rooms are small libraries of works bearing upon the subjects studied, but they appear to be mainly for the use of the professors. Great importance seems to be attached to cavalry, and there are four hundred horses kept for purposes of cadet instruction. A vacation and furlough of two months is given in summer, besides a few days at Christmas and Easter.

The daily routine begins at five A.M., and the entire day till nearly nine P.M., with proper hours for meals, and short intervals of free time, is devoted to work. There is a lecture in the morning, and the afternoon is usually spent in the lighter duties—one hour and a half in drawing, and the remainder out-of-doors.

The cadets are required, on Sundays, to attend religious service, which is provided both for Catholics and Protestants. In discipline, the battalion is managed in every way like a regiment, the non-commissioned officers being taken from the cadets themselves. The exact extent of authority and limit of punishment which every officer, professor, and non-commissioned officer can exercise and inflict is specified by law, the punishment ranging from two days' drill—the limit of a corporal's power—to thirty days' close arrest by the commandant. The fear of dismissal is, however, a wholesome check, as in that event the cadet, who has agreed to serve the state for seven years, must spend the remainder of his term in the ranks.

The closest surveillance is at all times exercised over the pupils. They are not permitted to converse aloud in the school-building, even out of study-hours. All the doors have glass windows from the hall, where an officer, always on duty, can see all within. Where the halls, following the form of the rectangular courts, cross each other, there are stations, with seats and tables, for the officer or non-commissioned officer on duty. Frequent night inspections are made in the dormitories, where the utmost quiet is maintained. Foreigners attending the school enter into no contract to serve the state, and, on the first infraction of the rules, are quietly dismissed. The treatment of cadets differs very little from that of private soldiers, and their uniform is very similar to that of the French infantry. They are allowed very little liberty; their food is of the plainest kind; they are forbidden to read newspapers, and have scarcely any thing in the way of recreation; nor would there be time, were there the opportunity. There is no privacy in domestic arrangements, a complete absence of luxury, and the life is not at all different from that of the ordinary barrack.

The course of study is designed to apply in the second year what has been studied in the first year, or, more properly, the first year is devoted to completing a good education, and the second to making the officers. It is regretted by the authorities that both years can not be devoted to military subjects, but the very imperfect condition of French education makes the present arrangement imperative. The course is largely literary, and but little mathematical, differing radically, in this respect, from the Polytechnic. A knowledge of mathematics is taken for granted, and only a short review of the practical portions, such as logarithms, mensuration, etc., is now required. There is a strong inclination to abandon even this. The pupils have the choice of studying either English or German, but must take one of the two. The first year's course comprises descriptive geometry, physics, geography and statistics, general literature, modern history, German or English, the theory of drill, and drawing. That of the second year includes topography, fortification, artillery, military art, military legislation and administration, military hygiene, German and English, theory of drill, and drawing. The cadets of each arm are instructed only in the drill and theory of their own arm, but the infantry cadets are taught riding. Artillery students are taught only the service of the piece, and learn nothing of manœuvre. Fencing and gymnastics are taught, but not swimming. A good deal of attention is given to practical field-work, and all the cavalry cadets, and those of the infantry who can ride well are required, while mounted, to make sketches and reconnaissances of roads and surrounding country.

About five-sixths of the students choose the study of German instead of English, but many more speak English than German. The reason of this is, that the better portion of the French people cause English to be taught their children in infancy.

The examinations are held by an examining jury, appointed by the Minister of War, who are entirely disconnected with the school. In the first year's examination, and in that alone, they are assisted by the professors. The first twenty-five or thirty of the class are said to evince ability, and pass good examinations; then come a hundred who pass fairly, after which there is a remarkable falling off. All but eight or ten in each class usually pass, and such of these as maintain a good moral character are permitted to go on in the school for another year. About forty of those who graduate highest are permitted to compete each year for half the number of places in the Staff School, and this is about the only source of competition. The industry of the pupils is indifferent—the thirty or forty who graduate well being men who, from natural character, would stand high in any school.

Saint-Cyr furnishes the great majority of the officers of the staff of the army, and about one-third of the officers of the line, the other two-thirds coming from the ranks. There is a wide difference of opinion in France as to the usefulness of officers who are educated here, as they are apt to resign. Those who remain in the service get rapid promotion. While in the lower grades two-thirds have risen from the ranks, it will be found that among the field officers about the same proportion are graduates of Saint-Cyr.

The old French idea of promotion from the ranks, growing out of the great success of the first Napoleon, who adopted it, seems to be prevalent throughout their whole military system. A sufficient number of officers are educated to keep up the scientific element of the profession, while the bait of promotion is held out to those in the ranks. Any one who carefully watches the workings of this plan can not fail to observe its debasing effect upon the army. It is an attempt to make a quart out of a pint —something out of nothing. Before such a system can be successful, the people must be elevated, or there must be universal service, which necessarily brings ability into the army. The Prussians, who have done both, and who successfully base their system of officering their army upon the best education of the nation, have given the most exalted character to their army, and at the same time encouraged civil education.

STAFF SCHOOL OF APPLICATION.

The Staff School of Application, which is situated in Paris, and is intended for the training of young officers especially for staff duty, next claims attention. The Staff Corps in time of peace contains thirty-five colonels, thirty-five lieutenant-colonels, one hundred and ten majors, three hundred captains, and one hundred lieutenants. Practically, all are educated here. Occasionally officers from the line may exchange into the staff by passing the final examination at the Staff School, and considerable advantage is gained in the way of promotion by those who, upon attaining the rank of captain in the staff, which usually requires about three years to accomplish, then exchange into the line. Examples of this class include generals Trochu and M'Mahon. The Staff Corps is the most aristocratic in the army, and considerable feeling exists against it. The career is chosen early in life, and by many who, however talented, fail entirely to develop practical aptitude, so that inefficient officers are always found in the corps; and it is thought by the best men in the army that these duties could be better performed by officers chosen for proved ability after a few years' service with their regiments. The superiority of the Prussian system, which embodies the latter principle, can not be questioned.

The Staff School, established in 1818, has a two years' course, and about twenty-five enter each year. The number of vacancies varies somewhat from year to year, with the casualties in the Staff Corps. The number is made up by giving places to two or three students of the Polytechnic, who are put, without examination, at the head of the list. Of the remainder, double the number required are taken from the graduates at Saint-Cyr, and an equal number of young lieutenants promoted from the ranks, if they will present themselves, all of whom are examined competitively. It is not unusual, however, for not more than eight or ten officers from the ranks to present themselves at the examination, and then not more than two are generally successful.

Many important modifications are being made in this school. In addition to a fixed number who graduate at once into the Staff Corps, an equal number of the highest upon the class-lists at Saint-Cyr will be educated here, and attached for two years to a regiment, in an arm of the service different from that to which they belong. Then they will join their proper arm and regiment, and be liable to detail for staff duty at all times, while they add to the professional knowledge of their regiment, and in time of war will be available to expand the regular staff establishment.

The programme of studies is wide, and is principally military, and of a practical character. A great deal of labor is done out-of-doors in sketching and drawing. Great attention is given to riding, and the German language is thoroughly taught. The use of instruments is also acquired, and practical exercises of all kinds are a prominent feature of the course. Mathematics are not studied. The system of lectures to the entire class is employed with scarcely any text-books, excepting a hand-book of staff duty—a kind of guide to staff officers. The students are all commissioned as officers on joining the school, which is presided over by a brigadier-general, assisted by a corps of twenty-one professors. On graduating, which few fail to do, the pupils are at once given the rank of first lieutenant. Here, as at Metz, many who graduate high at the Polytechnic and Saint-Cyr, find themselves near the foot at the close of the course.

As positions are already secured, there is very little competition, and only enough application to pass the examinations. The graduates, although officers of the staff, are required to serve two years each with the cavalry and infantry, and one year with the artillery. They are then given the rank of captain, and duty in their own corps, and, while captains, are required each year to furnish a certain number of topographical drawings and military reports of surveyed country, which are submitted to the War Office.

LA FLÈCHE.

The only remaining military school of much importance in France is La Flêche, which is the last of a large number formerly established for the diffusion of military education among the youth of France. The others were suppressed, on the just ground that a purely technical education was not, upon the whole, advantageous to youth; and this one is retained, to give a purely civil education to the orphan sons of officers and non-commissioned officers, and to those disabled in service who are unable to educate themselves. Four hundred pupils are educated here annually, and are admitted from the age of ten until nineteen. No examinations are held, save to determine what class the candidates for admission shall enter, and no student can remain after he is nineteen years old. Three hundred are gratuitous pupils, and the remainder pay one hundred and twenty dollars a year, admittance in each case being based entirely upon service-claims. The school has a military organization and discipline, is under a brigadier-general, and has a full corps of professors, who are mostly civilians. On graduating, the pupils may enter the military service through the regular school at Saint-Cyr, or remain in civil life, as they elect.

OBSERVATIONS.

It will be seen that in France the military schools do not, as in Prussia, form a distinct department, but are under the Minister of War, and also that only about one-third of the officers of the army are, of necessity, educated men, while in Prussia all must be so. It will be also noticed, that at the French schools there is almost a total absence of moral control, while in Prussia the opposite is true.

The great lack of a good preparatory education is loudly complained of in France, and most of the first year in all the military schools is required to make up for this deficiency. The almost total neglect of mathematical subjects at all the special schools is very noticeable. The course at the Polytechnic is general, and the exact sciences enter into it largely. The great attention given everywhere to drawing, and all practical subjects of a military character, is very striking. The idea seems to be to take the French mind as it is, and adorn it, rather than, by a careful course of exact study, to improve it. There is, in fact, a disposition to diminish the already moderate mathematical element in the military education, and to increase the literary studies. In the French system, the entire school course is given before service is seen, while in Prussia a certain amount of actual service must precede any theoretical course at the schools; nor is there in France, as in Prussia, any provision for recognizing, utilizing, and educating the talent of young men who have, by a few years' service, developed mental superiority.

It may not be amiss to compare these schools, in a few particulars, with our own at West Point. The Prussian system, which makes service universal, and in the highest degree respectable—even aristocratic—is enabled to secure the best possible officers without entire dependence upon exact school instruction; but in France we find, as with us, a partially voluntary military system, an attempt to make officers without previous training, and schools where the state endeavors to keep up the science of the profession by educating a portion of its officers.

The distinctive differences between the French and American systems are, that in France study and instruction are forced, under constant surveillance, and carried on in the lecture-room with very little use of text-books, while ours is almost entirely a course of voluntary private study of text-books, the recitation and blackboard being merely to test the students' actual progress in knowledge. Theirs is largely a practical course, including some literature, and very little mathematics; ours is largely mathematical, with about the same amount of literary study, and much less attention to drawing, with a practical course less extended in some respects, but vastly more general and thorough in others. While French students are but slightly educated in tactics and drill, except in their own arm, and the infantry and cavalry receive but a two years' course, and the standard of proficiency is so low that ninety-five per cent. graduate, our own school gives a thorough four years' course of civil education, embracing the whole range of exact sciences, makes each cadet proficient in every branch of service, and sets the standard of study so high that but thirty-three per cent. of the cadets can reach it. Theirs is little else than barrack life, and it is doubtful if this system can develop personal character of that high order sought at West Point, where each cadet is made to work out by himself, in his own way, his various tasks, while living like a gentleman in his separate room, paying great attention to neatness, the toilet, and the bath, and controlled through his own sense of uprightness and integrity, rather than by surveillance.

The school buildings nowhere approach the excellence, neatness, and appropriateness of our own, nor did the cadets, wherever I met them, show the trimness and manliness of those at West Point. These comparisons will apply pretty generally to the English military schools, so far as I have been able to understand them. They are all institutions of special courses, and do not undertake to give a complete military education in all the arms.

After seeing much of the best of the European armies, I believe that at the breaking out of our war our little regular army was officered by better technical soldiers than any army in the world, and this I believe to be due to West Point. There was much, however, in the academy that greatly impaired its usefulness. Although many graduates went with the South—the number is much less than is popularly supposed, only amounting to one-half of those from the South, and one-fifth of the whole number then in the army, while senators, members of the House of Representatives, judges of the Supreme Bench, and bureau officers went with their states *en masse*—I can see in this no argument against this school. Those who rebelled went with their section, in obedience to a general sentiment existing in the South, and not as a consequence of their West Point education. The reason why so large a proportion of our army officers seemed to espouse the Southern cause, is due to the fact that the War Department had for a long time been under exclusively Southern influences, and the prominent, desirable places were held by Southern men. The great trouble was, that the army had become exclusive, and separated from the sympathies of the people. General Scott himself had forgotten that the true purpose of West Point education was to leaven our volunteer forces, and was often heard to utter the absurdity, that the regular army, then ten thousand strong, must be kept intact, to fall back upon in case the volunteers failed. The adjutant-general of the army interposed all possible obstacles to the regular officers serving with volunteer troops, while the officers themselves were often open in their denunciation of volunteers, and did not see that, good or bad, the volunteers were all that we had; and that if not good, it was our duty to make them so. Many captains preferred to remain with their companies rather than take a volunteer regiment. Such a spirit is fatal to military enterprise. The volunteers were of ourselves—no better, and no worse; and if we excelled them in any particulars, it was only by reason of the superior advantages of a West Point education, graciously given us by the country. The faith in West Point officers was greatly shaken by these causes, and those of us who took volunteer commands had much to contend against; were looked upon with distrust by many, and faintly supported by our friends, while our honest efforts to secure discipline were viewed as absurd martinetisms. Before opportunity occurred to prove capability and good intention in the actual business of war, many were displeased by this feeling, and returned to their companies. Could our army be brought so nearly in accord with the people as to dissipate any apparent social antagonism, I believe that our officers would hold the same elevated place they have done heretofore among the military establishments of the world, and be loved and respected at home. Cadets, while clinging firmly to the high *esprit* which has always distinguished them, should endeavor to appreciate more truly their relations to and dependence upon civil society, and cease to look upon civilians with contempt. The expression "d—d cit" was an academical household phrase during my time at West Point. A large class of our officers, made up from the staff corps of the regular army, from which the higher general officers of the Army of the Potomac were principally drawn, forgot also that they were the servants of the people, and acted upon the theory that in their high places they were the masters—a legitimate conclusion from the foregoing sentiment. Those officers were, scientifically, the best men we had, and ought to have given us the best service; but they were unavailable, and the country found it necessary to relieve them of their commands. What I have described has always been, and still is, a strong argument against West Point, not as a technical training-school for officers, but on account of its effect upon them as citizens; and unless the cadets themselves will see and avert this danger, it may sooner or later destroy our military academy.

CHAPTER XI.

GERMAN CIVIL SCHOOLS.

I APPROACH this subject with diffidence, as my limited time in Germany deprived me of the opportunity of personal observation, and obliged me to gather much information at second-hand. The British Government Commissioners' reports are the latest and best authority. The Rev. Mark Pattison, of Lincoln College, Oxford, who was sent out as commissioner in 1861, has written an able and instructive pamphlet upon elementary education in Germany; but the fact that he has viewed the whole subject from the high Anglican point of view, has somewhat biased his report. Mr. Matthew Arnold, also, in 1868, published a brochure, called "The Schools and Universities of the Continent," of great value from its research, and liberal and comprehensive views. Mr. J. Kay, M.A., an English philanthropist, in 1850, published, in two volumes, a work entitled "The Social Condition and Education of the People," which goes deeply into German social and school life. In the summer of 1831, M. Victor Cousin was sent by the Ministry of Education of France on a tour of inspection in Germany. Nearly one-half of M. Cousin's report is occupied with Prussia, and he is to-day considered the best authority upon German primary education; but his account was mostly taken from a scheme of Von Altenstein, the educational minister of that time, which never became a law, and remains to this day in the archives of the Minister of Education in Berlin. In fact, Prussia has no written general law upon education, and never has had.

Our own country has furnished the best accounts of German education. In 1837, Dr. Alexander Dallas Bache, LL.D., then director of Girard College, was commissioned by that institution to make an educational tour in Europe, which occupied two years. His report was published in 1839, and covered six hundred pages. It treated the whole subject of education, including even reformatory, industrial, and hospital instruction, and is careful and correct. In 1843, Mr. Horace Mann, then Secretary of the Board of Education of Massachusetts, made a school tour in Europe at his own expense, and published a short account of the same in his next annual report. His report, although general, was just and accurate, and was republished in Europe, where it was considered the best authority upon the subject. With the exception of the report of a French commissioner sent out by his Government in 1854, these are about all the valuable publications upon educational matters, and some of them are too special, and others too general, to be of much service.

It is the general impression in our country that the schools of the several states of Germany originated in, and are maintained by, the arbitrary will of their Governments, without regard to the wishes of the people. Nothing could be more erroneous than this impression. The history of education in Germany is a part of the national history, and the schools are a genuine offshoot and part of national life, strongly rooted in the soil, and maintain a wonderful uniformity throughout all German Europe, with perhaps the best development in German Switzerland and Holland. Various antagonistic influences operate upon the schools—the ecclesiastical against the secular, and the central against local authority; but all unite in a common purpose for the improvement and perpetuation of education; and while each has in turn held superior control, and introduced new theories and methods, they have all left behind a portion of good.

NORTH GERMAN EDUCATION GROUNDED IN THE REFORMATION.

The present educational sentiment in Germany dates from the Reformation. With the exception of Luther, the great reformers of Germany were distinguished friends of classical learning, while the Romish party was hostile to culture. The leading intellect of the nation began to work eagerly together through the schools, to elevate and enlighten the masses. From that to the present day the first and highest purpose of German statesmanship has been to educate the people. About the middle of the last century the schools flagged, and seemed fast becoming mere torpid Church appendages. The school-masters were theological students, who made a trade of teaching until they could get a parish. At this epoch, Frederick the Great, whose civil projects and labors were not less remarkable than his military exploits, called to his service, in 1773, the renowned Frederick Augustus Wolf, and installed him in the University of Halle. This was the beginning of a new era, and laid the foundation of the classical scholarship of Germany.

PRIMARY EDUCATION.

The German schools are better in the Northern than the Southern States, in Protestant than in Catholic communities. In Austria, although the system is not wanting, education lacks the power and influence which characterizes it in Prussia. The following remarks relate to the Prussian system. In the absence of any organic school law like that of France, the public control of schools is exercised through administrative orders and instructions. It has for its basis the following articles, promulgated in 1794:

"Schools and universities are state institutions, having for their object the instruction of youth in useful information and scientific knowledge.

"Such establishments are to be instituted only with the previous knowledge and consent of the state.

"All public schools and public establishments of education are under the supervision of the state, and must at all times submit themselves to its examinations and inspections.

"Whenever the appointment is not, by virtue of the foundation or by special privilege, vested in certain persons or corporations, it belongs to the state.

"Even when the immediate supervision of such schools and the appointment of teachers is committed to certain private persons or corporations, new teachers can not be appointed, and important changes in the constitution and teaching of the school can not be adopted, without the previous knowledge and consent of the provincial school authorities.

"The teachers in the Gymnasia and other higher schools have the character of state functionaries."

In the Prussian Constitution of 1850 is the following provision:

"Every one is free to impart knowledge, and to found and conduct establishments for instruction, when he has proved to the satisfaction of the proper state authorities that he has the moral, scientific, and technical qualifications which are requisite. All public and private establishments are under the supervision of authorities named by the state."

With these principles as a basis, administrative control can be exercised without much difficulty. The foregoing regulations may be said to form part of the common law of Prussia, for they belong to every citizen's notion of what is right and fitting in school concerns. It is a mistake to suppose that the Prussian Government exercises a grasping and centralizing spirit in dealing with education. On the contrary, it makes the local administration as complete as possible, while taking care that education shall not be left to accident and caprice.

The state has always been an important school patron, and has always exercised its rights of patronage. Royal foundations are very numerous in Prussia, and in all Prussian schools of royal foundation the patronage remains vested in the crown to this day. This gives security to a large number of excellent schools. The control of schools for a long time resided in a ministerial body, to whom the affairs of both school and Church were intrusted; but in the great movement of civil and military reconstruction in Prussia under the Stein ministry, after her humiliation by Napoleon, the School Board was abolished, and an educational department created, at the head of which was Wilhelm von Humboldt. He held this position but two years, and was succeeded by Von Altenstein. Humboldt, however, may be considered as the inaugurator of the modern order of schools in Germany. His first recorded words upon the subject are: "The thing is, not to let the schools and universities go on in a drowsy and impotent way of routine, but to raise the culture of the nation ever higher and higher by their means." And this may be taken as the motto of his administration of public instruction.

Humboldt had associated with him two technical counselors. This number has since been increased to eight. The Minister of Education and the Under-Secretary of State for the Educational Department exercise the entire central authority over school affairs. In Prussia it is not the central minister who takes the most direct and important action, but rather the local authorities representing the crown.

By a principle of the Lutheran Church, the crown was its supreme head; and as the sovereign nominated the consistories, who acted in matters pertaining to schools as well as church, he was actually at the head of school matters. This, however, was not true of Catholic schools, as his authority extended only over the Protestant Church. To remedy this, at the period of reorganization already referred to, a board of directors of public instruction was appointed in each government district. These boards act for the crown, are in immediate relation with the central ministry, and are, in fact, the local school authorities. The lists of the men who have composed these provincial boards embrace the names of the most distinguished scholars of Germany. Some change has taken place in the organization of the local boards, but their general character has remained the same to this day.

The state of Prussia proper is divided into nine provinces, and these again into twenty-six governmental districts or departments, and each one of these subdivisions has its provincial or district school board.

In all of the Protestant states of Germany, both Church and State acknowledge obligations in respect to education, but in no two states is authority exercised alike. In Prussia, the higher schools are nearly exempt from Church influences, while in other states we find them almost entirely controlled by the Church. Everywhere a certain number of each school board must be clergymen.

For convenience, the organization of Prussian education will be considered as it existed before the war. The centre of home administration in Prussia is the Ministry of the Interior. Immediately under this minister are the presidents of the nine provinces—Prussia, Posen, Silesia, Pomerania, Brandenburg, Saxony, Westphalia, Hohenzollern, and the Rhine. These are divided into departments, presided over by prefects. All these officers are appointed and removable by the Minister of the Interior, and each is assisted by a council composed of two sections, one of which is called the Consistory for Church Affairs, and the other the Board for School Affairs. Although these officers are dependent upon and report to the Minister of the Interior, yet in all matters concerning the schools and the Church they report to the ecclesiastical and educational minister.

The departments are divided into circles, administered by an officer called a "landrath," who reports to the prefect of his department, and has associated with him a school superintendent, whose superintendency is usually co-extensive with the circle.

We see here a parallel line of duties passing through the same general heads of authority, and then dividing at the central power. There is practically a division of responsibility, so that primary education is controlled by departmental authority, while the provincial government regulates higher or secondary education. A portion of the council of the departments must belong to each of the forms of religion recognized by the state, Protestant and Catholic; but the minister of the parish is everywhere the local manager of the elementary school, and has a multitude of books and registers to keep, which are subject to the inspection of the superintendent.

Many of the smaller states had, before their absorption by Prussia, general laws minutely regulating school matters. Prussia has assumed jurisdiction over this subject, doubtful points being ruled as they arise by ordinances or circular letters, which serve as precedents for the future. Each administrative department may issue such ordinances, which, when they have received the approval of the Central Government, are authoritative in all the other departments; but great care is exercised in drawing up such rescripts. The minister first sends copies to all of the departmental governments, directing reports upon them, and not until all of these reports are received and carefully discussed by the Educational Bureau is final action taken upon the rescript. This scrupulous procedure occasions delay, but insures precision and consistency. The schools of Prussia may be classed as follows:

First. The Primary or Common Schools, which are accessible to all.

Second. The Higher or Secondary Schools, comprising the upper Burgher Schools, Real Schools, Progymnasia, and Gymnasia.

Third. The Universities.

The circle or diocese, the smallest state division, controlled by a civil officer, called a landrath, is of variable size and population, and may contain six or eight, or as many as forty parishes. Associated with the landrath is the superintendent, who is an ecclesiastical officer, and the departmental agent for the control of the schools of his circle or district. Each parish has one elementary school or more, according to the requirements and ability of its inhabitants. Each school has one building for school purposes, containing one or more rooms, according as the means and need of the school require one teacher or more. The limit of each of these schools has been fixed at eighty scholars, but it is common for a hundred to attend. This regulates the size of the building, which is usually of brick, with a tiled or shingled, and sometimes a thatched roof, and ordinarily contains the quarters of the teacher.

It is usual to place these buildings in the centre of the villages and towns, upon public grounds, and to separate them from other buildings by areas and fences, and the parish church is commonly embraced in the same inclosure. Within, the seats, with desks attached, and shelves beneath for books, are usually ranged in two rows, with an aisle between, the teacher's desk at the end opposite the door, and blackboards and maps on the walls. Here are taught the elementary branches, including reading, writing, the ground rules of arithmetic, and the history and geography of Germany. Religious instruction is also given.

In order to bring the youth to these schools, Germany has adopted a compulsory system. In every state, except Hamburg and Frankfort-on-the-Main, all of the children of both sexes between prescribed ages, ordinarily from six to fourteen, are compelled to attend school. Some states merely require a certain number of years of schooling, and leave the parent to choose whether it shall be at home or in school, and if the latter, at what school. This was the Prussian law until 1851, when it was changed so as to prescribe what school the child should attend.

Regular attendance at the school is required, and, to effect this, it is made the duty of the pastor and school-master to use all their moral influence to cause parents to send their children punctually and regularly. This failing, the police force is used. The police-office of the place makes out a list of all children of school age, and hands it to the local School Board connected with each school, which is then responsible for the children's attendance. The teacher keeps a list of absentees, marking those as *inexcused* who are absent without cause. The Board admonishes the parent, and if absence is repeated, the parent is fined, and, in default of payment, sent to jail. Sometimes the master, after a sufficient time, sends a messenger around each morning to their homes and gathers up the absentees. The usual hours of school are from eight o'clock till noon, and from two o'clock till four in the afternoon; but in many farming communities, in the summer, the children attend from four o'clock until eight in the morning, in order to assist in the farm labor afterward.

In Saxony the number of years of compulsory instruction is eight, and for each day missed a day is added, which must be made up before the parent can have control of his child's time. This seems to have worked better than any system of fines. It is made the duty of the police to inform the School Board of all new families that come into the parish, and the entire system is found to work easily and certainly. In many cases where the interests of labor and school conflict, half-day schools are established; and in some places there are two classes of schools, one for the children of parents who do not require the labor of their children, and one for those who can spare them but a part of the day.

Within the past ten years, the cotton manufacture has been largely developed in Saxony, and the children employed in this branch of industry have a fixed number of hours for school—some in the morning, others at evening, and others during the day. In nearly all of the states the minimum limit of age at which children can be employed in factories is fixed by law. The mill-owners are allowed to have their own schools if they desire, upon becoming responsible that the children shall receive a certain amount of instruction. The law is very strict with these capitalists, and should they deprive the children of the prescribed education, they would forfeit their right to employ infant labor. These examples show that the universal law of compulsory education accommodates itself easily and satisfactorily to the demands of industry.

The law is everywhere enforced, though with different degrees of rigor, but is most uniformly carried out in Prussia. In 1856, there were in that state twenty-four thousand two hundred and ninety-four public elementary schools, attended by two million seven hundred and twenty-eight thousand four hundred and seventy-two children. Seventy thousand two hundred and twenty pupils attended private schools. There were two million nine hundred and forty-three thousand two hundred and fifty-one children of school age, leaving only one hundred and forty-four thousand five hundred and fifty-nine who were not in school. Of those not in school, a large number were receiving private education at home. Some were boys in the lower classes of the higher institutions, and the remainder were sickly, or mentally deficient. Occasionally a migratory family escapes altogether. The gypsies, of whom there are many in Germany, are often regular attendants, and show industry, quickness, and good behavior. These figures do not indicate the degree of regularity of attendance, nor is it easily determined, but it is known to be good. Even the people of Germany criticise the compulsory system; but it all amounts to little, compared with the great fact that the class whose children attend these schools is well satisfied. The schooling is compulsory only in name, and the school has taken so deep root in the social habits of the German people, that, were the law repealed, there is no doubt that the schools would continue as full as they are now.

In Frankfort, where there is no compulsory law, and where many families have immigrated to escape the more rigorous law of the other German states, the children of school years are as regularly sent to school as in any other German city. It is often said that this submission to the school law is due to the docility of the German character; but it is the opinion of those who have had the best opportunities to know, that the general attendance is not so much in obedience to law as to the deliberate approving judgment of the people.

Mr. Kay says:

"There is nothing more untrue than that the central authority has all to do with the schools, that there is no local liberty of action, and that there is no union between Church and school.

"The generally supposed oppression of the Government in school matters has not the slightest foundation in fact. It is this simple religious parochial system, which has been abused and vilified in every possible way. It has been called tyrannical, illiberal, irreligious, and has been stigmatized by every opprobious epithet that ignorance and bigotry could invent. But the truth in the end will conquer, and Germany will one day be lauded by all Europe as the inventor of the system securing, in the best possible manner, her education, guided by the best intelligence, fostered by local activity, local sympathy, and the cordial sympathy of the Christian religion."

Mr. Pattison says:

"There is difference in populations in respect of capacity of education, differences, whether rightly or wrongly referred to race, that are certainly real. Even an elementary school is still an exotic among a population like that of the Mark, whose intractable speech-organ opposes an obstacle to it upon the threshold. Their next neighbor, on the contrary, the Missnian Saxon, whose dialect has become the standard speech of Germany, has appropriated more language before he goes to school than the other has learned after he has been several years. There is, perhaps, no more apt subject of culture among the German people than the Saxon. His speech-organs are flexible, his tones varied, and his ear delicate, and he learns with rapidity and pleasure. He takes readily that education which develops the faculties, but his pliability renders him less fit for that which consists in the inculcation of a fixed system of ideas. In a Saxon school far more is learned, and the taste much more cultivated, than in a Prussian school, but certainly a feebler moral training is given. The gentler nature and more lively fancy of the Saxon could not bear the more severe discipline under which the Prussian thrives."

In Germany one will be surprised to see how little interest is felt in school matters, and how little will be known of their system by people whose children may be at the time in the school, where they glide along unnoticed. This may be ascribed to a peculiar trait of nearly all people on the Continent, who seem to think it equally reprehensible not to thoroughly know their own business, and to know any thing else. This to Americans, who make it a part of their duty to know every thing, is often very vexatious. The German school-masters complain bitterly that this lack of interest weakens the schools, and renders them less efficient. Many charge this defect to the fact that school affairs are so completely locked up in the custody of Government officials, and argue that an increase of local authority would correct the evil. This opinion is fast gaining ground in many of the German states; and if we find no trace of it in Prussia, it is because the school system of that country is but just reaching the stage through which it has already passed elsewhere. There are, however, many things which the state can do better than local authority, such as the furnishing of competent teachers, and keeping the wants of growing communities supplied with school-houses and appliances. There is a disposition, however, in the more intelligent portions of Germany to take hold of school matters, and make considerable sacrifices in behalf of this interest. Communities often punish, by parish labor, failure to send children to school, and with a result greatly superior to that obtained by fines and imprisonment. A report upon this subject says, very wisely:

"The most effectual means of making children attend regularly is the way in which the master treats them. If he understands the art of making the children feel it pleasant to be at school, the desire to come there becomes a motive too powerful for the parents to be able to resist."

Already bodies of school delegates have been organized in nearly all of the large towns and cities of Prussia, and in Berlin in particular, and have had, so far, a most beneficial effect in bringing the scholars and people more closely in sympathy. The departmental governments look upon them with jealousy, but they are steadily gaining ground.

Private schools have heretofore been little known in Germany, but are now on the increase, as is private teaching by tutors in families. This will have a tendency to weaken the present centralized system, as well as to build up a class spirit of exclusiveness, and will endanger the preservation of that air of courtesy and good-breeding now so generally diffused throughout the lower classes. The habit of universal attendance at the day-school is one of the most precious traditions of German family life. The children of the humblest artisan, the shop-keeper, and the peasant, may be seen pursuing their studies together on the same bench with the children of the rich and the noble. The schools are very attractive. Each must have an open space about it, usually handsomely arranged. A play-ground is always provided. The whole area is carefully drained and made wholesome, and the children are never kept in more than an hour and a half at a time, when they go out, and all play together on a perfect equality. This feeling must last through life, for in the army I saw only the same courtesy from officer to soldier that was natural to expect from soldier to officer.

The prevailing opinion that compulsory attendance is a modern despotic system, founded on some theory of the right of the sovereign over the child, is incorrect. The system dates from the earliest period of the Reformation, and attendance at school was recognized as a religious duty long before it was made obligatory by a law of the state. From the time of Luther's address to the municipal corporations of Germany in 1524, this duty has been recognized, whether enforced by legislation or not. It was the distinction of the Protestant child that it should be taught to understand the doctrines and duties of its religion, and it was the duty of the Church to see that all of its children were instructed. In Brandenburg the royal edict dates from 1573; but this, and all other laws upon the subject which have been respected by all the German states during these hundreds of years, only defined an obligation universally admitted as one of the first duties of the citizen and member of the Church. Compulsory education in Germany never had to contend with an adverse public sentiment—not because the spirit of personal liberty was wanting, but because, since the Reformation, there has never been a time when it was not thought part of parental duty to have children properly taught.

Any one may establish a private school, but he must first obtain a license from the Government, and must also show that the public schools in his neighborhood do not afford sufficient school accommodations. Even after this his school is subject to all the inspections, and his teachers to all the examinations, provided in the case of public schools. He can fix his own rates of charges, but his programme of instruction must be ample; and although he can make private arrangements to accept scholars at a lower rate, he can not, as a consequence, abate the amount of instruction. There are in Prussia thirty-six hundred private teachers, against thirty-three thousand who teach in public schools.

In all large places there are also "schools for further improvement." These are mostly secondary and evening schools, and use the same rooms as the other schools. They are attended principally by apprentices at trades, who have learned imperfectly what should have been learned before confirmation, and by those who desire to carry their education farther still, pursuing their trades at the same time. All young men, on being apprenticed, are examined, and unless they can read, write, and cipher with facility, are sent to these schools. Young men can not enter them until after confirmation, but there is no limit of age afterward, and among the pupils are found journeymen, apprentices, mechanics, merchants, school-masters, and government clerks. There are also infant-schools, or, more properly, infant homes, supported entirely by charity, where poor laboring people can leave their children for care during the day-time.

INSPECTION OF SCHOOLS.

We will now notice how the system of inspection is carried on to insure the efficiency of these schools. Each circle, as we have seen, has its superintendent, who controls church and school matters, and who must be a clergyman. He is the school inspector for his district, and his duties are extensive and various. He must visit, direct, control, and take general charge of all school matters, form the classes, adjust the order of studies, settle points in dispute, encourage or direct the masters, and influence parents to send their children. He, in connection with the landrath, audits all school accounts, attends to the erection and repair of suitable buildings, and once in three years must send to the provincial governments estimates for these purposes. He receives no extra pay for these services, which are considered part of his ministerial duty, but his actual expenses, when traveling, are paid. He must make an annual report to the department conformable to the following rules. The report must be modeled on the plan of well-arranged oral statement; it must comprise a plain uncolored statement of facts, keeping each topic separate; when a professional opinion is required, it must be supported by grounds, the law, and the facts; each definite suggestion must be in the form of a separate report; the report must be written in a clear, legible hand, on the right-hand page of a sheet of paper, and date, place, and title on the opposite page.

The duty of these superintendents originally related especially to religious teaching, but has for a long time been general. There is also the local inspector, who is the pastor of the parish, and who exercises the same power over the school of his parish as the superintendent does over the district. Every school has its local board of managers, of which the pastor is a member, and usually chairman. He is compelled to visit his school at least once in a week, where a book is kept in which he must record, in his own hand, his visit, what the classes were doing, how they acquit themselves, the number present, and any event or information that may seem noteworthy. At the end of the year this book must be sent to the departmental government, where it undergoes scrutiny. His duties are by no means easy or few. He must acquaint himself with the children, and with all the internal affairs of the school, attend all meetings of the School Board, assist and support the teacher, and act as a medium between the teacher and the parents. He must see that the list of absentees is correctly kept, grant exemptions to children when necessary, allow leaves of absence of two or three days to the teacher, see that religious instruction differing from the faith of parents is not imparted to the children, and, when Protestants and Catholics attend the same school, appoint fixed hours of religious instruction in each week, and attend closely to the preparation of children for confirmation. He also keeps the school and church records.

As the local inspector is a crown officer, he is not always in hearty sympathy with the people. Experience proves that his religious influence in bringing children into the schools is more potent than law or punishment. This pastoral supervision over the schools was not created by royal edict, but grew out of duty in connection with religious and afterward secular instruction.

SUPPORT OF SCHOOLS.

Only a passing notice can be given to the subject of the support of these schools. As many of the people are very poor, the rate in the elementary schools is almost nominal; but a nominal rate is fixed for all scholars, rich and poor.

Nearly every country has endowment funds applicable to school purposes. These funds have arisen, to some extent, from bequests of charitable people, but mainly from secularized Church property. The money has nearly all passed into the hands of the Government as trustee, which manages it with great circumspection. The whole amount of annual revenue in Prussia from this source is about four hundred and eighty thousand thalers, a small portion of which is applicable to Church purposes. The great burden of school expense is borne by local taxation. This may be divided into three classes: first, the school fees paid by the children, which are so low as to be within the means of all; second, the local rate; and, third, general taxation. Of these three sources of revenue, the second bears the principal burden; for the rule is, that the children shall pay only a sum within the means of all, and that the general Government shall not be called upon until the locality has done its utmost. It is not left to the option of the district to say what schools it will have, but it must have schools and teachers enough for the requirements of all its children.

These are rules that hold good in all parts of Germany, but the mode of enforcing them differs. In Saxony, for instance, each department is permitted to fix its own rating-book, in which every family is taxed a sum proportioned to the ability of the family to pay, the law fixing the limit at fifty groschen as the minimum, and fifteen thalers as the maximum yearly payment. If this fails to cover costs, application is made to the department. The treasury of the department is divided into four funds—the Church Fund, the School Fund, the Poor Fund, and the Town Fund. The School Fund is made up of various small perquisites, and by direct taxation—first by a regular poll-tax, and then by a rated property-tax. This is but one of many methods of imposing school taxes. In Prussia taxation varies in every department and district; but, as a general rule, each family is taxed according to its pecuniary ability, and may pay in money or kind. The whole cost of schools seems to an American remarkably small.

The pay of teachers had always been loudly complained of as pitiably small, until 1852, when, in Prussia, the general Government, without fixing any sum, directed the departments to investigate the subject, and to permanently raise the salaries of teachers to such a sum as they should deem sufficient, having due regard to the usages of the locality and costs of living.

The local boards are variously made up in different states, but each school or union of schools has one. They correspond to our trustees, but are more active, and give the subject of education greater attention. In Würtemberg, the Church Board is also the School Board. In Saxony, the "Board of the Commune," corresponding to the "Circle" in Prussia, undertakes this duty; and when the commune is too large for this, special boards are appointed by the main board. In Prussia, and in several other states that have copied from her, each school has its own board, the rule generally observed in their formation being, that first, the patron, if there is one; second, the clergyman; third, the municipal authorities; fourth, the householders, shall be represented. The householders usually choose their own representative. The landrath, however, is given great power in rejecting, and, under certain circumstances, may himself appoint the householder delegate. The Board are the trustees of all school revenues, properties, lands, and houses; regulate taxation, grant exemption to scholars who desire it for longer periods than one week, and are responsible for the proper repairs of school buildings.

The school delegates, of which mention has been already made, usually exist in large towns, for the administration of city schools. They are democratic in spirit, and are looked upon with considerable jealousy. Their success, however, is steadily increasing, and they are everywhere infusing new life into school matters, by interesting a higher order of men in the work of teaching. They have almost entire control of the schools of Berlin, and these institutions deserve a special notice.

BERLIN SCHOOLS.

Berlin is rich in schools of almost every grade, but is not, like many capitals, a great centre of education, as it is of politics and trade. These institutions are constituted with a view to the education of the children of Berlin, and are all day-schools—boarding-schools not being known there until very recently. Children from abroad often go there to be educated, but usually live with friends, or in families, and attend as day-scholars. The schools are evenly scattered over the city, so that for the whole circuit of twenty miles there is no child of six years who can not easily walk four times a day to and from an elementary school. Older children, who require the advantages of the higher schools, find them equally accessible. There are, in all, about three hundred schools, of which one-half are elementary. They are of all denominations, to suit all religions, and are nearly all under control of the city authorities.

The administration of all city affairs is lodged with a body of thirty-four members, called the *City Magistracy*, appointed by the Provincial Council; but school matters are kept in the hands of a board of delegates, formed of two paid delegates, six members of the Magistracy, twelve members of the Municipal Council, three members chosen by the people, three school superintendents, and a Jewish rabbi. These members of the delegation are formed into committees, to each of which appropriate duties are assigned.

Each school has its Board, constituted as before described, with the clergyman of the parish as chairman. Below the Board are the head teachers, with whom they transact the business of the school, and above are the Board of Delegates, to whom they are directly responsible, and who in turn must report to the Provincial Council of Brandenburg, and they to the educational minister. These are the links which connect the individual school with the central authority. About one in eight of the entire population of Berlin are in school, at a cost to the city, over and above school fees, of about three hundred thousand thalers annually, or five dollars to each child—a sum equivalent to about twelve per cent. of the entire city expenditure. The excellence and cheapness of education in Berlin is attracting large numbers of foreign young men, and even women, especially Americans. The steps by which the schools have arrived at their present degree of excellence, through this system of compulsory attendance and religious training, are exceedingly interesting and instructive, but can only be glanced at here.

METHODS OF TEACHING.

The Primary School was originally but a catechismal school, conducted by theological students under the officers of the church, or by the pastor himself. It was an exclusively Protestant institution, born with the Reformation, and grounded in its principles—first, that "not incorporation with the visible Church, but individual faith, is the means of salvation;" and, secondly, that "true public worship is not a transaction of the priest, but the joint act of the congregation." Out of these two ideas grew the policy of general Christian instruction, and by degrees the secular education now provided in the elementary schools. Luther knew only the Latin schools, for in his day there were no others designed for the higher classes and candidates for the Church. Education had at first but one purpose—to teach religion; and when children learned to read, it was that they might read the Bible. From this aim, Protestant Germany has never swerved nor changed. Even during the philosophical reaction against religion, in 1763, we find royal authority directing the enforcement of the regulation that "The people's schools shall avoid all abstractions, but be Christianly taught in reading, writing, and arithmetic, catechism and Bible history." Stein, who found Germany at the feet of France, saw that she could be saved only by fostering a more vigorous national life, and sought successfully to secure this end through her common schools. This was the first innovation upon their ecclesiastical character, and they were made largely a political instrument, not to advance personal ambition, but for a great national purpose. The higher institutions have mostly shaken off ecclesiastical authority; and, though religion still retains its original place in the people's school, it stands merely upon a footing of equality with other departments of knowledge. Formerly each denomination had its separate school, unless one sect largely predominated, in which case children of different creeds attended the same school, and were instructed at stated times by their respective pastors.

The Catholics at first objected to these provisions, but soon acquiesced. Frequent attempts at proselyting were, however, discovered, and resulted always in the removal of the teacher. But a more potent agency which law can not reach, and which is everywhere observable, even in our own country, was the silent influence of the belief and practices of the majority. This has a power over children that nothing can resist. It was accordingly announced, in 1822, that mixed schools had practically failed; and the minister, Altenstein, gave notice that "such establishments will be no longer the rule, and will exceptionally be allowed only when obviously necessary, and when such coalition is the free choice of the two congregations acting under the advice of their respective clergy, and with the approval of the temporal and spiritual authority."

Matters remained pretty nearly upon this footing until 1848, when a strong effort was made by the higher classes to sever secular and religious instruction. This project found almost universal favor in the National Assembly, but gained no footing with the people; and school property was so largely owned by the Church, and the pay of teachers in many quarters so dependent upon the Church, as to make the change practically out of the question. The matter ended at that time by incorporating in the new constitution the following article, which is still in force, viz.:

"ART. 24. In the ordering of the public schools, regard shall be had, as far as possible, to denominational relations. The religious instruction in the people's school is under the conduct of the respective bodies."

This leaves it very much with the people themselves, and the general tendency is toward a separation of schools by the lines of the different denominations. Of the four million Prussian school children, about two-thirds are Protestant, and the remainder Catholic, except a small Jewish element of about forty thousand. The latter give no trouble in school matters. They do not fear proselyting, and are always ready and glad to avail themselves of the schools of either sect, and often have their own.

Considerable difficulties have sprung up from time to

time in different parts of Germany between the Lutherans and the Calvinists, who often claim, and have, separate schools. There are also Baptists and other dissenting denominations, which have occasioned some trouble by demanding distinct privileges under the law. The recognized churches ask for protection against the dissenting churches, but the reply is made that to accede to this claim, would be contrary to Prussian constitutional law. Upon this point the ecclesiastical minister says to the Prussian Chamber of Deputies:

"The danger to the state would be much more alarming, did we anticipate that, owing to defective religious instruction of the dissenting preachers, a generation would grow up without the fear of God, the foundation of all social order. Serious as the consideration is, it can not justify a deviation from right and justice, nor would it be reason enough for further legislative restraint upon liberty, since experience teaches that political repression is itself a cause of these aberrations of the instinct of freedom in the domain of religion, while a healthy and vigorous religious life readily absorbs them. From the ground I occupy as ecclesiastical minister, I most heartily welcome the abandonment of all further attempts at police coercion of innocent religious meetings, whatever be the religious tenets of the parties. Such attempts have more or less the character of religious persecutions, and are in harmony neither with the traditions of the monarchy nor its present constitution. Still less do they serve the interests of the two great religious communities between which the nation is divided. The two churches would be subscribing a testimonial to their own spiritual poverty, if they relied on such means for sustaining themselves. Christianity overcame the world by free convictions, and will continue to maintain and extend itself by this force alone. In forming its decision, the Government has not overlooked the political inconvenience which may arise from the view we have adopted. It may happen that the children may never have been taught the commandments—those first axioms of every civil society—'Thou shalt not steal,' 'Thou shalt do no murder,' 'Thou shalt not take the name of the Lord thy God in vain.' All this rests, not on our heads, but on the heads of those who are charged by God and the law with the bringing up of these children. The result at which we have arrived is not only the only legal, but the only practical cause; for what influence can the school have when it is at war with the family—when the children hear at home that what they have learned at school is idle and superstitious nonsense? On the two Christian churches rests the duty of seeking that which was lost, not by violence and repressive measures, but in the way of love—endeavoring, by precept and example, to recover that which has gone astray."

All the children of dissenting families are required to attend school, but there is no enforcement of religious teaching different from that of their parents. At fourteen every child is allowed to choose its own religion; nor can the parent who leaves his Church take with him his young children, but at the proper age the child chooses what religious body it will join.

Much discussion has taken place in Prussia as to whether early education should be based upon the child's reason or memory, and whether its religious training should begin with its tenderest years, or be left until confirmation, to become the labor of the pastor. The present inclination seems to be toward the strict Lutheran practice of early religious teachings.

School is opened and closed with prayer, in which the children join. This service consists of the Lord's Prayer, morning and evening benediction, to which are added other prayers in common use in the churches. The Creed and Ten Commandments are sometimes added, and the prayers and collects appropriate to church days. At church festivals the school-rooms are decorated with flowers, evergreens, or immortelles, and appropriate hymns are sung.

It is the duty of the teacher to inculcate the observance of the Sabbath, and the obligation of attendance at church on all holy days, and himself to set the example. Sermons and lectures, suited to the comprehension of young children, are frequently delivered in the school-room, either by the teacher or pastor. The regulations repeat that "the Bible is the field in which the Christian elementary school has to solve the problem of how to ground and build up the Christian life intrusted to it." The Bible is never used as a reading-book, but the historical parts of the Old and New Testaments are taught through the whole course, and select portions of the psalms, epistles, and prophets are read by the higher classes as a religious exercise.

The catechism of Luther is mechanically taught in the schools, in order that the pastor may initiate the child into the sense of Church doctrine. The learning of hymns holds an important place in elementary instruction, and about fifty are committed to memory during the course. This closes the subject of the religious portion of elementary instruction. The rules regulating it are very full, and beautifully and tersely expressed.

CHAPTER XII.

GERMAN CIVIL SCHOOLS—*Continued*.

The great aim in German schools is practical usefulness. The time was when a school was judged by the extent of its teaching, but now the quality of instruction has become the criterion of excellence, and the tendency is to select subjects which bear on practical life, and to teach them in a simple, elementary, but thorough way.

Mr. Pattison says of the Prussian schools: "They may aim at little, but the principle is to achieve it. It may look too little to the cultivation of the imagination, but it is possessed of a practical spirit which permits of no showing off. A Prussian *schulrath*, in visiting a school, may be blind to many faults, but his eye is quick as lightning to detect the least pretentiousness or hollowness in teaching."

It is one great advantage of a centralized school government, that all incentive to the exhibition of superficial accomplishments is taken away. There are public examinations, but they are never converted into exhibitions. The elementary school is not to communicate knowledge, but to qualify the child for certain simple operations. The instruction must be thorough, but it must be elementary. The master's business is not to talk, or even question, but to make the scholars practice. It is not enough that the child knows how, it must show that it knows how by facility of performance; and a pupil is treated like an apprentice, who learns his trade by merely being set to work at it. The elementary school must confine itself to that elementary skill which every citizen needs, whatever his calling may be. What the child has to learn is not so many distinct subjects, but the connected use of his sight, hand, and voice.

The subjects taught in a one-class village school, teaching twenty-six hours per week, are as follows: religion, six hours; reading and writing, twelve hours; ciphering, five hours; and singing, three hours. This plan may be varied so as to add an hour for drawing; and in larger towns, where there are more classes, natural phenomena may be studied, and sometimes natural history and the geography of Germany and Europe.

In the summer season many village schools become half-day schools for such children as are needed on the farms; and the remainder have more time devoted to them, and can thus get over more subjects. These half-day schools are shown by experience to be equal to the full-day schools in bringing forward the children in their studies, as those who are present receive more attention, and the children are not fatigued by being carried through all-day exercises. Reading and writing are taught simultaneously. There is no part of elementary teaching to which the scientific mind of the Germans has been more successfully applied than this. Long experience has brought the method to wonderful perfection.

From the deaf and dumb institution, through all the grades of infant-schools and reading-classes, the cultivation of the speech-organ is an object of assiduous attention. Many seminaries have deaf and dumb institutes attached to them, not merely that the students may learn the art of teaching such pupils, but because it has been found that the principles of language instruction can be best studied in this its most difficult form. The great number of provinces and district dialects present rare difficulties in teaching, "high" German being a new and foreign tongue to some, but it is strictly maintained as the school language.

The analytical mode of learning language is banished from the elementary schools. In the higher institutions this is, of course, not the case; but the development of the thinking powers is now recognized as no part of the work of the elementary schools, and the mother-tongue must be learned by use. The language instinct which every child possesses must be cultivated by assiduous exercise, of which reading, spelling, and writing are only so many different forms. Various methods of learning to read are used, none being prescribed; but nowhere, for the last thirty years, except in the more backward parts of North Germany, has the one so common with us been employed—beginning with the names of letters, and the spelling of words with these names. There is no standard reading-book, and it is found very difficult to produce one that shall meet all requirements. It must be the guide in literary style, and a book of practical grammar, natural history, and useful knowledge, in concise and entertaining form. It must also be free from moral teaching, which is left to its proper place. It must, in fact, be a portable encyclopedia of useful knowledge, suited to the comprehension of children.

In the great majority of the common schools and all of the higher ones, a delicacy and beauty of handwriting is acquired which is unrivaled by any other people. Writing is taught either from lithographic copies, graded as the child advances, or, when there is time, by the teacher direct from the blackboard, explaining and writing every curve, line, and motion, and followed by the children in the copy. There is much said of an American system which is gaining ground at the schools. Arithmetic is taught in a purely practical way, and fatiguing mental exercises are prohibited. The pupils are made perfectly familiar with units before going on with tens, and know these well before proceeding to hundreds.

When geography, history, and the natural studies are taught, they come either directly or suggestively from the reading-book. In geography the child must first know the spot where it then is, and then extend its knowledge to contiguous regions — all being co-ordinated from the place which the scholar actually sees and knows.

Mr. Mann gives so graphic an account of a geography lesson, as to tempt me to repeat it in full:

"The teacher stood by the blackboard, with the chalk in his hand. After casting his eye over the class to see that all were ready, he struck at the middle of the board; with a rapidity of hand which my eye could hardly follow, he made a series of those short diverging lines, or shadings, employed by map engravers to represent a chain of mountains. He had scarcely turned an angle or shot off a spur, when the scholars began to cry out: 'Carpathian Mountains,' 'Hungary,' 'Black Forest Mountains,' 'Würtemberg,' 'Giant's Mountains,' 'Riesen Gebirge,' 'Silesia,' 'Metallic Mountains,' 'Erz Gebirge,' 'Pine Mountains,' 'Fichtel Gebirge,' 'Central Mountains,' 'Mittel Gebirge,' 'Bohemia,' etc., etc. In less than half a minute the ridge of that grand central elevation which separates the waters that flow north-west into the German Ocean from those that flow north into the Baltic, and south-east into the Black Sea, was presented to view, executed almost as beautifully as an engraving. A dozen crinkling strokes, made in the twinkling of an eye, represented the head-waters of the great rivers which flow in different directions from that mountainous range; while the children, almost as eager and excited as though they had actually seen the torrents dashing down the mountain sides, cried out: 'Danube,' 'Elbe,' 'Vistula,' 'Oder,' etc. The next moment I heard a succession of small strokes or taps, so rapid as to be almost indistinguishable; and hardly had my eye time to discern a large number of dots made along the margins of the rivers, when the shouts of 'Lintz,' 'Vienna,' 'Prague,' 'Dresden,' 'Berlin,' etc., struck my ear. At this point in the exercise the spot which had been occupied on the blackboard was nearly a circle, of which the starting-point, or place where the teacher first began, was the centre; but now a few additional strokes round the circumference of the incipient continent extended the mountain ranges outward toward the plains, the children calling out the names of the countries in which they respectively lay. With a few more flourishes, the rivers flowed onward toward their several terminations, and, by another succession of dots, new cities sprang up along their banks. By this time the children had become as much excited as though they had been present at a world-making. They rose in their seats, they flung out both hands, their eyes kindled, and their voices became almost vociferous, as they cried out the names of the different places which, under the magic of the teacher's crayon, rose into view. Within ten minutes from the commencement of the lesson, there stood upon the blackboard a beautiful map of Germany, with its mountains, principal rivers and cities, the coast of the German Ocean, of the Baltic and Black Seas, and all so accurately proportioned, that I think only slight errors would have been found had it been subjected to the test of a scale of miles."

Drawing is carried no farther in the common schools of North Germany than simple free-hand drawing; but in South Germany the study is made more of.

Singing is taught by ear and by note. It is not carried beyond church music and the national airs, and the children must sing in church the next Sunday the pieces they have learned during the week. Mr. Mann says:

"The Prussian teacher has no book. He needs none. He teaches from a full mind. He does not cumber or darken the subject with any technical phraseology. He observes what proficiency the child has made, and then adapts his instructions, both in quality and amount, to the necessity of the case. He answers all questions, and solves all doubts. It is one of his objects, at every recitation, so to present ideas, that they shall start doubts and provoke questions. He connects each lesson with all kindred and collateral ones, and shows its relation to the every-day duties and business of life; and should the most ignorant man, or the most destitute vagrant in society, ask him 'of what use can such knowledge be?' he will prove to him in a word that some of his own pleasures or means of subsistence are dependent upon it, or have been created or improved by it."

These are the routine matters taught in the elementary schools. The scope of the system may seem narrow, but is not so in reality. The experience of years of deliberate trial is that, from seven to fourteen, children can not learn more than the mastery over the rudiments and means of future cultivation—the organs of speech and song, the material of language, the relations of numbers, the pen and the pencil. The child is not to be taught to know, but to do; not to acquire knowledge, but to develop capacity.

It may be desirable that children should have industrial training or artistic culture, or learn instrumental music or physical science; but average boys and girls can not do these things without sacrificing the elementary skill which can best be acquired in childhood. The efforts to restrict the elementary school to acquisition of this skill have not been efforts to keep down the education of the masses, but to place it on the only solid foundation. The duties of the elementary school are not arbitrarily defined, but define themselves as soon as it is understood that they end at fourteen.

Prussia must provide a general system of higher schools, to take up education where the common schools leave it, before she can fully merit all the praises usually given her; but how many there are of our own States that fall far below what she now accomplishes!

In thickly populated communities and large cities, various grades of higher schools already exist, introductory to secondary education; but there is a great deal of Government prohibition regarding them, and the children who may attend them. Under more liberal treatment, these would go far toward supplying the higher education which is necessary. It is sometimes said, in criticism of the German system, that the individual scholar is lost in the class, like a soldier in a company; that the programme of studies is too inflexible, and the supervision too minute.

An observer and traveler in 1842 pronounced the Prussian educational system "a deception practiced for the paltry political end of rearing the individual to be part and parcel of a despotic system of government; of training him to be either its instrument or its slave, according to his social station;" while one hears in all parts of Germany that the national school-masters at that very time were sowing the seeds of democracy, which burst forth six years later.

One notices in Germany a want of individual energy of character. Mr. Horace Mann says upon this subject:

"When the children come out of the school-room, they have little use for the knowledge acquired there, or their faculties that have been developed; their resources are not brought into demand; their powers are not roused nor exercised. Our common phrases—'The activities of life,' 'The responsibilities of citizenship,' 'The career of action,' 'The obligation to posterity,' would be strange-sounding words in a Prussian's ear. The Government steps in to take care of the subject almost as much as the subject takes care of his cattle. The subject has no officers to choose, no inquiries into the character of his candidate to make, no vote to give. He has no laws to enact or abolish. He has no questions about peace or war, finance, taxes, tariffs, post-offices, nor internal improvements to decide or discuss. He is not asked where a road shall be laid or a bridge shall be built—although in one case he performs the labor, and in the other supplies the materials. His sovereign is born to him, the laws are made for him. In war, his part is not to declare it, or end it, but to fight it, and pay for it. The tax-gatherer tells him how much he has to pay; the ecclesiastical authority plans a church he has to build; his spiritual guide prepares a confession of faith all ready for his signature. He is dictated alike how he must obey his king, and worship his God. Now, although there is a sleeping ocean in the bosom of every child that is born into the world, yet if no freshening, life-giving breeze ever sweeps across its surface, why should it not sleep in dark stagnation forever?"

OF THE ELEMENTARY SCHOOL-TEACHERS.

In nearly all German states the administration undertakes to test the fitness of the teacher for his office, and to educate him for it; and in no state can any person without a certificate of fitness teach either in a public or private school. Until 1810, no certificate was required, but private patronage of schools often abused its trust, and William von Humboldt, while at the head of the Department of Education, instituted the test of trial. Afterward a year's preparation was required; but at present a three years' course is prescribed at schools specially provided for the purpose. There are not less than sixty of these schools, called seminaries, in Prussia for the education of elementary school-teachers. A few of these are private schools, but in system and course do not differ from the Government establishments. A young man must have received the elementary schooling of the country, and been confirmed; and, as he can not enter until the age of eighteen, the four years after his confirmation are usually passed in preparation for the seminary. The seminary buildings are not usually imposing, but suffer from the parsimony with which the school in Prussia is always treated. They are scrupulously clean, well ventilated, have large and abundant maps, large engravings, and blackboards.

The cost of board is usually about forty thalers a year; and as the students do all their own serving except cooking, the whole expense is but little more than that of board. The entrance examination is easy, little being required beyond the elementary course. Great caution is exercised, however, as to the moral qualifications, and private life and character of the candidate, who must know Luther's catechism by heart, and the principal doctrinal texts of both the Old and New Testaments. The instruction is distributed over three years, as follows. The first year is occupied with bringing the pupil within the influences of the place, and making him feel what it is that he should become. In the second year he goes over more thoroughly the ground he has already traversed at school; and during the third is drilled in model schools, and has lessons in school management. The religious instruction runs on through the whole of this time, but is not so much a branch of teaching as a paramount influence.

The school subjects are classified as follows: Religion,

language, history, geography, natural history, arithmetic, writing, drawing, singing, theory of music, use of violin, piano, and organ. The subjects are divided among four teachers, known as a director, head teacher, music-teacher, and fourth teacher. There is something approaching barrack life in these schools, and military exactitude in the studies—the hours of labor and recreation being distributed as in the Prussian military schools. Nothing like familiarity is permitted between the teachers and pupils, and the closest watch is kept over the lives and conduct of the latter. To enter a beer saloon is forbidden, and to be seen smoking is certain dismissal. There is no idle time either for teacher or scholar. The first examination takes place at the end of the three years' seminary course, when others may be examined for the office of school-master. They are called "wild men," to distinguish them from trained men, and, in addition to the usual examination, are required to present a host of testimonials upon a multitude of points. This examination for all is very severe, and those accepted are rated as "very good," "good," and "sufficient." The graduates are at once assigned to some province as provisional or assistant teachers, and attached to schools. After three years' duty, they are again examined, mainly on their performance as teachers during those years, and, if found worthy, become full teachers.

In Prussia, the teacher, on receiving his definite appointment, must take the oath of allegiance, and, since 1850, the oath of the constitution. In Saxony, the teacher is sworn "to remain faithful to the pure evangelical doctrine as the same is contained in Holy Scripture, and expounded and set forth in the first unaltered Augsburg Confession and in Luther's Catechism, and diligently and purely teach the same."

The following are from the "Official Seminary Regulations of Prussia:".

"SCHOOL MANAGEMENT.

"There shall be taught school management for not more than two hours in the week. This may continue for the first year—a simple picture of the Christian school in its first origin, and its relation to family, Church, and State.

"In the second year the object and the arrangement of the elementary school may be explained, and the proper principles of elementary Christian instruction expounded.

"In the third year the pupils may be taught their future duties as servants of the Church and State, and the means of improvement after they leave the seminary; but the greater portion of this time will be with the lessons of the practicing school."

The regulations upon the religious portion of the seminary course are exceedingly full and explicit, covering many pages, and conclude as follows:

"Religious instructions conducted according to these principles will form teachers clearly aware of what they have to do, possessing within themselves a sufficient knowledge of the word, doctrine, and life of the Evangelical Church. It will open to them the entrance upon a God-fearing life, in which they may find practical experience of the course by which God leads us from sin to justification by faith, which worketh by love. To this end the whole life in the seminary must be brought under the discipline of the Word and the Spirit. Pupils and teachers alike must draw from the fountain of grace, and the community must exhibit a pattern of common Christian life."

These regulations take up in succession each subject of study, and describe its use and the method of teaching in full and perspicuous terms. Of knowledge of nature, they say:

"Natural history shall be taught in the first and second year classes two hours a week—not in a strictly scientific way, nor adopting any classification. The principal indigenous plants and animals shall be brought before the pupils, and described to them. In botany a foundation for future study shall be laid. They shall be taught to distinguish the principal native minerals and rocks. A popular description of the human body shall be given. The pupil should acquire a love for nature and natural occupations, and a practical direction should be given to this branch of instruction by constant reference to gardening, agriculture, industry, and trades. In the third year the student may advance into natural philosophy, which shall always be treated in an experimental way, without mathematical formulæ. The common instruments, machines, and mechanical powers may be explained to them, with the phenomena of heat, electricity, and magnetism."

Of writing, the regulations say that it

"Shall be taught with a special view to obtaining a plain and flowing hand, and, secondly, to learning how to set clear copies of single letters and strokes in proper succession for the school. The copies executed by the pupils are to be at once exercises in caligraphy and an intellectual discipline. The method of teaching to write is to be learned along with the practice in writing."

Special instructions are given for teaching the violin, organ, piano, and in vocal music; also in gymnastics and gardening.

The position of teacher in Germany is one of the highest respectability, as well it should be. They are a body of educated, courteous, refined, moral, and learned men, laboring with earnest enthusiasm among the poorest class of their countrymen. They are devoted to their duties, have strong fraternal feelings, and often hold conferences among themselves to discuss matters of general professional interest. The Government has recognized the value of their influence and their power for good, and has done its part in making the position of the teacher enviable.

The effect of the labors of the teachers upon the people of Germany is beyond belief. The curse of poverty has been almost removed. One sees, apparently, no poor children; all are well and cleanly clad; all are courteous; all have bright, intelligent faces; and one is incredulous when told that some of them are peasants' children.

On my way from Frankfort to Berlin, at nearly all the stations, when for a moment I could get off the train, I always saw young ladies, neatly and prettily dressed, serving soup, bread, and meat to the sick and wounded soldiers returning from France, and, on recognizing my uniform, as they always did, they would address me in good English, asking many questions of our country, and of our views of the war. We have many lessons yet to learn from these same much-ridiculed German people, and perhaps in nothing can they teach us more than in this making of thoroughly good school-teachers.

Every town has its newspapers, and the poor all read them, several often clubbing together for that purpose. Their houses are scrupulously clean and constantly whitewashed, the villages neat and orderly, and the lands beautifully cultivated. If any are unable to pay the school rate, or to clothe their children well enough to go to school, the neighborhood at once provides what is necessary. They have no poor-schools. Mr. Kay says:

"On arriving at one of the towns, I engaged a poor man as guide. I asked him to take me to see some of the schools where some of the poor were educated, and told him I wished to visit the worst schools. He answered me, 'Sir, we have no bad schools here, our schools are all good.' I said, 'Well, take me to the worst you know.' He answered again, 'I don't know any poor ones, but will take you to where my children go.' It was a lofty and handsome building, five stories high and sixty feet broad. In the two upper stories, all the teachers, ten in number, resided; on the lower floor there were ten class-rooms, twenty feet long, fifteen feet broad, and fourteen feet high, fitted up with parallel rows of desks, maps, drawing-boards, and school-books. Five of these rooms were for boys, and five for girls. The desk stood in front of all, and the walls were covered with maps, pictures, and blackboards. All of these were suited to the age and attainments of the children for whom the rooms were destined, and the children, after remaining a year and a half in one, were passed to the next. The children were so clean and respectably dressed that I could not believe they were the children of poor persons. I expressed my doubt to my guide. His answer was, 'My children are here, sir;' and then, turning to the teacher, he requested him to tell me who were the parents of the children present; the teacher made the children stand up one after another, and tell me who their parents were. From them I learned that two were the sons of counts, one the son of a physician, one of an officer of the royal household, one of a porter, and others of mechanics, artisans, and of laborers who were too poor to pay for their children's education, and whose children were clothed and educated at the expense of the town. They all sat at the same desks together; they were all clothed with equal respectability. In their manners, dress, cleanliness, and appearance I could discern no striking difference.

"After spending some time in the different class-rooms, the quiet and order of which were admirable, I went to the town-hall to see the chief educational authority for the city itself. Outside his door I found a poor woman waiting to see him. I asked her what she wanted. She said she had a little girl of five years of age, and that she wanted to persuade the minister to allow her to send her little daughter to school a year before the legal age for admission. I said to her, 'Why are you so anxious to send your child to school so early?' She answered, smiling at my question, 'The children learn at school so much which is useful to them in after life, that I want her to begin as soon as possible.' I thought to myself, this does not look as if the people dislike being obliged to educate their children."

THE HIGHER EDUCATION OF GERMANY.

If I have devoted a large portion of my space to elementary education, it is because in it we find Germany's vital power and pure religion. Above this we find the higher schools, where is about one scholar to every four or five hundred inhabitants, while in the elementary schools the proportion is one to eight.

In all large cities and rich populous communities are also found the "Middle Schools," which are just what the name implies—their purpose being to give such children as require it a middle grade of education, between the fixed elementary course and the scientific or classical course. These schools are attainable as yet only by the more favored classes, who live in large communities; but in the city of Berlin there are not less than twenty or thirty thousand pupils in them, and it is now the great want of German education that they be increased and made general.

The first grade of secondary school is the "Burgher School," the character of which is indicated by its name.

It differs little from the Middle School, and in many cases is identical with it, but generally provides a more advanced course, and leads directly to the next higher order—the "Real School." The actual difference between the Burgher School and the Middle School is, that while the latter is intended to finish the education of boys who can not go to the higher schools, the former is preparatory to a further course of study. It has a municipal character, and is intended to supply only the wants of the locality.

THE REAL SCHOOL.

The "Real School" forms a higher and distinct order, and is largely scientific, and intended to complete the education of young men destined for callings which do not require a university education. They are divided into three classes, and Latin is required in the highest. As education here leads to a business career, English and French are both taught. The Real School has a full course of nine years, which is so arranged that pupils can leave at intermediate stages. This excellent order of schools was introduced as early as 1738, but struggled against great discouragement, and did not gain firm footing until 1832. Prussia has now not far from a hundred of these schools, and they form one of her best educational features.

THE GYMNASIUM.

The "Progymnasium" and "Gymnasium" are classical schools which lead directly to the university. A general plan for all is fixed by the state, but great latitude of detail is left to the schools themselves in filling in their programmes. Prussia proper has about two hundred of these schools. They all have a state character, and are subject to state inspection, must bring their accounts to be audited by a public functionary, and can have no masters whose qualifications have not been strictly and publicly tested. We find in these higher secondary schools of Prussia, before her new acquisitions, with a population of eighteen millions, seventy four thousand pupils; while France, with thirty-six millions, has but sixty-six thousand of such scholars; and England and Wales, with twenty-three millions, but sixteen thousand.* The total expense of these schools in Prussia, in 1864, was two million five hundred and eighty thousand six hundred and eighty-four dollars; of which the fees made up about one-half, one-fourth was borne by municipalities, and five hundred and twenty-six thousand seven hundred and seventy-two dollars by the state.

The public schools are all very popular, and are greatly preferred to private schools, of which there are ten large ones in Berlin, and a few in other large cities. They have also a great advantage over private schools, as all professional men in Germany must pass through the universities, the examination for entrance to which is founded on the public school course, and is conducted by a commission composed largely of the faculties of the Gymnasia. In fact, the examination-test in Prussia does not amount to much. What is sought is that the student shall pass a certain number of years under instruction. This really trains him, while the examination-test does not. The thoroughness of Prussian education can be illustrated in no better way than by describing here the preparation necessary to matriculate in one of her universities.

Before 1788, it was an easy matter to enter one of these institutions. One only had to bring a letter of recommendation from the school he left, and show some knowledge of Latin. In that year a royal edict was promulgated re-

---

* There were also in the private higher schools of France some forty thousand or fifty thousand scholars, and a larger number in Prussia.

quiring that the pupil be examined both at the lower school on leaving, and also on presenting himself at the university. The examination embraced science and language. In 1794, after complaints that the universities had many unprofitable students, who merely came to escape military duty, strict rules were made; but there was no uniform plan of examination, and the regulations were still insufficient. Humboldt next inaugurated a uniform plan for the examination of candidates for the university, and the result was recorded in each case under the heads "qualified," "partially qualified," and "not qualified." The universities, however, from a desire to fill their catalogues, soon admitted all three grades of candidates. This evil is now corrected.

All candidates are examined at the Gymnasia, and but two grades of certificates given—"qualified" and "unqualified"—and no one without a certificate of "qualified" can matriculate; but those not qualified may be present at the lectures, and are known as "*extenue*," although their parents are advised to continue their preparation. The examining commission is very carefully constituted. The examination covers the mother-tongue, Latin, Greek, French, mathematics, physics, geography, history, and divinity, and, if the candidate is intended for the Church, Hebrew. The paper work lasts a week, and if the candidates fail in this, the *viva voce* examination is not tried. Many subjects are prepared by the school authorities, and the examiners select any they may see fit for the candidate. They report on each performance, "insufficient," "sufficient," "good," or "excellent," and no other terms are admitted. Each member of the commission must sign the certificate, to which the school authorities add a report as to the character of the candidate for conduct, diligence, and attainments. If, after being found "unqualified," he still insists upon going to the university, his position is exceptional; he can attend lectures, and is registered in a book specially kept for that class of students, but his time at the university does not count for a degree. He may return to a gymnasium and be examined once, and only once more, but his time at the university does not count to his advantage until after he has passed this examination.

All who enter for the three learned professions, and for teachers in the high schools and universities, must pass through the regular university course and graduate. Those, other than gymnasium students, who present themselves to the Certifying Board, although required to produce testimonials, are more gently dealt with by the Board, and those who fail to gain their certificates may still attend lectures with the same class from the Gymnasia.

The Prussian authorities understand how unreliable a test of scholarship and capacity an examination is, and aim to make it only such as a fair scholar of average ability and diligence may at the end of his school course come to with a quiet mind, and without a painful preparatory effort.

Great security and dignity is given to all school officials in Prussia, and the law protects them from all harsh treatment by the central authority. The minister may suspend for a short period, but can not dismiss. Every one in Prussia, of all politics and creeds, joins in bearing testimony that public instruction is in no way made a political instrument, and that it could not be; that the state administration of the schools and universities is fair and right, and that public opinion would not permit them to be governed by political interests. The truth seems to be, that the state has such faith in culture and in its schools that it will not permit them to be sacrificed to any other interest.

The scale of salary for all these high-school officials

ranges from three hundred and seventy-five dollars for a master of the lowest grade, to one thousand five hundred dollars a year for a director of the highest. This is in full for every thing; and when house-room and other allowances are furnished, a per centum is deducted. Some of the higher functionaries in some of the universities receive as much as three or four thousand dollars a year.

THE UNIVERSITIES.

I will only glance at the universities, and close the subject. It is the function of the university to develop into science the knowledge a student may bring with him from the secondary school, while it directs him toward his chosen profession. Prussia has seven universities—at Berlin, Bonn, Breslau, Greifwalde, Königsberg, Münster, and Braunsberg. They have two hundred professors, and about seven thousand students, although many Prussian scholars go to Heidelberg, Leipsic, Göttingen, and Jena. They all differ in many points of detail, but their general management is alike. None of them can boast of antiquity like those of France or England. They all have some property and some funds, but are mostly supported by their scholars, and the state steps in to pay the rest. The professors are appointed by the minister, but they act very independently of him in the management of their universities. The university authorities are as follows: first, a rector, who is chosen by the professors from among themselves, and is responsible for its discipline; then the university senate, elected in the same way, who, with the rector as chairman, administer internal affairs; then the faculties—of theology, law, medicine, and philosophy—who are required to administer their own departments, and are responsible for the attendance of their scholars. All the full professors and assistants are a teaching body, and, in connection, so arrange the course of lectures that all the ground to be gone over shall be covered, free liberty of choice of subjects being given as far as possible. Besides the regular professors, there are private professors. If a young man of learning wishes to become a private professor, he makes application, and is permitted to lecture before a committee of the faculty, who examine him, and, if he passes, authorize him to use the lecture-rooms when not required by the regular professors, and to lecture upon any of the subjects covered by the university course. He gets no regular pay—only fees—and attendance upon his lectures counts in the student's favor. As the private professor has a reputation to make, and the example of distinguished men before him, he works hard, while the regular professors, not to be outdone, are also driven to their best performance. The plan is ingenious, and makes it impossible for professors to lapse into routine, as is so often the case in our own institutions. The number of private and full professors in a university is generally about equal. The course is three years in theology, law, and philosophy, and four in medicine. The fees in each course of lectures range from four to ten dollars; but there are a few free scholarships, and an arrangement exists by which poor students can pay for their lectures by their services after graduating. Professors are also authorized to admit without charge many who are not able to pay. About every third scholar works hard—the others indifferently. Students are marked only for the lectures they attend, and the examination-test can not compensate for absence. In fact, without a satisfactory attendance, the student can not get his certificate of authority to appear for examination at all. This examination consists of three or four days of paper-work, and six or eight hours of *viva voce*. For lawyers and clergymen there is a second examination three years afterward.

In conclusion, what is perhaps most admirable in Germany is, that while material progress is rapid, culture is also a living power. Petty towns have their universities that are celebrated throughout the world, and the King of Prussia and Prince Bismarck oppose the departure of a great savant from Prussia as they would the loss of national power. Were you to ask a Prussian the tangible advantage of this system of education, he would reply that it had enabled their trained business men in every part of the world to beat all other people, with equal terms as to capital; and M. Durey, the late educational minister of France, says, "The young men of North Germany, all over the Continent, are securing, by reason of their better instruction, a confidence and command in business which the young men of no other nation can dispute with them." Who of us has failed to see something of this in America? And if you ask them how they effected their astonishing successes in Austria and France, they will reply, by thoroughly learning their business on the best plan by which it was possible to teach it to them. This is the merest sketch of what might, with interest and advantage, be expanded into volumes.

The influence of the German people is destined to be great, and will be exercised for good and peaceful ends. They may go to war, for war is sometimes necessary to secure peace. We felt this German power in our war, and know for what it was applied. No European nation can again attack them, except their near neighbor Russia, with whom there is the warmest relation of friendship and fraternity. And the other great nation of the future—ourselves—can have no other wish or interest than to join this moral alliance, and secure those ends which will best promote the good of mankind.

CHAPTER XIII.

FRENCH CIVIL SCHOOLS—EARLY HISTORY.*

POPULAR education has sprung out of the ideas and necessities of modern times, and elementary schools for the poor are institutions of recent history. With secondary schools it is different. They have a long history, going back, through a series of changes in every European country, to the very beginning of its civilization. The rich and noble houses always had their schools, although not all of their class were educated. All the countries of Western Europe had, in the feudal and Catholic Middle Ages, their monasteries and universities, which furnished teachers and controlled education, and the great centre and head of all was the University of Paris. Here came Roger Bacon, Dante, and Charles IV., the founder of the first university of the German Empire. It was to Paris that the rival popes referred their disputes for final decision; and in Asia, in foreign cities, on battle-fields, among statesmen, princes, priests, and scholars passed this word of recognition, "*Nos fuimus simul in Galaudia,*" the Rue de Galaude being an old street in the Latin quarter.

Roman civilization had established a system of schools in Gaul before her overthrow by the barbarians in the fourth century; but during the confusion that followed from the fourth to the twelfth centuries, the schools of France were confined to the monasteries. During the

---

* I am indebted for much that is in this chapter to the Reports of Professor Arnold, commissioner for the British Government to investigate and report upon the education of the Continent.

ninth century some provisions were made by the pope for the instruction of children outside the Church, and Charlemagne caused a school to be opened on a scale of great magnificence for the education of the young nobility, which, however, fell into disuse at his death.

THE UNIVERSITY OF PARIS.

In the first year of the thirteenth century the great school of Paris received its charter and the name "University of Paris," and, forty-nine years later, the first college of the University of Oxford was founded. Four nations composed the University of Paris—France, Picardy, Normandy, and England. It embraced a faculty of arts, which was pre-eminent, and of theology, law, and medicine. For a long time the chancellor of the Cathedral of Notre-Dame was academical chief of the university, both having a common seal. At last the university struck a seal of its own, which the pope ordered broken. The scholars rose in insurrection, and drove the chancellor out of the city. The matter was referred to the pope, who, after several years, yielded to the wishes of the university. The license to teach, the great goal of the university course, was still held by the ecclesiastical power (the chancellor of the Cathedral), and not until this was granted could the academic degree be awarded. Not only was the university thus hampered and circumvented by the great Metropolitan Church, but the mendicant orders intruded themselves upon it in every way, claiming the privileges of university students, to which they were at last admitted by the pope.

The university at one time, with its dependencies, comprised a third of the population of the city. It was exempt from taxation, its own courts administered justice, and it exercised complete power over Paris by threatening to close its lectures unless permitted to carry its measures. It adopted the plan of instruction by means of lectures, and seems, in this respect, to have left an impress upon schools in France which they still retain. In the fourteenth century colleges sprang up rapidly over France; and branch universities were established at Orleans, Angers, Toulouse, and Montpellier, among whose students we find the names of Erasmus, Rabelais, and Loyola.

The glory of the University of Paris was in its faculty of arts. Its course embraced grammar, rhetoric, and dialectic, besides arithmetic, geometry, astronomy, and music. This was the liberal course of the Middle Ages, and came direct from the schools of ancient Rome. Rhetoric embraced poetry, history, and composition, and dialectic took in the whole scope of philosophy. Unhappily the university did not follow the growth of the times, nor teach the new studies of the *Renaissance*, and animate by them the French schools, of which it was the head. Ramus, the representative in the university of the new order of things, who was attached to the College of Navarre, passed his life in bitter conflict with the university, and was twice condemned—once for his anti-Aristotelian heresies, and once for Calvinism. A retrograde spirit infected the university, and the colleges and schools of France, which everywhere depended upon it.

THE COLLEGE OF FRANCE.

The College of France, an institution founded by Fráncis I., and disconnected from the university, for the first time in France made Greek and Hebrew a part of the course, and established chairs for mathematics, philosophy, medicine, surgery, anatomy, and botany. This institution was spared by the Revolution, while all others perished.

THE JESUITS.

The Jesuits now came to successfully dispute the province, so long held unchallenged by the university. During their hundred years of unfettered teachings, ending with their dissolution in 1762, they established eighty-six colleges in France. This example was followed by the various monastic orders. The resources of the university were still intact, but the administration was no better than the instruction. Among the resources of the university were the post-office and the office of public conveyances, but it was compelled to render these up to the Government for the sum of one hundred and fifty thousand livres annually. The university undertook also, as part of the transaction, to make its instruction gratuitous. In 1764, the Jesuit schools were closed, and the members of the order expelled from France. The loss of their services as teachers was soon most seriously felt. Rousseau, among writers, and Turgot, among statesmen, paid great attention to schemes of education, and, by 1789, the public was roused to the great want of a new and better system.

THE SCHOOLS DURING THE REVOLUTION.

For twenty years after the Revolution, France did little for education except to build up and tear down. In 1791, the colleges were all placed under control of the state. In 1792, the university was abolished. In 1793, the property of the colleges was confiscated to the state, and later in the same year all the great public schools and the university faculties were suppressed. In 1792, Condorcet brought before the Committee of Public Instruction his memorable educational plan. He proposed a secondary school for every four thousand inhabitants, a college for each department, nine lycées for the whole of France, and crowned all by a National Society of Sciences and Arts, like the present Institute of France. The expense was to be borne by the state. Condorcet perished with the Girondists, and the reconstruction of public education did not begin until after the fall of Robespierre. Daunau's law of 1795 bore many traces of Condorcet's plan, and established primary schools, central schools, special schools, and, at the head of all, the Institute of France—the last a memorable and enduring creation. Normal schools, the Polytechnic, and the School of Mines, were also founded. But the country was too unsettled to carry on so considerable a work, and the scheme finally proved a failure. Private schools did better, but it was left for Napoleon, when he became first consul, to organize public instruction.

Fourcroy's law of 1802 took for its basis the secondary schools, both private and public. The Government aided them by providing houses, scholarships, and the pay of teachers. The course of studies was greatly enlarged, and a competent corps of inspectors furnished by the state. The work was now begun in earnest, and by 1810 was fully organized. In order to make the matter clear, it will be necessary to enumerate the civil divisions of France, and also to ask what had been done, if any thing, for the education of the poor.

MUNICIPAL DIVISIONS OF FRANCE.

France contains a population of about thirty-six millions, and is divided into eighty-six departments, corresponding in a measure to our States, and again into three hundred and sixty-three arrondissements, to which we have nothing nearer than our Congressional districts. There are, also, two thousand eight hundred and fifty cantons, like our counties, and thirty-six thousand eight hundred and twenty-six communes, like our townships. The departments, arrondissements, and communes, each have a separate civil administration, and are respectively presided over by a prefect, a sub-prefect, and a mayor, each assisted by a municipal council and a deliberative body. The three classes of functionaries, prefects, sub-prefects, and mayors are appointed by the central Government, and the deliberative bodies are elected by the people. The municipal councils are nominally elected by the people, but the law provides that the prefect of a department has the power to dissolve any municipal council and replace it by one of his own naming, and he usually exercises this power. This very complete organization was established by the First Consul in 1800.

THE CHURCH IN FRANCE.

Three forms of religious worship are recognized in France — viz., Roman Catholic, Protestant, and Jewish, and the ministers of all three are salaried alike by the state. The Roman Catholic is the religion of about thirteen-fifteenths of the people of France. There are about five million Protestants and seventy thousand Jews.

The Christian Church has, from the earliest ages, in France, recognized the duty, and claimed the right, of controlling public education, and an examination of the archives shows no lack of edicts and instructions from bishops to clergy to open free schools for the poor, where the children of the faithful might receive the elements of instruction. From the fourth century to the sixteenth, the village priests were enjoined to collect at their dwellings a certain number of readers and train them in the study of letters, as well as in the ministry of the altar. The extent of instruction thus given by the clergy, or the number receiving it, is nowhere stated, but their own published lamentations at their failure to carry out their duty induces the belief that it amounted to very little. The state in France has maintained, against the pope and its own subjects, the right to govern public instruction. Charlemagne even assumed and exercised the right to personally examine his bishops, to assure himself that they had not neglected their learning. Only once, for a short time during the Reign of Terror, has instruction ever been free in France.

Until the fifteenth century popular education in France bore little fruit, being controlled almost entirely by one class of society—the clergy. During all this early period, any poor peasant-boy might enter a monastery, join some order, and rise to learning and fame; but this, practically, opened the way to but very few. The collections of autographs run back only to the fifteenth century, for the simple reason that but few, even of the great, could before that time write their names. It is easy to imagine what was the education of the poor and lowly.

The unparalleled impulse given by the Reformation to popular education in Protestant countries can scarcely be estimated, or its advantages realized. Primary instruction in Scotland, Holland, and Protestant Germany dates from this epoch, and our own comes directly from it. France could not escape the great agitation of the time, but failed to found any lasting system. The Church interposed and the king yielded whenever any measure was urged looking to the education of the poor, and not strictly subject to ecclesiastical authority. The clergy endeavored to retain their influence by means of their own religious orders, and in 1789 there were twenty religious societies engaged in giving instruction to the poor of France. Their efforts had, however, for a long time been devoted almost exclusively to the rich, and it is not clear to what extent they benefited society.

BRETHREN OF THE CHRISTIAN SCHOOLS.

The order most worthy of special notice, and which still exists, and plays an important part in the education of the poor of France, is the "Brethren of the Christian Schools." It dates from 1679, and was founded by Jean Baptiste de La Salle, who was connected with the cathedral at Rheims, and resigned his position to execute his plan. He was a man of great zeal and piety—one of the very few who understood the deplorable state of ignorance of the poor of his country. He drew up, for the guidance of his order, a set of statutes, which, unchanged, still control it. He also composed a hand-book of method, which has scarcely been surpassed. He died in 1719, after having consecrated a life of singular devotion to the one idea of instruction for the poor. His work was destined to do more in the way intended than that of any other Frenchman of modern times.

Dispersed by the Revolution, the Brethren were restored by Napoleon, and at the Restoration owned, and taught in two hundred and ten houses. In 1848 they had in France nineteen thousand four hundred and fourteen schools, and taught one million three hundred and fifty-four thousand and fifty-six children. The Brethren devote themselves to the teaching of boys in all things that pertain to an honest and Christian life. They are not forbidden to receive the rich into their schools, but their business is with the poor, and toward them they are directed to manifest special affection. No brother is allowed to take orders. Their vows are poverty, chastity, and obedience, and to teach without fee or reward; and these vows are only taken for three years at a time. They are always to go in companies of threes, and to keep at their houses a store of school-books and materials for sale to their scholars at cost price. They are not permitted to talk gossip with their pupils, and are required to be sparing of punishments. Such are the rules to which this remarkable association owes its vitality. The pious founder, to whose thoughts the misery flowing from the debasement and ignorance of the poor was always present, and with whom its relief was a passion, took every precaution not to found an order of monks instead of an order of school-teachers. He prohibited bodily mortification, strictly limited the number of fasts, and dissuaded the brothers from taking perpetual vows. Other societies endeavored to imitate this, but none with much success. The order can not make itself felt in the poorest and most needy parts of the state; for, as the brothers always live by threes, the poor villages can not support them, when they might support a single teacher. The state still sees its lowest orders sunk in the deepest ignorance.

LOUIS XIV.—COERCIVE CATHOLIC EDUCATION.

Louis XIV. endeavored to reach all classes, but was actuated by motives so base, so unlike those which inspired M. de La Salle, as to defeat his own efforts. He bethought himself of the village school-master as a powerful and useful instrument in his work of forcible conversions, and, in a royal edict of 1698, ordered that the children of heretics be taken from their families at five years of age, to be brought up in Catholic schools. As these schools did not exist, they were ordered; and in them were to be taught to both sexes " the mysteries of the Catholic, apostolic, and Roman religion." Reading, and even writing, might also be taught. The edict went on to prescribe that the villages should be taxed for the support of their respective schools. Nothing came of this scheme. The era of the Revolution was approaching, when an impetus was to be given to the instruction of the poor such as was never felt before. Little is known of the real condition of primary instruction at this time, except the work of the various mendicant orders, which was meagre enough. The French poor were without instruction, except the Bible lessons by the village priest.

In the report of establishments of public instruction required by the revolutionary government, the columns for primary instruction are blank, and there are no data from which to estimate its condition. It is known that village schools occasionally existed, and that in 1789 one boy in thirty-one between the ages of eight and eighteen years was receiving secondary instruction of some kind, while in New England nearly every family sent one son to college.

No one could teach unless approved by ecclesiastical authority, and the curé usually appointed the teacher, often one of his own creatures. Mr. Arnold says: "At the beginning of this century the instruction of the most of the French people remained very little changed from what it was in the Middle Ages. In conversing with workingmen, I found that most had been to school at some time, their fathers more rarely, and their grandfathers never."

EFFORTS OF THE CONVENTION.

The Revolution busied itself with schemes for universal education, which all classes called for. The clergy claimed still more strongly their right to control it. It was agreed that "public education should be so modified as to be adapted to the wants of all orders in the state, that it might form good and useful men in all classes of society." Turgot had already drawn up a plan of a uniform national system, but, not satisfied with it, the Assembly appointed a commission, with M. de Talleyrand as its secretary, which, after two years of faithful, laborious inquiry, presented the draft of Condorcet's law just upon the eve of the adjournment of the Assembly. It only had time to resolve, "that there shall be created and organized a public instruction, gratuitous in respect to those branches of tuition which are indispensable for all men." At the next meeting of the Assembly, Condorcet presented an amended law, but the Convention now replaced the Assembly, and little was done except to extirpate such imperfect instruction as had already managed to maintain life in France. Much was destroyed when there was nothing to replace it, and the University of Paris fell in the common ruin. So complete was this destruction that Fourcroy, the chief agent of Napoleon in restoring the schools, declared to the Convention that France was fast relapsing into barbarism.

The Convention had a sincere desire to re-establish public instruction on a firm and just basis, but the times were not propitious. It has given France, however, two admirable institutions of learning, the usefulness of which she can never cease to appreciate—the superior Normal School and the Polytechnic. It discussed and passed laws establishing a general system, and adopted a programme embracing the subjects estimated by the Assembly as "indispensable for all men." "The children of all classes," so reads the law, "are to receive that primary education, physical, moral, and intellectual, best adapted to develop in them republican manners, patriotism, and love of labor." They were to learn "those traits of virtue which most honor freemen, and particularly those features of the French Revolution best adapted to elevate the soul, and render men worthy of liberty and equality." The law made women eligible as teachers, but disqualified women of noble family, or who belonged to any religious order, or who had been named for the post of teacher by a noble or ecclesiastic. Such was the popular feeling in France against the Church and nobility, that it was not deemed necessary to make any such restrictions with regard to men.

The Convention could do all this, but could not furnish common schools, and in despair, in December, 1793, abandoned the attempt, and declared that teaching was free—requiring only certificates of citizenship and morality. The state undertook to pay the teachers, and to compel parents to send their children. The next year another decree increased the conditions of the teacher's eligibility, and made the whole neighborhood of his school a censor over his acts. The system was patched each year, with partial results, and swimming, gymnastics, and military exercises were finally added, as "acquirements indispensable for all men." This seemed to be its culmination, for, in the next year, 1795, Daunau's remarkable law readjusted the whole scheme of public education, beginning with the primary schools, and ending with the institute. This law did more for primary education than any thing that had gone before, and endured until 1833. By this law the elementary programme was reduced to reading, writing, and ciphering. It abolished the fixed salaries of teachers, and left them to be paid by three-fourths of the pupils, provided indigent scholarships for the other fourth, and removed the obligation of parents to send their children. We see how the promise of the early Assembly to give free schooling to all was carried out. M. Guizot, in reply to the question, "What did the French Revolution do for popular education?" answers, "*Un deluge de mots, rien de plus.*" In respect to the actual establishment of popular instruction, this is undoubtedly true, yet it is generally conceded that the Revolution made it impossible for France subsequently to found a system which was not both secular and national. It is claimed that by this much was gained. The four or five years preceding 1799 saw France greatly reduced by her extravagant wars, and her general administration in neglect and confusion. Her schools formed no exception to this, and Napoleon set to work in earnest at the task—which has shed such imperishable glory on the consulate—to use his own words—of "founding a new society, free alike from the injustice of feudalism and from the confusion of anarchy." Of his peaceful labors, modern French administration, the Condorcet schools for the middle and upper classes, the Legion of Honor, the Code, the University, are living monuments. Primary schools received attention also, but the first great need was to rescue those on whom France rested, and who saved her society from the ruin in which it had fallen.

NAPOLEON AND THE SCHOOLS.

On the 1st of May, 1802, the law was made which regulated secondary instruction, and gave it, in the main, the form which it wears to-day. For the feeble, decaying central schools of the Convention—mere courses of lectures, without study and without discipline—the law substituted the communal colleges and lyceums, with a rigid course of sustained study and an iron discipline, and enlarged the exclusively mathematical and scientific course so as to include the classics.

Only a single article in the new law referred to schools for the poor. They were continued, and put under the supervision of prefects and sub-prefects. A house was provided for the teacher, and he was authorized to collect his pay from his pupils. Thorough investigations were made through all the departments to learn their needs. Nearly all complained bitterly of the almost total dearth of primary instruction, and many prayed for the re-establishment of the religious orders which had formerly taught the poor.

THE UNIVERSITY OF FRANCE.

By the law of May, 1806, the University of France was called into existence. The law reads: "There shall be formed, under the name of Imperial University, a body with the exclusive charge of tuition and of public education throughout the empire." The whole instruction of France was thus placed under a government of grand masters, councilors, and rectors. "No school, no establishment of learning whatever, can be formed outside the pale of the university, and without the authorization of its chief." It was well endowed by the state, and became a great civil corporation with vast vested rights.

Created an endowed corporation, not a mere department of the state, the university bore a character of independence which all modern governments in France are apt to regard with suspicion. Napoleon did not create it hastily, but assigned his reasons as follows:

"His majesty has organized the university as a corporate body, because a corporate body never dies, and because in such a body there is a perpetual transmission of organization and spirit. It has been his majesty's desire to realize, in a state of forty millions of people, what Sparta and Athens accomplished—what the religious orders attempted in our own day, but failed for want of unity. His majesty wants a body whose teaching shall be free from the influences of the passing gusts of fashion—a body that may keep moving, even though Government is lethargic—whose administration and statutes may be so thoroughly national that no one shall lightly lay his hands upon them."

These designs have not wholly failed. But disliked by the Bourbons, hated by the clergy, decried by the friends of unrestricted instruction, ill-supported by successive ministers incapable of Napoleon's elevated views, the university has been unable to maintain its exclusive privileges and its corporate character.

In 1824, it was made a ministerial department; in 1833,

its special appropriation was suppressed; and in 1851, its property was passed over to the state. But the minister of public instruction is still the head of the university, and his chief assistants are its functionaries, graduated in its faculties and inspired by its traditions. That transmission of a corporate spirit wished for by Napoleon has been accomplished, while the exclusive privileges which the growing tendencies of the age would not tolerate have been withdrawn, and from the corporate spirit the members of the university derive an independence, a self-respect, and a disinterestedness which distinguish them from the whole body of French officials.

The University of France has not the traditions of ancient universities, nor great estates, but it has features which compensate for the absence of all it does not possess —intelligence and equity.

It is scarcely necessary to trace the attempts to establish primary instruction during the First Empire. They were little else than a repetition of previous efforts, and met with like failures. In 1808 inquiries were again instituted into the condition of primary education. About one-half of the communes were found to be without instruction, and, where the schools still existed, teachers were found old, infirm, and unsuited to their duties. Napoleon sincerely wished to secure the instruction of the poor under proper restrictions, but was compelled, like the clergy before him, to acknowledge his failure. As the investigation progressed further, the deplorable state of national ignorance became more and more apparent. There was one happy exception. The Congregation of Christian Schools was beginning to re-appear, and was everywhere highly useful. Every possible help was given it by the state, and the result leaves nothing to regret except that it was not sooner restored.

"Perhaps no better criticism can be produced by the performance of the university upon primary schools," says Mr. Arnold, "than its table of expenditures—the entire sum, from first to last, being eight hundred and fifty dollars, and even this was paid by the minister of education from a contingent fund, and not from the funds of the university." The university was, in truth, never provided with funds for so great an undertaking, nor with a working staff suitable for such a purpose. Primary instruction was really in a state of torpor, and required a treatment more radical and extended than any one, if we except M. de La Salle, had as yet comprehended. The conscription, also, had the effect to harass and exhaust the lower people, until they cared very little for instruction or any kindred thing. Napoleon, aware of his error, took a really admirable step to rectify it, by establishing the first normal school at Strasbourg in 1810, and continued, up to the battle of Waterloo, abortive efforts to elevate by culture the poor of the empire. To the Restoration is due the credit of having for the first time perceived the necessity of aiding popular education by national funds.

SCHOOLS UNDER THE RESTORATION.

The primary schools up to this time had died for want of sustenance. That they would have lived long had they received aliment, is doubtful. Other Governments decreed programmes and systems; this one decreed money. In 1816, it gave ten thousand dollars to buy books and models for the schools of the poor. It reorganized schools, transferred the authority over them to a new set of officials, raised the standard of teachers, and provided for independent Protestant schools in Protestant neighborhoods. But the instruments left by the Revolution were not suitable for the easy working of a monarchy. In public instruction, like every thing else, the monarchy was constantly striving to assert its old traditions in the face of a legal situation of which it was not master, and it perpetually failed.

One of its first acts was to strike at the university and deprive it of its control of education, upon the ground that its power was too absolute, and incompatible with the paternal intentions and liberal spirit of the new Government. The re-appearance of Napoleon gave respite to the university; but the empire, more timid and moderate than before, did nothing to improve the schools.

The moment the order of the Christian Schools found itself relieved from the empire, it endeavored to shake off the yoke of the Imperial Institute. It directed its brethren not to appear for examination, and maintained that, since the order had never ceased to have a legal existence, all its ancient rights should revert to it, and in 1818 it was decided that exemption from examination be given the brethren. In 1824, primary instruction was surrendered entirely to the clergy. The law reimposed Latin as the language of the college lectures, and still continued the clergy as salaried servants of the state, and refused to heads of families the privilege of disposing of their own property.

In many such ways the Government alienated its friends and raised up powerful enemies, yet it always evinced warm solicitude, and sometimes liberality, toward education. In 1828, it restored to local school committees their lay element, taken away four years before, and in the same year gave back to the university the primary schools.

The little sum of ten thousand dollars, appropriated by the state for primary education, had been steadily enlarged, until, in 1830, it was sixty thousand dollars, and the one primary normal school at Strasbourg, bequeathed by the empire, had the same year increased to thirteen. Considerable progress seems to have been made; yet, say the committee of investigation: "It was externally more specious than internally sound." The ordinance of 1816 required all teachers to have certificates of examination, but the religious orders were allowed to evade it by presenting their letters of obedience in place of certificates. Others usually avoided their examinations, and often enough a communal school was represented solely by the schoolmaster's certificate. Of the twenty thousand communes with schools of some sort in 1834, hardly half owned their own school-houses. The remainder held their sessions in barns, cellars, stables, in the open porch of the church, and often in the one poor room of the teacher, in which he cooked, ate, slept, and reared his family. When school premises existed, they were often dilapidated hovels, windowless, fireless, without ventilation, reeking with moisture and fruitful of epidemics.

GUIZOT'S ADMINISTRATION OF SCHOOLS.

M. Guizot assumed control of the Educational Department of France in 1833, and sent no less than five hundred inspectors throughout the length and breadth of the country to determine accurately the condition of elementary schools. This is the first thoroughly effective step, commensurate with the work in hand, ever taken in France in the interest of primary education. On their report was based the law of 1833, which still, little altered, regulates the education of that country. This commission has left a most deplorable record. The teacher was often a petty tradesman, leaving his classes every moment to attend to a customer; many were drunkards, many were cripples. The list of vocations in which teachers were engaged outside of their schools is laughable, and the experiences encountered in making this sort of inquisitorial investigation would fill many volumes, which would read like fiction. The apathy everywhere found was very disheartening, and instead of the gratitude they reasonably looked for, the inspectors everywhere met resistance in some form, and were often not permitted to lodge in the village where they had prosecuted their inquiries.

THE MONARCHY OF JULY AND THE SCHOOLS.

We have seen how almost every Government that has ruled France since the Reformation has made popular education a necessity, has endeavored to establish it, and how miserably they have failed. We will now see how the monarchy of July, composed as it was of men who had long revolved the problem of popular education, performed its part in this great act.

The members of the Government were mostly élèves of the university, thoroughly imbued with its spirit, and soon showed that they intended schools to be controlled by an educated body. In the year 1831 teachers were required to be thoroughly examined and certified. In the next two years thirty new primary normal schools were created, and the budget for primary education was increased to two hundred thousand dollars; and in June, 1833, the new law, carefully drawn by a commission, of which M. Cousin was reporter, and M. Guizot chairman, was passed.

The law of 1833 is so truly the root of the present system of schools in France as to deserve especial notice. It was full of good sense, fruitful ideas, toleration, and equity, and had the great merit of attaining more nearly than any other enactment the object which it had in view. It founded for the first time in France a national elementary education. Succeeding legislation has subverted many of its important provisions, but the essential ones remain intact. What was before merely recommended was now made obligatory, and ways provided for its fulfillment. At first the law contemplated a provision for girls' schools, but this was deferred until 1836—the date of the first important legislation upon female popular education in France.

The Convention had at first exaggerated what was indispensable in primary education, and had afterward too much reduced it, which error was copied by Napoleon. This left a large class requiring more than the limited schedule of the primary schools, yet not requiring the course at the communal colleges. To supply this want, the law created a secondary primary instruction, embracing what may be called a good French education. For the great lower class, for the masses of France, an elementary primary instruction was instituted. To the Convention's list of subjects were added the elements of grammar, religious teaching, and instruction in weights and measures. This would have been a great step in advance, if the intent of the law had been carried out.

The law also made teaching free, requiring only that the teachers should furnish satisfactory testimonials of capacity and morality. It was necessary to found public schools almost everywhere, as the places where primary instruction was most needed were those where private enterprise was least active. Each commune was, therefore, required to re-establish, either alone or in conjunction with adjacent communes, at least one elementary school, to which were to be admitted no longer only a fourth or fifth part, but all of the indigent children of the locality, without fee. Parents were to be at all times consulted, and their wishes observed as to the denominational instruction of their children. The commune, the department, and the state were to jointly control these schools, and bear the expense of their support—the primary obligation resting on the commune, and the department, with the help of the state, making up any deficit. Many communes owned large school properties, while many were indigent. This was, in short, the machinery for the first efficient system of primary schools in France. Even this provision was meagre, being equivalent to about one school to a township in our Northern States.

For teachers, a house and forty dollars yearly salary were provided, with an additional amount to accrue from fees, fixed by the Municipal Council, and collected by the tax-gatherer. A fund, from which to pension retired teachers, was also provided for by a "drawback" from teachers' pay. Each department was required to establish a normal school. Local authority over schools and teachers was wisely guarded, and an appeal given in proper cases.

Such are the main features of the law of 1833, remarkable for the wisdom of its provisions, and the energy with which it was executed. M. Guizot realized that the weak point of his law was the incapacity of local authorities to carry out the part intrusted to them, and endeavored, by a series of letters and pamphlets, to communicate his own zeal to others, and to awaken that local interest and independent activity the lack of which is the defect of French civilization. He succeeded imperfectly in this, but he did establish the schools on a firm foundation, and won confidence in his own zeal and capacity.

The results of the law of 1833 were remarkable. In five years the number of normal schools increased to seventy-six, and furnished instruction to more than two thousand five hundred teachers. The elementary schools accommodated three million five hundred and thirty thousand one hundred and thirty-five children of both sexes— a proportion to the population almost as great as is found in Switzerland or Holland. The state also, in 1836, established girls' schools, nearly on the same footing as boys', and normal schools for preparing their teachers; also infant-schools and working-men's schools. These were all successful and popular, and, until the *coup d'état*, all worked with some measure of success.

Two defects ultimately became apparent in the system. In the first place, the local school authorities were inefficient. The fact was, and is now, that the country districts of France lacked men who were both able and willing to superintend primary education. It was to create such a class that Guizot labored so zealously, and here he failed. Public opinion can be guided, but men can not be improvised for such an emergency. In the second place, the pay of the teachers was insufficient. The law had made them influential and respectable, but left them poor. Government was devising means to correct this evil, when the republican government fell. A circular sent to the teachers on the eve of the elections exhorted them to use their influence for the return of sincere Republicans, and to "combat the popular prejudice that prefers a rich and lettered citizen, stranger to the peasant's life, and guided by interests at variance with peasants' interests," to the "honest peasant endowed with natural good sense, and whose practical experience is better than all the book-learning in the world."

CHAPTER XIV.

FRENCH CIVIL SCHOOLS—*Continued.*

THE "COUP D'ÈTAT" AND THE SCHOOLS.

AFTER the *coup d'état*, a commission was ordered to investigate and report upon the primary schools, and the workings of the law of 1833. The report of this commission condemned the teachers as overambitious, their training as injudicious, and their conduct toward spiritual and temporal authorities as disrespectful. Some discreditable occurrences in one of the most secluded departments of France were used as swift witnesses against the entire system. It was claimed that the statistics of crime showed an increase; public prejudice was aroused; and the religious orders were again brought forward to take a leading part in education. Sentences of dismissal and suspension were pronounced against lay-teachers, often for no other reason than the utterance of strong republican sentiments. On the dispassionate inquiry made at the instance of the university most of these teachers were finally reinstated; the complaints against overtraining and the normal schools gradually died away, and a few years later the Government freely acknowledged itself in the wrong.

In the years 1850, '52, and '54 the law of 1833 was amended, and made more efficient. M. Guizot's plan for the payment of teachers was improved by commuting the fees for an equivalent in salary. As an offset to this, a class of probationary teachers was organized upon less pay until after three years' service in the lower grade, when they were made full teachers. The salary of these teachers was now fixed at one hundred dollars per annum, and that of the full teachers of primary schools was only twenty dollars more. Communes were authorized to increase this sum, which was often done, but at no extra cost to the state.

The supervision and moral direction of the primary schools were given to the mayors and curés. The prefects were armed with extraordinary powers, but acted mainly upon the recommendations of academy inspectors. There were sixteen Academies of France, all branches of the university. Each had assigned to it a number of departments over which it had educational supervision. A functionary known as an academy inspector had the chief control of primary instruction, and acted in such matters conjointly with the prefects. The central authority was vested in "The Imperial Council of Public Instruction." The minister always presided at its meetings, and the members were appointed by the imperial power. To this body were referred all laws and decrees on education, the course of study at the schools, and all matters of this nature. The new law, like the old, guarantied and secured religious liberty. Rectors were charged by M. Guizot that in public schools no child of a different denomination from that of the majority should be constrained to take part in the religious instruction and observances of his fellow-scholars. Parents were to be invited and requested to cause such children to be taken at suitable times to join in the services of their own church, and clergymen were invited to visit the house during the week to give them suitable religious instruction in their own faith. Similar provisions were made for the higher schools. The new law has improved somewhat upon this. Whenever a commune contains sufficient numbers of each sect, different denominational schools are at once established; when not, the council decides that children of different denominations shall attend the same institution, under regulations which secure freedom of worship. Clergymen of different denominations have equal access to such schools, in order to watch over the instruction of their own flocks; and, notwithstanding much ignorant assertion to the contrary, there is no doubt that the liberty proclaimed by law is maintained in practice. To this the chiefs of the principal Protestant communities in France bear ample and positive testimony.

That provision of the law of 1833, which proclaimed the right of all indigent children to free instruction, had been taken advantage of by those not entitled to the privilege. To prevent this abuse, the new law compelled the mayors to make out an annual list of indigent pupils. This did not work well, and now the whole matter of indigent scholarships is in the hands of the prefects.

M. Guizot's scheme for intermediate instruction never succeeded, the poor being satisfied with the primary schools, and those able to do better aiming for the communal colleges. This feature was supplanted in the new law by a provision establishing a second grade of primary schools. Any communal authority may ask, and gain, from the departmental council the higher course for its school. Girls' schools were left about as they were found. They were all under public supervision and inspection. Lay boarding-schools are inspected by a committee of ladies appointed by the prefect, and certificates of capacity must be obtained by their teachers; but for the Sisters letters of obedience are sufficient.

PRESENT CONDITION OF SCHOOLS.

This is the legal condition of primary education in France. It is not easy to get at the real state of education there at this moment, or rather at the beginning of the war. For the past year few or no statistics upon educational subjects have been published, or, in fact, collected. In 1857, there were in France sixty-five thousand one hundred primary schools. Of these, thirty-nine thousand six hundred were attended by boys, seventeen thousand were attended by both sexes, and twenty-five thousand five hundred were exclusively girls' schools. The tendency in France is more and more to separate the sexes in education. The number of children who received instruction was three millions eight hundred and fifty thousand. Of these, two millions one hundred and fifty thousand were boys, and one million seven hundred thousand were girls. Of the whole number, two millions six hundred thousand paid for their scholarships, and the remainder, one million two hundred and fifty thousand, were free or indigent scholars.

The amount of instruction received by each pupil may be estimated by the whole cost, which was but forty-two million five hundred thousand and twelve francs, or about two dollars each. These calculations do not include the infant schools, numbering two thousand six hundred and eighty-four, under the direction of the empress, nor the practical and working-men's schools, which were supported by the empire. It is difficult to learn much about these schools, the Government reports showing little upon the subject.

French officials in the lower grades are very poorly paid, and those connected with the schools form no exception to the rule. The school inspectors, who come next after the teachers, are functionaries of the greatest importance, yet they receive only from four hundred to five hundred dollars a year, and a little more than a dollar a day for expenses. The minister of public instruction gets twenty thousand dollars a year, besides a house and many perquisites connected with his office.

SCHOOL BUILDINGS AND MANAGEMENT.

The buildings used for school purposes are usually adapted, not built, for the purpose. In Paris the school buildings are very handsome, and elaborately fitted up, but in the country districts they will not bear comparison with our own. It is not uncommon, in country villages, to see "*Ecole Publique*" over the door of a miserable-looking building whose doors lead directly into the filthy street, and flanked by a green-grocer's store and a beer-shop.

One of the public primary schools of Paris is in the Rue du Faubourg Montmartre, and may be taken as a fair specimen of its class. It is held in a large and imposing building, and accommodates four hundred pupils, equally divided between the sexes, which are separated. The rooms are all high and well-ventilated, the walls made non-conductive of sound, and each school has an open and a covered play-ground. The covered play-ground is a general feature of large, well-conducted schools throughout France. It is a large room, on the same level as the first floor, and often open at one side, as at Saint-Cyr. Here, in the middle of the day, the children take their meal, which they bring in their little baskets. The rooms are fitted up with short desks and seats, the walls generally bare of maps, but covered with blackboards. A map of France, one of Europe, a crucifix, and a bust of the reigning sovereign, are the invariable ornaments of every public school. The boys have two large rooms, in which they are taught reading, writing, grammar, arithmetic, history, and geography. The instruction is generally given to the whole class at once. The girls are all gathered in one large room, and there is one school-mistress for them all, assisted by fourteen monitresses, who receive about eight francs a month. The order in both schools is excellent.

Instruction and books in the communal schools of Paris, and most of the large cities, are entirely gratuitous. Although this is done to place the schools within the reach of the very poor, the well-to-do, except the born aristocrats, attend, often to the detriment of the poorer classes. The law, although strict enough on this point, is usually evaded by the mayors, whose business it is to administer it, by permitting the teachers to submit for approval their own lists, which are accepted without inquiry. The teachers, except some of the Christian Brothers, prefer in their schools the better clad, better trained, and more creditable child of well-to-do parents, to the often ragged and unclean offspring of the poor. A teacher's pardonable pride in having his pupils respectable, and in winning, through his scholars, the favor of their parents, readily accounts for this. This is more noticeable in the girls' schools; and there are communes where, of five Sisters engaged for the purpose of public instruction, one alone attends to the education of the poor in one great class; the other four to the smaller number of the well-born. The education which the nation provides for the poor is thus subordinated to the interests of others, sometimes to the exclusion of its lawful recipients. Mr. Arnold, however, thinks there are comparatively small numbers of children anywhere in France who do not at some time receive some instruction in the schools.

In the Rue de la Gaurdier there is a girls' school, with two hundred scholars, held by the Sisters, and, attached to it, an infant-school of one hundred. There is a community of sixteen Sisters here, of whom five have charge of the schools, and the remainder perform daily acts of charity in the neighborhood. The city of Paris has recently bought and presented to the Sisters their modern school premises. The order and neatness in this school are unsurpassed, but the instruction is ordinary. The Sisters teach the elementary branches very well, but, for scholarship, the lay schools for girls in Paris are said to surpass those of the religious orders, while in the remainder of France the opposite is the case. There is, nevertheless, something singularly pleasing and attractive in these Sisters' schools. There is the fresh, neat school-room, always cheerful, clean, and tastefully decorated, and a prevailing spirit of order and affection. The refinement and gentleness of the Sisters themselves speaks of tranquillity, innocence, and happiness. The law of France does not recognize perpetual vows, but it is very unusual for a Sister to quit a religious life after she once embraces it. Fatigue and ill health may compel her to give up teaching, but she becomes a visitress, or nurse, or labors in the dispensary, and devotes her life to the afflicted and necessitous. I found them everywhere among the wounded and the sick. Wherever misery came, there came also a Sister to relieve it.

One of the schools of the Christian Brothers stands in the Rue du Roche. It is kept by four members of the brotherhood, and is divided into four classes of one hundred each. The instruction of such immense classes is necessarily somewhat superficial. It is doubtful if any teacher of children can do justice to more than twenty-five or thirty in a class. The children are kept perpetually writing, and but little oral questioning is resorted to.

The Brothers often quit their order after their three or six years, and return to civil life, their purpose in joining the order being rather educational than religious. They are qualified to act as teachers two years earlier than the lay teachers, and thus are enabled to leave home much sooner. There is no doubt of the great good performed by this brotherhood, and it has always retained the favor of Government. The French people outside of Normandy, Alsace, and Lorraine, prefer the religious to the secular schools. With regard to the Sisters' schools, Mr. Arnold says: "There can not be a moment's doubt but their schools are beyond the reach of competition." In Paris it is a bad sign of the respectability of a family to prefer a lay to a religious school for its boys, and the same is true in the country where religious schools are accessible.

At Blanquefort, a well-built village of two thousand inhabitants, near Bordeaux, Mr. Arnold visited a school, of which he says:

"I found at the public school sixty boys on the books, and forty-three in attendance. The room was large, airy, well lighted, fitted up with desks, and the children at work under monitors. There was a map of France, and several small ones on the wall. Their reading was good, grammar good also; their geography good only in Europe; of history they knew nothing; their writing was fair, and arithmetic excellent. Their school-books were generally positively bad, and, as everywhere else in France, their reading-books embraced a series of moral lessons without substance, without style, and repulsive by their monotony. There is no really good series of school-books in France.

"The boys were cheerful, and under good discipline; some six were without shoes and stockings, but they were generally children of parents in comfortable circumstances. One in six were free scholars; the remainder pay two francs a month.

"The master's house is attached, and the law prescribes three rooms as his allowance. His pay was twelve hundred francs a year.

"The girls' school is but a few yards distant. The law does not provide this, but villages near large cities are usually provided for by the city, or at least assisted by it. This one was held in a bad, ill-ventilated building, without play-ground, and kept by the school-master's wife. Forty-eight girls had their names on the books, and twenty-eight were present. They were the children of families who did not live as servants. Their stock of information was very limited, but their reading, arithmetic, and needle-work were good. Fifteen were free scholars.

"We now visited a school kept by the Sisters. Six of them work here together, renting their school-building, and receiving only twenty dollars yearly from the department. Two Sisters have charge of the infant school, the remainder the girls' school. The propriety, neatness, and order which reigned here was most striking, and most favorably in contrast with the school just left. The cleanliness and order were beautiful. Flowers were arranged everywhere, and the furniture and fittings were a marvel of freshness. Fifteen were admitted as indigents; the remainder pay two francs a month. Forty-three girls and forty-eight infants were present. Boards and Bible pictures covered the walls. Instruction did not go far in the infant-schools. —affection seeming to control in their treatment; yet they knew their letters, and looked clean and happy, and went through their simple exercises prettily, and in excellent training. In the girls' school instruction was good."

The foregoing are specimens of the schools in the flourishing portions of France. The following is an example of another kind:

"At St. Martin de Touche, a village of eight hundred souls, a few miles from Toulouse, the school was in a poor building, ill-ventilated, with an uneven brick floor, and no play-grounds. This school is entirely free, being supported by the city of Toulouse. There were twenty-eight boys present. They all wore wooden shoes. The boys read pretty well, knew a little of geography, less of history, but their writing, grammar, and arithmetic were good. The master's wife had a class of six little boys in an adjoining room. She had formerly taught the girls of the village, but the Sisters had just opened a school, and all the girls had gone there. There were forty present at this school."

There are other schools, mostly private, both Protestant and Catholic, throughout France; but they are all under the law, and so nearly like those already described, that these may be taken as examples of the elementary schools of the country.

PRIMARY NORMAL SCHOOLS.

The normal schools, one to each department, are also included in primary instruction. The course is alike in all, and corresponds with that in the elementary schools; but many students pass beyond this meagre programme. The course occupies three years, and there are about fifty scholars in attendance at a time in each school. Paris has no normal school for primary instruction, but depends upon her attractions to draw the best teachers from the provinces.

Examinations are held each year, and those who fail are not permitted to go on. Great stress is laid upon methods of teaching, but the course of studies is exceedingly limited. A student who has passed the teachers' course may continue his studies considerably beyond this. There seems to be a constant fear of making students rather than school-masters, and the course would seem to us far too meagre. Students agree, on entering, to serve as teachers for ten years, and the best scholars receive some aid from the state. Agriculture and horticulture form a part of the course, and, besides being a profitable kind of instruction, are very popular.

SECONDARY INSTRUCTION.

France has sixty-three lyceums and two hundred and forty-four communal colleges. These are connected with the state, receiving assistance and gaining dignity and efficiency from the relationship. They all, in fact, receive aid from the state, the departments, the communes, and private benevolence, and in them all scholarships are provided for poor and deserving scholars. These schools are for the higher and middle classes of society, and serve excellently to blend the two. There is no law nor influence excluding from them the great under-class of France, yet it is very rare to find the sons of peasants here. In all these schools arrangements for boarding, discipline, hours of work and recreation, are regulated by Government, and are uniform.

The Minister of Public Instruction is at the head of this vast organization, and is assisted by the Imperial Council of Public Instruction—a specially organized body for the direction and control of schools. Each religious denomination, Catholic, Protestant, and Jewish, as well as all the learned professions and great interests of France, are represented in it. Among the names of the councilors we find M. Milne Edwards, M. Michael Chevalier, M. Dumas, M. Ravoisson, M. Le Verrier, and M. Nisard. This council is consulted on all important matters pertaining to schools. Next after this council come the eighteen branches of the great University of Paris, or Institute of France. This institution is composed of parts or branches, each located at the leading city of the province to which it is assigned. It uses the lecture-rooms of the schools established there, and has supervision of the schools of that portion of the territory of France which is allotted to it.

The lyceums and communal colleges have each their council of administration also.

THE LYCEUMS AND COMMUNAL COLLEGES.

The administration of the *lycées* is in the hands of a provisor, a censor, and steward, who take no part in teaching, but admit the scholars, correspond with parents, keep the accounts, and regulate discipline. Each *lycée* has two chaplains, and is supervised by its own council of administration. The professors give their lectures, and then have nothing further to do with the school until the next day. Then the masters take control, and are at all times with the boys, in school and out, and supervise their conduct. They direct them in preparing their lessons, attend them at their meals and at exercise, and sleep in their dormitories. The professors, and in fact the masters, must have passed the various examinations and taken the degrees, and are not allowed to be ignorant of the subjects which they teach.

The same general plan of instruction seems to be followed everywhere in the higher schools of France. A chief professor of the highest order of attainments in his subject gives a general lecture to a whole class, who take notes. They then retire to rooms of study, and there, under the direction of masters, go over repeatedly the topics of the professor's lecture until they are familiar with them. They all sleep in large dormitories like barracks, still under direction of masters, and their whole course is one of suppression and restraint, very different from our system, which requires lessons to be worked out by independent, almost free study.

The communal colleges are provincial, and their course of study and general character vary with the wants and condition of the people of the different communes.

SUPERIOR NORMAL SCHOOL.

The Superior Normal School for preparing professors for the higher public schools of France is situated in the Latin quarter, not far from the Polytechnic. It is a beautiful building, and here, after a three years' course, the higher professors are graduated. The select from all the academies of France present themselves here, and undergo a competitive examination for the scholarships. Three hundred and forty-four were examined at one time for thirty-five vacancies. There are usually about one hundred and ten scholars, and their intellectual character is extremely high. The school has twenty-three professors, and its course is about equally scientific and classic. It is not probable that another so complete and select a school exists in Christendom. M. Nisard is at its head; and among its graduates are such men as M. Bénard, Jules Girard, M. Cousin, M. Villemain, M. Taine, and M. Prévost Paradol.

The pay of a superior French professor is from three hundred to two thousand dollars a year, according to grade. He has three or four hours of duty a day, and afterward is entirely free. Around every great school a number of small ones always spring up, sometimes rivaling the parent institution, and employ the same professors at different hours—thus adding considerably to their incomes. There is a regular system of promotion, according to length of service and merit, and the younger members carry on their studies for the higher grades while attending their classes.

In the lycées boys are admitted at eight years of age, and have an eight years' course. Their first examination amounts to but little, but each year afterward the course must be well learned. The studies are not very different from those of our own good academies; but gymnastics, music, and drawing are made a part of the course. The schools are divided into eight forms, each occupying a year. A large number of the boys prepare here for the Polytechnic, Saint-Cyr, and other special schools, many of the best preferring the superior normal school.

THE SEVEN GREAT LYCEUMS OF FRANCE AND THEIR DEPENDENCIES.

Paris has, besides her other great schools, seven immense lycées, where the full course is given. In these, six thousand boys are educated, and around each of the schools is a small colony of private schools, pursuing the same course and employing the same professors. They are all under Government inspection. The arrangement of study in all is similar, although the buildings themselves are very unlike. They all have immense dormitories, clean refectories, dispensaries, and infirmaries, with their attendant Sisters of Charity; bath-rooms and kitchens, with stores of bread, wine, soup, meat, vegetables, and pastry, with all the appliances for preparing food. A boy has in them his board and lodging, instruction, books, writing material, clothes, washing, medical attendance, medicines, and warming and lighting, for two hundred and fifty dollars a year; and it is all excellent, and the sick-rate remarkably low. The food is limited, but sufficient. The pupils' day is long, and somewhat exhausting. They rise between five and six, and spend ten hours with their lessons, and about two at meals and recreations. Nearly all the schools have attached to them beautiful gardens, rendered attractive no less by their real beauty than the interest which the students take in their cultivation.

It would be a most interesting theme, if space permitted, to go through this vast machinery of French secondary instruction. The public schools of France afford to the higher and middle classes secondary, or high instruction for sixty-six thousand boys, while private schools, of a like good character, giving the same course, and under the same Government inspection, educate fifty-two thousand. Thus one hundred and eighteen thousand of the upper classes receive every eight years this instruction, or about fifteen thousand graduate each year. This gives roughly an idea of the extent of this education in France. It all has a religious character, but great pains are taken not to impede the freest action and development of religious thought. Nearly all of this vast number of schools have their characteristic excellence; as, for example, in mathematics, physics, or letters, law, medicine, or one of the various state services.

Such a thing as *fagging* or *hazing* is not known in France. The constant supervision by masters would prevent it, and it would be repugnant to the natural tastes of French people. The same of flogging; and the good sense of mankind everywhere seems to have set in decidedly against both these barbarisms. At the end of each quarter a written report of progress and conduct is sent to parents.

The attention formerly given to Latin and Greek is being gradually transferred to the modern languages. There has been recently a movement to condense the course, and make it more practical, by taking a boy from twelve to sixteen years of age through four years of practical study, tending more directly toward the calling he intends to follow, and also by making each year complete within itself, so that the boy, if called at any time to quit the schools, will have completed a course, though perhaps a short one. This change has been loudly called for by the active, enterprising middle classes, and has been, to some extent, successfully made. The great difficulty seems to be to find a sufficiently large number of this class at any one point to give such schools support.

The French mathematical course is very full, and excellently taught, but is more confined to special schools than is generally supposed. Favor toward it and the natural sciences seems on the increase. While the old notion that a superior social stamp is given by a classical education is prevalent, the tendency of modern thought in France, as well as elsewhere, is against it, and the craving for an education that deals with accurate facts is clearly growing.

THE UNIVERSITY.

The superior or university instruction in France is in the hands of several great faculties of professors established at various points, who teach those only who wish to pass beyond the bachelor's degree. There are five faculties of superior instruction—one each of theology, law, medicine, science, and letters. They form the eighteen branches of the great University of Paris. Sciences have ninety-eight chairs, letters eighty-six, theology forty-two, and law ninety-eight. No barrister can practice until he has attended lectures at a faculty of law for three years. Medicine has sixty-one chairs, and before one can practice, a four years' course at lectures is necessary.

Outside of these faculties and schools, there are a great many very important institutions of learning of almost every possible special character. The most celebrated of these is the College of France, before referred to, founded, with many others, at the Reformation, and now the sole survivor. It has thirty-one professors, among whom we find the names of Flourens, Coste, Franck, Laboulaye, Michel Chevalier, Sainte-Beuve, and Paulin Paris, and covers with its instruction all the most important provinces of human culture.

If we should undertake to criticise so grand and complete a system of higher education, it might be said that there is too much control by the central Government, too much prescribing to teachers the precise course they shall follow, and too much authorization required everywhere, and that education is too much limited and shackled. This is of course due to the character of the people, who must be controlled in every thing. The system is religious and dogmatical, but recognizes the rights of conscience. The state has steadily refused to make the Roman Catholic the religion of France, although it is the religion of four-fifths of its people. The state has undertaken to put education within reach of all her people, and to provide teachers for them. The teachers have, however, never been properly paid, and, but for the fact that they are exempt from the conscription, could not be kept up as a distinct profession. Education is not compulsory, nor is there any sentiment in France that favors such a course.

Of the condition of the mass of the French people I have hardly spoken. Tourists, writers, and humorists are silent upon the subject. Mr. Kay, who has written so much and so well upon elementary schools in Germany, and small proprietorships in France, says nothing upon the former subject. Mr. Arnold reached them once at Toulouse. Mrs. Blunt has given us light in her magazine articles, but the actual condition of the great mass of French peasantry is to the world a sealed book. We have seen that the state has provided a primary school for about every six hundred of her people, corresponding to about one to each of our townships. At some time, about two-thirds of the children of France attend these schools, and a portion, perhaps half of them, perhaps more, pass through the primary course. The rolls of the army and other statistics and sources of information, show that somewhere between twenty-five and thirty-five per centum of the population can not read or write. Of the half who attend the primary schools irregularly, the amount of instruction is exceedingly limited, and the primary course itself is very elementary. Mr. Arnold says that the people of France are "not in the least bookish," and are "almost incredibly ignorant;" and, as regards the peasantry: "The merits of the French school system are undoubtedly more in the probable future than in the present or past, but the schools are there; and in the rise of the people in wealth and comfort is probably the only obligation that can draw these people to them."

THE COMMON PEOPLE OF FRANCE.

After the third of the nation who can not read or write, there comes another third whose acquirements scarcely amount to any thing. One boy in about three hundred of the inhabitants passes through the higher institutions, corresponding to our high schools and colleges, and one in about fifteen hundred receives an education of the first order.

This ought to give some notion of the condition of the French people in respect to education. In viewing the great struggle with Prussia, this subject, I fear, has not received due weight. The common people of France seldom read books. They have no magazines, and newspapers are scarcely known among them. A city like Rheims, Rouen, or Asnières, of fifty or sixty thousand inhabitants, usually publishes two or three little sheets, about such as we always find in every village of four or five hundred inhabitants in Kansas or Nebraska, and not more than a hundredth part of the population read them. The peasantry of France comprise upward of twenty-five million of the population, and, in villages of four or five hundred up to two or three thousand, one would look in vain for that leaven of respectable society which we find everywhere in our own country. The exceeding ignorance of these people is, of course, accompanied by superstitious and groundless suspicion. They are little controlled by reason, but seem, like the people of the South in our war, to possess the faculty of believing whatever is favorable to themselves. This peculiarity M. Gambetta availed himself of in forcing public feeling in France by the grandest series of falsehoods ever told from a chair of state. It was this that led them to condemn and execute as a spy every man who could not account for himself to their liking, and that caused their non-combatants to fall upon the wounded and isolated German soldiers and slay them, always believing that their own people would at once recover the ground.

We have no population that at all corresponds to the poorer peasantry of France. Even the mountain inhabitants of East Tennessee and Kentucky are vastly superior in intelligence and character, though not in morality, to the French peasantry. The old men are vicious, and wear a fierce and dismal expression of countenance; while the old women, usually with a white cloth about their heads, have faces as totally blank and destitute of any human expression as many of the lower animals. The children usually have round, fat, unintelligent faces. The young men, during my stay in France, were mostly with the army, and the young women were attractive only from the universal charm of youthful maidenhood.

These people live by agriculture and the common trades, in villages of a few hundred inhabitants. Their houses are usually of stone, one and a half stories high. Near the front door, which always opens directly on the street, is kept the compost heap for enriching the little farm. In Paris I have seen thousands of men, who labored upon the roads with a horse and cart, living in the streets, and sleeping under their carts upon an old sheepskin, from one year's end to the other—their poor old faces showing no more animation, hope, or happiness, than the horse which was their only companion. I fear that our people who visit France keep their eyes generally toward Paris, the Tuileries, the Bois du Boulogne, and the Grand Opera, and see little of real French life.

The following is an extract from an article by a member of a French and English ambulance, published in "Macmillan's Magazine," and gives an average view of the peasantry:

"If I am asked what was the attitude of the peasants during the war and between the two armies, I reply that their behavior was the most lamentable of all the lamentable spectacles in this unhappy struggle. It is among the peasants that the results of ignorance and selfishness have exhibited themselves in the most striking manner. In the Ardennes the people were not heroic; but at any rate they assisted the French army, helped the wounded, and were not utterly vile before the enemy; but in Normandy and the

Beauce, where I was afterward stationed, the state of demoralization was frightful. The peasants were too selfish to make the least sacrifice for their own soldiers, and thus, both from fear and from interest, became subservient to the Germans, furnishing them with subsistence and other assistance. With rare exceptions, they did nothing for the wounded; but if we happened to be successful in an action, I can not describe the low ferocity with which they turned upon the Germans, before whom they had recently been cringing. At Oucques the ambulance had some difficulty in preventing two wounded Bavarians from being massacred by the people. At St. Leonard, a peasant actually amused himself with pulling the broken leg of a German, for the mere sake of causing him torture. At Ouzoner, the people thronged round a solitary wounded officer, and assailed him with threats and insults of all kinds; and their stupidity was equal to their wickedness. They were constantly mistaking us for Germans, on account of our flag and the ambulance cross on our sleeves. They were certain that we were in communication with the Prussians, because we were not afraid of them, and accused us of firing rockets to point out the position of the army to the enemy. At Sammanthe, they were convinced that the Prussians had come, because our ambulance was established there; and at Ouzoner, it was believed that we had plundered the wounded, and that our only object in nursing the patients was to make money. I do not deny that devoted hearts and souls above the common were to be met with. I have heard from peasants, of both sexes, golden words, which will remain in my recollection as long as I live; but the great majority, even when intelligent, are shamefully demoralized and scandalously profligate, selfish, and wicked. Quarrels and scandals rage with fury in the villages, and even in the families themselves things occur which are too bad to be mentioned."

It is to be hoped that we shall no longer look on France as an example of civilization worthy of admiration and imitation.

CONCLUSION.

I claim little originality for the foregoing pages. I was compelled, by my limited time in Europe, to avail myself largely of the labor of others, and have written the book at a remote frontier post, without libraries, and compelled to rely upon the courtesy of our ministers at Berlin, Paris, and London for the necessary volumes of reference. I thank these gentlemen for their kind assistance.

I found much to admire in the simple, earnest life of the German people, who have accomplished so much by rational and persistent labor, and I have tried to be just in my criticisms upon French character and methods.

Our own service should derive important lessons from the Franco-Prussian war, and I submit this work to the public, and especially to my brother officers, as my contribution toward that result.

APPENDIX.

ADMINISTRATION OF THE PRUSSIAN ARMY.

Subsistence Department.

In time of peace, when there is no commissary officer on duty with troops of the standing army, or the subsistence of troops by the proper department is attended with unusual difficulty, supplies may be furnished by the *commune* in which the troops are quartered. While on a peace footing, officers may, and usually do, draw money commutation for their rations; but when the army is mobilized, every person in it, without regard to rank or grade, is entitled to one ration in kind daily, and no more, and commutations are not then allowed.

The ration consists of twelve ounces of fresh or salt beef, or smoked beef, or mutton, or two-thirds of a pound of salt pork; one pound and a half of bread, which may be increased to two pounds, without meat; four ounces of rice, and four ounces of barley or grits, or eight ounces of peas or beans; one half-pound of flour, or three pounds of potatoes; four ounces of salt, and four ounces of green, or three ounces of roasted, coffee.

The commanding general directs which of the component parts of the ration shall be issued.

The cost of the ration is about twenty-one cents.

In an enemy's country, supplies are obtained, as far as practicable, by requisitions upon the inhabitants through their own civil officers, if possible; but no more than the home price for the articles so obtained is paid under any circumstances. Requisitions, when made by the order of the commanding general, must be facilitated by all commanding officers.

In addition to the ration, the Subsistence Department furnishes dried fruit, sauerkraut, and such vegetables as can be obtained or transported.

Extra issues of whisky or brandy may be made in the field, on the order of the commanding officer, in cases of unusual fatigue or exposure. The ration is one gallon to forty-eight men.

Under similar circumstances the ration may be increased to one pound of beef, one third of a pound of rice or barley and grits, or two-thirds of a pound of peas or beans, and four pounds of potatoes.

In cases of lack of sufficient transportation, the commanding general may reduce the ration, specifying what parts and quantities thereof shall be issued.

Beer, wine, tobacco, and butter are not usually kept by the Subsistence Department, but the commanding general may authorize the issue of these articles, when they can be obtained. A ration will then consist of one quart of beer, one pint of wine, and three ounces each of butter and tobacco.

When troops are transported by railway or steamboat, an extra allowance in money is paid to the commanding officers of regiments or detachments for procuring refreshments for the troops on the line of travel. This allowance is as follows per man: For a trip of from 8 to 15 hours, 8 cents; from 15 to 31 hours, 15 cents; from 31 to 39 hours, 23 cents; from 39 to 47 hours, 30 cents; for every eight hours' travel beyond forty-seven, eight cents is paid.

Commanding officers are required to see that each man carries with him, when traveling by rail or boat, at least one pound of bread, and a suitable quantity of salt pork and whisky, as a reserve ration.

In case there should be no proper accommodations for men on the line of travel, subsistence stores, with butchers and bakers, are sent forward, under charge of a commissioned officer, and warm meals are prepared in advance of the arrival of the troops.

The issues of subsistence stores must in every case be witnessed by a company officer or a pay-master, and commanding officers of posts or pay-masters are required to thoroughly inspect all articles received.

The hides of beeves slaughtered for the use of troops are returned to the Subsistence Department, and, when sold, the proceeds of the sale are turned over to the troops to whom the beef is issued.

When issues of salt meats are made, there is a suitable deduction for salt and brine.

Commutation is allowed for the bread ration when it is not drawn in kind.

The refreshment addition for troops while traveling is always paid in advance—sometimes daily, and sometimes for the whole tour.

An increase of the ration is usually authorized by the War Department upon the issuing of the order placing the army upon a war footing.

Pay Department.

There is no Pay Department proper in the Prussian Army. The troops are paid tri-monthly by a pay-master, who is a regimental officer, and belongs to the battalion staff, and who, besides paying the troops, disburses and keeps the accounts of all the other funds of the regiment, under the direction and supervision of the Regimental Board, as is explained under "Internal Economy of Regiments." The money for the payment of troops is received by the regimental commander, together with allowances for the other funds, from the War Department, and the pay-master's duties are those of a treasurer and cashier, under the direction of the commanding officer and Regimental Board.

Internal Economy of Regiments.—Administration of Funds and Duties of Regimental Boards.

The commanding officer is president of the Regimental Board, and superintends the whole cash business; and should the funds of the regiment become exhausted, is authorized to draw within certain limits upon the general War Fund.

The second member, the lieutenant-colonel, superintends the business of the pay-master, and is required to know that the books and accounts are properly kept and balanced. The lieutenant-colonel has special functions relating to all accounts of his regiment, is responsible for their accuracy, and excused from all field exercises. All organizations manage their own funds, supplies of clothing, and entire equipment.

The pay-master, who is an officer of the regiment, receives and counts the different regimental funds, keeps each in its proper safe, and disburses them. He directs the correspondence, calculations, and book-keeping, and makes all payments. He does not attend drills or field manœuvres.

The troops are paid by the pay-master on the 1st, 11th, and 21st of each month.

Private deposits are not allowed to be made in the regimental safes, but officers are allowed to receive the savings of their men until the amount reaches $10, when it must be deposited to draw interest.

The Regimental Board has charge also of the funds for keeping in order clothing and equipments, including signal equipments and arms, and for the messing arrangements.

Contributions are made monthly to the fund for officers' widows, and to the officers' clothing fund.

The fund for the assistance of officers actually in want was instituted by the War Department in 1869, and is for the benefit of officers below the grade of captain.

At the mobilization the garrison troops receive stated amounts for this last fund, and for the other funds mentioned.

The board of officers for the management of funds in different organizations is made up as follows: in an infantry or artillery regiment, the regimental commander, one staff officer, one captain, two first and two second lieutenants; in a chasseur or rifle battalion, the commander, one chief of squadron, one first and two second lieutenants; in an engineer subdivision, one staff officer, or captain, and one first lieutenant; and in a subdivision of train troops, one staff officer and one captain. At the Military Academy the management of the funds rests with the Directory.

The Additional Pension Fund for artillery officers is kept up by donations from officers of artillery, pay-masters, and administration officers. It is managed by a board of officers selected from the Artillery Brigade of the Guards at Berlin. Disbursements are made quarterly from this fund to invalided officers. This board manages also a fund for the relief of widows of artillery officers.

The Review Fund accrues from sales of worn-out tools and unserviceable ordnance and building material, and from rent of refreshment booths on the review ground. It is applied to payments for damages done to fields and crops during manœuvres, and for miscellaneous purposes.

Each battery and company of artillery receives a fund ranging from 7\frac{20}{100}$ to 8\frac{80}{100}$ monthly for repairs of harness, gun-carriages, and for making targets, etc.

Savings of any of these funds may accumulate to $100; but when that amount is reached, one-half goes to the General War Fund.

Besides the funds named, there are others of minor importance. Among them are those for education of soldiers, for medical attendance and medicines for wives and children of soldiers, for horse medicines, for regimental bands, for libraries and military charities, for swimming schools, and for the decoration of cemeteries.

Clothing.

The commanding officer of a regiment, or other distinct organization, is responsible for the clothing and entire equipment of his command, and general officers are held to a like responsibility in respect to their commands.

There is for every department of troops a clothing board, or commission, composed of the prefect, a pay-master, and one or more officers. In artillery regiments the officer in charge of the tailor-shop is always a member of this commission.

No arrangement exists for furnishing troops in the field with clothing, as it is assumed that the supply furnished each soldier on taking the field will last until his return.

All material for the manufacture of clothing is furnished to the tailors, who are enlisted men, and is by them made up for the different regiments.

The refuse material is sold, and the proceeds transferred to the fund for equipment.

All articles of clothing, except gloves and ear-coverings, are twice inspected before issue.

Non-commissioned officers and privates, except one-year volunteers, are furnished with all articles of clothing and equipment required during their term of service.

Only invalided soldiers are allowed to retain their worn-out clothing; all others turn it in, and it is replaced by new articles.

Soldiers going to hospital turn in their clothing, except shirts, and are furnished with suitable clothing by the Hospital Department.

Troops changing station receive extra under-clothing in order to keep themselves clean *en route*, but must turn it in upon arrival at their destination.

Soldiers discharged for disability during the winter months, if of feeble constitution, are furnished an overcoat, which must, however, be turned in to the proper authority upon their arrival at home.

The expenses for altering clothing and repairing boots are paid from the General Contingent Fund.

The expenses of washing and cleaning the linen suits are borne by the Public Fund, managed by the board, as before explained.

All enlisted men are entitled to an outfit of clothing gratis. This for each man in the infantry: One cap with cockade, one dress-coat, one linen jacket, one pair cloth trowsers, one pair linen trowsers, one pair drawers, one pair stockings, one stock, one great-coat, one pair mittens (leather for non-commissioned officers, cloth for privates), one pair ear-coverings, one shirt, one pair boots, one pair shoes, and two pairs half-soles.

In the mounted service each man receives: One cap with cockade, one linen jacket, one stock, one pair kersey trowsers, one pair cloth trowsers re-enforced with leather, one pair stable trowsers, one pair drawers, one shirt, one pair stockings, one great-coat, one pair long boots, one pair shoes, one pair gloves, and one pair ear-coverings.

For school and acrobatic exercises, there are furnished each non-commissioned officer, in addition to the above, one linen jacket and pair trowsers, and one pair light shoes.

In garrison, each soldier receives: Two double blankets in winter and one in summer, one coverlet, one mattress, one pillow, and two sheets. The garrison administration pays for the washing of the bed furniture, but each man pays for the washing of his own clothes.

Other Provisions of the Prussian Army.

Persons on furlough do not receive commutation of their allowances, but officers and officials on court-martial service, or like duty, interfering with the discharge of their customary functions, receive all of their allowances in full.

The forage ration is of two kinds—light and heavy. The heavy ration consists of eleven and one-fourth pounds of oats, three pounds of hay, and three and a half pounds of straw. The light ration is the same, except that the amount of grain is ten pounds. Heavy rations are issued to horses of the cavalry and artillery, and to horses belonging to general officers and officers of their staffs, officers of the war ministry, of the engineers, intendance, administration high officials (civil officers transferred for special military service in war), officers in charge of transportation and pack-trains, postilions, and sutlers. All horses not belonging to any of the above branches draw light rations of forage.

When oats can not be obtained, the equivalent per pound is: Of barley, one pound; of rye, one pound; of middlings, one and one-fifth pounds; of hay, two and one-eighth pounds, and of straw, five pounds.

When forage is issued by measure instead of weight, a heavy ration is one and one-half pecks of oats, and a light one, one and one-fourth pecks.

Forage for officers' horses is drawn as usual while the officers are on furlough for six months; but after that time the issue ceases.

Receipts are given the contractors or other parties furnishing forage, on which payments are made by the officers receiving it; but no officer having a command less in numbers than a company is authorized to give such receipts.

In the receipts, the different arms or branches of the service for which forage was drawn must be mentioned.

The actual delivery of forage supplies to troops must be witnessed, and such supplies thoroughly inspected at the time by a company officer or paymaster.

Expenditures for writing material, printing, office-furniture, stamps, seals, etc., are made from the proper fund, as explained under the head of funds.

Commanding generals of armies and army-corps furnish their own office-furniture.

Expenses for apprehension, subsistence, and delivery of deserters are paid from the recruiting fund.

All expenses attending the sales of condemned horses are paid from the proceeds of such sales.

Every distinct organization of troops at the mobilization carries with it a certain amount of ready-money proportioned to its size, as a reserve fund, sufficient to cover all its expenses for fifty days.

The administration is, in like manner, furnished with a reserve fund for sixty days.

These reserve funds are to meet unexpected contingencies and emergencies, and are in addition to funds for the regular supplies and equipment.

Horses are furnished in part by purchase by the state, and partly in kind by the civil commune.

All horses for military purposes must conform to a fixed standard as regards height, age, condition, etc., and must pass a board of inspectors, consisting of two commissioned officers and a veterinary surgeon.

Horses captured from the enemy must be turned over at once to the officers in charge of the horse dépôt.

Every civil official called into service at the mobilization receives two or three months' salary in advance.

Should his salary as a military be higher than a civil official, he receives only the pay of the civil position.

Civil officials on the retired or pensioned lists, called upon for military duty as officers or officials of the administration, receive the pay of the positions to which they are assigned.

Officials of the commune are looked upon as state servants.

All civil officials are examined before assignment to military duty.

Officials, during temporary suspension of their duties, receive half-pay.

What is known as the immobile part of the army consists of such levies as are called in, and form a part of neither the mobilized standing army, nor the reserves, nor garrison troops.

The regulations for payment of these troops are the same as for the army on peace-footing.

At the conclusion of a war and the disbandment of the extraordinary forces called in, the troops of the line, or standing army, return to the condition of peace-footing; the reserves and landwehr are put upon the furlough condition. Officers called into service from the pension list, and civil officials taken from their ordinary positions, return to the places occupied by them before mobilization. Pay-masters, however, are retained on the war-footing for a time sufficient for the settlement of their accounts.

The allowance of transportation for officers' baggage depends upon the size and nature of the command with which the officer travels.

An officer commanding a column of not more than three hundred men is allowed one saddle-horse and one two-horse wagon.

In a command of two companies exceeding four hundred men there is allowed to each officer one saddle-horse, but only one two-horse wagon for officers' baggage.

Three companies are allowed three saddle-horses and a four-horse wagon; and in all cases where surgeons accompany commands, each is allowed a saddle-horse.

Loads for wagons are as follows: For a two-horse wagon, seven hundred and fifty pounds; for a four-horse wagon, one thousand pounds; and for a six-horse wagon, two thousand pounds.

If horses can not be obtained, oxen are used, based on the estimate of draught power of three oxen being equal to that of two horses.

Expenses incurred on a march, for equipments and keeping in order of clothing, for horse-shoeing, horse medicines, and for repairs of means of transportation, are paid by the officer in command, who takes receipts for all amounts so disbursed.

When soldiers are taken sick on the march, and there is no surgeon on duty with the command, they are taken to the nearest suitable house, and a civil physician summoned to attend them. A physician so called in is entitled to collect for each man thirty cents for each visit.

Soldiers sent to hospital receive an addition to their pay ranging from sixteen cents daily for the highest grade of non-commissioned officer to a *per diem* of three cents for a private.

Pay of the Prussian Army.

The following table shows the yearly pay of officers of the Prussian Army on a peace footing. On a war footing the actual amount is largely increased by certain allowances paid them, and at all times the actual amount received varies with the kind of duty performed.

Designation.	Thal.*
General of Infantry	4000
Lieutenant-general	4000
Major-general	3000
Cavalry staff-officer—Colonel	2600
Infantry " "	2000
Lieutenant-colonels of Cavalry	1800
" Infantry	1600
Majors of Cavalry	1800
" Infantry	930
Captain of Cavalry, Artillery, or Engineers—1st Class	1800
" " " " —2d Class	720
" Infantry—1st Class	1200
" " —2d Class	600
" Guards Regiments—1st Class	1408
" " —2d Class	720
First Lieutenant of Guards, Cavalry, Artillery, Train, and Pioneers	420
" " Infantry	360
Second " Guards	388
" " Mounted Artillery	372
" " Foot Artillery	360
" " Cavalry and Train	336
" " Infantry	300

Monthly Pay of Enlisted Men.

Designation.	Thal.	Gros.
Sergeants of Cavalry, Artillery, Pioneers, and Train—1st Class	12	00
" " " " " —2d Class	10	00
" " " " " —3d Class	8	00
" Infantry—1st Class	10	15
" " —2d Class	8	15

* The thaler is composed of 30 groschen, valued in American money at 73 cents.

Monthly Pay of Enlisted Men.

Designation.	Thal.	Gros.
Corporals of Cavalry, Artillery, Pioneers, and Train—1st Class	9	00
" " " " " —2d Class	8	00
" " " " " —3d Class	6	15
" Infantry—1st Class	7	15
" " —2d Class	6	15
" " —3d Class	5	00
Privates of Artillery	5	00
" Cavalry and Trains	4	00
" Infantry	3	15

The following table shows the daily pay of what are known as high officials, who are civilians called into service for the performance of their usual vocations with the army:

Designation.	Thal.	Gros.
Chief Surgeon at Army Head-quarters	3	15
Assist. " " "	3	00
Corps Auditor	2	15
Division Auditor	2	00
" Chaplain	2	00
Secretary	1	24
1st Staff Surgeon at Head-quarters of a Department	2	15
2d " " " " "	2	00
3d " " , " "	1	24
Pay-master " "	1	24
OFFICIALS OF THE ADMINISTRATIONS.		
Field Intendant	3	00
" Intendance Counsel	2	15
Intendance Assessor	2	15
" Secretary	1	24
Calculator at Field Intendance	1	24
Assistant Calculator at Field Intendance	1	12
Pay-master	2	00
" Accountants	1	12
Assistant Pay-master	1	00
Field-supply Master	2	00
" -magazine Controller	2	00
" " " Assistant	1	00
Assistant Veterinary Surgeon } at Horse Dépôt	1	24
Pay-master }		
AT FIELD HOSPITALS.		
Chief Staff Surgeon	2	15
Assist. "	2	00
" Surgeon	1	24
Staff Apothecary	1	24
Field "	1	24
Chief Hospital Inspector	2	00
Assist. " "	1	12
Hospital Secretary	1	12
POST-OFFICE.		
Field Postmaster	2	00
Chief Post-office Secretary	1	24
Assist. " "	1	12
Inspector of Field Telegraph	2	00
Clerk " "	1	24
LOW OFFICIALS.		
Baker	1	00
Surgical Instrument-maker		24
Laborer in Field Apothecary Department		12
" " " Post-office		24
Gunsmith and Saddler		24
Postillons and Drivers		12

Officers and soldiers on sick leave receive full pay, but on ordinary furlough pay stops after six months.

Officers in confinement, or suspended by sentence of court-martial, receive no pay after the forty-sixth day of such confinement or suspension.

Prisoners of war receive no pay during absence from their commands.

Officers and officials in hospitals receive full pay.

In case of death, the family of the deceased receives one month's pay, called a grace-salary, and on this creditors of the deceased have no claim.

Pay-masters and officials of administrations receive, to enable them to settle their accounts, pay for four months after the disbandment of troops with which they have served.

Hospital nurses and assistants are paid per month as follows:

	Thal.	Gros.
Hospital Assistant in charge before nine years' service	9	15
" " " after " " "	11	15
" " in general service	7	15

Soldiers who have occupied civil positions under the state or commune, when called into service, receive their pay as before.

Extra pay, according to length of service, is given to drummers, buglers, and band musicians.

Soldiers on duty as clerks at head-quarters of general officers may receive pay not to exceed that of a first-class sergeant of infantry.

Veterinary surgeons receive six thalers additional monthly pay when attending the horses of more than one squadron, battery, or ammunition, provision, or pontoon train; and a further addition of four thalers per month is paid them for attending the horses at the head-quarters of a general, or of a chasseur or pioneer battalion.

Soldiers under ordinary arrest or confinement receive full pay. When under close arrest or confinement, they forfeit four cents daily; and this deduction must pay for their washing.

Non-commissioned officers, as color-bearers, when under arrest, forfeit all pay except sixteen cents daily.

Sick men in the reserve hospitals receive pay as if on peace footing.

Soldiers when sick and cared for by private persons receive the pay of the hospital on the rolls of which they are borne.

Holders of the military Merit Cross receive three thalers per month additional pay; and those holding the military Honor Token of the first-class, one thaler monthly.

The best marksman of a regiment receives also additional pay, but for one year only.

Officers employed on the construction of fortresses receive additional daily pay as follows: Staff officer, 75 cts.; captain, 60 cts.; lieutenant, as fortification secretary or bureau assistant, 30 cts.

A sergeant on duty in construction of fortress as wall-master receives 25 cts. additional pay daily.

Chaplains are paid by the Field Intendance and from a special fund.

Officers and soldiers upon taking the field may arrange to have one half of their pay paid to their families, and these payments are made by the Field Intendance.

Officers on duty at the different head-quarters may have one half of their pay turned over to their families by the War Department at home.

All such payments to families are made monthly in advance, and continue whether the officer be in arrest, or sick, or on duty, and, in case of death, do not cease until the end of the current month.

Veterinary surgeons of the staff receive twenty-five thalers per month; veterinary surgeons, eighteen thalers; and assistant veterinary surgeons, fifteen thalers; and all receive daily six cents as extra subsistence money.

A battalion commander receives thirty thalers per month, and a battalion adjutant ten thalers per month extra pay.

Officers of the Intendance of Divisions and of the General Field Intendance are paid 1500 thalers annually.

The pay of the Field Railway Department is as follows:

	Thalers.	Groschen.
Chief of a division, daily	3	15
" construction "	2	15
Road-master........ "	1	15
Accountants, watchmen, and telegraph guards, daily	2	00

While in the enemy's country, the chief of a division receives five thalers daily.

When on duty in the Railway Department, soldiers receive pay as follows:

	Thalers.	Groschen.
Sergeant (as accountant), monthly	8	00
Clerks, monthly	3	00
A gens d'arme, monthly	1	15
Carpenters and privates, daily	0	8

The annual salaries of the telegraph inspector and telegraph secretary of the Railway Department are respectively 1700 thalers.

Pay of the Landwehr.

During the annual drills a captain of Landwehr receives daily two thalers fifteen groschen; a first lieutenant, one thaler; and a second lieutenant, fifteen groschen. Travel pay is received in addition.

Should drills be continued over the time ordered, pay is received for the actual number of extra drill days.

Landwehr officers promoted during drill receive increased pay from date of promotion.

At the discretion of the brigade commander, officers of the Landwehr absent from drill by reason of sickness may receive full pay.

Landwehr officers who belong also to the line, ordered on semi-weekly drills with the Landwehr, draw half-pay in the line and full pay as officers of Landwehr.

Extra Money Allowances in the Prussian Army.

Upon the mobilization of the army, an extra allowance is made by the Government for the purpose of providing an outfit for field service. It is as shown in the following table:

APPENDIX.

	Thalers.
Colonel commanding regiment	150
Regimental adjutant—Second lieutenant	35
" surgeon—Captain	90
Staff " "	90
Assistant " "	45
Battalion commander	90
Company " —Captain	70
First lieutenant	35
Second "	30
Battalion adjutant—Second lieutenant	35
Pay-master " "	35
Gunsmith	52

Mounted officers receive, as Horse Equipment Fund, the following:

	Thalers.
Regimental commander	40
" surgeon	40
Assistant "	20
Battalion commander	20
Company "	20
Regimental and battalion adjutants and pay-masters, each	20

Horses, saddles, and bridles for officers and officials are furnished in kind for equipment of officers taking the field.

Persons who provide their own horses are allowed one hundred thalers each for them, if they are found serviceable by the Board of Inspectors.

For wagons furnished the army, and lost or destroyed in service, the following amounts are paid:

	Thalers.
For a two-horse wagon	150
" four- " "	300
" six- " "	350

Members of the Cadet Corps promoted to lieutenants, and non-commissioned officers promoted to commissions in the infantry or administration, receive twenty thalers in the infantry, and forty thalers in the cavalry and artillery.

The War Department also allow to sergeants promoted while on active service an equipment fund of one hundred and fifty thalers.

Loss of uniforms and equipments in line of duty incidental to active service validates a claim for seventy thalers.

Officers or officials who, from nature of disease or injury, are obliged to undergo treatment at medical institutions other than military hospitals, are allowed one hundred and fifty thalers as assistance-money by reason of increased expense.

Officers and officials of the enemy held as prisoners of war receive a monthly allowance, in advance, of twenty-five thalers.

When such prisoners are in hospital undergoing treatment, one third of their allowance is deducted.

Eighteen thalers is paid as a premium for each serviceable horse captured from the enemy.

A pay-master on duty at a military prison, charged with the disbursements thereof, receives a monthly addition of two thalers for every fifty men; four thalers for over fifty and less than one hundred, and five thalers for more than one hundred and less than one hundred and fifty.

An addition of forty cents monthly is made to the pay of military prisoners for activity and general good conduct.

The leisure hours of prisoners are employed in work for themselves and at school, and a prisoner acting as instructor receives weekly forty groschen. One half of this amount is deducted for his tobacco and whisky, and the remainder is saved and paid him at the expiration of his sentence.

Soldiers in charge of prisoners always receive an addition to their monthly pay. This addition is, for a sergeant, eight thalers; for a corporal, four thalers; and for a private, two thalers.

Travel pay to enlisted men is as follows: First-class sergeants, color-bearers, and veterinary surgeons, daily, forty-five groschen; second-class sergeants, corporals, buglers, musicians, and assistant veterinary surgeons, daily, thirty-seven groschen.

Lieutenants detailed as instructors in technical schools receive nine thalers per month additional pay.

Officers on duty at the artillery school receive fifty thalers per year additional pay.

An officer detailed for topographical duty has an addition to his pay of twenty thalers monthly. To officers on duty connected with trigonometrical surveys forty groschen *per diem* is allowed for traveling expenses.

Engineer officers on special duty connected with their department receive: staff-officers, one thaler and twenty-four groschen; captains, twenty-seven groschen; and lieutenants, fifteen groschen, daily.

Officers of the Military Academy attending the spring and fall manœuvres receive eight thalers per month during absence from the Academy on such duty.

Eight thalers per month is given to officers who hold medals for bravery in action during the years 1813, 1814, and 1815.

Premiums are paid to soldiers of Polish extraction for proficiency in learning the German language. In a company the best scholar receives five thalers, and the second best three thalers per annum.

*Organization of the Army of the North German Confederation.**

The army of the North German Confederation comprises the contingents of twenty-two different States, of a total area of 154,898·95 English square miles, and a total population of 29,906,217. These twenty-two States are:

	Area in sq. m.	Population.
1. Kingdom of Prussia	131,442·22	24,039,608
2. Kingdom of Saxony	5,586·1	2,423,401
3. Grand Duchy of Mecklenburg Schwerin	5,016·7	560,618
4. Grand Duchy of Saxe Weimar	1,356·9	282,928
5. Grand Duchy of Mecklenburg Strelitz	1,017·0	98,770
6. Grand Duchy of Oldenburg	2,388·3	315,022

* In addition to the Army of the North German Confederation, there were operating against France the armies of Bavaria, Würtemberg, and Baden, since absorbed into the North German Army.

	Area in sq. m.	Population.
7. Duchy of Brunswick	1,377·30	302,792
8. Duchy of Saxe-Meiningen	924·1	180,335
9. Duchy of Saxe-Altenburg	493·2	141,426
10. Duchy of Saxe-Coburg-Gotha	735·12	168,851
11. Duchy of Anhalt	865·4	197,041
12. Principality of Schwarzburg Rudolfstadt	361·3	75,116
13. Principality of Schwarzburg Sondershausen	321·2	67,533
14. Principality of Waldeck	418·4	56,807
15. Principality of Reuss (elder line)	102·5	43,889
16. Principality of Reuss (younger line)	309·4	89,097
17. Principality of Schaumburg Lippe	165·4	31,186
18. Principality of Lippe Detmold	423·3	111,352
19. Free town of Lübeck	107·1	48,538
20. Free town of Bremen	95·80	109,572
21. Free town of Hamburg	152·93	305,196
22. Province of Upper Hessia	1,236·8	257,499

These numbers refer to the population of the States in 1867, when the last census was taken.

The military forces of these twenty-two States, forming the North German Confederation, are recruited, according to Clause 57 of the Constitution, from all ranks and classes of society, substitution not being permitted. The King of Prussia is, by the provisions of Clause 63 of the Constitution, commander-in-chief. The military forces of the North German Confederation consist of the army, the navy, and the landsturm. The army is divided into the standing army and the landwehr.

THE STANDING ARMY.

The standing army is the army always available for immediate warlike operations. It forms the nucleus of the military forces of the Confederation, and consists of the Corps of the Guards, the First, Second, Third, Fourth, Fifth, Sixth, Seventh, Eighth, Ninth, Tenth, Eleventh, and Twelfth Army Corps, and the Hessian Division. Every army corps consists of infantry, cavalry, artillery, jägers or sharp-shooters, engineers, and the military train. The different army corps of the North German Confederation on a peace footing are subdivided as follows:

THE CORPS OF THE GUARDS.

The Corps of the Guards consists of two divisions of infantry, one division of horse, one brigade of artillery, one battalion of engineers, one battalion of military train, one company of castle guards, the institution for invalids at Berlin, and the Leib Gendarmerie.

FIRST DIVISION OF INFANTRY OF THE GUARDS.

1st Brigade of Infantry of the Guards.—1st Regiment of the Guards; 3d Regiment of the Guards; 1st Regiment of Landwehr of the Guards; one battalion of Jägers of the Guard; one Lehr infantry battalion; the schools for non-commissioned officers at Potsdam, Juelich, and Bieberich.

2d Brigade of Infantry of the Guards.—2d Regiment of the Guards; 4th Regiment of the Guards; Regiment of Fusileers of the Guards; 2d Regiment of Landwehr of the Guards; one company of Invalids of the Guards.

SECOND DIVISION OF INFANTRY OF THE GUARDS.

3d Brigade of Infantry of the Guards.—1st Regiment of Grenadiers of the Guards (Emperor Alexander); 3d Regiment of Grenadiers of the Guards (Queen Elizabeth); one battalion of Sharpshooters of the Guards; 1st Regiment of Landwehr Grenadiers of the Guards.

4th Brigade of Infantry of the Guards.—2d Regiment of Grenadiers of the Guards (Emperor Francis); 4th Regiment of Grenadiers of the Guards (Queen); 2d Regiment of Landwehr Grenadiers of the Guards.

DIVISION OF CAVALRY OF THE GUARDS.

1st Brigade of Cavalry of the Guards.—Regiment of Gardes du Corps; Regiment of Cuirassier of the Guards.

2d Brigade of Cavalry of the Guards.—Regiment of Hussars of the Guards; 1st Regiment of Lancers of the Guards; 3d Regiment of Lancers of the Guards.

3d Brigade of Cavalry of the Guards.—1st Regiment of Dragoons of the Guards; 2d Regiment of Lancers of the Guards; 2d Regiment of Dragoons of the Guards.

ARTILLERY BRIGADE OF THE GUARDS.

Field Artillery Regiment of the Guards; Siege Artillery Regiment of the Guards.

FIRST ARMY CORPS.

FIRST DIVISION.

1st Brigade of Foot.—1st East Prussian Regiment of Grenadiers, No. 1 (Crown Prince); 5th East Prussian Regiment of Foot, No. 41; 1st East Prussian Regiment of Landwehr, No. 1; 5th East Prussian Regiment of Landwehr, No. 41; Reserve Battalion of Landwehr, No. 33.

2d Brigade of Foot.—2d East Prussian Regiment of Grenadiers, No. 3; 6th East Prussian Regiment of Foot, No. 43; 2d East Prussian Regiment of Landwehr, No. 3; 6th East Prussian Regiment of Landwehr, No. 43.

1st Brigade of Horse.—East Prussian Regiment of Cuirassiers, No. 3 (Count Wrangel); Litthau Regiment of Dragoons, No. 1 (Prince Albrecht of Prussia); Litthau Regiment of Lancers, No. 12.

SECOND DIVISION.

3d Brigade of Foot.—3d East Prussian Regiment of Grenadiers, No. 4; 7th East Prussian Regiment of Foot, No. 44; 3d East Prussian Regiment of Landwehr, No. 4, 7th East Prussian Regiment of Landwehr, No. 44.

4th Brigade of Foot.—4th East Prussian Regiment of Grenadiers, No. 5; 8th East Prussian Regiment of Foot, No. 45; 4th East Prussian Regiment of Landwehr, No. 5; 8th East Prussian Regiment of Landwehr, No. 45.

2d Brigade of Horse.—1st Regiment of Leib Hussars, No. 1; East Prussian Regiment of Lancers, No. 8.

To the First Army Corps further belong the 1st Brigade of Artillery, consisting of the East Prussian Field Artillery Regiment, No. 1, and the East Prussian Siege Artillery Regiment, No. 1; further, the East Prussian Battalion of Jägers, No. 1; the East Prussian Battalion of Engineers, No. 1; and the East Prussian Battalion of Military Train, No. 1.

Attached to the 1st Division is also the company of invalids for East and West Prussia.

SECOND ARMY CORPS.

THIRD DIVISION.

5th Brigade of Foot.—1st Pomeranian Regiment of Grenadiers, No. 2 (King Frederick William IV.); 5th Pomeranian Regiment of Foot, No. 42; 1st Pomeranian Regiment of Landwehr, No. 2; 5th Pomeranian Regiment of Landwehr, No. 42.

6th Brigade of Foot.—3d Pomeranian Regiment of Foot, No. 14; 7th Pomeranian Regiment of Foot, No. 54; 3d Pomeranian Regiment of Landwehr, No. 14; 7th Pomeranian Regiment of Landwehr, No. 54; Reserve Battalion of Landwehr, No. 34.

3d Brigade of Horse.—Pomeranian Regiment of Cuirassiers, No. 9 (Queen); Regiment of Dragoons, No. 3; 2d Regiment of Pomeranian Lancers, No. 9.

FOURTH DIVISION.

7th Brigade of Foot.—2d Pomeranian (Colberg) Regiment of Grenadiers, No. 9; 6th Pomeranian Regiment of Foot, No. 49; 2d Pomeranian Regiment of Landwehr, No. 9; 6th Pomeranian Regiment of Landwehr, No. 49.

8th Brigade of Foot.—4th Pomeranian Regiment of Foot, No. 21; 8th Pomeranian Regiment of Foot, No. 61; 4th Pomeranian Regiment of Landwehr, No. 21; 8th Pomeranian Regiment of Landwehr, No. 61.

4th Brigade of Horse.—Pomeranian Regiment of Dragoons, No. 11; Pomeranian Regiment of Hussars, No. 5 (Blucher); 1st Pomeranian Regiment of Lancers, No. 4.

The artillery of the 2d Army Corps is the 2d Brigade of Artillery, consisting of the Pomeranian Field Artillery Regiment, No. 2, and the Pomeranian Siege Artillery Regiment, No. 2. The Jägers of the 2d Army Corps are the Battalion of Jägers, No. 2. The engineers of the corps, the Battalion of Engineers, No. 2; and the military train of the corps consists of the 2d Battalion of Military Train.

Attached to the 2d Army Corps is also the institution for invalids at Stolp.

Attached to the 4th Division is also the company of invalids for Pomerania and Posen.

THIRD ARMY CORPS.

FIFTH DIVISION.

9th Brigade of Foot.—1st Brandenburg Regiment of Leib Grenadiers, No. 8; 5th Brandenburg Regiment of Foot, No. 48; 1st Brandenburg Regiment of Landwehr, No. 8; 5th Brandenburg Regiment of Landwehr, No. 48.

10th Brigade of Foot.—2d Brandenburg Regiment of Grenadiers, No. 12 (Prince Charles of Prussia); 6th Brandenburg Regiment of Foot, No. 52; 2d Brandenburg Regiment of Landwehr, No. 12; 6th Brandenburg Regiment of Landwehr, No. 52.

5th Brigade of Horse.—1st Regiment of Brandenburg Dragoons, No. 2; East Prussian Regiment of Dragoons, No. 10;* 2d Regiment of Brandenburg Lancers, No. 12; 1st Regiment of Brandenburg Lancers, No. 3 (Emperor of Russia).

SIXTH DIVISION.

11th Brigade of Foot.—3d Brandenburg Regiment of Foot, No. 20; 7th Brandenburg Regiment of Foot, No. 60; 3d Brandenburg Regiment of Landwehr, No. 20; Reserve Battalion of Landwehr, No. 35, 7th Brandenburg Regiment of Landwehr, No. 60.

12th Brigade of Foot.—4th Brandenburg Regiment of Foot, No. 24; Regiment of Brandenburg Fusileers, No. 35, 8th Brandenburg Regiment of Foot, No. 64 (Prince Frederick Charles of Prussia); 4th Brandenburg Regiment of Landwehr, No. 24; 8th Brandenburg Regiment of Landwehr, No. 64.

6th Brigade of Horse.—Brandenburg Regiment of Cuirassiers, No. 6; Brandenburg Regiment of Hussars, No. 3 (Ziethen); Schleswig-Holstein Regiment of Lancers, No. 15.

The artillery of the 3d Army Corps is the 3d Brigade of Artillery, consisting of the Brandenburg Regiment of Field Artillery, No. 3, and the Hessian detachment of Siege Artillery, No. 11. The Jägers of the 3d Army Corps are the Brandenburg Battalion of Jägers, No. 3. The engineers of the Corps are the Brandenburg Battalion of Engineers, No. 3; and the military train is the Brandenburg Battalion of Train, No. 3.

Attached to the 6th Division is the company of invalids for the province of Brandenburg.

FOURTH ARMY CORPS.
SEVENTH DIVISION.

13th Brigade of Foot.—1st Magdeburg Regiment of Foot, No. 26; 3d Magdeburg Regiment of Foot, No. 66; 1st Magdeburg Regiment of Landwehr, No. 26; Reserve Battalion of Landwehr, No. 36, 3d Magdeburg Regiment of Landwehr, No. 66.

14th Brigade of Foot.—2d Magdeburg Regiment of Foot, No. 27; 4th Magdeburg Regiment of Foot, No. 67; Anhalt Regiment of Foot, No. 93; 2d Magdeburg Regiment of Landwehr, No. 27; 4th Magdeburg Regiment of Landwehr, No. 67; Anhalt Regiment of Landwehr, No. 93.

7th Brigade of Horse.—Magdeburg Regiment of Cuirassiers, No. 7; Westphalian Regiment of Dragoons, No. 7;† Magdeburg Regiment of Hussars, No. 10, Altmark Regiment of Lancers, No. 16.

EIGHTH DIVISION.

15th Brigade of Foot.—1st Thuringian Regiment of Foot, No. 31; 3d Thuringian Regiment of Foot, No. 71; 1st Thuringian Regiment of Landwehr, No. 31; 3d Thuringian Regiment of Landwehr, No. 71.

---

* From the 2d Brigade of Horse, attached to the 5th.
† Attached to the 7th Brigade of Horse from the 14th Brigade of Horse.

16th Brigade of Foot.—4th Thuringian Regiment of Foot, No. 72; Schleswig-Holstein Regiment of Fusileers, No. 86;* 7th Thuringian Regiment of Foot, No. 96; 4th Thuringian Regiment of Landwehr, No. 72; 7th Thuringian Regiment of Landwehr, No. 96.

8th Brigade of Horse.—Schleswig-Holstein Regiment of Dragoons, No. 13; Thuringian Regiment of Hussars, No. 12.

The artillery of the 4th Army Corps is the 4th Brigade of Artillery, consisting of the 4th Regiment of Field Artillery and the Magdeburg Regiment of Siege Artillery, No. 4. To the 4th Army Corps further belong the Magdeburg Battalion of Jägers, No. 4; the Magdeburg Battalion of Engineers, No. 4; and the Magdeburg Battalion of Military Train, No. 4.

Attached to the 7th Division is also the company of invalids for Saxony.

FIFTH ARMY CORPS.

NINTH DIVISION.

17th Brigade of Foot.—3d Posen Regiment of Foot, No. 58; 4th Posen Regiment of Foot, No. 59; 1st West Prussian Regiment of Landwehr, No. 6; 1st Lower Silesian Regiment of Landwehr, No. 46; Reserve Battalion of Landwehr, No. 37.

18th Brigade of Foot.—2d West Prussian Regiment of King's Grenadiers, No. 7; 2d Lower Silesian Regiment of Foot, No. 47; 2d West Prussian Regiment of Landwehr, No. 7; 2d Lower Silesian Regiment of Landwehr, No. 47.

9th Brigade of Horse.—West Prussian Regiment of Cuirassiers, No. 5; 1st Silesian Regiment of Dragoons, No. 4; Posen Regiment of Lancers, No. 10.

Attached to this Division is the company of invalids for the province of Silesia.

TENTH DIVISION.

19th Brigade of Foot.—1st West Prussian Regiment of Grenadiers, No. 6; 1st Lower Silesian Regiment of Foot, No. 46; 1st Posen Regiment of Landwehr, No. 18; 3d Posen Regiment of Landwehr, No. 58.

20th Brigade of Foot.—Westphalian Regiment of Fusileers, No. 37; 3d Lower Silesian Regiment of Foot, No. 50; 2d Posen Regiment of Landwehr, No. 19; 4th Posen Regiment of Landwehr, No. 59.

10th Brigade of Horse.—Kurmark Regiment of Dragoons, No. 14; 2d Regiment of Leib Hussars, No. 2; West Prussian Regiment of Lancers, No. 1.

The artillery of the Fifth Corps is formed by the 5th Brigade of Artillery, consisting of the Lower Silesian Regiment of Field Artillery, No. 5, and the Lower Silesian Siege Artillery Regiment, No. 5. To this Corps further belong the Silesian Battalion of Jägers, No. 5; the Lower Silesian Battalion of Engineers, No. 5; and the Lower Silesian Battalion of Military Train, No. 5.

---

* Attached to the 8th Division from the 9th Army Corps.

SIXTH ARMY CORPS.

ELEVENTH DIVISION.

21st Brigade of Foot.—1st Silesian Regiment of Grenadiers, No. 10; 1st Posen Regiment of Foot, No. 18; 1st Silesian Regiment of Landwehr, No. 10; 3d Lower Silesian Regiment of Landwehr, No. 50; Reserve Battalion of Landwehr, No. 38.

22d Brigade of Foot.—Silesian Regiment of Fusileers, No. 38; 4th Lower Silesian Regiment of Foot, No. 51; 2d Silesian Regiment of Landwehr, No. 11; 4th Lower Silesian Regiment of Landwehr, No. 51.

11th Brigade of Horse.—Silesian Regiment of Leib Cuirassiers, No. 1; 2d Silesian Regiment of Dragoons, No. 8; 1st Silesian Regiment of Hussars, No. 4.

TWELFTH DIVISION.

23d Brigade of Foot.—1st Upper Silesian Regiment of Foot, No. 22; 3d Upper Silesian Regiment of Foot, No. 62; 1st Upper Silesian Regiment of Landwehr, No. 22; 3d Upper Silesian Regiment of Landwehr, No. 62.

24th Brigade of Foot.—2d Upper Silesian Regiment of Foot, No. 23; 4th Upper Silesian Regiment of Foot, No. 63; 2d Upper Silesian Regiment of Landwehr, No. 23; 4th Upper Silesian Regiment of Landwehr, No. 63.

12th Brigade of Horse.—3d Silesian Regiment of Dragoons, No. 15; 2d Silesian Regiment of Hussars, No. 6; Silesian Regiment of Lancers, No. 2.

The 6th Brigade of Artillery, consisting of the Silesian Regiment of Field Artillery, No. 6, and the Silesian Regiment of Siege Artillery, No. 6, forms the artillery of the Corps. To the Corps belong also the 2d Silesian Battalion of Jägers, No. 6; the Silesian Battalion of Engineers, No. 6; and the Silesian Battalion of Military Train, No. 6.

SEVENTH ARMY CORPS.

THIRTEENTH DIVISION.

25th Brigade of Foot.—1st Westphalian Regiment of Foot, No. 73; Hanoverian Regiment of Fusileers, No. 13; 1st Westphalian Regiment of Landwehr, No. 13; 5th Westphalian Regiment of Landwehr, No. 53.

26th Brigade of Foot.—2d Westphalian Regiment of Foot, No. 15; 6th Westphalian Regiment of Foot, No. 55; 2d Westphalian Regiment of Landwehr, No. 15; 6th Westphalian Regiment of Landwehr, No. 55.

13th Brigade of Horse.—1st Westphalian Regiment of Hussars, No. 8; 2d Hanoverian Regiment of Lancers, No. 14.

FOURTEENTH DIVISION.

27th Brigade of Foot.—Lower Rhine Regiment of Fusileers, No. 39; 1st Hanoverian Regiment of Foot, No. 74; 3d Westphalian Regiment of Landwehr, No. 16; 7th Westphalian Regiment of Landwehr, No. 56.

28th Brigade of Foot.—5th Westphalian Regiment of Foot, No. 53; 2d Hanoverian Regiment of Foot, No. 77; 4th Westphalian Regiment of Landwehr, No. 17; 8th Westphalian Regiment of Landwehr, No. 57; Reserve Battalion of Landwehr, No. 39.

14th Brigade of Horse.—Hanoverian Regiment of Hussars, No. 15; Westphalian Regiment of Lancers, No. 5.

The complement of artillery for the Corps is formed by the 7th Brigade of Artillery, consisting of the Westphalian Regiment of Field Artillery, No. 7, and the Westphalian Regiment of Siege Artillery, No. 7. To the Corps belong also the Westphalian Battalion of Jägers, No. 7; the Westphalian Battalion of Engineers, No. 7; and the Westphalian Battalion of Military Train, No. 7.

EIGHTH ARMY CORPS.
FIFTEENTH DIVISION.

29th Brigade of Foot.—East Prussian Regiment of Fusileers, No. 33;* 5th Rhenish Regiment of Foot, No. 65; 1st Rhenish Regiment of Landwehr, No. 25; 5th Rhenish Regiment of Landwehr, No. 65.

30th Brigade of Foot.—2d Rhenish Regiment of Foot, No. 28; 6th Rhenish Regiment of Foot, No. 68; 2d Rhenish Regiment of Landwehr, No. 28; 6th Rhenish Regiment of Landwehr, No. 68; Reserve Battalion of Landwehr, No. 40.

15th Brigade of Horse.—Rhenish Regiment of Cuirassiers, No. 8; 1st Rhenish Regiment of King's Hussars, No. 7.

SIXTEENTH DIVISION.

31st Brigade of Foot.—3d Rhenish Regiment of Foot, No. 29; 7th Rhenish Regiment of Foot, No. 69; 3d Rhenish Regiment of Landwehr, No. 29; 7th Rhenish Regiment of Landwehr, No. 69.

32d Brigade of Foot.—Hohenzollern Regiment of Fusileers, No. 40; 8th Rhenish Regiment of Foot, No. 70; 4th Rhenish Regiment of Landwehr, No. 30; 8th Rhenish Regiment of Landwehr, No. 70.

16th Brigade of Horse.—2d Rhenish Regiment of Hussars, No. 9; Rhenish Regiment of Lancers, No. 7.

The complement of artillery of the Corps is furnished by the 8th Brigade of Artillery, consisting of the Rhenish Field Artillery Regiment, No. 8, and the Rhenish Siege Artillery Regiment, No. 8. The Jägers of the Corps are the Rhenish Battalion, No. 8; the engineers, the Rhenish Battalion, No. 8; and the train, the Rhenish Battalion, No. 8. To the 8th Army Corps belongs also the so-called Inspection of the garrison of Mayence, consisting of the 2d Posen Regiment of Foot, No. 19; the 4th Rhenish Regiment of Foot, No. 30; the 1st Hessian Regiment of Foot, No. 81; and the 1st Nassau Regiment of Foot, No. 87.

NINTH ARMY CORPS.
SEVENTEENTH DIVISION.

33d Brigade of Foot.—Magdeburg Regiment of Fusileers, No. 36;† 1st Hansetown Regiment of Foot, No. 75; 2d Hansetown Regiment of Foot, No. 76; 1st Hansetown Regiment of Landwehr, No. 75; 2d Hansetown Regiment of Landwehr, No. 76.

---
* Attached to the 29th Brigade of Foot from the 1st Army Corps.
† Attached to the 33d Brigade from the 4th Army Corps.

34th Brigade of Foot.—Grand Ducal Mecklenburg Regiment of Grenadiers, No. 89; Grand Ducal Mecklenburg Regiment of Fusileers, No. 90; Grand Ducal Mecklenburg Battalion of Jägers, No. 14; 1st Grand Ducal Mecklenburg Regiment of Landwehr, No. 89; 2d Grand Ducal Mecklenburg Regiment of Landwehr, No. 90.

17th Brigade of Horse.—1st Grand Ducal Mecklenburg Regiment of Dragoons, No. 17; 2d Grand Ducal Mecklenburg Regiment of Dragoons, No. 18; 2d Brandenburg Regiment of Lancers, No. 11.

EIGHTEENTH DIVISION.

35th Brigade of Foot.—1st Rhenish Regiment of Foot, No. 25; Schleswig Regiment of Foot; Schleswig Regiment of Landwehr, No. 82.

36th Brigade of Foot.—2d Silesian Regiment of Grenadiers, No. 11; Holstein Regiment of Foot, No. 85; Holstein Regiment of Landwehr, No. 85; Reserve Battalion of Landwehr, No. 86.

18th Brigade of Horse.—Magdeburg Regiment of Dragoons, No. 6; Schleswig-Holstein Regiment of Hussars, No. 16.

The complement of artillery of the Corps consists of the 9th Brigade of Artillery, formed by the Schleswig-Holstein Regiment of Field Artillery, No. 9, and the Schleswig-Holstein Detachment of Siege Artillery, No. 9. The Jägers of the Corps are the Lauenburg Jägers, No. 9; the engineers number one battalion, viz.: the Schleswig-Holstein Battalion of Engineers, No. 9; and the military train consists of the Schleswig-Holstein Battalion, No. 9.

TENTH ARMY CORPS.

NINETEENTH DIVISION.

37th Brigade of Foot.—East Friesland Regiment of Foot, No. 78; Oldenburg Regiment of Foot, No. 91; East Friesland Regiment of Landwehr, No. 78; Oldenburg Regiment of Landwehr, No. 91.

38th Brigade of Foot.—2d Westphalian Regiment of Foot, No. 16; 8th Westphalian Regiment of Foot, No. 57; 1st Hanoverian Regiment of Landwehr, No. 74; Reserve Battalion of Landwehr, No. 73.

19th Brigade of Horse.—Westphalian Regiment of Cuirassiers, No. 4; 1st Hanoverian Regiment of Dragoons, No. 9; Oldenburg Regiment of Dragoons, No. 19.

TWENTIETH DIVISION.

39th Brigade of Foot.—7th Westphalian Regiment of Foot, No. 56; 3d Hanoverian Regiment of Foot, No. 79; 3d Hanoverian Regiment of Landwehr, No. 79.

40th Brigade of Foot.—4th Westphalian Regiment of Foot, No. 17; Brunswick Regiment of Foot, No. 92; 2d Hanoverian Regiment of Landwehr, No. 77; Brunswick Regiment of Landwehr, No. 92.

20th Brigade of Horse.—2d Hanoverian Regiment of Dragoons, No. 16; 2d Westphalian Regiment of Hussars, No. 11; Brunswick Regiment of Hussars, No. 17; 1st Hanoverian Regiment of Lancers, No. 13.

The complement of artillery of the Corps consists of the 10th Brigade of Artillery, formed by the Hanoverian Regiment of Field Artillery, No. 10, and the Hanoverian Regiment of Siege Artillery, No. 10. The Jägers of the Corps are the Hanoverian Battalion of Jägers, No. 10, the engineers are the Hanoverian Battalion of Engineers, No. 10; and the train consists of the Hanoverian Battalion of Military Train, No. 10.

ELEVENTH ARMY CORPS.

TWENTY-FIRST DIVISION.

41st Brigade of Foot.—Pomeranian Regiment of Fusileers, No. 34;* Hessian Regiment of Fusileers, No. 80; 1st Nassau Regiment of Landwehr, No. 87; 2d Nassau Regiment of Landwehr, No. 88.

42d Brigade of Foot.—2d Hessian Regiment of Foot, No. 82; 2d Nassau Regiment of Foot, No. 88; 2d Hessian Regiment of Landwehr, No. 82; 3d Hessian Regiment of Landwehr, No. 83; Frankfort-on-the-Main Reserve Battalion of Landwehr, No. 80.

21st Brigade of Horse.—Rhenish Regiment of Dragoons, No. 5; 2d Hessian Regiment of Hussars, No. 14.

TWENTY-SECOND DIVISION.

43d Brigade of Foot.—2d Thuringian Regiment of Foot, No. 32; 6th Thuringian Regiment of Foot, No. 95; 1st Hessian Regiment of Landwehr, No. 81; 6th Thuringian Regiment of Landwehr, No. 95.

44th Brigade of Foot.—3d Hessian Regiment of Foot, No. 83; 5th Thuringian Regiment of Foot, No. 94; 2d Thuringian Regiment of Landwehr, No. 32; 5th Thuringian Regiment of Landwehr, No. 94.

22d Brigade of Horse.—1st Hessian Regiment of Hussars, No. 13; Thuringian Regiment of Lancers, No. 6.

TWENTY-FIFTH (GRAND DUCAL HESSIAN) DIVISION.

49th Brigade of Foot.—1st Regiment of Foot, No. —; 2d Grand Ducal Hessian Regiment of Foot; 1st Grand Ducal Hessian Battalion of Jägers; 1st Grand Ducal Hessian Regiment of Landwehr; 2d Grand Ducal Hessian Regiment of Landwehr.

50th Brigade of Foot.—3d Grand Ducal Hessian Regiment of Foot; 4th Grand Ducal Hessian Regiment of Foot; 2d Grand Ducal Hessian Battalion of Jägers; 3d Grand Ducal Hessian Regiment of Landwehr; 4th Grand Ducal Hessian Regiment of Landwehr.

25th Brigade of Horse.—1st Grand Ducal Hessian Regiment of Chevaux-legers; 2d Grand Ducal Hessian Regiment of Chevaux-legers.

To the Hessian Division belong also a detachment of field artillery, a company of engineers, and a detachment of military train.

To the 11th Army Corps further belong the 11th Brigade of Artillery, consisting of the Hessian Regiment of Field Artillery, No. 11, and the Brandenburg Regiment of Siege Artillery, No. 3; the Hessian Battalion of Jägers, No. 11; the Hessian Battalion of Engineers, No. 11; and the Hessian Battalion of Military Train, No. 11.

---

* Detached from the 2d Army Corps.

TWELFTH (ROYAL SAXON) ARMY CORPS.
TWENTY-THIRD DIVISION.

45th Brigade of Foot (1st Saxon).—1st Regiment of Grenadiers, No. 100; 2d Regiment of Grenadiers, No. 101 (King William of Prussia); 1st Regiment of Landwehr, No. 100; 2d Regiment of Landwehr, No. 101.

46th Brigade of Foot (2d Saxon). — 3d Regiment of Foot, No. 102 (Crown Prince); 4th Regiment of Foot, No. 103; 3d Regiment of Landwehr, No. 102; 4th Regiment of Landwehr, No. 103.

To this 1st Saxon Division of Foot, No. 23, belongs also the Regiment of Royal Saxon Sharp-shooters, No. 108—unlike the arrangement in Prussia, where the sharp-shooters are not part of a division.

TWENTY-FOURTH DIVISION.

47th Brigade of Foot (3d Saxon).—5th Regiment of Foot, No. 104 (Prince Frederick August); 6th Regiment of Foot, No. 105; 5th Regiment of Landwehr, No. 104; 6th Regiment of Landwehr, No. 105.

48th Brigade of Foot (4th Saxon). — 7th Regiment of Foot, No. 106 (Prince George); 8th Regiment of Foot, No. 107; 7th Regiment of Landwehr, No. 106; 8th Regiment of Landwehr, No. 107.

To this 2d Royal Saxon Division of Foot, No. 24, also belong the 1st Royal Saxon Battalion of Jägers, No. 12, and the 2d Royal Saxon Battalion of Jägers, No. 13; whereas the Prussian jägers do not form part of a division.

It is also to be noted that the 1st and 2d Royal Saxon Divisions, Nos. 23 and 24, do not each include a brigade of horse, like the Prussian divisions. The cavalry of the kingdom of Saxony forms a division by itself, consisting of two brigades. The 1st Royal Saxon Brigade, No. 23, is formed by the Regiment of Horse Guards, the 1st Regiment of Horse (Crown Prince), and the 1st Regiment of Lancers, No. 17; while the 2d Royal Saxon Brigade of Horse, No. 24, consists of the 2d Regiment of Horse, the 3d Regiment of Horse, and the 2d Regiment of Lancers, No. 18. Besides these, the 12th (Royal Saxon) Army Corps has, as its complement of artillery, the 12th Brigade of Artillery, consisting of the Field Artillery Regiment, No. 12, and the Detachment of Siege Artillery, No. 12; the Chief Arsenal (Haupt Zeughaus); the Battalion of Engineers, No. 12; and the Battalion of Military Train, No. 12.

Infantry of the Standing Army.

The whole infantry force of the standing army of the North German Confederation consists consequently of 9 regiments of Guards, 109 regiments of the line, of three battalions each, and 1 battalion of sharp-shooters of the Guards, 1 battalion of jägers of the Guards, and 16 battalions of jägers or sharp-shooters—making a total of 118 regiments of foot and 18 battalions of jägers, or 372 battalions.

The staff of each of the 118 regiments of infantry consists of 1 officer of the staff, as commander; 1 major, as fifth officer of the staff (that is to say, besides the commander of the regiment and the commanders of each of the three battalions); 1 lieutenant, as adjutant; 1 non-commissioned officer, as clerk; and the regimental band, numbering 48 men in the five old regiments of the Guards and the 4th of the Guards (Queen), and 10 men (32 others are taken from the état of the companies, as assistants) in the old Prussian regiments of the line, Nos. 1–40. In the four new regiments of the Guards, except the Queen Regiment, mentioned before, and the new regiments of the line, the band is formed by 10 men (and 12 from the état of the companies). To the staff of each regiment belong also one chief physician of the staff, two physicians of the staff, and three assistant physicians; the chief physician being at the same time the special physician of the 1st battalion of the regiment, the other two staff physicians the special physicians of the other two battalions, with 1 assistant physician for each battalion. Each battalion of all regiments of the line, on a peace footing, has a strength of 18 officers and 532 men. The battalions of the five old regiments of the Guards number 22 officers and 684 men. The five old regiments of the Guards referred to are the 1st Regiment of Foot Guards; the 2d Regiment of Foot Guards; the Regiment of Grenadiers of the Guards, No. 1 (Emperor Alexander); the Regiment of Grenadiers of the Guards, No. 2 (Emperor Francis); and the Regiment of Fusileers of the Guards. Each battalion of jägers consists of 22 officers and 532 men, in peace.

The whole force of the infantry of the North German Confederation, exclusive of the staffs of divisions, army corps, and higher commands, or, in other words, of the 118 regiments of foot (6714 officers and 190,668 men) and the 18 battalions of jägers (396 officers and 9612 men), on a peace footing, amounts to 7110 officers and 200,280 men. The 118 regiments of foot and the 18 battalions of jägers, on a war footing, number 8450 officers, 380,596 men, 14,854 horses, 2124 wagons of baggage, etc.

Each battalion, in war, has 1 wagon with munition, containing from 16,710 to 16,940 cartridges, and 1290 explosive cartridges, 12 axes, 10 spades, etc.; 1 wagon containing the cash-box of the battalion and accounts, articles of uniform in reserve, and the tools and requisites for the shoe-makers and tailors of the battalion; 1 cart containing drugs and medicines; 1 wagon for the officers' equipage; and 4 horses with pack-saddles.

There are some slight changes in the arrangement for the fusileer battalions and the jäger battalions. Each battalion consists of 4 companies; each company is subdivided into smaller commands of about 20 men each, commanded by a non-commissioned officer. 'On a peace footing there are from 6 to 8 such commands, in war generally 12; two or three of them together are commanded by an officer. Such a body is called an inspection, but does not rank as an intermediate command between the captain of the company and the commands of the non-commissioned officers.

There is hardly more than a nominal distinction between the different regiments of foot, those regiments called the regiments of fusileers and the battalions of jägers forming the light infantry. The fusileers have no bayonets on their guns, but use their short swords instead. The jägers are armed with rifles admitting of greater precision in taking aim. The jägers, as well as the fusileers, are used in the offense as well as the defense. The jägers are, as far as possible, recruited from those persons who wish to become gamekeepers and foresters, and have been assistants to such before entering the army. It will be seen from this that these troops are therefore specially adapted to act in mountainous and wooded districts with advantage.

The gun of the North German infantry is the needle-gun of Dreyse; admits of firing five times in a minute, and carries well to a distance of 800 yards. Some alterations which are to be made will no doubt improve the needle-gun. At present it is heavier, and certainly not as good as the French Chassepot.

Cavalry of the Standing Army.

The cavalry of the standing army of North Germany consists of 10 regiments of the Guards—viz.: 2 regiments of cuirassiers, 2 regiments of dragoons, 3 regiments of lancers (Uhlans), 1 regiment of hussars, 1 regiment of Saxon, and 1 regiment of Grand Ducal Hessian chevaux-legers; and of 66 regiments of the line—viz.: 8 regiments of cuirassiers, 19 regiments of dragoons, 17 regiments of hussars, 18 regiments of lancers, and 4 regiments of horse. The sum total of the cavalry is, consequently, 76 regiments, of 5 squadrons each. In case of mobilization, one squadron remains in the garrison, forming the nucleus of supplements to be sent to the field as re-enforcements. A regiment of horse on a peace-footing numbers 25 officers, from 713 to 716 men, and 672 horses; in war, 23 officers, 653 men, 705 horses, and 7 wagons. The 76 regiments of horse represent a force of 1896 officers, 54,122 men, and 50,938 horses, in peace; and 1748 officers, 49,428 men, 53,380 horses, and 532 vehicles, in war.

The cavalry is divided into heavy and light cavalry, and men and horses are selected with regard to this. The heavy cavalry serves for a regular fight against opposing cavalry in masses. The light cavalry serves more as éclaireurs. They are armed with rifled breech-loading carbines, and, in case of necessity, dismount and fight as infantry against infantry, an instance of which occurred during the last war, where a village occupied by a superior force of French infantry was stormed by a squadron of hussars who had dismounted and fought as infantry. The cuirassiers are heavy cavalry, armed with sword and pistol.

The Uhlans, or lancers, are also counted heavy cavalry, but in reality occupy an intermediate position between light and heavy cavalry; their arms are sword, pistol, and lance. The dragoons, hussars, and the Saxon and Hessian regiment of horse form the light cavalry.

The influence of the numerous public and private studs which have existed for centuries in Germany, especially in East Prussia, Mecklenburg, and Hanover, has been very beneficially exercised, and the breed of horses in the army is very enduring and strong.

The Artillery of the North German Army.

The artillery of the North German Confederation consists of 1 regiment of field artillery of the Guards, 12 regiments of field artillery and 1 Hessian detachment of field artillery, 1 regiment of siege artillery of the Guards, 8 regiments of siege artillery, 4 detachments of siege artillery, and 1 detachment of artificers.

The field artillery is especially used for attacking in the open field the advancing lines of the enemy, while the siege artillery is designed for siege operations, and in the field to attack the fortifications of the enemy. Every field artillery regiment consists of 3 detachments of foot, of 2 batteries of six-pounders and 2 batteries of four-pounders each, and 1 detachment of horse, of 3 batteries of four-pounders.

On a peace footing each battery numbers 4 guns; in war, 6. The whole force of the field artillery in war is, consequently—taking into consideration that the 12th Regiment (Royal Saxon Corps) numbers 1 battery more than the Prussian regiments, 164 batteries of foot and 39 batteries of horse, making a total of 203 batteries, and 1218 guns—482 six-pounders and 736 four-pounders. Every siege artillery regiment consists of 2 detachments, of 4 companies each, making a total of 88 companies.

It is to be noted that while the privates in the different services of the artillery are trained only for their special service, every artillery officer receives an instruction which makes him completely conversant with all the different branches of the artillery, and enables him to take a command in any of them.

The field artillery of North Germany is armed with rifled four and six-pounders of cast-steel. They fire grenades, grape-shot, and shrapnel shells. Grape-shot is only used at a distance of 600 yards and less, especially when the guns are in danger of being taken, and in fortresses when a breach in the wall has been effected by the enemy. They are fired from guns which are not rifled.

The foot batteries, so called because the men serving the guns are not on horseback, as those of the batteries of horse are, are principally employed in assisting the infantry, and the batteries of horse in supporting the attacks of the cavalry. Of course, according to the exigencies of the case, exceptions to this general rule frequently occur.

The siege artillery is armed with rifled 6, 12, and 24 pounders, smooth-bore 6 and 12 pounders, and smooth-bore 7 to 50 pound mortars. The siege artillery is also armed with rifled mortars, which throw bombs of the heavier kind to a height of 3000 feet. The detachment of artificers is commissioned with the preparation of fire-works, rockets, fuses, etc., which require particular attention and skill. The German guns are all breech-loaders.

A detachment of field artillery of foot consists of 1 officer of the staff, 6 captains, 13 lieutenants, 73 non-commissioned officers, 368 men, 160 horses, and 16 guns, in peace. A detachment of field artillery of horse, in peace, consists of one staff officer, 3 captains, 10 other officers, 43 non-commissioned officers, 231 men, 216 horses, and 12 guns. A detachment of siege artillery, in peace, consists of 1 staff officer, 5 captains, 13 other officers, 61 non-commissioned officers, and 340 men. The whole force of the field artillery, in peace, is 1137 officers, 22,391 men, 9328 horses, and 808 guns; that of the siege artillery, 501 officers and 9798 men. A detachment of field artillery, in war, numbers 18 officers, 610 men, 516 horses, 24 guns, and 41 vehicles. The whole force of the field artillery, on a war footing, consists of 1262 officers, 54,177 men, 53,195 horses, 1284 guns, and 5288 vehicles. The strength of the siege artillery in war is variable, according to the requirements of the campaign.

The Engineers.

There are 13 battalions of engineers, and 1 company of Hessian engineers. Every battalion—except the 12th (Saxon) battalion, which consists of but 3 companies—consists of the 1st company, who are pontonniers; the 2d and 3d companies, who are sappers; and the 4th company, who are miners. There are in all 52 companies of engineers. Every battalion of engineers, excepting the Saxon battalion, numbers 18 officers, 495 men, and 6 other persons.

The whole force of the engineers, in peace, is 162 officers, 3078 men, 1633 horses, and 324 vehicles. In war they number 228 officers, 9378 men, 2288 horses, and 380 vehicles, besides 13 pontoon trains (which are, however, hardly ever all mobilized), of 65 officers, 2899 men, 3601 horses, and 533 vehicles.

The engineers are more of a technical than a tactical body, but are as regularly drilled in military matters as any other troops, and carry, along with their special tools, guns of the same description as the infantry. The pontonniers are charged with the building of bridges in war, the sappers with the attack of fortresses and fortifications from above ground, the miners with attacks of the same description under ground.

The Train.

The train consists of the military organized troops for the transport of munitions, provisions, pontoons, field telegraph utensils, and the appliances for field railways, field hospitals, etc., and furnishes drivers for the baggage and munition carts of the mobilized troops. There are 13 battalions of train, and a Hessian detachment. Every battalion consists of two companies and 1 depôt, and numbers 12 officers, 225 men, 4 other persons, 121 horses, and 24 vehicles. In peace the train numbers 162 officers, 3078 men, 1633 horses, and 324 vehicles; in war, 404 officers, 19,465 men, 16,841 horses, and 2615 vehicles.

The sum total of the forces of the North German Confederation, in peace, including staffs, non-attached officers, and administrations, is 12,976 officers, 306,194 men, 63,718 horses, 810 guns, and 324 vehicles. The sum total of the troops available for the field, in war, including the higher staffs, commands, administrations, head-quarters, 4 field railway detachments, 4 field telegraph detachments, munition depôts, etc., is 13,037 officers, 537,990 men, 158,007 horses, 1284 guns, and 13,180 vehicles. There are, besides, the supplements, numbering 3295 officers, 184,647 men, 22,724 horses, and 252 guns; also troops which remain at home as occupation forces, numbering 7100 officers, 214,124 men, 23,323 horses, 234 guns, and 390 vehicles; so that the sum total of the military forces of North Germany, in war, amounts to 23,432 officers, 936,761 men, 204,054 horses, 1770 guns, and 13,570 vehicles.

THE END.

VALUABLE STANDARD WORKS

FOR PUBLIC AND PRIVATE LIBRARIES,

PUBLISHED BY HARPER & BROTHERS, NEW YORK.

☞ *For a full List of Books suitable for Libraries, see* HARPER & BROTHERS' TRADE-LIST *and* CATALOGUE, *which may be had gratuitously on application to the Publishers personally, or by letter enclosing Five Cents.*

☞ HARPER & BROTHERS *will send any of the following works by mail, postage prepaid, to any part of the United States, on receipt of the price.*

MOTLEY'S DUTCH REPUBLIC. The Rise of the Dutch Republic. By JOHN LOTHROP MOTLEY, LL.D., D.C.L. With a Portrait of William of Orange. 3 vols., 8vo, Cloth, $10 50.

MOTLEY'S UNITED NETHERLANDS. History of the United Netherlands: from the Death of William the Silent to the Twelve Years' Truce—1609. With a full View of the English-Dutch Struggle against Spain, and of the Origin and Destruction of the Spanish Armada. By JOHN LOTHROP MOTLEY, LL.D., D.C.L. Portraits. 4 vols., 8vo, Cloth, $14 00.

NAPOLEON'S LIFE OF CÆSAR. The History of Julius Cæsar. By His Imperial Majesty NAPOLEON III. Two Volumes ready. Library Edition, 8vo, Cloth, $3 50 per vol.
  Maps to Vols. I. and II. sold separately. Price $1 50 *each*, NET.

HAYDN'S DICTIONARY OF DATES, relating to all Ages and Nations. For Universal Reference. Edited by BENJAMIN VINCENT, Assistant Secretary and Keeper of the Library of the Royal Institution of Great Britain; and Revised for the Use of American Readers. 8vo, Cloth, $5 00; Sheep, $6 00.

MACGREGOR'S ROB ROY ON THE JORDAN. The Rob Roy on the Jordan, Nile, Red Sea, and Gennesareth, &c. A Canoe Cruise in Palestine and Egypt, and the Waters of Damascus. By J. MACGREGOR, M.A. With Maps and Illustrations. Crown 8vo, Cloth, $2 50.

WALLACE'S MALAY ARCHIPELAGO. The Malay Archipelago: the Land of the Orang-Utan and the Bird of Paradise. A Narrative of Travel, 1854–1862. With Studies of Man and Nature. By ALFRED RUSSEL WALLACE. With Ten Maps and Fifty-one Elegant Illustrations. Crown 8vo, Cloth, $3 50.

WHYMPER'S ALASKA. Travel and Adventure in the Territory of Alaska, formerly Russian America—now Ceded to the United States—and in various other parts of the North Pacific. By FREDERICK WHYMPER. With Map and Illustrations. Crown 8vo, Cloth, $2 50.

ORTON'S ANDES AND THE AMAZON. The Andes and the Amazon; or, Across the Continent of South America. By JAMES ORTON, M.A., Professor of Natural History in Vassar College, Poughkeepsie, N. Y., and Corresponding Member of the Academy of Natural Sciences, Philadelphia. With a New Map of Equatorial America and numerous Illustrations. Crown 8vo, Cloth, $2 00.

WINCHELL'S SKETCHES OF CREATION. Sketches of Creation: a Popular View of some of the Grand Conclusions of the Sciences in reference to the History of Matter and of Life. Together with a Statement of the Intimations of Science respecting the Primordial Condition and the Ultimate Destiny of the Earth and the Solar System. By ALEXANDER WINCHELL, LL.D., Professor of Geology, Zoology, and Botany in the University of Michigan, and Director of the State Geological Survey. With Illustrations. 12mo, Cloth, $2 00.

WHITE'S MASSACRE OF ST. BARTHOLOMEW. The Massacre of St. Bartholomew: Preceded by a History of the Religious Wars in the Reign of Charles IX. By HENRY WHITE, M.A. With Illustrations. 8vo, Cloth, $1 75.

LOSSING'S FIELD-BOOK OF THE REVOLUTION. Pictorial Field-Book of the Revolution; or, Illustrations, by Pen and Pencil, of the History, Biography, Scenery, Relics, and Traditions of the War for Independence. By BENSON J. LOSSING. 2 vols., 8vo, Cloth, $14 00; Sheep, $15 00; Half Calf, $18 00; Full Turkey Morocco, $22 00.

LOSSING'S FIELD-BOOK OF THE WAR OF 1812. Pictorial Field-Book of the War of 1812; or, Illustrations, by Pen and Pencil, of the History, Biography, Scenery, Relics, and Traditions of the Last War for American Independence. By BENSON J. LOSSING. With several hundred Engravings on Wood, by Lossing and Barritt, chiefly from Original Sketches by the Author. 1088 pages, 8vo, Cloth, $7 00; Sheep, $8 50; Half Calf, $10 00.

ALFORD'S GREEK TESTAMENT. The Greek Testament: with a critically revised Text; a Digest of Various Readings; Marginal References to Verbal and Idiomatic Usage; Prolegomena; and a Critical and Exegetical Commentary. For the Use of Theological Students and Ministers. By HENRY ALFORD, D.D., Dean of Canterbury. Vol. I., containing the Four Gospels. 944 pages, 8vo, Cloth, $6 00; Sheep, $6 50.

ABBOTT'S FREDERICK THE GREAT. The History of Frederick the Second, called Frederick the Great. By JOHN S. C. ABBOTT. Elegantly Illustrated. 8vo, Cloth, $5 00.

ABBOTT'S HISTORY OF THE FRENCH REVOLUTION. The French Revolution of 1789, as viewed in the Light of Republican Institutions. By JOHN S. C. ABBOTT. With 100 Engravings. 8vo, Cloth, $5 00.

ABBOTT'S NAPOLEON BONAPARTE. The History of Napoleon Bonaparte. By JOHN S. C. ABBOTT. With Maps, Woodcuts, and Portraits on Steel. 2 vols., 8vo, Cloth, $10 00.

ABBOTT'S NAPOLEON AT ST. HELENA; or, Interesting Anecdotes and Remarkable Conversations of the Emperor during the Five and a Half Years of his Captivity. Collected from the Memorials of Las Casas, O'Meara, Montholon, Antommarchi, and others. By JOHN S. C. ABBOTT. With Illustrations. 8vo, Cloth, $5 00.

ADDISON'S COMPLETE WORKS. The Works of Joseph Addison, embracing the whole of the "Spectator." Complete in 3 vols., 8vo, Cloth, $6 00.

ALCOCK'S JAPAN. The Capital of the Tycoon: a Narrative of a Three Years' Residence in Japan. By Sir RUTHERFORD ALCOCK, K.C.B., Her Majesty's Envoy Extraordinary and Minister Plenipotentiary in Japan. With Maps and Engravings. 2 vols., 12mo, Cloth, $3 50.

ALISON'S HISTORY OF EUROPE. FIRST SERIES: From the Commencement of the French Revolution, in 1789, to the Restoration of the Bourbons, in 1815. [In addition to the Notes on Chapter LXXVI., which correct the errors of the original work concerning the United States, a copious Analytical Index has been appended to this American edition.] SECOND SERIES: From the Fall of Napoleon, in 1815, to the Accession of Louis Napoleon, in 1852. 8 vols., 8vo, Cloth, $16 00.

BALDWIN'S PRE-HISTORIC NATIONS. Pre-Historic Nations; or, Inquiries concerning some of the Great Peoples and Civilizations of Antiquity, and their Probable Relation to a still Older Civilization of the Ethiopians or Cushites of Arabia. By JOHN D. BALDWIN, Member of the American Oriental Society. 12mo, Cloth, $1 75.

BARTH'S NORTH AND CENTRAL AFRICA. Travels and Discoveries in North and Central Africa: being a Journal of an Expedition undertaken under the Auspices of H. B. M.'s Government, in the Years 1849–1855. By HENRY BARTH, Ph.D., D.C.L. Illustrated. 3 vols., 8vo, Cloth, $12 00.

HENRY WARD BEECHER'S SERMONS. Sermons by HENRY WARD BEECHER, Plymouth Church, Brooklyn. Selected from Published and Unpublished Discourses, and Revised by their Author. With Steel Portrait. Complete in 2 vols., 8vo, Cloth, $5 00.

LYMAN BEECHER'S AUTOBIOGRAPHY, &c. Autobiography, Correspondence, &c., of Lyman Beecher, D.D. Edited by his Son, CHARLES BEECHER. With Three Steel Portraits, and Engravings on Wood. In 2 vols., 12mo, Cloth, $5 00.

BOSWELL'S JOHNSON. The Life of Samuel Johnson, LL.D. Including a Journey to the Hebrides. By JAMES BOSWELL, Esq. A New Edition, with numerous Additions and Notes. By JOHN WILSON CROKER, LL.D., F.R.S. Portrait of Boswell. 2 vols., 8vo, Cloth, $4 00.

Harper & Brothers' Valuable Standard Works. 3

DRAPER'S CIVIL WAR. History of the American Civil War. By JOHN W. DRAPER, M.D., LL.D., Professor of Chemistry and Physiology in the University of New York. In Three Vols. 8vo, Cloth, $3 50 per vol.

DRAPER'S INTELLECTUAL DEVELOPMENT OF EUROPE. A History of the Intellectual Development of Europe. By JOHN W. DRAPER, M.D., LL.D., Professor of Chemistry and Physiology in the University of New York. 8vo, Cloth, $5 00.

DRAPER'S AMERICAN CIVIL POLICY. Thoughts on the Future Civil Policy of America. By JOHN W. DRAPER, M.D., LL.D., Professor of Chemistry and Physiology in the University of New York. Crown 8vo, Cloth, $2 50.

DU CHAILLU'S AFRICA. Explorations and Adventures in Equatorial Africa: with Accounts of the Manners and Customs of the People, and of the Chase of the Gorilla, the Crocodile, Leopard, Elephant, Hippopotamus, and other Animals. By PAUL B. DU CHAILLU. Numerous Illustrations. 8vo, Cloth, $5 00.

BELLOWS'S OLD WORLD. The Old World in its New Face: Impressions of Europe in 1867-1868. By HENRY W. BELLOWS. 2 vols., 12mo, Cloth, $3 50.

BRODHEAD'S HISTORY OF NEW YORK. History of the State of New York. By JOHN ROMEYN BRODHEAD. 1609-1691. 2 vols. 8vo, Cloth, $3 00 per vol.

BROUGHAM'S AUTOBIOGRAPHY. Life and Times of HENRY, LORD BROUGHAM. Written by Himself. In Three Volumes. 12mo, Cloth, $2 00 per vol.

BULWER'S PROSE WORKS. Miscellaneous Prose Works of Edward Bulwer, Lord Lytton. 2 vols., 12mo, Cloth, $3 50.

BULWER'S HORACE. The Odes and Epodes of Horace. A Metrical Translation into English. With Introduction and Commentaries. By LORD LYTTON. With Latin Text from the Editions of Orelli, Macleane, and Yonge. 12mo, Cloth, $1 75.

BULWER'S KING ARTHUR. A Poem. By EARL LYTTON. New Edition. 12mo, Cloth, $1 75.

BURNS'S LIFE AND WORKS. The Life and Works of Robert Burns. Edited by ROBERT CHAMBERS. 4 vols., 12mo, Cloth, $6 00.

REINDEER, DOGS, AND SNOW-SHOES. A Journal of Siberian Travel and Explorations made in the Years 1865-'67. By RICHARD J. BUSH, late of the Russo-American Telegraph Expedition. Illustrated. Crown 8vo, Cloth, $3 00.

CARLYLE'S FREDERICK THE GREAT. History of Friedrich II., called Frederick the Great. By THOMAS CARLYLE. Portraits, Maps, Plans, &c. 6 vols., 12mo, Cloth, $12 00.

CARLYLE'S FRENCH REVOLUTION. History of the French Revolution. Newly Revised by the Author, with Index, &c. 2 vols., 12mo, Cloth, $3 50.

CARLYLE'S OLIVER CROMWELL. Letters and Speeches of Oliver Cromwell. With Elucidations and Connecting Narrative. 2 vols., 12mo, Cloth, $3 50.

CHALMERS'S POSTHUMOUS WORKS. The Posthumous Works of Dr. Chalmers. Edited by his Son-in-Law, Rev. WILLIAM HANNA, LL.D. Complete in 9 vols., 12mo, Cloth, $13 50.

COLERIDGE'S COMPLETE WORKS. The Complete Works of Samuel Taylor Coleridge. With an Introductory Essay upon his Philosophical and Theological Opinions. Edited by Professor SHEDD. Complete in Seven Vols. With a fine Portrait. Small 8vo, Cloth, $10 50.

CURTIS'S HISTORY OF THE CONSTITUTION. History of the Origin, Formation, and Adoption of the Constitution of the United States. By GEORGE TICKNOR CURTIS. 2 vols., 8vo, Cloth, $6 00.

DOOLITTLE'S CHINA. Social Life of the Chinese: with some Account of their Religious, Governmental, Educational, and Business Customs and Opinions. With special but not exclusive Reference to Fuhchau. By Rev. JUSTUS DOOLITTLE, Fourteen Years Member of the Fuhchau Mission of the American Board. Illustrated with more than 150 characteristic Engravings on Wood. 2 vols., 12mo, Cloth, $5 00.

GIBBON'S ROME. History of the Decline and Fall of the Roman Empire. By EDWARD GIBBON. With Notes by Rev. H. H. MILMAN and M. GUIZOT. A new cheap Edition. To which is added a complete Index of the whole Work, and a Portrait of the Author. 6 vols., 12mo, Cloth, $9 00.

HARPER'S NEW CLASSICAL LIBRARY. Literal Translations. The following Volumes are now ready. Portraits. 12mo, Cloth, $1 50 each. Cæsar.—Virgil.—Sallust.—Horace.—Cicero's Orations.—Cicero's Offices, &c.—Cicero on Oratory and Orators.—Tacitus (2 vols.).—Terence.—Sophocles.—Juvenal.—Xenophon.—Homer's Iliad.—Homer's Odyssey.—Herodotus.—Demosthenes.—Thucydides.—Æschylus.—Euripides (2 vols.).—Livy (2 vols.).

DAVIS'S CARTHAGE. Carthage and her Remains: being an Account of the Excavations and Researches on the Site of the Phœnician Metropolis in Africa and other adjacent Places. Conducted under the Auspices of Her Majesty's Government. By Dr. Davis, F.R.G.S. Profusely Illustrated with Maps, Woodcuts, Chromo-Lithographs, &c. 8vo, Cloth, $4 00.

EDGEWORTH'S (Miss) NOVELS. With Engravings. 10 vols., 12mo, Cloth, $15 00.

GROTE'S HISTORY OF GREECE. 12 vols., 12mo, Cloth, $18 00.

HELPS'S SPANISH CONQUEST. The Spanish Conquest in America, and its Relation to the History of Slavery and to the Government of Colonies. By Arthur Helps. 4 vols., 12mo, Cloth, $6 00.

HALE'S (Mrs.) WOMAN'S RECORD. Woman's Record; or, Biographical Sketches of all Distinguished Women, from the Creation to the Present Time. Arranged in Four Eras, with Selections from Female Writers of each Era. By Mrs. Sarah Josepha Hale. Illustrated with more than 200 Portraits. 8vo, Cloth, $5 00.

HALL'S ARCTIC RESEARCHES. Arctic Researches and Life among the Esquimaux: being the Narrative of an Expedition in Search of Sir John Franklin, in the Years 1860, 1861, and 1862. By Charles Francis Hall. With Maps and 100 Illustrations. The Illustrations are from Original Drawings by Charles Parsons, Henry L. Stephens, Solomon Eytinge, W. S. L. Jewett, and Granville Perkins, after Sketches by Captain Hall. 8vo, Cloth, $5 00.

HALLAM'S CONSTITUTIONAL HISTORY OF ENGLAND, from the Accession of Henry VII. to the Death of George II. 8vo, Cloth, $2 00.

HALLAM'S LITERATURE. Introduction to the Literature of Europe during the Fifteenth, Sixteenth, and Seventeenth Centuries. By Henry Hallam. 2 vols., 8vo, Cloth, $4 00.

HALLAM'S MIDDLE AGES. State of Europe during the Middle Ages. By Henry Hallam. 8vo, Cloth, $2 00.

HILDRETH'S HISTORY OF THE UNITED STATES. First Series: From the First Settlement of the Country to the Adoption of the Federal Constitution. Second Series: From the Adoption of the Federal Constitution to the End of the Sixteenth Congress. 6 vols., 8vo, Cloth, $18 00.

HUME'S HISTORY OF ENGLAND. History of England, from the Invasion of Julius Cæsar to the Abdication of James II., 1688. By David Hume. A new Edition, with the Author's last Corrections and Improvements. To which is Prefixed a short Account of his Life, written by Himself. With a Portrait of the Author. 6 vols., 12mo, Cloth, $9 00.

JAY'S WORKS. Complete Works of Rev. William Jay: comprising his Sermons, Family Discourses, Morning and Evening Exercises for every Day in the Year, Family Prayers, &c. Author's enlarged Edition, revised. 3 vols., 8vo, Cloth, $6 00.

JEFFERSON'S DOMESTIC LIFE. The Domestic Life of Thomas Jefferson: compiled from Family Letters and Reminiscences by his Great-Granddaughter, Sarah N. Randolph. With Illustrations. Crown 8vo, Illuminated Cloth, Beveled Edges, $2 50.

JOHNSON'S COMPLETE WORKS. The Works of Samuel Johnson, LL.D. With an Essay on his Life and Genius, by Arthur Murphy, Esq. Portrait of Johnson. 2 vols., 8vo, Cloth, $4 00.

KINGLAKE'S CRIMEAN WAR. The Invasion of the Crimea, and an Account of its Progress down to the Death of Lord Raglan. By Alexander William Kinglake. With Maps and Plans. Two Vols. ready. 12mo, Cloth, $2 00 per vol.

KINGSLEY'S WEST INDIES. At Last: A Christmas in the West Indies. By Charles Kingsley. Illustrated. 12mo, Cloth, $1 50.

KRUMMACHER'S DAVID, KING OF ISRAEL. David, the King of Israel: a Portrait drawn from Bible History and the Book of Psalms. By FREDERICK WILLIAM KRUMMACHER, D.D., Author of "Elijah the Tishbite," &c. Translated under the express Sanction of the Author by the Rev. M. G. EASTON, M.A. With a Letter from Dr. Krummacher to his American Readers, and a Portrait. 12mo, Cloth, $1 75.

LAMB'S COMPLETE WORKS. The Works of Charles Lamb. Comprising his Letters, Poems, Essays of Elia, Essays upon Shakspeare, Hogarth, &c., and a Sketch of his Life, with the Final Memorials, by T. NOON TALFOURD. Portrait. 2 vols., 12mo, Cloth, $3 00.

LIVINGSTONE'S SOUTH AFRICA. Missionary Travels and Researches in South Africa; including a Sketch of Sixteen Years' Residence in the Interior of Africa, and a Journey from the Cape of Good Hope to Loando on the West Coast; thence across the Continent, down the River Zambesi, to the Eastern Ocean. By DAVID LIVINGSTONE, LL.D., D.C.L. With Portrait, Maps by Arrowsmith, and numerous Illustrations. 8vo, Cloth, $4 50.

LIVINGSTONES' ZAMBESI. Narrative of an Expedition to the Zambesi and its Tributaries, and of the Discovery of the Lakes Shirwa and Nyassa. 1858-1864. By DAVID and CHARLES LIVINGSTONE. With Map and Illustrations. 8vo, Cloth, $5 00.

M'CLINTOCK & STRONG'S CYCLOPÆDIA. Cyclopædia of Biblical, Theological, and Ecclesiastical Literature. Prepared by the Rev. JOHN M'CLINTOCK, D.D., and JAMES STRONG, S.T.D. 3 vols. now ready. Royal 8vo. Price per vol., Cloth, $5 00; Sheep, $6 00; Half Morocco, $8 00.

MARCY'S ARMY LIFE ON THE BORDER. Thirty Years of Army Life on the Border. Comprising Descriptions of the Indian Nomads of the Plains; Explorations of New Territory; a Trip across the Rocky Mountains in the Winter; Descriptions of the Habits of Different Animals found in the West, and the Methods of Hunting them; with Incidents in the Life of Different Frontier Men, &c., &c. By Brevet Brigadier-General R. B. MARCY, U.S.A., Author of "The Prairie Traveller." With numerous Illustrations. 8vo, Cloth, Beveled Edges, $3 00.

MACAULAY'S HISTORY OF ENGLAND. The History of England from the Accession of James II. By THOMAS BABINGTON MACAULAY. With an Original Portrait of the Author. 5 vols., 8vo, Cloth, $10 00; 12mo, Cloth, $7 50.

MOSHEIM'S ECCLESIASTICAL HISTORY, Ancient and Modern; in which the Rise, Progress, and Variation of Church Power are considered in their Connection with the State of Learning and Philosophy, and the Political History of Europe during that Period. Translated, with Notes, &c., by A. MACLAINE, D.D. A new Edition, continued to 1826, by C. COOTE, LL.D. 2 vols., 8vo, Cloth, $4 00.

NEVIUS'S CHINA. China and the Chinese: a General Description of the Country and its Inhabitants; its Civilization and Form of Government; its Religious and Social Institutions; its Intercourse with other Nations; and its Present Condition and Prospects. By the Rev. JOHN L. NEVIUS, Ten Years a Missionary in China. With a Map and Illustrations. 12mo, Cloth, $1 75.

OLIN'S (DR.) LIFE AND LETTERS. 2 vols., 12mo, Cloth, $3 00.

OLIN'S (DR.) TRAVELS. Travels in Egypt, Arabia Petræa, and the Holy Land. Engravings. 2 vols., 8vo, Cloth, $3 00.

OLIN'S (DR.) WORKS. The Works of Stephen Olin, D.D., late President of the Wesleyan University. 2 vols., 12mo, Cloth, $3 00.

OLIPHANT'S CHINA AND JAPAN. Narrative of the Earl of Elgin's Mission to China and Japan, in the Years 1857, '58, '59. By LAURENCE OLIPHANT, Private Secretary to Lord Elgin. Illustrations. 8vo, Cloth, $3 50.

OLIPHANT'S (MRS.) LIFE OF EDWARD IRVING. The Life of Edward Irving, Minister of the National Scotch Church, London. Illustrated by his Journals and Correspondence. By Mrs. OLIPHANT. Portrait. 8vo, Cloth, $3 50.

RAWLINSON'S MANUAL OF ANCIENT HISTORY. A Manual of Ancient History, from the Earliest Times to the Fall of the Western Empire. Comprising the History of Chaldæa, Assyria, Media, Babylonia, Lydia, Phœnicia, Syria, Judæa, Egypt, Carthage, Persia, Greece, Macedonia, Parthia, and Rome. By GEORGE RAWLINSON, M.A., Camden Professor of Ancient History in the University of Oxford. 12mo, Cloth, $2 50.

RECLUS'S THE EARTH. The Earth: a Descriptive History of the Phenomena and Life of the Globe. By ELISÉE RECLUS. Translated by the late B. B. Woodward, and Edited by Henry Woodward. With 234 Maps and Illustrations, and 23 Page Maps printed in Colors. 8vo, Cloth, $5 00.

POETS OF THE NINETEENTH CENTURY. The Poets of the Nineteenth Century. Selected and Edited by the Rev. ROBERT ARIS WILLMOTT. With English and American Additions, arranged by EVERT A. DUYCKINCK, Editor of "Cyclopædia of American Literature." Comprising Selections from the Greatest Authors of the Age. Superbly Illustrated with 132 Engravings from Designs by the most Eminent Artists. In elegant small 4to form, printed on Superfine Tinted Paper, richly bound in extra Cloth, Beveled, Gilt Edges, $6 00; Half Calf, $6 00; Full Turkey Morocco, $10 00.

SHAKSPEARE. The Dramatic Works of William Shakspeare, with the Corrections and Illustrations of Dr. JOHNSON, G. STEEVENS, and others. Revised by ISAAC REED. Engravings. 6 vols., Royal 12mo, Cloth, $9 00.

SMILES'S LIFE OF THE STEPHENSONS. The Life of George Stephenson, and of his Son, Robert Stephenson; comprising, also, a History of the Invention and Introduction of the Railway Locomotive. By SAMUEL SMILES, Author of "Self-Help," &c. With Steel Portraits and numerous Illustrations. 8vo, Cloth, $3 00.

SMILES'S HISTORY OF THE HUGUENOTS. The Huguenots: their Settlements, Churches, and Industries in England and Ireland. By SAMUEL SMILES. With an Appendix relating to the Huguenots in America. Crown 8vo, Cloth, $1 75.

SPEKE'S AFRICA. Journal of the Discovery of the Source of the Nile. By Captain JOHN HANNING SPEKE, Captain H. M. Indian Army, Fellow and Gold Medalist of the Royal Geographical Society, Hon. Corresponding Member and Gold Medalist of the French Geographical Society, &c. With Maps and Portraits and numerous Illustrations, chiefly from Drawings by Captain GRANT. 8vo, Cloth, uniform with Livingstone, Barth, Burton, &c., $4 00.

STRICKLAND'S (MISS) QUEENS OF SCOTLAND. Lives of the Queens of Scotland and English Princesses connected with the Regal Succession of Great Britain. By AGNES STRICKLAND. 8 vols., 12mo, Cloth, $12 00.

THE STUDENT'S SERIES.
    France. Engravings. 12mo, Cloth, $2 00.
    Gibbon. Engravings. 12mo, Cloth, $2 00.
    Greece. Engravings. 12mo, Cloth, $2 00.
    Hume. Engravings. 12mo, Cloth, $2 00.
    Rome. By Liddell. Engravings. 12mo, Cloth, $2 00.
    Old Testament History. Engravings. 12mo, Cloth, $2 00.
    New Testament History. Engravings. 12mo, Cloth, $2 00.
    Strickland's Queens of England. Abridged. Engravings. 12mo, Cloth, $2 00.
    Ancient History of the East. 12mo, Cloth, $2 00.
    Hallam's Middle Ages. 12mo, Cloth, $2 00.
    Lyell's Elements of Geology. 12mo, Cloth, $2 00.

TENNYSON'S COMPLETE POEMS. The Complete Poems of Alfred Tennyson, Poet Laureate. With numerous Illustrations by Eminent Artists, and Three Characteristic Portraits. 8vo, Paper, 75 cents; Cloth, $1 25.

THOMSON'S LAND AND THE BOOK. The Land and the Book; or, Biblical Illustrations drawn from the Manners and Customs, the Scenes and the Scenery of the Holy Land. By W. M. THOMSON, D.D., Twenty-five Years a Missionary of the A.B.C.F.M. in Syria and Palestine. With two elaborate Maps of Palestine, an accurate Plan of Jerusalem, and several hundred Engravings, representing the Scenery, Topography, and Productions of the Holy Land, and the Costumes, Manners, and Habits of the People. 2 large 12mo vols., Cloth, $5 00.

TYERMAN'S WESLEY. The Life and Times of the Rev. John Wesley, M.A., Founder of the Methodists. By the Rev. LUKE TYERMAN, Author of "The Life of Rev. Samuel Wesley." Portraits. 3 vols., Crown 8vo.

VÁMBÉRY'S CENTRAL ASIA. Travels in Central Asia. Being the Account of a Journey from Teheran across the Turkoman Desert, on the Eastern Shore of the Caspian, to Khiva, Bokhara, and Samarcand, performed in the Year 1863. By ARMINIUS VÁMBÉRY, Member of the Hungarian Academy of Pesth, by whom he was sent on this Scientific Mission. With Map and Woodcuts. 8vo, Cloth, $4 50.

WOOD'S HOMES WITHOUT HANDS. Homes Without Hands: being a Description of the Habitations of Animals, classed according to their Principle of Construction. By J. G. WOOD, M.A., F.L.S. With about 140 Illustrations. 8vo, Cloth, Beveled Edges, $4 50.

Harper's Catalogue.

The attention of gentlemen, in town or country, designing to form Libraries or enrich their Literary Collections, is respectfully invited to Harper's Catalogue, which will be found to comprise a large proportion of the standard and most esteemed works in English and Classical Literature—COMPREHENDING OVER THREE THOUSAND VOLUMES—which are offered, in most instances, at less than one-half the cost of similar productions in England.

To Librarians and others connected with Colleges, Schools, &c., who may not have access to a trustworthy guide in forming the true estimate of literary productions, it is believed this Catalogue will prove especially valuable for reference.

To prevent disappointment, it is suggested that, whenever books can not be obtained through any bookseller or local agent, applications with remittance should be addressed direct to Harper & Brothers, which will receive prompt attention.

Sent by mail on receipt of Six Cents in postage stamps.

Address   HARPER & BROTHERS,
                            FRANKLIN SQUARE, NEW YORK.

www.ingramcontent.com/pod-product-compliance
Lightning Source LLC
Chambersburg PA
CBHW050847300426
44111CB00010B/1168